Is the Sacred for Sale?

*The Old People in the desert
know that the Winds of Change are here.
It is time for the Dreamers
to respond to the Dream.*

Anonymous message between Elders, sent across the continents in 1999

Is the Sacred for Sale?

Tourism and Indigenous Peoples

Alison M. Johnston

London • Sterling, VA

Dedicated to all the children in this time

First published by Earthscan in the UK and USA in 2006

ISBN-13: 978-1-85383-859-0 paperback
ISBN-10: 1-85383-859-4   paperback
ISBN-13 978-1-85383-858-5 hardback
ISBN-10: 1-85383-858-6   hardback

Typesetting by Safehouse Creative
Printed and bound in the UK by Bath Press, Bath
Cover design by Susanne Harris
Front cover artwork by Mike Leach
The cover shows an authentic Aboriginal design by Mike Leach (St'at'imc) called 'The Sacred
White Raven Blanket', which depicts four white ravens holding the sun in balance. This
symbol reflects the Native American medicine wheel – an ancient symbol that represents the
balance of life.

For a full list of publications please contact:

Earthscan
8–12 Camden High Street
London, NW1 0JH, UK
Tel: +44 (0)20 7387 8558
Fax: +44 (0)20 7387 8998
Email: earthinfo@earthscan.co.uk
Web: **www.earthscan.co.uk**

22883 Quicksilver Drive, Sterling, VA 20166-2012, USA

Earthscan is an imprint of James & James (Science Publishers) Ltd and publishes in association
with the International Institute for Environment and Development

A catalogue record for this book is available from the British Library

Library of Congress Cataloging-in-Publication Data

Johnston, Alison M.
    Is the Sacred for Sale? : tourism and indigenous peoples / Alison M. Johnston.
        p. cm.
    Includes bibliographical references and index.
    ISBN 1-85383-858-6 – ISBN 1-85383-859-4 (pbk.)
1. Indigenous peoples – Economic conditions. 2. Indigenous peoples – Social conditions.
3. Indigenous peoples – Land tenure. 4. Sacred space. 5. Culture and tourism. 9.
Conservation of natural resources. I. Title.
    GN380.J64 2005
    305.8 – dc22

                                                                              2005015724

Printed on elemental chlorine-free paper

Contents

Contents

List of Figures and Boxes

Figures

Boxes

Prologue

Once we begin to see, we are doomed and challenged to seek the strength to see more, not less.

(Arthur Miller, cited in Oprah, April 2002, p42)

This book is not intended to speak on behalf of or in the place of Indigenous Peoples. It is written to help break the silence on critical issues of our time, affecting us all. It is about consumerism and our own role in it.

I have sat in many a United Nations forum, where Indigenous rights are being negotiated away by corporate nation states behind closed doors. I have also seen the struggle by isolated Indigenous Peoples to access international avenues for the protection of rights, as refuge from the global economy. In our time there is a deliberate, methodical yet politely disguised economic assault on Indigenous lands and Indigenous cultures, which few of us wish to acknowledge. It is a cycle that our society has acted out before, never graciously. This time it threatens life systems and our very existence.

I am one of many witnesses to our collective sleep, with a responsibility to speak out. We have been told to wake up, heal ourselves and choose conscious connection. The corporate system is no one's brother. Evidence is all around us in the systematic impoverishment of peoples and the destruction of ecosystems worldwide. We all were wired at birth with enough common sense to recognize this. Sacred knowledge inhabits us all, though we may choose to forget.

The views expressed are my own, shaped by my ongoing work with Indigenous Peoples across many time zones. A trip to Guatemala in 1985 made me want to understand. The sale of our family farm that same year was my own experience of the sacred being sold.

If what I have written here pushes you out of your comfort zone, or confirms what you have witnessed in your own life travels, let this be a small sign of hope.

With prayers for the humanity in all of us.

Alison Johnston
Written at Swena'7em
April 2005

Acknowledgements

Many beautiful souls carried me toward and through the writing of this book. I thank you all – for grounding me, for teaching me and for being a mirror.

I carried this book inside of me for a long time. With the help and encouragement of many it became real.

First I must thank Jonathan Sinclair Wilson of Earthscan Publications for overcoming jet lag in Nairobi to contemplate the idea of a cross-cultural book on tourism; as well as Camille Adamson, Victoria Brown and the whole Earthscan team for their unwavering respect toward the sensitive issues. Is the Sacred for Sale? stands as a question thanks to their leaps of faith and patience.

I sincerely thank all those who guided me on the narrow red road of story telling. Thank you Chief Garry John for your ongoing contributions, which enabled me to anchor this book at 'home'; Rosalin Sam for your kind support; Elder Ruby Dunstan for your incredible trust and for your profound example; Ron Gardner for all the inspiring talks on protocol; Meitamei Olol Dapash for your invaluable guidance across the continents; and Ratu Manoa Malani for helping the big picture to become possible. Thank you Lix Lopez for, afterward, taking it all to the next level – to where the dialogue belongs. I extend my deepest respect to all those who keep the sacred fires and ceremonies.

Many others also took turns guiding me on this journey of story telling. Thank you Anita Pleumarom for your tremendous insights; Nina Rao for your candour; and Fiona Archer for your frankness and dedication. You all have brought beautiful integrity to the realm of advocacy work. Further thanks to Kurt Kutay for your refreshing leadership and willingness to share the lessons.

Finally, I acknowledge the brave twosome who proofread the entire manuscript from a cross cultural perspective. Thank you Leah McIntosh for continually expanding my thoughts; and Millee Mackenzie for helping me see the 'end' and ensuring that I got there, to the new beginnings.

As for my beginnings, I am grateful to my parents for rooting me on our family farm; my grandparents who took me fishing and berry picking on the backroads; my Uncle Lou who told me the real history; as well as Patricia Deptford, Janet Wallace, Jim Roberts, Cora Shandler, Ian Millar, Lee Gass and John McAlpine, who each fine-tuned my compass along the way. I will never forget my horse Tako, who was a true teacher of life and dreams.

To all of my dear friends, I truly appreciate you accompanying me. The support and prayers of many have given me the strength to witness this story and to let it come through me.

Very special thanks go to my life partner Michael for his vision and appreciation of the old knowledge, and to our daughter Khamael for keeping me rooted firmly in now. Judianne Thomson and George Leach, and the Scotchman family at large, all helped me more than they know.

Is the Sacred for Sale? is a question belonging to us all. It is up to us each to find our place in the answer. This book is one small part of my own gratitude for life. Servabo fidem.

List of Acronyms and Abbreviations

AI   Amnesty International
AKTE   Working Group on Tourism and Development (Switzerland)
APEC   Asia Pacific Economic Cooperation Forum
BBC   British Broadcasting Corporation
CBD   United Nations Convention on Biological Diversity
CCA   community conserved area
Cdn$ Canadian dollars
CEESP   Commission on Environmental, Economic and Social
                  Policy (IUCN)
CEO   chief executive officer
CERD   UN Committee for the Elimination of Racial Discrimination
CI   Conservation International
COICA   Coordinating Body of Indigenous Organizations of the
                  Amazon Basin
COP   Conference of the Parties to the CBD
CSD   United Nations Commission on Sustainable Development
DFID   UK Department for International Development
ECOT   Ecumenical Coalition on Tourism (Hong Kong)
EEC   European Economic Community
ETE   Ecological Tourism in Europe (Germany)
EU   European Union
FSC   Forest Stewardship Council
GATS   General Agreement on Trade in Services (WTO)
GATT   General Agreement on Tariffs and Trade (WTO)

GDP	gross domestic product
GEF	Global Environment Fund/Facility
GNP	gross national product
GTZ	Gesellschaft für Technische Zusammenarbeit (Germany)
IADB	Inter-American Development Bank
IATA	International Air Transport Association
ICBG	International Cooperative Biodiversity Groups Program (Smithsonian Institute)
ICCROM	International Centre for the Study of the Preservation and Restoration of Cultural Property
ICOMOS	International Council on Monuments and Sites
ICT	Indian Country Tourism
IGC	Intergovernmental Committee on Genetic Resources, Traditional Knowledge and Folklore (WIPO)
IGO	intergovernmental organization
IIFB	International Indigenous Forum on Biodiversity (Indigenous caucus of CBD)
IIPT	International Institute for Peace Through Tourism
ILO	International Labour Organization
IMF	International Monetary Fund
IOC	International Olympic Committee
IPR	intellectual property right
ISCST	International Support Centre for Sustainable Tourism
ISO	International Organization for Standardization
ITB	International Tourism Bourse Fair (Berlin, Germany)
ITRI	Indigenous Tourism Rights International (US)
IUCN	International Union for the Conservation of Nature and Natural Resources (World Conservation Union)
IWGIA	International Work Group for Indigenous Affairs (Copenhagen, Denmark)
IYE	United Nations International Year of Ecotourism, 2002
kg	kilogram
km	kilometre
MBC	Mesoamerican Biological Corridor
MDG	Millennium Development Goal
NEC	national ecotourism council
NGO	non-governmental organization
OAS	Organization of American States
OMM	*Organización Mundo Maya*
PATA	Pacific Asia Travel Association
PCB	polychlorinated biphenyl
PIC	prior informed consent
PPP	*Plan Puebla Panama*

PR	public relations
RARE	RARE Center for Tropical Conservation (Arlington, Virginia, US)
SBSTTA	Subsidiary Body on Scientific, Technical and Technological Advice (CBD)
SWOT	strengths, weaknesses, opportunities and threats
TCE	traditional cultural expression
TIES	The International Ecotourism Society
TILCEPA	Theme on Indigenous and Local Communities, Equity and Protected Areas (IUCN)
TIM Team	Tourism Investigation and Monitoring Team (Thailand)
TK	traditional knowledge
TNC	The Nature Conservancy (US)
TRIPS	Agreement on Trade Related Aspects of Intellectual Property Rights
TRR	traditional resource right
TUI	Touristic Union International (Germany)
TWN	Third World Network (Malaysia)
UCLA	University of California at Los Angeles (US)
UK	United Kingdom
UN	United Nations
UNCHR	United Nations Commission on Human Rights
UNCTAD	United Nations Conference on Trade and Development
UNDP	United Nations Development Programme
UNEP	United Nations Environment Programme
UNESCO	United Nations Educational, Scientific and Cultural Organization
UNGA	United Nations General Assembly
UNICEF	United Nations Children's Fund
UNPF	United Nations Permanent Forum on Indigenous Issues
US	United States
WCPA	World Commission on Protected Areas
WES	World Ecotourism Summit, 2002
WGIP	United Nations Working Group on Indigenous Populations
WHC	World Heritage Centre
WHIPCOE	World Heritage Indigenous Peoples' Council of Experts
WIPO	World Intellectual Property Organization
WPC	Fifth World Parks Congress, 2003 (Durban, South Africa)
WTO	World Trade Organization
WTO-OMT	UN World Tourism Organization
WTTC	World Travel and Tourism Council
WWB	Webber Wentzel Bowens
WWF-International	World Wide Fund for Nature

Chapter 1

Introduction

Must tourists destroy the things they love?
(George, 2004)

Ecotourism has an earthy appeal, but its cachet as a wonder industry is crumbling. As an industry, ecotourism is more damaging to life systems globally than all other industries combined. 'How?', you say – because this industry targets Indigenous Peoples' cultures and ancestral lands. It penetrates to the core, quickly, before anyone can comprehend what just happened or what it means to us all.

None of this talk of ecotourism concerns us, some think. After all, world oil supplies are forecast to run out as early as 2015.[1] So how much damage could the travel industry possibly do if airlines are, one day, grounded? Lots, if we are not careful about what we mean by 'eco' tourism. Lots, if we don't heed all the red lights in the biosphere today, saying that we must re-evaluate lifestyle, wealth and success. Our consumer fantasies – fanned by corporations – have deceived us about the relationships inherent to life.

Industrial ecotourism goes where we should not. It sells sacred lands, sacred knowledge systems, sacred ceremonial sites and sacred trusts simultaneously. It does this in an 'up close and personal' way, where cause literally meets effect. This is a destined meeting of peoples, to test us. When will we heal the cycle of industry abuse? When will we bring economics back into touch with life systems?

Ecotourism is a metaphor for where we stand today as a society. The ecotourism industry glamorizes both our vices and our virtues. By understanding its workings, we can see why choice – not chance – makes destiny, especially now.

This book encourages you to ask the vital questions. It invites you to find your own answers. We each need to choose with knowledge, conviction and dedication what kind of human relationships sustain and celebrate life, before our careening global economy takes us all beyond chaos.

Ecotourism: The chameleon industry

The ecotourism phenomenon

Ecotourism emerged in the US and Europe during the early 1980s as a hybrid concept, when 'sustainability' became a fashionable but serious concern. It is now known by a variety of names, from ethnic or nature tourism to adventure travel. The common element is a professed ethic of respect. Ecotourism is said to benefit local communities and the environment (see Box 2.2).

Growth of ecotourism became particularly strong following the first United Nations Earth Summit in Rio de Janeiro in 1992. This event persuaded governments to link 'development' (that is, economic growth) with the 'environment'. It also led to wide-scale privatization of development assistance, supposedly for poverty relief. Governments began to aggressively use foreign policy to create 'green' business opportunities. Many large conservation groups took on a quasi-corporate role as project consultants and brokers for development. During this period, ecotourism became a championed industry. There was considerable jockeying for positions in the tourism sector, with many governments frontrunners in the competition. The Philippines hosted the first ecotourism congress of the Pacific Asia Travel Association (PATA) in 1992, and proudly says that 'ecotourism has been a buzzword ever since' (The Philippines, 1999). Mesoamerica positioned itself as the first region of countries to collaboratively market ecotourism through the Mundo Maya (Mayan World) programme (see Chapter 7).

Many players were keen to assert their identity through ecotourism. Touristic Union International (TUI) of Germany took the corporate lead, hosting workshops on sustainable tourism at the United Nations (UN) in 1998. Conservation International (CI) and The International Ecotourism Society (TIES) emerged at the front of the non-governmental organization (NGO) pack, though essentially corporate entities. Both worked with the UN to frame 'stakeholder' programming for the UN International Year of Ecotourism (IYE) in 2002. They launched themselves as 'global' think tanks, flanked by the like-minded World Wide Fund for Nature (WWF-International) and The Nature Conservancy (TNC). Under their leadership the line between industry interests and conservation blurred.

Themes raised in Rio were echoed a decade later approaching the next Earth Summit. Klaus Toepfer, executive director of the United Nations Environment Programme (UNEP), called tourism '*the* most important sector in development because of the number of jobs and its growth' (Toepfer, 2002). At the World Summit on Ecotourism (WES) in 2002 the merits of ecotourism were emphasized. African delegates said: 'Ecotourism can bring benefits to the remote rural areas where the majority of our population lives.'[2]

Given these developments, 'ecotourism companies are convinced of their support' (Rao, 2002). More than one company owner attending the WES gushed: 'This is our opportunity in industry to save the Earth.' However, many groups witnessing this industry euphoria have urged caution. The feeling is not just 'too much, too soon', but there are also concerns about how the tourism industry is portraying 'sustainable' tourism. At the *Going Native* debate on tourism, hosted by The Netherlands Centre for Indigenous Peoples in 1999, it was reported that '"eco" tourism as practiced in the Philippines remains the same exploitative industry' (Palomo, 1999).

Since 1992 there have been several statements about sustainable tourism, each with their own take on ecotourism. Some emerged from industry initiatives such as the Pacific Asia Travel Association's (PATA's) Value-based Tourism Committee formed during the early 1990s (D'Amore, 1999). Others were products of government or NGO meetings, where delegates attempted to capture some meaning and importance from their work. Many of these statements were summarized for UN deliberations (Meyer and Garbe, 2001). But the majority are stand-alone efforts that have floated between meeting rooms and have never been put under the scrutiny of affected Indigenous Peoples.

Ecotourism fundamentalism has not eased over time. Proponents re-cite the alleged benefits, while opponents tally the costs. Often the only thing agreed upon is that the 'eco' of ecotourism implies virtue. The 'eco' name has always suggested certification. Most either applaud this brand recognition or react in outrage. With so many players claiming expertise on ecotourism, the voice of affected Indigenous Peoples has seldom been heard. Many industry associations, consultants and NGOs, who are vocal about ecotourism, speak a whole range of community truisms without taking the time to really know 'community' (that is, as constituency, partner or peer). There are a great many parties – on both sides of the ecotourism divide – which get heard simply because viewpoints of Indigenous Peoples continue to be suppressed. Policy developed in this elitist, fraternal environment is dangerously out of balance.

Indigenous Peoples have been widely featured in ecotourism marketing, but remain poorly informed of international dialogues on standards. They are asked to either believe in ecotourism or to reject it, depending upon who is present saying that they have Indigenous interests at heart. Industry interests say 'get on board', while NGOs of various stripes claim that only their own agenda is clean. More and more, Indigenous Peoples are rejecting these overtures and taking their own stands on sustainable tourism. At the United Nations Permanent Forum on Indigenous Issues in 2003, it was reported that tourism has severely damaged Indigenous lands (UN, 2003).

BOX 1.1   Indigenous Peoples get ready

KLM Royal Dutch Airlines' in-flight magazine sums up ecotourism:
With our insatiable quest for novelty, we are venturing further and further afield. No longer satisfied with lying on a beach for two weeks, we want to trek through the Andes, take a horseback safari through the Okavango Delta, climb Kilimanjaro or live like a headhunter in a Borneo longhouse (Davies, 2002, p16).

All these 'novelty' destinations are Indigenous Peoples' lands.

Biodiversity: The next wave of ecotourism

Today ecotourism is a revitalized topic globally due to the momentum of UN talks on biodiversity following the Rio Earth Summit in 1992. Governments are under pressure to implement principles agreed to in the *UN Convention on Biological Diversity* (CBD). At the same time, they are mindful of overstepping their respective comfort zones. Many regard international laws on the environment, human rights and Indigenous Peoples as a burdensome political dance. They are looking for 'solutions' that will bring kudos without setting costly precedents.

The search is on for financial incentives for biodiversity conservation.[3] At the CBD Ministerial Round Table in Slovakia in 1998, governments looked at tourism as an option. It was agreed that global guidelines on tourism might help to achieve *financial* 'sustainability'. Six months later the IYE was announced, with an emphasis on '[increasing] opportunities for the efficient marketing and promotion of ecotourism destinations and products on international markets' (WTO and UNEP, 2002).

Since then, tourism has become the sacred cow of biodiversity economics. Governments and allied institutions are advising: 'If you want to protect biodiversity, it must be made an economic asset. Ecotourism as a model of revenue generation is very important' (Toepfer, 2002). The ecotourism industry is supposedly progressive – that is, an alternative to more blatantly destructive commerce.

As yet, little clarity has been provided by world governments on how sustainability could be achieved in the so-called 'eco' tourism industry. At the 14th Global Biodiversity Forum in 1999, the World Conservation Union (IUCN) sought direction on policies, programmes and activities for sustainable tourism. Although ecotourism was already a prominent growth industry, there was, by then, only a weak definition of 'sustainable use'.[4]

By 2002, no headway had yet been made towards industry standards that would give comfort to impacted Indigenous Peoples or their communities. Nina Rao, Southern co-chair of the NGOs' Caucus on Tourism at the United Nations Commission on Sustainable Development (CSD), voiced concerns at the WES: 'Looking at biodiversity as an economic asset is extremely disturbing. We have always looked spiritually at this. Yet here we see this being eroded' (Rao, 2002).

The notion that 'eco' tourism could galvanize biodiversity conservation is now crumbling. In 2003 The Nature Conservancy proclaimed ecotourism 'an exciting new way to support conservation'.[5] But most international tourism NGOs oppose government promotion of ecotourism.[6] They have little faith in UN processes to define sustainable use, and caution that the tourism industry is speeding ahead with its vices intact (Equations et al, 2004). Independent scientific inquiries confirm that there is *reason* for outcry (Honey, 2004) (see Box 9.4). Animals put under the ecotourism spotlight are stressed out (Ananthaswamy, 2004) just like their human brethren.

Indigenous Peoples are being severely affected by the ecotourism industry. Globally, it is Indigenous ancestral territories that industry finds most marketable. In these 'biodiversity-rich' areas, conflict over industrial-style conservation and corporate-led development is mounting. Governments are therefore scrambling to manage perceptions. Select Indigenous Peoples have been singled out as 'eco' tourism success stories through programmes such as the Equator Initiative (which some sarcastically call the 'Oscars of Poverty').

Most Indigenous Peoples find that involvement with the ecotourism industry accelerates their loss of rights. For each Indigenous People or Indigenous community who benefits from so-called 'eco' tourism, there are countless others who do not. As such, many Indigenous leaders worldwide

---

BOX 1.2　Armchair travellers

A whole generation of television watchers has been exposed to images of distant exotic worlds and 'lost' tribes. The British Broadcasting Corporation (BBC) series *Life on Earth* 'was watched by 500 million people in 100 countries'. To make this epic, filmmaker David Attenborough 'travelled for three years through 40 countries' (Miersch, 1998, p14). Now there are a host of naturalist shows on cable networks, often at prime time. While this 'nature' film business is credited with raising awareness of conservation, it has also fuelled mass 'eco' travel to sensitive ecosystems – often Indigenous territories. Consumers can channel-surf across the places described in travel magazines, where 'Mother nature is at her most alluring' (*Condé Nast Traveler*, p106, 1999).

are challenging conventional thinking on tourism. They say that biodiversity conservation is another excuse for commercial access to Indigenous lands. UN assurances for the protection of 'traditional knowledge' have not allayed this concern (see Chapter 10).

Ecotourism: Global toolbox for community relief?

Industry structure and profits

Tourism is called the world's largest and fastest-growing industry.[7] It results in a transfer of US$25 billion from North to South annually[8] and is, for many impoverished Southern countries (for example, Vanuatu, Belize), the lead source of foreign exchange. As an industry of promise, it has immense momentum and clout.

While ecotourism accounts for just 5 per cent of international tourism, it is generating enormous debate. Industrialized peoples,[9] after degrading much of their own environment, are increasingly hungry for a tourism experience involving 'nature' or 'exotic' cultures. Many want to contribute to 'saving' endangered places and peoples – ironically, put at risk by our own consumer lifestyle. These trends have made ecotourism the most profitable marketing idea that the tourism industry has ever known. Ecotourism, the fastest-growing segment of tourism (CI, 2003), is expanding at over four times the rate of most other types of tourism.

Large and small tour companies alike are now selling travel packages that have an aura of heart and conscience. Still, it is rare that such cosmetic changes translate into any improvement for target communities or their neighbours. Although ecotourism has a higher profit margin than regular package tourism, there is not enough clearance (using industry profit formulas) to allow significantly different corporate practices.

From industry's standpoint, ecotourism must remain reasonably competitive with other market prices, or a number of companies would sabotage their own success. Many conventional tour operators profiting off mass tourism include ecotourism in their portfolio, albeit sometimes under different brand names. Large corporations such as TUI have captured a major share of the international 'eco' tourism market.

The structure of the ecotourism industry is thus vastly different from how it seems. It has several tiers, all interwoven by subcontracts, commissions and other industry fees. Indigenous Peoples whose lands and cultures are marketed are typically kept on the fringe and receive only dregs. At the community level, handshakes and contracts offer little protection. Most are negotiated under grossly lopsided conditions constituting duress.

Profit formulas for the ecotourism industry have four main features, all perpetuating colonial patterns:

1   *High volume sales*: the ecotourism industry needs to maintain a large, constant flow of tourists to be financially viable (in other words, economically sustainable).

2   *Classic trickle down*: there is usually no room in the corporate bottom line for meaningful benefits to reach the community level.

3   *Oppressive relationships*: target communities experience a loss of culture, identity and self-esteem.

4   *Post-traumatic stress*: community members may act out their grief through substance abuse, domestic violence, prostitution, corruption or crime.

One dilemma is that the ecotourism industry is self-regulated and companies seldom adhere to declared standards of practice. Where corporate integrity is maintained, the business often cannot withstand market pressures. Industry monopolies routinely swallow small companies seeking to develop a product more consistent with ecotourism ideals. Illustrating this trend is the UK, where the five largest ecotourism companies service approximately 40 per cent of the British market. Today we politely call such takeovers 'consolidation'. More 'modest' Indigenous economies are undermined by these predatory practices.

These industry trends are driven by a global travel market glutted with 'warehouse' deals, 'no frills' discounts and cut rates on the internet.[10] Aggressive mass marketing essentially fixes the price point for 'eco' tourism. Air travel prices are particularly influential (see Box 9.6). Tourists are accustomed to a certain ratio between air and land costs. A study by the British Association of Travel Agents shows that most 'eco'-minded tourists are prepared to pay only UK£6–£16 extra for their holiday (Davies, 2002, p20). A similar study in Germany found consumer willingness to pay just one additional US dollar (Christ et al, 2003, p36). This does not leave room in industry for true 'eco-'pricing (reflecting costs to life systems), let alone healthy exchange with Indigenous Peoples.

BOX 1.3   Extreme anthropology

The latest ecotourism thrill is 'extreme anthropology' (Spears, 2002). For US$33,000–$49,000 per person, TCS Expeditions (US) takes travellers on a three- to four-week odyssey with a private jet and scientists. Its 'Natural Wonders around the World' trip highlights mostly Indigenous territories, while the 'Heaven and Earth' expedition is mainly Indigenous sacred sites (www.tcs-expeditions.com). Once again, adventurers put culture under their microscope.

The double face of globalization

Industry interpretations of the ecotourism concept tend to be misleading. There are promises of community involvement and benefit-sharing. However, these are hard to substantiate in light of industry's worldwide impacts on Indigenous Peoples' ancestral title and rights. Industrial-style ecotourism is causing widespread loss to Indigenous Peoples of their customary lands, ceremonial centres (sacred sites), languages and knowledge that define them as a people. The emergence of cultural tourism as 'one of the hottest travel trends for the 21st century' (WTO-OMT, 1997) accentuates this crisis.

Cultural erosion is everywhere in the tourism chain of events. Most Indigenous Peoples need only look as far as the community market. Here the double edge of financial incentives is apparent. What happens when a family, and eventually an entire village or region, replaces the cultivation of an heirloom potato variety with potatoes that make better French fries? It is not only an immediate loss of genetic diversity and customary practices. There is a domino effect over generations. In the end, the youth is not only eating the French fries but buying the sugar-loaded commercial varieties. The family garden becomes smaller, young people leave their community for jobs and diabetes creeps in. It is a devastating cycle of culture loss with consequences that eventually spill across all world continents and populations.

Variations of this picture exist today in Indigenous communities worldwide. Tourism jobs lure impoverished families away from seasonal harvesting and food preparation. Meanwhile, tourism inflates the price of purchased food staples. This tightens the vice of poverty, increasing vulnerability to market pressures and all forms of abuse, especially corporate. Indigenous children from Manaus to Kathmandu are selling North American or European candies, cigarettes and postcards to tourists, instead of handmade items home produced from endemic crops. Many others are begging, shining shoes for small coins or get ensnared in sexual prostitution (Baker, 2004). There is a generation-wide loss of customary practices. This jeopardizes cultural identity (that is, 'peoplehood') – the very basis in international law for Indigenous Peoples' land rights and, hence, survival.

Already, such impacts are adequately documented to provide a sobering reference point. Looking at this literature some say that concerns raised by Indigenous Peoples are exaggerated. However, it must be remembered that 99 per cent of third-party analyses (for example, consultant reports, academic papers and mainstream NGO inquiries) lack the necessary familiarity, sensitivity and intimacy with the distinct issues raised by Indigenous Peoples to competently discuss or compare them. Most persons calling these 'pet' issues are themselves shaped by the corporate/consumer world. Few know the smell of soil or taste of water inside concerned communities, or the extent to which these biological lifelines (and our ability to appreciate them) are altered by industry. The question should thus be asked: *who* is being self-indulgent?

For these reasons most smaller grassroots-oriented NGOs working internationally on tourism see extreme conflict between tourism and biodiversity. At the International NGOs' Workshop on Tourism and Biological Diversity in Berlin in March 2000, the concerns of Indigenous Peoples were highlighted and marked as a priority by most participants.[11] During the 2004 World Social Forum, Southern tourism NGOs called for a social review of tourism – including the role of intermediary NGOs in promoting forms of 'sustainable' tourism that harm impoverished communities (see www.wsf-tourism.org).

Many independent tour operators who have made the effort to get acquainted with Indigenous Peoples share this perspective. Yvonne Mejia, a Peruvian tour operator who has worked with local communities for over 20 years, says they are 'the Cinderella of ecotourism' (Mejia, 2002).

Nonetheless, within the international institutions governing policy, candidness on the dangers of industrial ecotourism is rare. Too many institutions' mandates are entwined with the politics of biodiversity (that is, the economics of access and use). Most offer occasional commentary on risks, while pursuing programmes that elevate the risk. UNEP, for example, has stated that 'Ecotourism can severely damage the environment and create social and cultural pressures that undermine biological diversity' (Aloisi de Larderel, 1999). Yet, its Tour Operators' Initiative implicitly accepts conventional tourism, which thrives on mass bookings, unsustainable air travel and industry self-regulation (see www.toinitiative.org and www.uneptie.org/tourism).

BOX 1.4   Philanthropy at what cost?

The Great Escape Foundation has popularized the idea of ecotourism as philanthropy. Through its 2004 Global Scavenger Hunt, it sought to raise US$1 million for charities such as the United Nations Children's Fund (UNICEF) and Doctors without Borders (Griffin, 2003). On this 'anthropological adventure… Budding Indiana Jones (and Janes)' compete for US$100,000 in prizes (Andreeff, 2002). Can our materialism really heal what it destroys?

Product development

Product development in the ecotourism industry continues to be either high end or 'backpacker' oriented, but is becoming more eclectic. There are the standard appeals to nature-starved city folk – for example, kayaking remote archipelagos, hiking 'wilderness' areas or safaris across sprawling grasslands. On the other end of the spectrum are packages that target the neuroses created by our affluent but detached consumer life. These include a range of activities, from supposedly genuine 'shamanic' healing sessions or 'native wisdom' retreats (for instance, vision quests) to the televised *Eco-Challenge* (see Box 1.7) and *Survivor* competitions (see Box 1.8). Most forms of ecotourism have a serious impact upon Indigenous Peoples due to their location or cultural content.[12]

Among the several forms of tourism marketed or perceived as ecotourism, there is a common trend. Industry activities are generally characterized by:

- *Large gap between theory and practice ecotourism*: corporate commitment to the ideals of ecotourism seems strong but is usually weak. There is little due diligence in creating initiatives that could bring these ideals to life. Only a few independent companies such as Wildland Adventures and Journeys International have utilized a sizeable portion of their profits to sponsor community-owned programmes that 'walk the talk'.
- *Clustering of companies at popular sites*: ecotourism brochures all offer variations on the same theme. There is high repetition of destinations between companies. This means that most areas 'in vogue' with eco-tourists will experience intense and prolonged impacts – for example, the Maasai Mara Game Reserve in Kenya and Machu Picchu in the Andes Mountains, Peru. Today, these centres are considered 'ecotourism hubs' – the base from which so-called ecotourism can be expanded regionally. Industry interactions with locals there provide a disturbing precedent for future 'eco' tourism in new locales.
- *Penetration of vulnerable areas*: eco-tourists typically want to see the 'exotic' before it disappears (see Boxes 1.2 and 1.3) or upon hitting some life-cycle pinnacle in their own life.[13] This demand has led to mass tourism within sensitive ecosystems and wildlife corridors: logical 'no-go' zones for industrial development. It has also resulted in companies and conservation NGOs overriding Indigenous Peoples' ancestral title. Although these impacts are known, there are few cases of voluntary withdrawal by industry interests.[14]
- *Fifteen-year window of operations*: in the ecotourism industry, the precautionary approach of the *UN Convention on Biological Diversity* is absent. The average destination loses its unique features within just 15 years (Ashton, 1999). During this short time period, ecosystems are scarred and Indigenous cultures strain under consumer whims. It is a long road to recovery for communities, with spiritual reconnection being the critical step. Financial

mechanisms, compensation arrangements an⟍
industry 'benefits' cannot mitigate, repair or ju
damage.

The ecotourism market is unlikely to correct itself, despite th⟍
cial incentives. With companies all showcasing the same destin⟍
variations, there is an avalanche of impacts once a new 'produ᷅   ᴅiscov-
ered'. In this process there is also a progressive desensitizing of tourists. If
we don't flinch at the working conditions of porters on Mount Kilimanjaro,
in Tanzania, or on the Inca Trail, in Peru, we are unlikely to scrutinize
industry practice elsewhere. Few of us discern or shun forms of exploitation
that are *standard* within the ecotourism industry. Most travellers just want to
carry enough dry socks, bottled water and granola bars for their trek so that
there's no personal holiday crisis.[15]

Fundamental changes in industry practice require corporate disclosure, as well as international policies supporting Indigenous Peoples' ability to
protect their inherent and inalienable rights. There is no impassive solution.

BOX 1.5   **Setting the pace in Laos**

Laos opened to foreigners in 1989 and by 2003 was hosting 700,000 tourists.
Today, 'central Laos has all the makings of travel's last frontier: an unmapped
wilderness, a lost city, villagers unaccustomed to visitors' (Potts, 2003, p115). In
2002, North by Northeast Tours, a Thai travel company with Canadian roots, set
off to chart new turf. Using satellite mapping and a digital camera to mark its
'finds' – as well as local porters – its team ambled into 'the primitive village of
Ban Na… If we don't explore and sell it, others will' (Potts, 2003, p219).

Indigenous Peoples in the ecotourism equation

Government pragmatism

Indigenous cultures are *big* business for the ecotourism industry. The majority of prime ecotourism destinations worldwide lie within isolated Indigenous
territories, where Indigenous Peoples preserve the ecological legacy that elsewhere has been destroyed. There, high biodiversity remains due to knowledge
systems refined over millennia (Reichel-Dolmatoff, 1999). Eco-tourists will
spend a small fortune to see these 'pristine' lands, particularly when the trip
includes a chance to interact with 'authentic' tribal cultures.

Governments are savvy to the profits attached to tourism involving
Indigenous Peoples. In national ecotourism plans, products with Indigenous
content are coined 'value-added' tourism. Northern countries have poured

‌n money into quantifying this cultural premium and are now pushing ‌otourism' diversification onto debt-saddled countries of the South. Meanwhile, those whose economies are directly built on Indigenous lands are capitalizing firsthand (see Box 1.6). In New Zealand, a NZ$300 million government investment built the *Te Papa Tongarewa*, or national museum of Maori culture. This centre received 1 million visitors during its first five months of operation (Hinch, 1999). Canada has since created a permanent 2000 square metre exhibition on Aboriginal peoples at its Museum of Civilization (see www.civilization.ca). Culture showcases of this calibre help to anchor ecotourism; there is immense profit by association for countries branding their tourism industry with Indigenous images.

In tourism, governments are often more entwined with industry than elsewhere in the global economy. It can be difficult to distinguish the private sector from the public sector because of the level of state investment in tourism and the types of easements granted to industry. Several countries, such as Papua New Guinea, prominently feature Indigenous Peoples in their national travel brochures and websites.[16] Many national promotions foster an appreciation of everything 'folkloric' without any corresponding improvements in 'development' policy (that is, methods for free and prior informed consent). They push generic products that feed off nameless families, communities and peoples whom most governments would prefer to remain incognito.

Ecuador offers a prime example of government manoeuvring with respect to ecotourism. When it hosted the World Congress on Adventure Travel and Ecotourism in 1999, Indigenous peoples were featured in the welcoming and were asked to announce that 'the doors are open' to ecotourism. Yet, next door in the oil sector, government policy is also open access – endangering Indigenous Peoples in regions such as Pastaza, Ecuador. Needless to say, the congress did not indicate any magnanimous shift of national policy. The entertainment provided to congress delegates was a derogatory depiction of a Jívaro 'headhunter' dance. So why did Indigenous speakers participate? They were creating an opening to tell their own story. Through the conference organizers, some had arranged to make a headline presentation on how Indigenous nations such as the Cofán, Quechua and Hoarani developed their own tourism enterprises as a means of fighting oil development on ancestral lands.

Governments count on being able to develop international regimes for industrial access and use before Indigenous Peoples are fully conversant with the global economy or with avenues to protect themselves through international law. The goal in forums such as the CBD is to create policy quickly, before the process of policy development is encumbered with unwanted accommodations. Investment certainty comes before decency. If this line of political thought continues amongst world governments, the costs to humanity will be staggering.

BOX 1.6 **Colonizers host European tourists**

Canada and Australia both fund Aboriginal tourism commissions nationally in order to capitalize on strong European interest in Aboriginal tourism. Australia's Indigenous Affairs minister has stated that the country's 'greatest treasure is arguably its Indigenous peoples and their cultures' (ABC Network, 2002). In 2005 Australia launched the Aus$3.8 million 'Business Ready Program for Indigenous Tourism'. Canada, meanwhile, reports upwards of Cdn$2.9 billion annually from Aboriginal tourism (ATTC, 2003). In 2003, it invested Cdn$599,000 in Aboriginal Tourism Team Canada. It then sponsored a Cdn$2.5 million three-day conference on Aboriginal tourism in Whistler, British Columbia – site of the 2010 Olympics. Between 2000 and 2005, Canada aimed to attract 10.8 million visitors from Europe for 'native tourism' (Ogilvie, 2003). Can we call this sustainable?

Indigenous Peoples' vigilance

Indigenous leaders worldwide have identified industry-controlled tourism as one of the major threats to their peoples' cultures and to the integrity of ancestral lands. The ecotourism industry is of particular concern since it specifically targets ancestral lands. The crux is free and prior informed consent. However, the underlying concepts of 'development' and 'conservation' pushed by government also endanger Indigenous cultures.

In spite of the problems identified with this industry, some Indigenous Peoples continue to utilize the term ecotourism in a favourable way. The idea persists that in the hands of a community ecotourism can be 'good for the people'. Communities have expressed impatience towards the suggestion that industry may move too quickly for them to jump in or stay on board. Among this bunch, many have met the disastrous consequences of rushing forward; others have followed their own instinct to slow down or entirely shut down. The same lesson plays over and over: marketing before comprehensive community planning is dangerous.

In Canada's Alert Bay, British Columbia, the Kwakiutl have been keen to offer whale-watching tours in order to capitalize on local growth in the ecotourism industry. However, the whale pods in their vicinity landed on the national endangered species list due, in part, to pressure from aggressive outside eco-tour operators, just a few years into the local whale-watching boom. This is one case of many worldwide where Indigenous Peoples who are interested in tourism have found themselves caught in the backwash of industry's impacts, with opportunities foreclosed.

It remains that most Indigenous Peoples curious about the ecotourism concept lack access to information that is crucial for decision-making. Some pursue industrial-style 'ecotourism' because available snapshots of the industry seem benign enough. Others know of the community learning curve elsewhere and are forging their own cultural path. But many homegrown initiatives succumb to industry competition. For example, the Quechua and Aymara of Taquile Island, Peru, lost their community transport co-operative to outside interests. If a third party becomes the main interface to the consumer world, local control over access and visitation quickly becomes tenuous.

When Indigenous Peoples garner the resources to embark on their own assessment of the ecotourism industry, there are three main concerns that emerge:

1   *past grievances*: things that are sacred that have already been com-
     mercialized through tourism – for example, cultural images and
     sacred sites;
2   *current threats*: things that are sacred which are on the brink of
     tourism commercialization – for example, ceremonial and heal-
     ing practices;
3   *future vigilance*: other sacred elements of culture that are vulnerable
     to global tourism markets – for example, knowledge of medicinal
     plants.

Indigenous Peoples who access this information are informing sister communities that all encounters with the ecotourism industry warrant utmost precaution. A protective strategy, embracing the totality of industry's impacts, is critical.

Getting real about ecotourism

The 'eco' of tourism: Ecology or economics?

Ecotourism is widely marketed as corporations giving something back. It offers a convincing image of world community at a time when the wisdom of world government is being questioned. Through ecotourism, governments believe that the leadership and citizenship of the private sector can be proven. Many see it as a powerful rebuttal to the anti-globalization protests that are gaining momentum around the world today.

Several countries see ecotourism as a preferred way of financing environmental conservation. Some consider it a deterrent to the poaching or 'high grading' of endangered species. Others regard it an economic alter-native to intensive logging. There are many valid sounding arguments, often co-opted from NGO platforms (see Western Canada Wilderness Committee, 1997).

Ecotourism is, ultimately, a bailout strategy for economic growth.[17]

The industry does not challenge the fundamental causes of biodiversity loss, such as today's consumer lifestyle, wide-open trade regimes or corporate human rights violations globally. Instead, it specifically targets the most affluent of global consumers.[18] Their large disposable incomes and desire for status as connoisseurs of world travel make them a sought-after market niche. Most 'eco' tourists are veteran travellers who continue to log *plenty* of air miles.

The danger of ecotourism is that, as a lucrative growth industry, it is seductive over the short term. Several governments facing the collapse or costly restructuring of mismanaged extractive industries, such as fisheries (Nierenberg, 2003) or forestry, see ecotourism as a solution. Countries that have lost their edge on traditional tourism markets also are swinging toward ecotourism. There is a frontier mentality – with rapid investment and minimal regulation. As a result, the ecotourism industry itself has become a significant cause and accelerator of problems such as pollution and climate change.[19] NGOs coalitions warn that ecotourism is really just a new form of mass tourism, bringing globalized corporate profits at the price of localized hardship.

Testimonies from Indigenous Peoples confirm that ecotourism is highly oversold as a concept. Most say that ecotourism proposals look little different in character than other industry ventures in their midst. Their experience is that the ecotourism industry profiteers off Indigenous cultures, behind a mask of doing good.

Ecotourism and communities

After two decades of debate and practice, there are still differing opinions as to what qualifies as ecotourism. With industry departing so greatly from the original concept of ecotourism, opinions have become polarized. Most policy-makers maintain that the ecotourism industry has intrinsic value. Yet many ground workers believe that ecotourism involves even greater social and ecological costs than regular mass tourism. Vulnerable ecosystems are penetrated and Indigenous cultures are commoditized at industry's whim.

The ecotourism industry has not retooled itself in order to work with communities. It has simply transferred conventional business practices from other sectors. Nowhere is this more apparent than among Indigenous Peoples living in the biodiversity oases now fashionable for ecotourism, such as Laos (see Box 1.5). Industry's immediate focus upon 'discovery' of ancestral lands is typically product development, instead of establishing a trusted relationship with the people. This type of rapid assessment and pre-emptive investment shuts out communities. Indigenous Peoples have no real part in tourism development, project management or industry benefits.

While the ecotourism industry sells itself as being responsive to community needs, it is in reality a mixed group of business interests whose ethics compass leans to the political right.[20] The vast majority of companies are intimidated or put off by any prospect of having to learn to do business differently. They will push and then push more, posturing as necessary to obtain access permits from involved ministries. Government revenue objectives are satisfied, but at huge opportunity cost and direct loss to target communities.

Most Indigenous Peoples find it impossible to effectively challenge industry practices or government approval processes that threaten their ancestral territory and culture. In today's fiscal climate, business is rolling and communities are reeling. Few communities can rally the necessary support to get heard. Few see options beyond outright rejection of industry. While campaigns publicizing industry wrongdoings are increasingly the only recourse, communities put on such perpetual defence may underestimate potential allies.

Outside conventional industry, there is a minority who believes in ecotourism really assisting affected Indigenous Peoples. Some NGOs and small companies support the principle of self-determination even if getting there seems murky. Their commitment to relationship-building is usually sincere and can lead to good rapport if the terms for dialogue are mutually agreed from the outset. Initiatives such as 'Ethical Traveler' of the Earth Island Institute (see www.ethicaltraveler.com) are still learning the ropes of such cross-cultural protocol, but are breaking trail, nevertheless. They give insights to how tourism supports or breaches fundamental rights.

On this more altruistic front the reviews are mixed. Most organizations playing a support role to Indigenous Peoples are aware of the involved human rights issues, but have limited understanding of Indigenous rights, or Indigenous knowledge issues. They may inadvertently proceed in ways that compromise ancestral title and rights. For example, many conservation NGOs will support the creation of a protected area, without first understanding how this could negatively impact upon land rights and self-determination.

The irony is that while both mainstream and 'activist' versions of ecotourism are proclaimed a socially just alternative to conventional mass tourism, each tends to perpetuate the very relationships which economically and politically oppress Indigenous Peoples. Very few NGOs or companies advocating a 'conservation economy' take their cue from Indigenous Peoples, rather than attempting to provide answers or pirate recognition for innovation.

Ecotourism lessons

Personal growth for a price

Ecotourism brings the most affluent of consumers into the immediate midst of Indigenous Peoples.[21] It is a meeting of two worlds, which will result in either exploitation or healing. The outcome depends not just upon their mutual readiness, but also upon the intent and pertinent experience of any intermediaries involved in the exchange (such as tour operators or broker NGOs).

Most tourists are unprepared for the full experience possible through travel. Their decision to purchase an ecotourism holiday is seldom made with a real sense of context. It is like a graduation: out of the shopping mall and into exclusive designer boutiques.[22] Most who can afford such specialty travel will experiment, interchanging a luxury cruise or vineyard tour with a popular eco-tour, such as a safari or eco-lodge stay.[23] They are gravitating towards something different, without much reflection as to why.

The majority of these tourists are seeking to balance their lifestyle on a physical level. They want an experience that takes them away from city life, office pressures or household schedules. Usually their own livelihood comes from the very industries which threaten biological and cultural diversity worldwide. Most own shares – directly or via mutual funds, pension plans, life insurance or simple bank deposits – in a broad spectrum of implicated multinational corporations. Some hold an executive or management position in these companies. They seek a break from the structure they live in, without understanding economic globalization or its harsh societal and cross cultural impacts.

Only a minority of travellers opt for ecotourism because of the possibility of profound learning and growth. These rare individuals are in search of a personal experience that will touch them on multiple levels.[24] In many cases, they are seeking something esoteric or spiritual. In this quest, they are drawn to 'nature' and to Indigenous Peoples. Like conventional eco-tourists, they want balance; however, they already understand to some degree that their personal journey is connected to the global and cosmic whole.

BOX 1.7   Racing to the four corners

The Eco-Challenge race emerged as part of the 'adventure sports' craze in 1992 and a decade later was in full gear, sporting 'remote' destinations such as Sabah and Fiji. Sabah offered competitors 'a chance to explore one of the last truly wild places on Earth' on Dusun/Kadazan lands. The Fiji course took them, wearing their corporate sponsor's logo, through 'hunting grounds once home to cannibals' (see www.ecochallenge.com). With over 940 million households watching, 50 or so international teams dashed to the finish line, claiming: 'This is no holiday.' But on their heels came eco-tourists. Outdoor Travel Adventures offers 'post Eco-Challenge' trips, where 'you can spill your own sweat on the 2002 Eco-Challenge course' (Blakesley, 2003, p54).

It is true that relationships built through tourism *can* fundamentally change lives.[25] Through tourism it is possible for visitors to understand the connectedness of what Indigenous Peoples call the 'web of life'. For this very reason there is now an international movement promoting peace through tourism (D'Amore, 1999). Still, inside the ecotourism industry the potential for such a shift is low. Most companies have yet to move beyond dismissive or paternalistic communications and relationships with Indigenous Peoples. It is primarily *local* lives that are changed by tourism, further tipping global class and race relations out of balance.

From consumer to compatriot

Eco-tourists visiting the lands of Indigenous Peoples frequently comment upon the hardcore poverty. Many see it as an eyesore that they would prefer covered up; but some find it alluring and compelling. Tour companies read their clientele carefully in this regard. It is not just foreign tourists who become squeamish about poverty. Reactions can be especially pronounced among domestic tourists, living in denial to shield their own conscience. Fundamentally, *our* consumer attitudes determine the degree of benefits flowing from industry to target communities.[26]

Information on local circumstances is normally kept at the level of curiosity. There is often a romancing of poverty to integrate the trip experience with the tourist's own reality, which today is increasingly shaped by upscale lifestyle magazines urging consumer 'simplicity', like *Real Simple* or *Country Living* (US editions). This diet of seemingly non-offensive trip information is far from neutral. Anyone who has lived poverty knows that it is not romantic. Anyone familiar with the extreme indignities of Indigenous poverty knows its direct link to colonialism, industry profiteering and our own consumer habits.

What happens when eco-tourists come into face-to-face contact with Indigenous Peoples through tourism's brief encounters? This usually is the point where the tourist paddles forward, instead of risking a glimpse of 'cause and effect'. This is where the average tour operator sugar-coats the issue of 'underlying causes' – namely, corporate duplicity and our consumer complicity. No meaningful understanding is built of the link between cultural diversity and biological diversity. None of the core issues is touched concerning threats to biodiversity in such destination areas, or other affected world regions. In this respect, ecotourism is the perfect holiday from liability. We can pretend that we are doing good, while disowning our consumer selves.

Most eco-tourists are on board the holiday canoe to expand their understanding of the world, not to fundamentally challenge or dismantle it. They want to return home to continue their career, their studies, their family time or their retirement. They are searching for an adventure, fantasy or sabbatical, but not a life-shattering epiphany or calling. Successful tour companies know this buffer zone; their professional guides navigate towards a safety net. The idea is to give clients just enough taste of transformation that it will register as a 'peak experience' and excite them (or their friends) to sign up for the next trip. They do not want to lose clients to volunteer initiatives such as the Peace

Corps. Nor do they want to overface them and give business back to regular holiday companies.

Only in cases where the resident Indigenous People control their own exposure to tourism is there a prospect of a balanced exchange, leading to a relationship of respect, communication and collaboration. Some Indigenous Peoples such as the Cofán of Ecuador have hosted paying visitors at a separate village built specially for this type of intercultural exchange. The Cofán created a satellite 'community' as the base for guided cultural tours through their ancestral lands in the rainforest.[27] Zábalo differs fundamentally from its government-promoted counterparts, such as those exploiting the Kayan in Thailand (*The Nation*, 2003) or high-traffic DumaZulu in South Africa.

Tourists entering this type of experience very quickly learn the difference between artificial boundaries created by industry to mingle 'haves' with 'have nots', and natural boundaries created within communities to bring relationships into a healthful balance. They have the opportunity to experience firsthand what is sacred in this domain, and why the sacred is not for sale.

BOX 1.8 *Survivor* **affects survival**

The hit television series *Survivor* has brought new fanfare to ecotourism. This series, 'king of the TV jungle' (Gee, 2002), debuted in 2000 with 51 million viewers in the US alone. A few years and 50,000 applicants per episode later, it still drew 27 million loyal fans. Viewers were treated to a 39-day game between 'tribes', depicting Indigenous Peoples' lives as 'deprivation'. Meanwhile, an on-site crew of 250 backed up the 16 contestants (Hochman, 2001).

Through *Survivor*, we gawked at the mock 'Indigenous' experience and demonized 'nature'. The set featured tribal-sounding music, tribal-looking effigies and a 'tribal council' fire. Contestants ate worms and larvae. They painted their faces and wore bone and feather necklaces while eyeing the US$1 million prize: awarded for individualism, manipulation and betrayal – values opposite from those of Indigenous Peoples. We saw them dream of Doritos chips and spend US$400 on a hamburger. 'Great Aboriginal Father, be kind to us', said one forture seeker.

Survivor was a bonanza for several industries. Advertising companies posted hundreds of millions in revenue; Las Vegas casinos cashed in too. The show was touted as 'a template for all that America stands for' (Tremblay, 2001). Yet, there was no indication of royalties to Indigenous Peoples from the show or from its extensive spin-offs.

There has been a surge in ecotourism on ancestral lands as companies rush to issue brochures to *Survivor* destinations (*The Province*, 2001). In 2003, GAP Adventures featured tours led by former cast members. Tour groups were divided into three 'tribes' for friendly clashes in between traditional sightseeing (see www.gap.ca).

Death of a concept, birth of capacity

A decade ago, it was already old news that ecotourism is, in essence, a marketing brand, delivering more of the same types of industrial impacts. By 1992, it was well documented that vulnerable places and peoples are put in *further* jeopardy by the ecotourism industry. Even industry insiders were spreading the word about destructive practices. A handful of small owner operators and internationally experienced consultants went public with their appeals for better corporate ethics.[28] By this time, however, a profitable consulting industry had already built up around ecotourism, benefiting from the confusion around the concept. For the next decade, this group would recycle variations of the same information on ecotourism strategies and impacts.

The UN's announcement of 2002 as the International Year of Ecotourism gave new vigour to this money-making debate. Under the umbrella of the IYE and the *UN Convention on Biological Diversity*, a number of well-established, highly networked consultants and consultancy NGOs have proposed a fresh batch of 'best practice' studies and pilot projects. These are being embraced by world governments, policy institutions and affiliated development assistance agencies as if the period of reflection, 1992–2002, was a lost decade. There is a lot to gain for consultants plugged into corporate, government and multilateral contracts, now that ecotourism markets remain buoyant – and much to lose for Indigenous Peoples caught in the crossfire. Law firms are straddling the divide, providing the legal infrastructure for tourism deals.

For Indigenous Peoples whose ancestral territories are now declared 'biodiversity' zones, the ecotourism industry is becoming big news. There has been an array of broken promises about community involvement and benefits. Most communities caught in this grey zone of abuse are too cut off from the resources necessary for some form of corrective action. However, there is growing resolve among Indigenous leadership internationally to share information on ecotourism so that others can differentiate good from bad. Many Indigenous Peoples are choosing to walk their own cultural path with tourism, for their own reasons, leaving ecotourism deal-makers knocking at the door.

Consumers know little of the deception around ecotourism (in either corporate circles or the 'conservation' and 'development' communities), much less the costs of ecotourism to actual living, breathing communities. They judge ecotourism by what they smell and hear while ambling along a river, or traversing a walkway through the forest canopy. For most, knowing that these vibrant pockets of life exist is enough. To many of us this means that stewardship is happening. The natives must be happy, we think.

With Indigenous Peoples and consumers both being handed abbreviated information on ecotourism benefits and costs, it still falls to the 'experts' to determine the course of industry expansion. To date, few impact assessments completed by big-name consultants, billboard-size consulting firms or consultancy NGOs have responsibly touched upon the cautionary tales. Those that do are usually authored by parties who, as consultants, play both sides of the fence. What will another ten years of expert guidance look like? If the last 20 years are an indication, there will be little correction of distorted statistics on ecotourism until Indigenous Peoples have a leading role in the analysis.

To safeguard life systems on Earth, Indigenous leaders must guide impact assessments and performance audits concerning industry proposals for ancestral territories. The risk in identifying such an obvious step is that it will spawn a whole new generation of proposals from the consulting world. Already, consultants sniffing out new directions at international meetings on biodiversity and tourism realize that Indigenous Peoples will play a larger role in developing templates and tools for so-called 'sustainable' tourism. There are proposals for facilitation services rolling off their printers. Facilitated stakeholder consultations and facilitated capacity-building workshops will mark this 'new era' of ecotourism expansion, unless we realize our present crossroads in human relations with the sacred.

If the ecotourism industry wishes to gain credibility, the whole pattern of communications on sustainable tourism must change. The costs of industrial ecotourism currently filtered from target communities and (when possible) shared directly by Indigenous Peoples tells a straightforward story. Within government and industry there is acceptance – if not active policy – of an apathetic and often sloppy work ethic toward Indigenous Peoples. The whole industry is built on outdated formulas for 'community participation'. Most consultations ignore international law on the rights of Indigenous Peoples.

This book looks at new ways of working together with Indigenous Peoples, starting from a foundation of our personal self-knowledge. Today there is abundant rhetoric about consultation and capacity-building, but complete resistance to making the dialogue real. Companies fear costs, governments fear disrupted commerce, international bodies fear political maelstroms, consultants fear becoming redundant and many NGOs become threatened when there is nothing to critique. This protectionism represents a lot of energy to be harnessed.

By rethinking our roles and responsibilities, it is possible to rebuild sustainable economies. But do we share a sense of purpose in safeguarding life systems? Can we reach a place of mutual respect and care?

Conclusion

Given the conflicting data on ecotourism, and the poignant testimonies from Indigenous Peoples of industry's misdeeds, it must be stressed that 'no stone should be left unturned'. This is not a time to be cavalier about sustainability and play one 'expert' opinion off another. We are talking about *life systems*. The issues skirted by policy-makers are real – not just for affected communities, but for humanity and existence as a whole.

We need honesty in future talks on bio-cultural diversity. To date, the process for critical talks on 'sustainability' has served industry. In ecotourism, the principle of community participation is where dialogue begins, but also where it gets stuck. When cross-cultural issues such as rights and responsibilities enter the discussion it just thickens the mud, unless there is a guiding vision of beauty (that is, *life*) and soulful living for all.

Ultimately, it is spiritual terrain that needs to be covered. Few of us are willing to put on hip waders to walk into this heart of the debate. Yet, now is the time for courageous decisions. To break the impasse we need to reconnect head to heart. We need to bring our corporate/consumer world to conscious-ness with regard to impacted Indigenous Peoples, their ancestral lands and our profound *a priori* interconnectedness. Otherwise, this material world treads on sacred ground.

Reaching productive discussions on sustainable tourism will require:

- naming the real barriers to cross-cultural communication (such as racism);
- our moral commitment to developing a common understanding of economy-wide industry impacts;
- tolerance for unfamiliar concepts, practices and value systems;
- adherence to international law concerning the rights of Indigenous Peoples;
- willingness to let a policy process fail if it is not suited to the task;
- humility to start over as necessary, whether at the macro- or micro- level; and
- commitment to circle back to first principles (for example, human rights) when stuck.

Recommended reading

- *Contours* newsletter, issued by the Ecumenical Coalition on Tourism (Hong Kong), www.ecotonline.org
- *Cultural Survival Quarterly* (1999) feature issue on 'Protecting indigenous culture and land through ecotourism', summer edition
- Equations (India) newsletter and website, www.equitabletourism. org
- Indigenous Tourism Rights International (US), mailing list and website, www.tourismrights.org
- *Third World Resurgence* (1999) feature edition on 'Tourism,

globalization and sustainable development', no 109, March,
Third World Network

- Tourism Investigation and Monitoring Team (Thailand), newsletter and website, www.twnside.org.sg/tour.htm

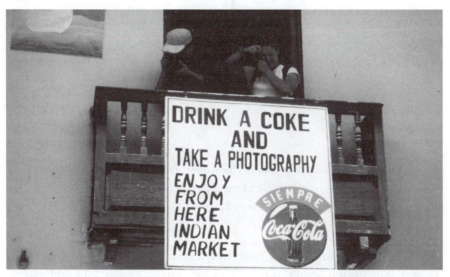

Figure 1.1 **Market at Pisac, Peru: A tourist favourite for telephoto adventures**

Figure 1.2 **Market at Pisac, Peru: Tourists zoom in on 'culture' for pennies per picture**

Chapter 2

Land Rights

Of all the 'ism', tourism is the worst. It has in its path all the neo-colonial patterns.

(Aga Khan, Muslim spiritual leader, cited in Tan, 2004, p3)

The fundamental issue of 'eco' tourism is land rights. All rights of Indigenous Peoples flow from ancestral title to the land. These are inherent and inalienable collective rights recognized under international law, vital to individual human rights. They include the right to self-determination, achieved through free and prior informed consent.

Looking at ecotourism, it is important to distinguish between industry's advances and Indigenous Peoples' own tourism enterprises, which are mislabelled as ecotourism. Some Indigenous Peoples have successfully used tourism to safeguard their ancestral territory. Through tourism they are exercising their title to ancestral lands. This may generate enough income to help sustain legal teams, or for broader advocacy campaigns to defend land rights. But for most, it is a strategic interface with the world, necessary to expose ongoing colonialism. The vast majority remain reliant upon funding for shelter from industry's abuse, which differs little between the various global industries.

While successes in Indigenous tourism do exist, most governments exaggerate the role of supportive policies and programmes. Policy is often used to make unilateral, statutory decisions over ancestral lands without regard for *a priori* rights. Moreover, many governments that are frontrunners in developing policy for 'sustainable' tourism, supposedly inclusive of Indigenous Peoples, are aggressively countering land rights in other areas of their national economy. This misconduct is widespread and an innate part of economic globalization.

Globally, the ecotourism industry is accelerating the loss of Indigenous Peoples' land rights. The industry is not only self-regulated but also highly transient. Companies essentially operate jurisdiction-free once licences, contracts or itineraries are in hand. Most governments will collaborate with industry on marketing, but otherwise remain 'hands off' to prevent corporate relocation. Exploited Indigenous Peoples have few options but resistance once land rights are bypassed through such a nebulous permitting process.

Indigenous leaders seldom discuss tourism without raising the subject of ancestral title. Indigenous Peoples' cultural understanding of title is that it is Creator-given and exists in perpetuity as a sacred responsibility. Business interests accustomed to land being bought and sold find this disconcerting. In their thinking, 'The business of business is business' (Iwand, 2003). Few companies are willing to enter dialogue on inter-generational responsibilities that span lifetimes. Their world consists of quarterly earnings and annual reports.

BOX 2.1   Cashing in on Indigenous lands

'According to UNDP [the United Nations Development Programme], 80 per cent of the world's remaining biodiversity is located in Indigenous territories' (Shaw, 2003). Today, like yesterday, industry activity within Indigenous Peoples' lands buoys global stock markets and currencies. During 2004, 'mutual funds focused on natural resources were the top performing group' (*Vancouver Sun*, 2004). However, there has been no corresponding security for Indigenous Peoples. Instead, industry is closing in with sudden intensity. The United Nations is parading its Millennium Development Goals (MDGs), saying that biodiversity will help to achieve them (UNDP, 2003). New economic powers such as China are making international investments and acquisitions. As this industrial machinery revs up, we are supposed to believe that ecotourism industry is somehow less invasive. Yet, it transports global consumers smack into the middle of Indigenous territories.

The politics of land rights

Outstanding grievances

The sovereignty of Indigenous peoples, though initially recognized by many European colonial powers, was quickly wallpapered over. It was a process called domestication, involving a series of legalized illegalities (Martinez, 1999, p30). Indigenous land rights were moved under colonial law. Today, these sordid details are no secret at the United Nations (UN). What remains hushed is the ongoing mission of certain 'upstanding' governments to utilize the UN and parallel bodies to suppress Indigenous Peoples. For the sake of industrialization, corporate governments are again orchestrating access to Indigenous ancestral lands.

World governments have framed Indigenous Peoples' land rights as a maverick political issue when, in the context of biodiversity and policy for sustainable use, they are more a technical matter requiring conscientious scrutiny. In international law, Indigenous land rights exist. They indicate underlying ancestral title with an inescapable economic component. The question is how to accommodate such title and rights without compromising their real meaning and function. How do we reorient ourselves, binding rights to responsibility?

To date, there has been no international inquiry or grievance body dedicated to the issue of Indigenous land rights and tourism. Nor has there been support for Indigenous Peoples to coordinate and relay critical information to relevant policy forums, such as the UN's first inter-agency meeting on sustainable tourism in November 2004. Third-party academic studies, nongovernmental organization (NGO) reports and consultant snapshots are the only visible paper trail of repeat industry offences. These disclosures offer a glimpse of the issues and their implications, but are not even a small shadow of Indigenous Peoples' own testimonies.

The major reason for this lack of due diligence on land rights is economic. Many governments are fast tracking private-sector proposals for so-called 'eco' tourism, regardless of whether they offer sustainable tourism. In effect, the subject of land rights is taboo in international and national policy talks on tourism. Most governments perceive Indigenous land rights as an arbitrary veto power on development, rather than a valid time-tested (in fact, *millennial*) system for sustainable relationships.

Initiating a coherent discussion on the issue of land rights is a challenge. It is a topic that leads to heated exchanges. Strong emotions are expressed by Indigenous leadership concerning corporate disregard for cultural concepts of title. Governments and industry, in turn, react with indignation and disdain – suggesting colonialism was the best thing that happened to Indigenous Peoples. Today, though, corporate racism and racist characterizations of colonial history are less defensible because of media exposés (Ayres, 2004). Even the popular press now reports on violations of land rights (Davies, 2002).

Whereas Indigenous defence of the land used to be ridiculed by industry as an eccentricity or inconvenience, it is now seen as a potential impediment to business. Since Indigenous Peoples began to converge on the UN in 1977 their international stature has grown. Many are skilfully using global political arenas when corporations, or industry as a whole, become too heavy-handed in their treatment of communities.[1] Others have put pressure on corporations by airing grievances within international markets[2] or bodies such as the World Trade Organization (WTO) and the credit-rating agency Standard & Poor's (Willcocks, 2004). In the tourism sector, as elsewhere, such land rights disputes are now a growth industry for law firms practising corporate law.[3]

Exchanges between Indigenous Peoples and NGOs tend to be more amicable, but not necessarily more informed. Several NGOs are vocal proponents of conservation strategies that may threaten ancestral land rights – for example, protected areas. Few truly concede to cultural protocols when setting foot in an Indigenous territory.[4] There is a lingering sense of primacy among a good many 'environmentalists'.

Despite these strained relationships around land rights, the topic keeps cropping up. Mention of land rights is now commonplace at major international policy forums. Indigenous Peoples are lobbying governments for an end to the impasse, especially in forums concerning the 'environment'. Their leadership has become adept at bridging spiritual and technical dialogues on sustainable use. This is creating a significant shift in relations. World governments now refer to 'traditional knowledge' as a component of biodiversity conservation, though they have yet to comprehend or heed sacred knowledge.

Barriers to meaningful dialogue

Much of the antagonism over land rights could be resolved by having a common base of information to guide talks. However, the world economy is thriving on misinformation. Perpetuating stereotypes about Indigenous Peoples and the alleged 'benefits' of colonialism (that is, 'development') is more profitable than healing colonial relationships.

Land rights are a prominent topic within international dialogues on sustainable tourism. This does not mean that they are incorporated within the discussion agenda. Core issues raised by Indigenous Peoples or supportive NGOs are usually deflected elsewhere. In the *UN Convention on Biological Diversity* (CBD) arena, one safety valve used is the programme of work on traditional knowledge. Governments rely upon this as a 'catch all' when hot issues concerning Indigenous rights come up.

Land rights were the proverbial 'hot potato' during the CBD's development of draft guidelines on tourism and biodiversity during 2001–2004. Many tourism 'experts' participating came to the CBD process late and thus had no exposure to the course of debate on land rights or traditional knowledge, both topics outside their expertise and personal social realm. None sought a catch-up briefing on Indigenous rights issues, nor was any briefing arranged for them. Key baseline information never reached this group, weakening the process.

Such bottlenecks indicate the need for due diligence. Strangleholds on information are common in tourism dialogues where land rights emerge as a topic. Resources such as the *UN Study on Treaties* (Martinez, 1999) are available but are not being referenced or applied. Volumes upon volumes of past statements by Indigenous Peoples to the UN, and to other world bodies, routinely get lost in the bureaucratic void. Meanwhile, mandated Indigenous leaders (who truly represent the Elders) are seldom identified or funded to participate. It is reasonable to ask: where is our conscience in policy forums? How can we reverse peer pressure so that fundamental rights actually matter?

There are now high-profile initiatives promoting tourism as a bridge to peace. The International Institute for Peace through Tourism has held annual summits since 1999. Although this forum attempts to bridge spiritual and technical dialogue, the handful of Indigenous delegates found that there was no place at the table except as glorified stakeholders (Smoke, 1999). This type of experience is reminiscent of ecotourism itself. Navaya Ole Ndasko, Maasai, asks: 'Can we really talk about peace through tourism? In whose image? In the image of Anglo-American "peace"?' (2003).

Breaking new ground

In the tourism sector, the learning curve around land rights is steep. The dialogue is shaping swiftly due to the intrusive nature of ecotourism. This is causing dangerous polarization. Most government negotiators are more inclined to duck the real issues through 'make work' projects on safe tangents (for example, supposed 'best practices', partnerships or certification) than to identify meaningful ways of accommodating co-existing titles. Many Indigenous delegates, meanwhile, are becoming stuck in an unimaginative vocabulary of dialogue which is reactive to government positions; they become more tied to a negotiating table than to the Elders, ceremonies or land. Both of these tangents lead to a replay of past grievances.

The lesson in this dynamic is twofold. First, recognized leaders (that is, mandated decision-makers) need to be involved on both sides for any visionary solutions to occur. Second, it takes a sense of fellowship (interconnection) to communicate effectively on divisive issues. Agreeing on a bilateral yet transparent process,[5] and giving the process a chance to succeed, are vital. Stakeholder forums are *not* the place for dialogue on Indigenous rights (see Chapter 8).

Advancing awareness of what land rights are and how they relate to sustainability requires a sincere willingness to learn. It is difficult to evaluate ecotourism impacts without first being sensitized to Indigenous Peoples' unique relationship with the land. This relationship has been acknowledged by the UN Commission on Human Rights (Daes, 1997), among many others. However, the average person (whether layperson or 'expert') lacks the background to recognize the rights-related impacts of ecotourism, or how these link to international law, global trade regimes and political processes that affect Indigenous Peoples.

Future dialogue forums on sustainable tourism need to reflect land rights as a core cross-cutting issue. Otherwise, we will end up mired in a debate that is not really the debate. Ancestral title is an *inclusive* concept, altogether different from exclusive jurisdiction (that is, property law) in European-based legal systems. Portraying it as a threat or diminishing it through sanitized dialogues on traditional (actually, sacred) knowledge only avoids real conversations about sustainability.

Untangling the myths

Ancestral title: Ownership versus guardianship

Indigenous Peoples worldwide have in common a distinct concept of land rights. Across Indigenous cultures, title and rights are passed down through families. This provides for the subsistence and welfare of family members. It carries major obligations that are understood community wide, usually by puberty. These rules of use, described as a sacred relationship, are incumbent upon all.

Ancestral title is based on oral history of sustainable use. It defines the types of relationships necessary for meeting the needs of present and future generations. Compromising this knowledge can carry the penalty of disentitlement, through banishment or even death. However, Elders will normally intervene to help families or communities heal imbalances before impacts spill over to affect others and reach this type of crisis point.

The main difference between Indigenous conceptions of land title and the exclusive ownership models used by world governments is not just the standards set in law or lore, but the consistency of standards. Today, countries are negotiating baselines for biodiversity conservation under the UN. The spirit of these negotiations is permissive (that is, biased towards industrial access and use) despite lip service to a precautionary approach. National legislation for environmental protection is only minimally enforced with respect to corporations.

In today's globalized economy, companies purchasing land – or rights to use land – need not practise progressive stewardship unless specific zoning (such as low-impact land use and/or alternative methods) is in place. Where restrictive zoning or covenants do exist, it is because biodiversity in the surrounding region is already adversely affected to a high degree. Companies operate across these various management zones as profitable, only modifying their practices when required. On average, corporate environmental performance is poor (Ayres, 2004). Unless local communities somehow raise the political and economic stakes, there is no impetus for companies or their host governments to change course.

Worldwide, Indigenous leadership is viewing such trends with dismay. Although customs vary within each Indigenous culture, a unifying characteristic, continent to continent, is a personalized relationship with the land. Indigenous Peoples normally consider the land to be sacred. In many Indigenous languages the word for 'land' translates to mean 'soul' or 'mother'. To respect the land is to respect not just oneself and each other, but also the Creator.

Under colonial duress some Indigenous Peoples have degraded or commercialized their own ancestral territory. Poverty can be a powerful wedge in cultural decision-making, and is still widely used as an instrument of colonization and assimilation. The 'use or lose' doctrine of colonial law is equally potent. It is painful for communities to watch the corporate cycle, its devastating effects on the land and how it lures their youth. Some are choosing with a heavy heart to accept industry's overtures, trying to steer this relationship towards a middle road.

Co-management attempts at cultural centres such as Uluru (Ayer's Rock, Australia) illustrate the challenge of mingling culture with commerce through industry formulas. In some famous cases, the commerce lacks either consensus or the blessing of the Elders and/or key spiritual authorities. Although all looks well, there may be 'inside' issues that go unreported in conventional case studies and sustainability auditing.

The promotion of ecotourism as a financial incentive for biodiversity conservation thus has an ominous side. Indigenous Peoples have heard this rationale for 'development' before and lived the ensuing poverty. The only difference now is that they themselves are being asked to forsake ancestral title through community participation. Industry has crafted a personable image to reach the next level of 'resource' extraction.

Infringement of Indigenous rights

Through the CBD, world governments are now aware of the onus potentially on them with respect to Indigenous Peoples' rights. There is no similar level of awareness among Indigenous Peoples themselves. Worldwide, *most* Indigenous Peoples do not know their rights or how to begin protecting them, let alone the array of UN agencies and world trade bodies where they are being chiselled away in the interest of commerce.

Nonetheless, many Indigenous Peoples are aware that industry sees community participation as a way of obtaining unfettered access to their lands. Yet again, 'new' economic opportunities are being imbedded in old assimilation models. As a result, the prospect of an Indigenous movement against tourism is growing. During the UN International Year of Ecotourism (IYE) in

2002, lead institutions strained to downplay the magnitude of reported 'local community' concerns.

Industry tends to ignore ground resistance until its market image is shaken. Plan 'B' only comes into play when inertia becomes more costly than risking new precedents. At this point, government may consider a peace dividend. Some countries have offered compensation packages of land and/or money to Indigenous Peoples when a traditional use area is slated for tourism development. In Huatulco, Mexico, and many other industry hubs, the insult (and injury) of purported consultation has led to prolonged cross-cultural conflict.

The objective of most compensation schemes is to convince Indigenous Peoples that title means *ownership*, not guardianship or spiritual connection. Governments want to privatize ancestral lands using ecotourism revenues as compensation (in other words, a 'financial incentive'). If such a deal can be reached, the issue of land rights is contained cost effectively because:

- *Ancestral title is partially extinguished*: the involved Indigenous People(s) lose their customary authority to press for sustainable investment – that is, industry reform – and must rely upon domestic legislation and policies instead.
- *Land rights are swept under domestic law*: appeals by Indigenous Peoples under international law become more complex, costly and controversial when domestic remedies fall short.

For government, it is a success when Indigenous Peoples file land claims. Filing such a claim is substantially different from actually exercising ancestral title or pursuing government-to-government dialogue on the basis of sovereignty. It signals recognition of, and submission to, colonial law. This shifts the burden of proof concerning title onto the claimants (Indigenous Peoples), releasing the concerned colonial government from its full obligations.[6]

Compensation for damages

There is no win–win scenario in compensation. Governments describe it as 'no net loss' strategy for conflict resolution. For Indigenous Peoples, though, it means total loss because their culture is subverted. Across Indigenous cultures, ancestral title is understood as a sacred duty to care for the land (that is, their ancestral territory) and for life systems as a whole. When this customary relationship with the land is severed there is no such thing as substitute lands. Sacred relationships are thrown into disequilibrium like in the corporate world. The whole process, compensation included, is a calculated form of genocide.

Indigenous Peoples' initial response to forced resettlement is often survival-oriented – for example, food security. Government valuation methods used to structure land swaps, land buyouts or other compensation assume that biodiversity has little inherent value except in the hands of 'capable' developers (namely, industry). They also deem Indigenous lives to be of less value (Mumba, 2004).[7] Thus, Indigenous Peoples are routinely allocated 'replacement' lands that are either unproductive or in another tribe's territory. During 2004, the Indigenous Peoples of Sabah, Malaysia, were alerted to such encroachment. A member of parliament 'called for a comprehensive survey on native idle land in the state with a view to developing it' for ecotourism (*Daily Express*, 2004).

Profound questions are being raised about government tactics. In international law, duress invalidates an agreement (Schulte Tenchkoff, 1999). Systematic discrimination, such as the poverty caused by inequitable land 'deals', constitutes duress. Compensation is therefore not an airtight legal remedy to what many governments consider their 'Indigenous problem'. Customary authorities (such as hereditary Chiefs or matriarchal lines), Eders and future generations of children can still invoke their people's ancestral title, appealing to the international community for support. Today, a number of Indigenous Peoples are doing just that. In 2005, the Chortí Maya shut down the Copán 'archeological' park in Honduras for five days to protest violated agreements.

This means an unsettled business climate for the tourism industry. Some independent small companies are several steps ahead of both government and industry at large in recognizing ancestral title. Examples include peer (as opposed to overrated 'partner') relationships or non-prejudicial land lease arrangements. New relationships of this kind, structured with mutual respect and openness, set useful precedents for ethical commerce. This is where the private sector has a leadership role to play in achieving sustainable tourism.

Getting the facts

Global status of Indigenous land rights

Internationally, the particulars of land rights vary significantly; but the globalization of corporate trade is quickly coalescing rights into one coherent issue. As Indigenous Peoples across continents compare their present circumstances, it is apparent that each is staving off similar corporate forces. In the context of tourism, there is a range of situations to consider (see Box 2.4).

This portrait of the ecotourism industry is not flattering. Nearly every major ecotourism destination globally sits within an Indigenous People's ancestral territory. There are severe rights violations at almost all of these destinations (see Box 2.4). Elsewhere, isolated peoples like the Jarawa (Andaman Islands, India) and the Tarahumara (Copper Canyon, Mexico) are bristling at being the new ecotourism sensations. Even where land rights are constitution-ally enshrined, industry is known to push every boundary of decency. The tribes of Papua New Guinea are bracing against Australia's heavy colonial hand in making their lands 'safe' for ecotourism (*Agence France Presse*, 2004). In Fiji Four Seasons Hotels and Resorts has pressured villagers on the Coral Coast to relinquish a sacred island, their final place of refuge. This is the land-scape view of industry that we need to digest.

Worldwide, there is now a continuum, across industries, of stand-offs between Indigenous Peoples and corporate interests. A poignant illustration is Bolivia, where several Aymara were killed in 2001 for seeking a voice in 'de-velopment', and charges of treason and sedition were laid against Indigenous leaders. As a result of such intimidation, some Indigenous Peoples have made bold counter-statements. The U'wa in Colombia have threatened suicide to prevent industrial-style development on ancestral lands (see Box 2.5). Others such as the Zápara in Ecuador have risked reprisal by putting their customary law on paper, banning further 'desecration' of their people's ancestral terri-tory by any outside business interests – whether public, private or 'non-profit' (Zápara, 2000). Often the greatest challenge for Indigenous Peoples is 'foreign aid' – for example, fiscal restructuring or foreign investment – dictated by the world's wealthier countries for the benefit of corporations and our global consumer class. Even where land rights are recognized, it is hard to hand an eviction notice to such a conglomerate of interests.

Across the global economy the lowest common denominator shapes operational standards. The ecotourism industry is no exception. Tourism com-panies claiming integrity will need to forge a convincing path with Indigenous Peoples, standing on their own respective character references (from the com-munity trenches where sacred knowledge is defended) as opposed to industry certification or other third-party audits and accolades.

BOX 2.2   Ecotourism: Heaven sent?

Ecotourism is any form of so-called 'sustainable' tourism that commercializes the collective cultural property of Indigenous Peoples without free and prior informed consent. This definition spans the range of marketing labels associated with ecotourism, such as nature, cultural, ethnic and adventure travel. Such tourism claims to be socially or environmentally responsible; however, the concepts and policies are usually developed by government and/or industry in isolation from the affected Indigenous Peoples or without appropriate dialogue. Globally, this tourism has accelerated the erosion and loss of Indigenous Peoples' ancestral title and rights behind a veil of 'doing good'. It often involves some shade of 'consultation' and promise of benefit-sharing, but is normally 'business as usual' (adapted from Johnston (2000)).

Impact of the private sector on land rights

For the ecotourism industry, access to Indigenous Peoples' territories has become primarily a legal exercise. In a short time frame, this industry's much proclaimed sanctity of community has been abandoned. Most companies are looking for expedient entry, not a lengthy community orientation. They are tuned in to government signals and will fulfil the necessary legalities, while exploiting whatever loopholes exist.

This self-contained approach to business is a pattern that many believed ecotourism would break. Instead, the industry has carried this same pattern to isolated rural areas where Indigenous Peoples are least equipped to respond. From Burma to Brazil there are repeated incidents of industry 'grabbing' ancestral lands. 'There are plenty of horror stories … like the 5000 villagers who lived among the hundreds of ancient pagodas in Burma given two weeks to leave' (Davies, 2002, p26).

Many Indigenous leaders believe that companies are making a calculated business decision of where to operate based upon land rights. In most regions globally, where ecotourism thrives there is racism towards Indigenous Peoples and open contempt for their rights. This enables a business culture of unapologetic profiteering. Newcomers tend to run with the herd, engaging local communities on the going terms. Consequently, altercations like strikes, road blockades and hostage-taking are increasing. The porters' strike at Machu Picchu, Peru, in September 2001 helped to shame the industry into changes in labour policy.[8]

Nevertheless, some ecotourism companies do have an altruistic side. These independent operators are often aware of legal and political irregularities in host countries towards Indigenous Peoples. They also tend to see through national rhetoric on ecotourism. This is a realistic group of companies, focused on achievable goals such as building a mutually beneficial relationship with a single Indigenous People or Indigenous community.

Many such companies make a tangible difference to Indigenous Peoples by venturing into new types of business relationships (including protocol agreements) – often at significant upfront cost. In doing so, they implicitly recognize land rights. Still, some inadvertently become an agent of government assimilation policy (for example, plans to integrate Indigenous Peoples into the regional or national economy).

There are extreme subtleties in how ecotourism can be used to negate land rights. Ecotourism initiatives claiming to promote biodiversity conservation are among the trickiest to read. They may give the impression of showcasing Indigenous ecosystem knowledge, while slotting Indigenous Peoples into programmes as unequal 'partners' in biodiversity conservation.[9] Many national ecotourism plans facilitate such assimilation.

Companies attracted to a particular country by seemingly coherent national planning for ecotourism can get caught in the doubletalk. They commence tours to a particular area, believing credible government consultation or other outreach has occurred with Indigenous Peoples. Yet, in many cases, no meaningful dialogue or verification of due diligence has taken place.

The norm is still industrial intrusion to Indigenous ancestral territories. This affects land rights on two levels: the central principle of free and prior informed consent is violated, with serious human rights implications, and customary practices supporting biodiversity are disrupted. In time, a people's distinct relationship with the land may be sufficiently fractured to jeopardize their ancestral title. This spills over to colonial courts, where a key legal test for title is continuous occupancy and use of the land.

Differing views on biodiversity

Biodiversity is a word used to describe the rich variety of life that makes up an integral ecosystem, habitat range or other biological whole. Since the first Summit in Río de Janeiro in 1992, it has been a benchmark in policy-making for the environment. Countries are now under pressure to plan industrial growth with internationally accepted biodiversity targets in mind.

Today, there often is false confidence in the biodiversity concept. Many people assume that it is a scientific precept; however, it is more political and economic than scientific. Its widespread acceptance and use shows just how entwined governments are with world corporations and research industries.

In practice, biodiversity is about trade-offs. It is a model for sustainability that is based upon an abbreviated understanding of the connectedness of life. The main function is zoning. Governments can use a biodiversity matrix to plot how they will alternate monocultures, clear-cutting or other intensive enterprises like mass 'eco' tourism with professed 'off-limits' natural pockets and corridors. Within this equation a balance is supposed to emerge.

Governments have promoted the biodiversity concept in political dialogues with Indigenous Peoples. They believe that it appeals enough to the interests of so-called 'traditional' cultures to redress grievances and get on with current business.

While Indigenous Peoples pushed hard in Río de Janeiro for sacred knowledge to be recognized as a vital foundation of biodiversity, most shake their heads at the biodiversity concept. Biodiversity is a government term suggesting knowledge, power and control over the 'environment'. Talking about it inside an Indigenous community draws many a blank stare. Indigenous leaders tend to see biodiversity programming as yet another 'development' scheme.

Indigenous Peoples are telling a different story than world governments about human impacts upon Earth cycles. Worldwide, many Elders are watching ecological thresholds. They say that being disconnected from our own soul and heart is taking humanity down a chaotic and self-destructive path. This is reflected in the melting glaciers, deciduous leaves that forget to drop and migratory birds that stay too long.[10]

Ancestral title reflects what scientists call biodiversity, but also embraces the totality of life (and death) relationships plus life (and death) choices, making the biodiversity concept appear unsophisticated. It speaks to the essential connectedness (interdependence) in which we live. This connectedness is as inviolable as the contract we each have with death. Violating it can bring death. In this small space between life and death the sacred is found.

One indicator of biodiversity loss is insecure land rights. Symptoms show quickly when Indigenous Peoples are denied their ancestral title. It is not possible to live partly inside the sacred circle of life. We are either living in healthy relationship with the biosphere or precariously outside it. The compromise-oriented programming of biodiversity is taking world governments towards a threshold where the Earth will not so gently call us back.[11]

It is time to rethink the wisdom of patterning 'eco' tourism after biodiversity alone. Love for life and love for fellow humanity need to enter the sustainability equation.

Poverty alleviation through ecotourism

Pro-poor tourism

The UN maintains that ecotourism can provide poverty alleviation, thereby inducing biodiversity conservation. During 2002–2003 the World Tourism Organization (WTO-OMT) and the United Nations Conference on Trade and Development (UNCTAD) launched the programme Sustainable Tourism for the Elimination of Poverty, calling it 'tourism liberalization with a human face'. The United Nations Environment Programme (UNEP), Conservation International (CI) and the UK Department for International Development (DFID) also advocated 'pro-poor' tourism (Ashley et al, 2001; Christ et al, 2003).

These initiatives have bought time for industry growth, distracting us from the discord of talks on 'sustainable' tourism. Through the *General Agreement on Tariffs and Trade* (GATT) and the *General Agreement on Trade in Services* (GATS) of the World Trade Organization (WTO), liberalization is well under way. The World Bank and the International Monetary Fund (IMF) are ushering a new league of countries towards mass 'eco' tourism. Northern 'donor' governments (the *takers*) have a pact to maintain and promote industry interests above all else. By 2004, talks had shifted to 'biodiversity and prosperity' under the CBD.

Actual costs of ecotourism are left out of these biodiversity formulas. 'Pro-poor' tourism pushes new industry products based on culture. While Indigenous cultures are characterized as an 'asset', there is no quantum for culture loss. Such costs are considered intangible and difficult to evaluate (Vellas, 2002). Therefore, Indigenous child labour in ecotourism hubs such as Cusco (Peru) and Chiang Mai (Thailand) factors in as gross national product (for example, gum or postcard sales), but *not* as a child's face or an indicator of violated land rights. Against this backdrop, the WTO-OMT appeal for poverty relief is highly manipulative. Pairing ecotourism with poverty gives the industry an almost divine status. If ecotourism can combat poverty, who could be against it?

It is more apt to ask how poverty shapes consent. Massive poverty in many of the rural areas that are profitable for ecotourism is like gold for cash-strapped governments. Poverty means pliable ground for government incentives and corporate proposals, including those advanced by the United Nations Development Programme (UNDP) via the WTO-OMT. It is the primary fuel – alongside petroleum – for economic globalization.

The 'pro-poor' argument is particularly disturbing in light of industry's penchant for Indigenous territories. Indigenous Peoples who are able to exercise their ancestral title are *not* poor. It is only when stripped of their lands, relocated and/or corralled into a colonial reserve that they live in the severest of poverty. Even then, they are not 'poor', if poverty is understood spiritually. Colonization has not eradicated sacred knowledge, though every effort to assimilate them is still made by most world governments.

Today, poverty is simply a twisted rationale for private-sector leadership. It is considered a barrier to biodiversity conservation because it is an overriding need (Higuero, 1999). Yet, governments *benefit* if Indigenous Peoples identify as being 'the poor'. Once communities experience this distance from their culture, they enter the orbit of 'consumerdom' where worth is relative and dignity requires acquisition. They are more likely to interact as passive recipients of 'development assistance' than as proactive rights holders.

For industry, ecotourism is a way of accessing the final frontier of Indigenous cultural 'resources'. After another ten years of this industrial-style ecotourism, it is predictable where the world's 350 million Indigenous Peoples will be. There will be even *more* material impoverishment due to culture loss. Indigenous Peoples are more valuable to the world economy if impoverished, because poverty does away with encumbrances like free and prior informed consent. It is pliability of workforce, not portability of human rights, which most world governments are after.

'Biodiversity economics' (McNeely, 1999) and 'natural resource economic analysis' (Higuero, 1999) ignore this architecture of the world economy. So do most other consumer models for social change. Although eco-tourists are described as socially aware, most are unlikely advocates for new economic relationships. Therapy, self-help merchandise and advertising that glorifies individualism have influenced a whole generation of consumers. 'Tough love' is now replacing our basic sense of humanity. We believe that some people choose to be where they are (that is, impoverished), overlooking our own direct (consumer) role in keeping them there.

BOX 2.3 **Indigenous Peoples: The losers amongst generic poor**

'Do not expect all the poor to benefit equally, particularly the poorest 20 per cent. Some will lose.' This appraisal of 'pro-poor' tourism was issued by the UK at the United Nations Commission on Sustainable Development (CSD) (DFID, 1999). Why do the race and gender implications not raise more eyebrows? Globally, Indigenous peoples are the poorest of the poor.

Benefits to Indigenous Peoples

Ecotourism cannot deliver poverty alleviation unless core international law is upheld instead of continually watered down. Worldwide, poverty among Indigenous Peoples is the product of violated land rights. 'Development', though billed as poverty relief, is a big player. For example, social forestry initiatives said to restore rights 'typically restrict commercial use by local people' (Forest Trends, 2003).

Although governments try to restrict interpretations of collective rights to food, ceremonial and social activities, Indigenous Peoples are a *rightful* player in the private sector. Most Indigenous Peoples have long traditions of trade that have helped to sustain their well-being. Today, economics remain vital to self-determination. Revitalized customary commerce is necessary for healthy, flourishing Indigenous cultures and communities.

While Indigenous Peoples generally have no cultural concept of land or resource ownership, ancestral title has become essential to beating poverty. Land rights flow from title (in other words, from responsibility) and are the core of Indigenous economies. Without these rights Indigenous Peoples are shut out of today's private sector. They cannot engage industry in sustainable enterprise via an equity role. Nor can they enforce codes of conduct. Their trade options, investment capability and management authority are essentially gone once lands are alienated to third parties.

The domestication of land rights under colonial law created a dependency relationship with colonizing governments (Martinez, 1999). Indigenous Peoples have endured systematic economic oppression, only to be ridiculed for receiving 'handouts' or not doing 'an honest day's work'. Although precedents now exist to negotiate royalties (such as 'pay the landlord' protocols), these breakthroughs are rare. It takes a critical mass of cultural healing and rebuilding to move companies in this direction. There must also be freedom from political harassment, disappearance, torture and murder. In many countries this does not exist. In 2004, the director of the Akha Heritage Foundation in Thailand was arrested after soliciting support for Indigenous land rights and repeatedly exposing practices of the ecotourism industry in Thailand (see www.akha.org).

In the tourism sector, Indigenous proposals for royalties are particularly hard to advance. Efforts are obstructed by the seemingly abstract nature of industry's day-to-day impacts. The softer the impacts are in conventional economic terms (especially culture loss), the easier it is for a company to obtain social licence for 'business as usual'. Thus, few Indigenous Peoples internationally have been able to negotiate with the ecotourism industry for independent revenue or livelihoods. Certification is an industry cover-up, useful to a company when Indigenous Peoples themselves won't vouch for corporate approaches (see Chapter 9).

Nonetheless, economic globalization is a double-edged force with respect to rights. Concentrated offshore control of ecotourism markets is stacking the odds against Indigenous Peoples. It gets harder and harder to preserve the principle, and fundamental right, of free and prior informed consent. However, globalization can bring new bearing upon national performance vis-à-vis international law if media are effectively alerted.

Some Indigenous Peoples are bypassing government and dealing directly with foreign companies to secure tourism benefits. Others are forging strategic alliances to stay a step ahead of industry and government. The Heiltsuk of Canada purchased the Koeye watershed, with funds from American philanthropists Howard and Peter Buffet, to outmanoeuvre developers pushing industrial forestry and 'eco' tourism (Heiltsuk Tribal Council, 2001).

The Maasai keep watch

Images of the Maasai's ancestral territory are synonymous with ecotourism. Maasai Mara in Kenya is called 'the world's most popular wildlife watching destination' (Lisagor, 2003, p92). The picture of the dusk on the Maasai Savannahs, countless wild zebras, wildebeast, elephants, hyenas, buffalo and lines of cattle led by their Maasai herders have been etched into tourists' cultural imagination of this land and its people. The area was turned into a national reserve in 1974; but there still is no compensation or return for the forcibly evicted Maasai. Today it supports over 50 tourist camps and lodges instead. On ecological grounds alone the outcomes are heinous. Industry practices are slow to change, despite the lodge certification programme of the Ecotourism Society of Kenya and the game park ethics programme of the Kenya Professional Guides Association. However, 'The wildlife lover ... may be blissfully unaware that Maasai ... have been evicted ... to make way for his environmentally friendly game lodge' (Davies, 2002, p21).

For the Maasai, the desecration of Maasai Mara is one of many 'development' crises in their midst (MERC, 2004). Both the Kenyan and Tanzanian governments continue to override Maasai sovereignty (Olol-Dapash, 1999, 2001, 2004). Today, as before, the Maasai Elders, leaders and Tribal Chiefs must contend with institutionalized land theft. Poverty is stalking Maasai children, while the global ecotourism industry reaps profits from Maasai lands. This leaves the Maasai few options but to seize media attention through well-timed clashes with industry. During the 1980s and 2000, Maasai warriors speared wildlife in Amboseli National Park to protest lost grazing rights and water access, cultural abuse and economic exploitation by the central government and the tourism industry in Kenya.

Government rebuff of the Maasai has enabled world conservation interests to parachute in with management services. Conservation International (of Washington, DC), for example, is developing biodiversity strategies in Kenya and Tanzania through its Critical Ecosystem Partnership Fund, which includes ecotourism. Past Maasai encounters with such conservation superstars have not been positive. The World Conservation Union (IUCN) management plan in Tanzania led to Maasai evictions from ancestral lands in Ngorongoro to make way for a 'protected' area, which now receives 100,000 tourists annually. Today, the Maasai are battling IUCN involvement in the sacred Naimina Enkiyio Forest, their last ceremonial ground (Ole Tiampati, 2004; WRM, 2004). This US$2.6 million IUCN project is funded by the European Union (EU). 'Powerful economic interests want the Forest of the Lost Child for tourism' (Ol-Dapash, 2005). They are flanked by white ranchers, hooked on the profits of 'private' game reserves (that is, re-privatized Maasai lands), and an international bag of eco-lodge disciples, whose liberal use of Maasai memorabilia and 'replicas' often undermines real community enterprise (see Ol- Dapash and Kutay, 2005).

In the midst of this ongoing encroachment, the Maasai have taken steps to exercise their ancestral title. During 2003, the Maasai began working with the support of Wildland Adventures (US) to develop their own *Ecotourism Principles and Code of Conduct*. The Maasai Environmental Resource Coalition and Wildland are now delivering joint tours, offering Maasai communities a direct tourism income through respectful cultural exchanges (Kutay, 2003; Mbaria, 2003). In 2005, *Outside* magazine called this 'the best Africa trip of the year'. Elsewhere, however, the Kenyan police and its paramilitary unit shadow the Maasai. In 2004, several Maasai were shot and killed, and many more arrested and charged for peacefully protesting government abrogation of a 100-year-old land agreement (see www.maasaierc.org) between the Maasai and the colonial authorities.

The battle of the Maasai will continue to be steep. The colonial legacy of England lives on. During 2003–2004, the UK government dealt a blow to Indigenous Peoples, unilaterally rejecting their collective rights which are enshrined in international law (Survival International, 2004). The UK also joined forces with its former colonies, Canada and Australia, and their comrade the US to block the *United Nations Draft Declaration on the Rights of Indigenous People*; Séguin, 2003; Oman, 2004). While Canada seemed to change its tune in late 2004, it already had laid tracks across the UN for a net extinguishment of Indigenous rights. Countries with an economic interest in Indigenous territories are discreetly applauding.

BOX 2.4 Land rights at world ecotourism destinations

Amazon region, Brazil

Brazil is a signatory of *International Labour Organization (ILO) Convention 169* and its constitution recognizes the territorial rights of Indigenous Peoples. Some Indigenous Peoples have secured reparation payments or demarcation of their territories. However, harassment and assassinations are the norm. According to Amnesty International (AI, 2003), Indigenous leaders are in increasing danger of human rights violations, including extra-judicial executions.

Trekking routes, Nepal

In Nepal, 'Indigenous nationalities are still considered untouchables by the Hindu *varna* system' (NEFIN, 2003). Many are classified as '*Rai* … an indistinct label that describes many distinct indigenous groups' (Darai, 2004). According to the International Work Group for Indigenous Affairs (IWGIA, 2004), there is a widespread attitude of '*jegare pani hune*' (whatever you like, you can do to them). Human Rights Watch (HRW, 2004) is challenging this caste-based discrimination through the United Nations (UN).

San (Bushmen) territory, Africa

In Botswana, the San were violently removed from the Central Kalahari Game Reserve to make way for ecotourism and other business. Next door in South Africa, the San Council has negotiated a role for their people as guardians of San heritage in the Drakensberg. However, the Khomani San face abuse by private tourism operators and state police following their successful land 'claim' in 1999 (Cultural Survival, 2004b).

'Hill tribes', Thailand

The Thai government denies citizenship to persons identifying themselves as Indigenous Peoples. The Assembly of Indigenous and Tribal Peoples of Thailand has appealed for Thailand to 'stop the arrest, harassment and threat' against those maintaining a traditional way of life and to cease oppressive measures against them 'travelling and gathering to demand recognition of their rights' (Cultural Survival, 2002). No turnabout is in sight.

Rainforests and pristine beaches, Hawai'i

Hawai'i is under illegal occupation by the US (Cultural Survival 2004a). During 2003–2005, the proposed *Akaka Bill* led to high controversy. This bill would terminate the nationhood of Hawai'i, bringing native Hawaiians under federal jurisdiction. Why worry? The same month that President Bush committed to respect tribal sovereignty nationwide, the US rejected Indigenous self-determination at the UN (Oman, 2004).

Kerala, India

During 2003, India launched a tourism campaign promoting Kerala as a religious and spiritual destination, with a harmonious legacy – just weeks after brutally suppressing Adivasis who protested their 'landlessness'. Conflict grew as government pursued ecotourism on the seized lands in the Muthanga Wildlife Sanctuary. In 2004, the National Assembly of Tribal, Indigenous and Adivasi Peoples denounced India's *National Policy for Tribals*.

Haida Gwaii, North America

Canada has no treaty, or other legal claim, to the Haida territory. In court, Canada has denied any constitutional obligation to consult over 'development' unless Aboriginal title is first proven. This ignores both Canada's own fiduciary (trust) duty, as well as the *United Nations Study on Treaties* guidance on burden of proof (Martinez, 1999, p46). The Haida have had to sue Canada to limit industrial logging of 'old growth' trees in their territory.

Uluṟu, Australia

Australia is still 'granting bucket loads of extinguishments of Native Title interests' (Simon, 2004). During 1999 and 2000, the United Nations Committee on the Elimination of Racial Discrimination condemned these extinguishments. Since then, Australia has refused entry to UN investigative committees. The Sovereign Union of Aboriginal Peoples continues to document and publicize Australia's genocide and its ongoing crimes against humanity.

Integrating land rights

Government accommodation of ancestral title

During May 1996, Calestous Juma, past executive secretary of the *UN Convention on Biological Diversity* (CBD), 'stressed that it is critical that Indigenous Peoples' rights be viewed and handled as not only political but also technical matters' (IPBN, 1996). Since then, governments have framed a dialogue supposedly addressing Indigenous Peoples' concerns about sustainability.

Article 8(j) of the CBD on 'traditional knowledge' is a focal point.[12] It looks ameliorative but squarely places compliance under domestic (that is, colonial) law.

During 2000, an open-ended working group commenced under the CBD to examine 'traditional knowledge' regarding biodiversity conservation. However, the process has cloistered Indigenous Peoples away from the main body of talks, especially technical dialogues on discrete topics like sustainable use (where tourism is scheduled) which occur through the CBD's Subsidiary Body on Scientific, Technical and Technological Advice (SBSTTA). There is no real mechanism to build trust, establish rapport or harmonize expertise. Nor is there reasonable consensus on how to care for life systems. On grounds of efficacy alone, the process is faltering.

The real paradox of this CBD process on traditional knowledge is that among Indigenous Peoples *land rights* are the basis of sustainability. When governments agree to respect, preserve and maintain 'traditional knowledge' as part of a master plan for biodiversity, but insist on omitting land rights from this dialogue, there is a fundamental short circuit. This body of sacred knowledge is intimately tied to land rights through ancestral title (that is, the customary practices binding people to the land in mind, body, spirit and emotions). For this reason, Indigenous leaders speak in terms of indivisible heritage. If Indigenous land rights and their inherent responsibilities continue to be denied, Article 8(j) simply facilitates more colonial manoeuvring around applicable international law. There is more legalized unlawfulness.

The ecotourism industry will create its own demise if standards for sustainable tourism follow the narrow biodiversity (CBD) prescription. Tourism featuring the territories and cultures of Indigenous Peoples cannot be sustainable in the absence of respect for ancestral title and rights. With land rights intact, Indigenous Peoples are able to:

- choose whether to pursue a tourism economy;
- set conditions for approval and operations of tourism enterprises;
- enforce protocol for visitation by industry, NGOs and institutional tour operators;
- access venture capital on an equitable basis.

These pivotal expressions of self-determination operationalize ancestral title – ensuring economic development that enhances cultural and biological diversity.

Jurisdiction jitters and sovereignty

Jurisdiction is the main reason that we see few tourism initiatives honouring ancestral title. World governments are focused on swift and exponential material gain, led by corporations. They recoil at the mention of any perceived jurisdictional issue (that is, 'competition') which could be a drag on this agenda. It is easier to classify land rights as an extremist demand than to grapple with them as an unassuming system for sustainability at the level of community, ecosystem or biosphere. The tenet 'The sacred is not for sale' is the ire of many an ambitious politician and business promoter.

It should not be dismissed that land rights are a jurisdiction issue. Land rights, land-use planning and regulation are intertwined. At the same time, the implications of jurisdiction should not be exaggerated. Most governments have misread and misconstrued Indigenous Peoples' assertion of sovereignty. In fact, many use 'sovereignty' arguments as a fear tactic for suppressing Indigenous land rights. This, ironically, has led to private landowners and industry rallying against their own displacement. Respected tourism professionals, who know nothing about ancestral title, raise the scenario of the 'balkanization' of areas. Overall, Indigenous land rights are framed as a power play rather than as a principled social contract guided by the society's Elders.

There is a vast cross-cultural divide between concepts of sovereignty. In the corporate world, money and science (which advances profit) are considered sovereign, whereas among Indigenous Peoples the Creator is sovereign. This is the spiritual underpinning of ancestral title. Traditionally, sovereignty is not about fee simple (in other words, privatized) ownership, winning the next bankroll for tourism or building the best situated eco-lodge. Sovereignty is a customary governance system under the authority of tribal Elders. It includes dispensing justice in accordance with natural law (that is, life systems). This ensures behavioural restraint when relationships (such as economics) veer out of balance.

Future discussions on sustainability need to contemplate the notion of co-existing title. This is a duality that many Indigenous Peoples are already familiar with. Several have the custom of shared use areas for sustenance. These territorial arrangements continue today and are normally a source of conflict only when European-style (that is, exclusive) title interferes – for example, through forced land 'claims' or forced compensation packages that demarcate economic borders.

In the tourism sector, co-existing title is the technical issue around land rights that demands our attention. The pressing question is: how does it work? There is no conundrum to solve here. Co-existing title is about relationship-building. We need to heal exploitative relationships among races, cultures, generations, classes and genders which have been normalized by colonialism and consumerism. The starting point is self-knowledge – understanding our *inalienable* and therefore sacred interconnection.

Seabed and foreshore disputes: Fiji and New Zealand

Few things are so hotly contested in the tourism sector as beach access. Many a government has ejected Indigenous Peoples from shoreline tracts in order to make way for tourism development. This brazen 'clean-up' is still something that industry expects. Beaches have become the domain of multinational corporations and developers.

Two recent disputes over foreshore and seabed ownership are elevating the issue of ancestral title. Both Fiji and New Zealand have new legislation concerning who has dominion over these areas. Other countries have watched these cases with unease, aghast at the spectre of other Indigenous Peoples seeking restitution of prime waterfront 'real estate'. Previously, state efforts to shore up title had emphasized land. Now their attention has turned offshore due to growing emphasis on the tourism and oil sectors.

The uproar began in 2003 when Fiji announced that it would transfer to Indigenous Peoples control of coastal areas, including coral lagoons, reefs and seabeds. Fiji, coming from a colonial history of Indirect Rule (wherein islands were ceded under a unique arrangement, not forcibly annexed like some Pacific islands), said 'it was "right" that local tribes should get the direct economic benefit … of international holiday makers' (*Stuff*, 2004). Following a cabinet decision, the Fiji government began developing a management plan to guide the transition. This means 'Foreshore lease rentals will no longer be paid to the state, but to the customary owners' (*Stuff*, 2004).

In practical terms, the Fiji decision involves no change for industry other than a different name on lease cheques. Nonetheless, the move 'alarmed the country's tourism industry' (*Seattle Times*, 2003). It was a case of projection. If Indigenous Peoples followed industry's lead and treated industry in the same way that it had treated them, blocking use, there was cause for concern.

In New Zealand, the reaction of government was swift and decisive. The government nullified a Court of Appeal decision giving the Maori Land Court a say in adjudicating customary ownership. The ruling Labour party then 'introduced into parliament legislation designed to cut off claims' by the Maori to the foreshore and seabed (Braddock, 2004; Christian World Service, 2004). The bill passed immediately, though government had 'pledged to protect customary rights' (*New Zealand Herald*, 2004). This could lead to privatization of the coastline. It has inflamed racism, though New Zealand markets itself to travel markets as 'sharing the breath of life'.[13]

New Zealand's strategy, which is to oppress the Maori in the notorious style of Canada and Australia (*New Zealand Herald*, 2004), is a sign of things to come. Worldwide, countries are watching Canada and Australia to see how they contain and put a cap on 'Indigenous issues' through consultation and other window dressing. In the name of national interest (which is *revenue*, not sustainability) colonial title is being sewn up. Priscillia de Wet of the Khoe

(South Africa) says 'eco' tourism is at the heart of this 'second wave of dispossession' (Auran-Clapot and Gygax, 2003).

The coastal zone impacts of tourism, already severe, will rapidly worsen on this track. The Maori, who under ancestral title are 'responsible for the foreshore and seabed' (Mutu, 2003), are restrained by the 'settler' (colonial) courts from enforcing sustainable use. Although Maori efforts to reassert title were vindicated in 2005 when the UN Committee on Elimination of Racial Discrimination (CERD) found the new *Seabed and Offshore Act* discriminatory, there is no overwhelming government pressure on New Zealand to retract the legislation. Yet again, the corporate ethic of taking has been reinforced over the cultural etiquette and customary practice of sharing.

BOX 2.5 | **Sacred trusts**

The U'wa of Columbia recently announced that they would choose suicide over industrialization. Decisions of this magnitude arise from a deep-seated understanding of responsibility. In many Indigenous cultures it is understood through customary law that the people have a sacred duty to protect ancestral lands, with their own life if necessary. The land, water and air are to be protected with your own life because they sustain all life. So what are we 'consumers' being called upon to give up amidst today's collapse of life systems? Is the uproar really over our supposed 'right' to consume and travel; or do our life values run deeper?

Getting beyond greed

Steps for the private sector

Ecotourism companies wanting to ensure that their operations are beneficial to Indigenous Peoples need to grasp the economics of land rights from a holistic perspective. What is for sale? By whom? On what conditions? Chapter 8 discusses the relationship side of this inquiry.

The main challenge to 'eco' tourism companies seeking a sustainable turnaround in their industry is its structure. Most tour operators promote travel to several continents simultaneously. This is how they attract and retain clients. In doing so, they move across a variety of government systems. It becomes difficult for them to grasp any single nation's interaction with Indigenous Peoples. Most companies can afford only a glance at national debates on biodiversity, corporate responsibility and Indigenous rights.

Independent companies sensing the connection between ancestral title and biodiversity conservation have a critical role to play in demonstrating alternative approaches to ecotourism. Some such as Wildland Adventures (US) have proven that it is possible to run viable operations while supporting self-determination by involved Indigenous Peoples. However, even these ethics-motivated businesses face a steep learning curve in terms of operational consistency. Should they lead tours for conservation organizations such as The Nature Conservancy (TNC) which are frequently lambasted by Indigenous Peoples for disregarding land rights?

Two basic sets of information are needed by companies to develop rights-sensitive programming:

1   *factual overview of land rights internationally*: the status of Indigenous
     Peoples' struggles with neo-colonialism, region to region,
     especially the human rights dimensions of biodiversity
     conservation;
2   *insight into ancestral title in proposed operating areas*: the meaning
     of ancestral title versus biodiversity locally, especially cultural
     protocol for dispensing collective rights and responsibilities.

Due to peer pressure, more companies may be compelled to operate with higher diligence towards Indigenous rights. During April 2002, the WTO made a pivotal ruling with respect to Indigenous Peoples. It held that unrecognized land title can be considered an unfair subsidy under free trade regimes. The tourism industry stands to be economically hit by this precedent, given its current push into isolated Indigenous territories via GATS.

Sacred sovereignty or materialistic sovereignty

Through colonization, legal systems asserting the European 'use or lose' doctrine of ownership have been used to appropriate land and resources from Indigenous Peoples. Entire species and ecosystems are stripped without any regard for the Indigenous People(s). Now the tourism industry is largely following suit with mass 'eco' tourism.

On this economic scale, even a small flow of royalties would counter poverty and dependency; ultimately, however, Indigenous Peoples are not asking for these dregs, but instead are urging industry to restructure altogether. They are challenging companies to downsize, to understand 'the sacred balance' described by famed ecologist David Suzuki (Suzuki, 1997) and to respect life. This implies a fundamentally different notion of equity than is embraced at an operational level by intergovernmental conservation bodies such as UNEP and the IUCN.

Underlying this appeal is a distinctly different understanding of contracts. Among Indigenous Peoples, contracts are seen as sacred instruments. They are regarded as personal pledge – an extension of one's birth covenant with the Creator. Put simply, one must be living in balance or the internal discord will spill over to affect family, community and all surrounding life. The only thing that can terminate our present contract of accountability is death. When our body expires, accountability enters another dimension.

In the tourism sector, Indigenous Peoples have shown themselves willing to turn incentive measures upside down. In order to safeguard their territories (so-called 'biodiversity'), many are taking steps to put tourism investments on unstable ground. Their direct action has been criticized as civil disobedience; recently, there have been accusations of terrorism (see Box 2.6). However, it should be understood in light of ancestral title – recognizing that the real bottom line is reverence for *life*, not economic growth at any cost. 'We are not a threat to the world... On the contrary, we hold out a hope, an alternative for humanity' (Valencia, 2005).

BOX 2.6	'War on terror' underwrites corporations and our consumer lifestyle

The US National Intelligence Council has earmarked Indigenous Peoples as 'threats to the security and hegemony of the United States' (Gonzalez, 2005). Why? Because their ancestral lands are now, more than ever, *the* strategic acquisition for corporations. Amnesty International warns that the so-called 'war on terror' ... is threatening to expand to Latin America, targeting Indigenous movements that are demanding autonomy and protesting free-market globalization' (Gonzalez, 2005). Quietly, beneath our radar, areas are being secured for investment.

Conclusion

Internationally, the economic imperative of tourism is helping to expose government agendas on biodiversity. It is clear that governments want commercial access to Indigenous Peoples' lands. The greater revelation is the extent to which land rights are violated and cultures prostituted. There is a corporate race to break bread with, and make dough from, so-called 'lost' tribes.

This whirlwind of investment brings two systems of governance face to face. On the one hand, there are corporate governments, seeking access to lands in perpetuity for development purposes, regardless of impacts. On the other hand, there are Indigenous Peoples who have inherent and inalienable collective rights under ancestral title, and identify themselves as the keepers of sacred sovereignty. Our attempted industrialization of life has made this a fated meeting.

During the next decade we will determine what kind of moral character we want to live and die by. Today there is a brotherhood of Anglo nations (the UK, Canada, Australia, New Zealand and the US) which poses a grave threat to Indigenous Peoples worldwide and, hence, to us all. There is also an upswell of grassroots civil protest against the destructive forces of consumerism and economic globalization. Will we continue with our relentless material pursuits, or remember our common humanity?

We must be open to understanding ancestral title, on all its levels. It is not enough to talk about tourism 'benefits', 'fair trade' tourism or 'pro-poor' tourism. These third-party approaches treat Indigenous Peoples as an addendum to industry, and condone profitable industry practices (such as excessive air travel and systemic land rights violations), which clearly are *not* sustainable. Indigenous rights, in contrast, are a natural baseline hinging upon responsibilities, which if respected give rise to sustainable livelihoods.

Recommended reading

- Daes, E.-I. (1997) *Indigenous Peoples and Their Relationship to Land*. UN Economic and Social Council, Commission on Human Rights, 20 June
- Daes, E.-I. (2002) *Working Paper on Indigenous Peoples' Permanent Sovereignty over Natural Resources*. UN Economic and Social Council, Commission on Human Rights, 31 July
- Gilbert, K. (1994) *Because a White Man'll Never Do It*. Angus and Robertson, Sydney
- Martinez, M. A. (1999) *Study on Treaties, Agreements and Other Constructive Arrangements Between States and Indigenous Populations*. UN Economic and Social Council, Commission on Human Rights, 22 June
- Stavenhagen, R. (2001–2007) UN Special Rapporteur on the Situation of the Human Rights and Fundamental Freedom of Indigenous People, Various reports issued to UN Economic and Social Council, Commission on Human Rights, see www.unhchr.ch/indigenous/rapporteur.htm
- Trask, H.-K. (1999) *From a Native Daughter: Colonialism and Sovereignty in Hawai'i*. University of Hawai'i Press, Honolulu
- United Nations Permanent Forum on Indigenous Issues website, www.un.org/events/indigenousforum/

Figure 2.1 **Two visions of earth stewardship: Indigenous or industrial**

Industrial Vision: Biodiversity	Indigenous Vision: Sacred Lands
Colonial: based on domination	Millennial: based on co-existence
Flows from science – without/above Creator	Flows from conscience – with love for all Creation
Directed by experts – moved by ego	Guided by Elders and Ancestors – moved by humility
Managed by components – for economic planning	Envisioned as connection – for safe-guarding sacred life systems
Governed by access and use agreements – negotiable	Governed by customary protocol – time tested and non-negotiable
Incentive to exploit – financial	Prohibitions to ensure respect – sacred
Manipulation of 'legal' terminology – for profit	Maintenance of holistic systems of governance – for balance
Linear system of buying and selling divorced from real limits	Cyclical understanding of life and life relations
Instant gratification for our own indulgences	Timeless considerations for the generations behind and before us
'Takers'* who care for themselves	'Leavers'* who care for others

* See Quinn (1992)

Figure 2.2 **Aboriginal Tent Embassy in Canberra, Australia: The real story of colonialism**

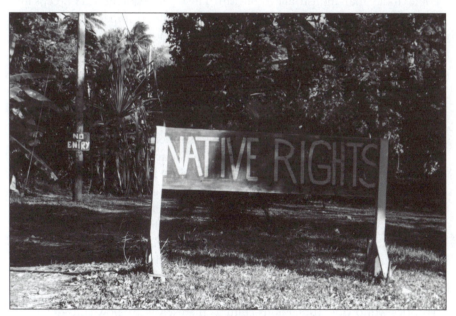

Figure 2.3 **Remembrance sign erected on island of Molokai, Hawai'i**

Chapter 3

Self-Determination of Indigenous Peoples

> **We, the Indigenous Peoples, walk to the future in the**
> **footprints of our ancestors.**
> *(Kari-Oca Declaration, Earth Summit 1992, Brazil)*

From an international perspective there is no greater threat to Indigenous Peoples today than industrial ecotourism. The ecotourism industry creeps into the deepest recesses of culture and community life. It impacts the full spectrum of rights and is responsible for rights violations on all levels. Globally, no other industry single-handedly endangers the spiritual core of Indigenous cultures to such an extent.

Tourism is now an epidemic among Indigenous Peoples, holding little or no long-term benefit locally (*Abyia Yala* 1999, p1). Definitions of ecotourism would have us believe otherwise. The International Ecotourism Society (TIES) says that ecotourism 'sustains the well-being of local people'. The World Conservation Union (IUCN) and The Nature Conservancy (TNC) call it environmentally responsible travel that provides for 'active socio-economic involvement of local peoples'. These definitions suggest that we finally have an industry committed to ethical commerce. However, as industry grasps for new labels such as 'sustainable' tourism, its track record lingers to remind us of the ongoing 'green wash' and now 'browning'. Indigenous Peoples are their realizing that ancestral lands have been inventoried and annexed for conventional tourism under the pretext of saving 'biodiversity'.

The ecotourism industry has made a beeline for profit inside Indigenous territories worldwide. Indigenous cultures themselves are now considered 'up for grabs'. As a result, culture loss is pandemic. Lands held in trust under customary law 'from time immemorial', 'from time out of mind' and 'from the Dawn of Creation' are straining under rapid industrialization. While some

Indigenous Peoples have managed to fend off unwanted tourism or develop healthy tourism alternatives, exploitation remains industry's recipe for profit. Consumer expectations of 'fee for service' relationships shape most exchanges, not local rights, interests or needs.

Many of us have little compassion for this situation of Indigenous Peoples. As holiday makers we have a hard time imagining tourism as a destructive force locally. In the consumer world we make household purchases such as the next trip without significant barrier. The logic is that if we can do it, so can they. So why all the fuss by Indigenous leaders over self-determination? Why the misgivings about such an 'easy' and 'light' industry?

Our consumerism and consumer attitudes are a colonial carry-over. This makes it is hard for us to see the racism within ecotourism.[1] But them emulating us is the premise of 'progress'. On one hand, there is our impulse to be voyeurs to Indigenous cultures; on the other hand, there is the assumption that Indigenous Peoples should want to be like us, in lifestyle and modes of business. Governments talk of reconciliation and capacity-building while engineering dependency. This seed of disunity was inculcated within us as children. Nursery rhymes such as Robert Louis Stevenson's 'Foreign Children' taught us all about colonialism. In school, children are still fed a curriculum based on Manifest Destiny; today it is known by the euphemism of 'economic globalization'.[2]

This is the footing of the global ecotourism industry. The business formula applied is the *same* as that used in other industries. Through ecotourism governments are promoting industrial ideas about conservation, development and social order. What would it take to heal these economic relationships which now endanger life systems globally? Can we reach any mutual understanding on the urgent need for new relationships?

Indigenous Peoples' encounters with industry

Concentrated impacts

The mass promotion of ecotourism by industry is now happening globally. Although Indigenous Peoples are central to industry's marketing of ecotourism, they seldom can secure fair terms of trade.[3] Even rarer is the choice of whether to participate in tourism. Not even 1 per cent of 'Indigenous' travel products on the world market are owned by Indigenous Peoples.[4] The ecotourism industry has turned Indigenous Peoples into landmarks and their ceremonies into spectacles. While the impacts upon cultural survival and biodiversity are devastating, most affected communities are too marginalized to challenge business practices. Some, such as the Toda of India, have at first entreated visitors to tell other travellers to come (Isaacson, 2002, p104), but usually with no idea of ecotourism's slippery slope. Groups such as the Cordillera Ancestral Development Centre (the Philippines) are racing to tell other Indigenous Peoples to beware.

Many non-governmental organization (NGO) observers describe the ecotourism industry as negligent and fraudulent. These allegations are not made for shock value. The concentration of impacts upon Indigenous Peoples is real; it exposes not just industry's ways, but also our own consumer complacency. The ecotourism industry routinely goes off limits, for example, it:

- markets Indigenous territories and cultures without appropriate consent – profiting from rights violations;
- commercializes Indigenous sacred sites, ceremonies and knowledge – violating customary law;
- competes to find 'lost tribes' – sensationalizing culture loss;[5]
- gives a false sense of consultation, consent and benefit-sharing – contravening international law.

The extent of these problems inside the ecotourism industry is poorly understood.[6] There is a tendency to react in disbelief, and our denial can very quickly shift into tacit support for the status quo. It is easier to look at supposedly 'past' ethical issues such as apartheid or slavery than to examine similar issues existing here and now, with identical overtones. Few of us benefiting from consumer culture (for example, travel perks) want to know the complexity of global dynamics supporting it. Issues like exploitation are simply not welcome topics if they hit a personal chord. Graphic violations of international law affecting Indigenous Peoples go largely ignored.

In Russia, a prominent Yupik leader exclaimed: 'We hate it when Indigenous People are treated like objects'. In the Russian far east and north, tourism is 'killing their culture' (George, 2004). Only when tourism is controlled directly by Indigenous Peoples is there prospect of healthy interchange. The successful Jemez Pueblo (Rice, 2001; see www.jemezpueblo.org) and the Blackfeet relationship with Global Volunteers (Barton, 2003; see www. globalvolunteers.org) in the US offer refreshing relief from the global replays of abuse.

> **BOX 3.1 Bankrolling the pioneers**
>
> Today, major corporations such as HSBC Bank send professional staff on 'eco' tourist expeditions with conservation groups like Earthwatch, all expenses paid (Kaufman, 2004). Staff are expected to revitalize, experience the frontier spirit and then return invigorated for bank business. The irony, of course, is that banks finance the liquidation of biodiversity. The World Bank and Inter-American Development Bank are pushing mass 'eco' tourism.

Sadly, the controversy around ecotourism is diminishing world governments' appetite for dialogue rather than elevating it. Industry's 'successes' in economic terms give it tremendous leverage in sailing past scrutiny.[7]

Stacked odds

The economic promise of the ecotourism industry, and its metamorphoses in order to keep an ethical image among consumers, make it difficult for Indigenous Peoples to confront. Public empathy for concerns is usually low. We are all more inclined to cling to 'feel good' images than embrace the possibility of our own lifestyle causing harm.

While Indigenous Peoples are thwarted from asserting their rights on this front, industry is poised for action. It is routine for companies in such an image-sensitive business to hire troubleshooters for public relations. Communications consultants are discreetly brought in to patch up public perception; sometimes, legal injunctions are also pursued. In business, the cost of premium consultants and lawyers is simply factored in as overhead, whereas for Indigenous Peoples these same resources are normally out of reach. If litigation ends up the best hope for justice, chance of a fair trial is compromised on economic grounds alone.

Companies need to rethink the messages they send, and what relationships they reinforce, through accepted business practices. Until the fear of terrorism erupted in September 2001, businesses could readily purchase risk insurance to safeguard against political upheavals. Through this they enjoyed a degree of protection against protests, including demonstrations by Indigenous Peoples. This type of contingency planning has shaped how the corporate world relates to marginalized communities. Today, tourism-related security initiatives are proliferating. These may soon target Indigenous Peoples if industry access to 'biodiversity' (that is, Indigenous ancestral lands) is perceived as threatened.[8] Templates already exist in some countries; there are police units monitoring Indigenous 'extremists', which are deployed when altercations over so-called 'resources' hit a political nerve.

If the ecotourism industry wants to engage Indigenous Peoples in a way that naturally draws community support, it must be willing to learn who it is talking to, what these people's experiences and aspirations are and why the right to self-determination is so passionately defended. Companies need to learn how to approach business as a *holistic* relationship. This means cultivating a family ethic (on the understanding that we are all related), not piggybacking on anthropologists or other intermediaries. It demands real soul-searching on options, as opposed to mere strategic planning (such as the adversarial 'SWOT' analysis of strengths, weaknesses, opportunities and threats). Otherwise, business agreements are staged and tour companies are just another opportunist travelling through.

> **BOX 3.2** **Advertising monopoly**
>
> 'PR' agencies in financial centres such as New York City and London specialize in grooming companies for controversy. Most have a conflict of interest towards representing Indigenous Peoples due to their roster of corporate clients who are active in resource-rich Indigenous territories. How many market 'biodiversity' yet lack even one Indigenous client? How many offer price breaks to affected Indigenous Peoples for catchy city billboards?

New directions for corporate ecotourism

Industry's task

The pressure to consult with Indigenous Peoples is building across industries. Developments such as the *United Nations Draft Declaration on the Rights of Indigenous People* have given a new context to global commerce. The difference with ecotourism is that consultation is not an add-on, but a founding principle.

The principle of community participation, which includes benefit-sharing, is *central* to the ecotourism concept. Purists see it as a continuum, rather than a single act of outreach during impact assessment. Industry, however, finds this a burdensome ideal. Few companies selling so-called 'eco' tourism have taken steps to satisfy even the most basic interpretations of local involvement, especially in regions of high poverty. From project conceptualization forward, there usually is minimal dialogue with affected communities. Diligence is particularly low towards Indigenous Peoples because racial, class and religious prejudices tend to cross-fertilize across business sectors.

Within the ecotourism industry there is occasional peer censure over environmental standards, but little concerning the social aspects of operations. Much of the laxness in relations with Indigenous Peoples stems from corporate interpretations of due diligence – and the ongoing passing of the 'buck' (that is costs) between industry and government. There are a number of outstanding questions, such as:

- Which body of law should govern consultation: domestic law in the company's home country; national laws in the host country; international law; or customary law of the involved Indigenous People(s)?
- Whose standard of consultation should apply: the government's policy; corporate, NGO or academic versions; or cultural protocol stipulated by the affected Indigenous People(s)?
- Whose responsibility is it to identify and approach the affected people(s) and communities: government's; the private sector's;

hired consultants'; or other intermediaries'?

- Must a proponent contact all identified local communities or can one or two be considered representative?
- What type of follow-up is necessary to confirm that the 'necessary' persons are reached?

These issues, elaborated upon in Chapter 8, require mention here since the integrity of consultation is so frequently disputed. When industry interests or NGO interest groups seek endorsement, consultations tend to meander completely around Indigenous Peoples' right to self-determination. We must tune into these money and turf games and demand better. Recent NGO initiatives such as the South North Tourism Route in South Africa (Heaton, 2004) and Ban Jalae Hilltribe Life and Culture Centre in Thailand (Pasimio, 2004) claim to offer tourists an experience 'through the eyes of Indigenous Peoples'; however, it is difficult to determine who controls what in such projects since most press releases originate from involved NGOs or are filtered through government.

BOX 3.3   **Extinction profitable**

'Bird watchers get more enjoyment spotting a rare bird than they do spotting a common one' (Sierra, 2003). And what about tourists? The old pastime of people-watching is alive and well. 'Indigenous cultures are particularly attractive' if perceived as endangered 'or at least under siege' (Gardner, 1997, p14). The Pachamama Alliance (see www.pachamama.org) offers the ultimate telephoto adventure. 'We will have the rare privilege of interacting with the Achuar People in the early stages of their contact with the modern world.'

Terms of reference

The primary question with respect to ecotourism is who can give consent. Who can say whether industry is welcome? Who can confirm if its performance is satisfactory? This becomes a very personal enquiry once we are honest about the number of us either opening the way for industry, or blazing along on its heels.

Dialogue on consent is difficult for a number of reasons. The first practicality is that most industry liaisons or 'go-betweens' with communities do not understand who the local Indigenous People(s) are, or how to make respectful contact. Moreover, most 'experts' hired to handle community relations have a sketchy understanding of cultural protocol. The questions of appropriate protocol and representation can be confusing from the outside. Class or caste attitudes – layered on top of cultural prejudices – often blind us, though we insist otherwise and like to see ourselves as 'objective'.

Within or between Indigenous Peoples, there is often ambiguity about representation identity, too. Answers may vary depending upon the length of colonization or degree of racism experienced. Some confidently know their identity and freely speak of their historical relationship with the land or spiritual traditions. Others are reluctant to openly associate with their culture due to the oppression this continues to bring in some colonial societies. These differences affect the strength of cross-cultural dialogue, especially when communications are rushed.

It is not uncommon for Indigenous Peoples to identify themselves by government terms, like 'Indian', which are generic, rather than by the real name of their people. This muting of identity has been one of the 'successes' of colonialism. Getting Indigenous Peoples to internalize such labels, and the prejudices these derogatory terms carry, is a powerful tool for governments to control the course of development. It strips away the self-esteem of the people; in time, many no longer want to associate with their own customary practices.

Due to these dynamics, there is no agreement yet on how best to define Indigenous Peoples for the purpose of evaluating the ecotourism industry's delivery on promises. There is a lot at stake for everyone involved, all balancing upon whether the free and prior informed consent of the affected people exists or not. Nationally and internationally, there is a deliberate confusion of terms among world governments (Schulte-Tenckhoff, 1999), which benefits industry. As tourists, we like to plead ignorance, though rumblings of the disquiet inevitably reach us. Usually, we hear of some human rights fiasco but then shrug it off as 'over there'.

It is a war of words that has a long political history. Will governments broaden their mandate beyond economics, enabling Indigenous self-determination according to international law? Or will long-standing policies of assimilation continue, in the name of making Indigenous 'issues' more manageable? Many Indigenous leaders feel that there is a blend. They see terms such as 'biodiversity' and 'ecotourism' being utilized by government in order to repackage the same old colonial relationships.

Such plays on terminology and 'truths' have put Indigenous leaders on guard. Many feel that governments are using ecotourism to further national (that is, corporate) goals of economic integration and economic growth. This conventional 'development' formula disregards even basic safeguards for sustainable use. It also hides an array of human rights questions. Thus, most leaders have low faith in industry's pledge to reform, regardless of how it presents 'sustainable' tourism.

Proposed remedies

Increasingly, Indigenous Peoples are seeing through all the eco 'tourisms'

– particularly ecotourism cloaked in the brown skin of 'consultation' and 'benefit-sharing'.

While identity is a central issue now addressed by Indigenous Peoples worldwide who are fighting industrial exploitation, it holds particular urgency relative to ecotourism. The ecotourism industry thinks of Indigenous Peoples as *product*.[9] At the World Ecotourism Summit (WES) in 2002, Indigenous Peoples were described as 'culturally rich societies' and 'traditional cultures'. This type of patronizing cliché gets translated in tourism brochures as colourful, folkloric and frozen in time. It transforms Indigenous Peoples into something for industry to behold, instead of customary landholders to whom it is beholden. In rural Taiwan, as elsewhere, Aboriginal cultures are transformed into 'historical caricatures of themselves' (Munsterhjelm, 2002, p53).

Efforts to clarify the principles and rules of engagement have met with considerable resistance. Barriers like geography and sovereignty are being raised by world governments. Some, for example, point out the disagreement in Asia and Africa over validity of the term 'Indigenous Peoples' – though this terminology and the rights that it confers are being upheld regionally (IWGIA, 2004, p456; Tebtebba Foundation, 2003, p102). Others highlight the varied circumstances of Indigenous Peoples between continents, or from North to South. So long as governments pull the debate to this petty level, most 'consultation' is damaging. The question of how to legitimately seek consent still lurks.

Amid this discord, a handful of prominent international institutions such as the World Bank have seemed to fill the void by developing consultation models specific to Indigenous Peoples. These initiatives carry their own complications since they are driven by a development agenda that endangers Indigenous Peoples and insatiably consumes biodiversity. They function primarily as a wedge for profitable lending, investment and consultancy opportunities in Indigenous territories. Where there is fanfare over community participation, it usually signals deceit.

As Indigenous Peoples become better linked with one another through international exchanges (for example, UN meetings, the internet, solidarity trips or NGO alliances), they are gaining fresh perspective on the constant 'shape shifting' within development policy. They see how hybrid programmes such as ecotourism are marketed to them. They know that new flavours of corporate 'buy in' like certification are usually sour beneath the surface.

The relentless commercialization of 'resources' is now backfiring on world governments. Instead of convincing Indigenous Peoples to chase profit and embrace corporate thinking, it is injecting many with new vitality and cultural pride. Around the question of trade, a revitalized sense of identity and understanding of rights is growing. Many Indigenous Peoples are circling back to their spiritual strengths, rejecting in principle the very notion of industrial-style development and looking to their own customs of trade instead. Peoples like the Maasai in Kenya and the Bhotia in India are crawling out from beneath distorted bottom-rung jobs such as 'porter', 'night watchman' and 'chambermaid' to resume their ancestral role as guardians (Olol-Dapash, 2003; Rana et al, 2003, p3).

At the United Nations Working Group on Indigenous Populations (WGIP) in Geneva, Indigenous Peoples have pushed for self-identification as the international standard to solve the question of identity. WGIP deliberations (Daes, 1996) and *International Labour Organization* (ILO) Convention 169 support this. Adopting this standard for consultation and for negotiations on world trade would help to demystify what constitutes free and prior informed consent. Nevertheless, acceptance by world governments is slow due to the economic interests they guard.

The ecotourism industry has a chance to centre itself by listening to this debate in the international arena. Indigenous leaders are communicating clearly to the world who their peoples are and what gifts they bring to the global dialogue on sustainability. Their message is that economic relationships cannot continue on the present course – in either biological or spiritual terms. By sharing this knowledge, they have indicated very clearly what the missing dimensions are. Are we prepared to learn? Or will we continue to press on as if commerce can proceed out of balance?

BOX 3.4   Rights and wrongs

Indigenous Peoples' right to self-determination as peoples (also called nations or tribes) is affirmed in several resolutions adopted by the United Nations General Assembly, including:

- *Declaration on the Inadmissibility of Intervention in the Domestic Affairs of States and the Protection of their Independence and Sovereignty (1965);*
- *International Covenant on Civil and Political Rights (1966);*
- *Declaration on the Preparation of Societies for Life in Peace (1978);*
- *Manila Declaration on the Peaceful Settlement of International Disputes (1982);*
- *Declaration on the Right to Development (1986).*

The *Draft United Nations Draft Declaration on the Rights of Indigenous People* is fought by the UK, Canada, Australia, the US and New Zealand because it teases apart the three tiers of rights of Indigenous Peoples, stipulating both individual and collective rights from the starting point of self-determination (Schulte-Tenckhoff, 1999). If the document survives their battering with any degree of integrity, it will be a small miracle. Compliance would be costly for countries that profit off rights violations!

Who are Indigenous Peoples?

Colonized Peoples

Indigenous Peoples are the customary landholders in the majority of areas worldwide that are now popular for ecotourism. The common thread among Indigenous cultures, continent to continent, is a unique relationship with the land, expressed and carried through their spirituality (Daes, 1997). This relationship is often described as a guardian role. It is essentially a birth covenant to care for life systems and future generations.

Through colonialism there has been calculated damage to Indigenous governance systems (that is, ancestral title). Globally, governments have awarded ambitious entrepreneurs and companies open access to Indigenous territories. Today, the remnants of 'biodiversity' are strategically mapped, supposedly for protection. However, the maps have led industry back into Indigenous territories with new intensity and precision; our corporate/consumer world now feeds primarily off these lands. Some Indigenous Peoples have responded by reconnecting with their Elders to strengthen cultural practices, for the safeguarding of life systems. But many are driven by extreme poverty to accept jobs or business ventures that break their own cultural protocols about living in relationship with the land. By design, colonial 'landlessness' forces desperate measures.[10]

Today, colonial policies are being meticulously reworked to further integrate Indigenous Peoples into the global economy. Methods have included persuasive ideologies such as 'development' and 'sustainability', which give the appearance of consent and progress. Although Indigenous Peoples describe this systematic advancement of industry as genocide,[11] their own eyewitness accounts of colonization are dismissed. Those of us benefiting from colonization (now typecast as 'consumers') do not want to know what is unlawfully taken from elsewhere to provide our comforts. In our society of 'disposable' income, most just want reassurance that more 'goods' are coming, not how. Supply and demand are narrow economic terms lacking much ethical context.

Indigenous Peoples know first-hand the human costs of our globalized consumer economy. In some regions the progression of colonial impacts has been documented through oral history. In others, the Elders still have firsthand memory of events. Shared colonial histories include violent dispossession of land (such as massacres), deliberate introduction of disease (for example, smallpox), forced labour and brutal separation of children from families for 'education'. Today, variations on this theme abound, with the worst cases often occuring in countries held in high esteem internationally. Many countries still sanction surveillance, imprisonment, torture and political killings of Indigenous Peoples. Human rights abuses are especially prevalent in protected areas, which are a magnet for ecotourism but often employ coercive conservation (see Chapter 6). Ethical NGOs like Survival International and Cultural Survival are helping to publicize the ongoing abuses.

Worldwide, the legacy of colonization is similar. There are distinct repercussions for Indigenous Peoples:

- Indigenous Peoples are the poorest of the poor globally, for whom the most basic consumer products (such as vaccinations, nutritious 'whole' foods and footwear) are priced beyond reach.
- Most identify with the South since demographics vary little between Northern and Southern Indigenous Peoples (for example, poverty, child mortality, life expectancy and relevant literacy).
- Surviving families undergo generations of recovery (including cycles of suicide, physical and emotional abuse, alcoholism and other self-medicating addictions).
- Healing and capacity-building both have 'glass ceilings' if pursued through funded programmes, due to government policies designed to foster continued dependency.

This legacy of colonialism is evident in ecotourism. Few Indigenous Peoples have the wherewithal to exercise their right to self-determination by standing squarely on their feet in negotiations or other dialogue with industry. The situation of the San Peoples of Africa tells a global story. 'The community is sitting in the driver's seat, but is then told by five consultants and two expatriates how to drive' (Thoma, 2000). Donors and their institutional or NGO partners typically set the course, while claiming to support something community based. This is the case now in Karala, India, where a new international think tank for 'eco' tourism development is underway – despite Karala's own abysmal conduct with respect to Indigenous Peoples and so called 'biodiversity' (really, Adivasi ancestral lands; see Box 2.4 and Radhakrishnan, 2005). Few communities left in the wake can piece together a livelihood with dignity. The Meyagari Women's Group of the Samburu in Kenya, which sells exquisite beadwork to passer-by safari goers, is a rare success story.

BOX 3.5   The New World Order

… although the UN General Assembly resolution 1514 proclaims colonization as a violation of international law … a doctrine of denial and complicity exists among the government states of the Western hemisphere to block implementation by the Indigenous Nations and Peoples of the right to decolonization (Acosta, 2003).

Rights holders

Due to recent colonial history, new development programmes that seem more sympathetic with Indigenous Peoples have met resistance. Locally, catch phrases like 'biodiversity' and 'ecotourism' are not being embraced to the extent that governments had hoped. Nor are the general principles associated with them, such as conservation or the protection of 'traditional' lifestyles, as envisioned by development agencies and donors. Indigenous Peoples are questioning these concepts rather than endorsing them because of the conflict of interest of involved agencies.

While a great many governments use foreign policy to portray themselves as polite and progressive with respect to Indigenous Peoples, this is often primarily a public relations strategy. Many countries that appear to be advocating on behalf of Indigenous Peoples have a covert diplomatic agenda. This is common where financial stakes are high. In global talks on biodiversity and tourism, there has been skilful diplomacy by a number of countries seeking a financial windfall from 'eco' tourism. Germany, for example, has been highly involved and stands to benefit from the expansion of domestic tourism companies, such as the German Touristic Union International (TUI), operating offshore.

Definitions of Indigenous Peoples, and interpretations of applicable international law on Indigenous rights, are formed in this policy environment. Frequently, those countries with poor records concerning relationships with Indigenous Peoples are shaping the international standards. Their conduct at home can differ markedly from what they publicly advocate. Some, such as Australia and Canada, are known to quietly subjugate Indigenous Peoples through economic and legal instruments or police intimidation.[12] Others such as Mexico, Ecuador and Brazil continue to sanction more overt violence, especially in rural areas off the mainstream media track.

It is vital to know the nuances of such issues when evaluating the conditions under which tourism could benefit Indigenous Peoples and support their customary practices. Currently, development policies detrimental to Indigenous Peoples far outnumber those that reinforce their right to self-determination. Nationally and internationally, there is minimal public- or private-sector compliance with core international law. Trusted hoteliers such as Méridien and Delta have chosen to pursue investments on sacred lands declared 'no-go' areas by Indigenous Peoples in Tahiti and Canada, respectively (Pambrun, 1998, p33; IPSM, 2004). Tourism Concern (UK) is conducting a campaign to challenge 'sweatshop' labour standards now colouring the industry worldwide.

Powerful voice in the global economy

Today there are an estimated 350 million Indigenous Peoples worldwide.

Biodiversity-rich Indigenous territories are a prime motivator for governments to try out 'new' formulas for development.

World governments are fully aware that, globally, Indigenous Peoples occupy the lands most valuable for economic development (Chandler, 2002). Their foreign affairs ministries are responsible for creating diplomatic openings to these 'resources'. There is now a proliferation of intergovernmental negotiations on 'environment' topics concerning Indigenous Peoples.

Negotiations and work programmes on Indigenous 'issues' are now under way across the UN system, in the United Nations Development Programme (UNDP), the United Nations Environment Programme (UNEP), the United Nations Educational, Scientific and Cultural Organization (UNSESCO), the United Nations Conference on Trade and Development (UNCTAD) and the United Nations Commission on Human Rights (UNCHR), to name just a few. Complementary talks are held within arenas such as the World Trade Organization (WTO) and the World Intellectual Property Organization (WIPO). All are initiated under the pretence of benefiting Indigenous Peoples; but together they serve to ease industrial access to the Earth's remaining 'resources'. Beneath the undulating niceties and assaults of diplomacy (and all the North–South jostling), there is a tacit agreement among countries to move forward a 'clean' economic agenda on biodiversity, with unfettered access to Indigenous territories. Contradictions between the *UN Convention on Biological Diversity* (CBD) and WTO trade agreements illustrate this orchestration of interests. Cultural diversity and 'traditional knowledge' are praised and promoted, but thoroughly undercut.

Most Indigenous Peoples lack the baseline information and resources necessary to demand good faith in international standard-setting. Nevertheless, there is a critical mass of Indigenous leadership plugged in who warn that the current system of policy development is unsustainable (see Chapter 10). At the 2002 UN Earth Summit in Johannesburg, Indigenous delegates delivered the *Kimberley Declaration*, decrying corporate control of 'sustainability' policy. Since then debates on international regimes for access and benefit-sharing have heated up, with Northern countries taking an aggressive stand. Indigenous Peoples are the loudest voice of dissent, despite their suppressed and often makeshift representation in world forums: 'Governments are afraid of us.'

Globalization of the sacred

Old World economics
The globalization of economics is old news to Indigenous Peoples whose lands have been annexed and siphoned of 'resources' through colonialism. Its only new feature today is the packaging. There is now lip service at the UN

to Indigenous Peoples as global stewards of biodiversity; at the same time, an elaborate international framework is being laid out to draw Indigenous Peoples deeper into the global economy. Through environmental accords and development programming, Indigenous Peoples are being encouraged to sign onto the very economic regimes that suppress them.

Internationally, the public and private sectors are working together to present a set of incentives to Indigenous Peoples. This is aimed at what the corporate world calls integration, yet has the effect of assimilation. Corporations, like governments, are aware that Indigenous Peoples inhabit the remaining biodiversity-rich areas of the world – which offer the highest prospects for investment. Efforts are thus being made to court them, industry to industry. The offerings are usually meagre (stakeholder consultation as opposed to equitably structured dialogues), but are enough to make some impoverished communities feel acknowledged or even optimistic. From Mali to the Arctic, deal-making is moving at a fast pace. Methods vary little from one economic sector to another. Tourism, singled out as a financial incentive under the CBD, is particularly active.

One Tribal Chief watching variations of 'development' policy for the last 30 years notes:

> For years governments have been determined to extinguish Indigenous nations. They have created laws and policies to make this 'legal'. But now they figure that the best way to extinguish us is to convince us to cut down our own tree. This is what we call neo-colonialism. It is all driven by economics. Governments inject their principles into you through development programmes and then persuade you to use their philosophies on your own people. Those generations that are the roots of our tree, our children and Elders, will then never know who they are, because the tree has been made into lumber; the lumber is used to build a house on cement foundation (Leach, 2002).

This type of credible feedback from properly mandated Indigenous leaders who have an overview of policy development is not being heeded. World policy forums are fast-tracking trade agreements and industry guidelines, maintaining that conventional industry is the answer to what NGOs have called 'the biodiversity crisis' (Khor, 2002).

New World solutions

The globalization of biodiversity 'solutions' such as ecotourism or so-called sustainable tourism is now being finessed through the international policy system. Tourism is a major agenda item in the *General Agreement on Trade in Services*

(GATS) negotiations of the WTO.[13] The effect will be to reduce restrictions on foreign ownership, increasing franchising and other licensing arrangements (Pleumarom, 1999). This, alongside laxer aviation treaties facilitating mass travel (Jones, 2003), is a blow to the original concept of ecotourism. Indigenous Peoples' right to self-determination, although protected in international law, will be further eclipsed by globalized mass tourism.

At the World Ecotourism Summit (WES) in 2002, the ethical dimensions of development were raised. Representatives from East Africa stated that the major obstacle to sustainability on the African continent is the unwillingness of development 'partners' to understand their local perspectives: 'People come and take, but they don't give back. We don't have a problem; it is the world that has a problem.' The World Rainforest Movement says that this attitude of taking permeates the global economy: 'the present "development" pattern throws Indigenous People away. They are brutally dispossessed in the name of conservation, or they are deceived in the name of development' (WRM, 2003). These statements echo Indigenous Peoples' own communiqués to world governments.

Ecotourism is one of the most potent forms *ever* of colonial development. The industry penetrates Indigenous cultures,[14] often just by treading on ancestral lands. Within Indigenous cultures the land is synonymous with the people, and often translates to mean soul. The land is said to mirror the Creator (for example, the rivers being its life blood), meaning that the Creator dwells in it. Indigenous ceremonies, knowledge and customary practices are therefore all impacted by indiscriminate 'eco' tourism, whether or not a direct or indirect target of industry. This leads to a rapid succession of culture loss and biodiversity impacts, beyond those immediately apparent.

Given the links between cultural and biological diversity, ecotourism seldom entails a simple transaction or straightforward audit where Indigenous Peoples are concerned. It is imbued with ideals and theories that seem a perfect fit with Indigenous values, such as respectful and responsible visitation. However, these supposed features have been manipulated into a rationale for economic growth – that is, top-down development prescriptions. This is why the 'Trojan horse' analogy is so often used to describe ecotourism (Tan, 2002). Corporations have a utilitarian view of ecotourism. So do scientists hungry for patents, geologists after oil and churches seeking converts. Ecotourism provides cover for a range of colonial pursuits.

Klaus Toepfer, director of UNEP, met with the handful of Indigenous delegates attending the WES. As a seasoned bureaucrat he was able to reflect their concerns back to them in a thoughtful way. 'Are we not globalizing a very specific way of thinking? Water used to be considered sacred across cultures. Now we are pricing water in order to protect it, because the value of respect is no longer there' (Toepfer, 2002). What Toepfer did not concede is the current role of the UN in exporting this consumer ideology.

Worldwide, Indigenous Peoples have rejected the commercialization of life-sustaining elements because their Elders say the waters, lands and atmosphere intermingle with us in delicate balance.[15]

BOX 3.6 **Churches groom flocks for 'development'**

Who would ever guess? Originally, the Catholic Church helped to dispossess, 'tame' and enslave Indigenous Peoples. Today, evangelical churches with corporate ties are spreading a doctrine of submission. Ecotourism is the new tool for many church emissaries. Overland Missions (US) leads treks into regions like the Amazon. Several groups, such as the Center for World Indigenous Studies, are outspoken against this practice. (Daley, 2003)

Market madness

Cultural colour on world markets

The ecotourism industry has found Indigenous cultures useful for selling 'nature' products. To industry, culture means 'value-added' sales. Whether trips feature a visit to a local community or merely offer Indigenous Peoples as a scenic backdrop to other sightseeing and recreation, similar images are used to advertise. More than 50 per cent of ecotourism brochures portray encounters with Indigenous Peoples or their ancestral lands.

In most instances, Indigenous Peoples have no means of knowing when or where they are being marketed, or by whom. This is particularly true among Southern Indigenous Peoples due to the extreme communication barriers they face. Living in impoverished rural areas and communicating by word of mouth or battery-operated radio do not lend to easy monitoring of industry practices. Peoples like the Maya of Guatemala and the Maasai of East Africa regularly appear in brochures without any genuine consent or negotiated conditions (such as royalties, prohibitions or agreed roles and responsibilities). Northern Indigenous Peoples are also considered open season by the tourism industry. During 1999, photos of an unnamed sacred site and mysterious 'Indian' chief were splashed across travel posters at tram shelters in Berlin advertising trips to the US. Similar marketing now pervades the internet.[16]

Caricatures of Indigenous Peoples can be found in tourist quarters everywhere. In ecotourism destinations, postcards and cheap cultural knock-offs are sold *en masse*, as if resident Indigenous Peoples had some choice in being a target of tourism. Elsewhere, there is an assortment of fake merchandise sold or marketed without any cultural or even geographic context. This includes wooden Indians outside souvenir shops in cities like Glasgow, Quebec City and Santo Domingo; masks and effigies of Indian Chiefs sold alongside wooden clogs in Amsterdam's touristy flower market; and North American dream-catchers sharing a shelf with plush koala bears at trinket shops in Canberra. Most of this 'cultural' paraphernalia is made in China. In Malaysia, tourists can buy 'Australian' Aboriginal didgeridoos, mass produced in Sarawak – a double-barrelled rights infringement hitting ancient cultures on two continents:

> Tourism goes right to the heart of who we are as a Peoples. Our culture and our way of life are on the line. We have seen our eagle feathers and sweetgrass used as icons to market tourism to the world (Smoke, 1999).

What these aberrations show is the storytelling power of tourism. Globalized tourism has carried the same stereotypical images far and wide. We are now on the brink of countries trying to carve out tourism brand names such as 'Natives in Nature' or 'Tribal Trails'.[17] Ecotourism is pushing markets in this direction. Rather than promoting travel that is tolerant of diverse cultures, it harnesses one overwhelming consumer culture.[18] Illustrating this are porters at the Panama City airport, whose shirts read '*Cultura Turistica*' in 2001. The tourist culture is indeed supreme in Central America. But it is the Kuna and other Indigenous Peoples of Panama who fast become acquainted with visitors, not the other way around. For most tourists, jaunting from one destination to another on annual vacation, there is a superficial blur of Indigenous identities. Ecotourism marketing accentuates this with its frequent omission of factual information about Indigenous Peoples.[19]

The ecotourism industry is highly mobile and dispersed, with offshore offices, unlike the Indigenous communities which it passes through. Economic globalization and the advent of tourism marketing Indigenous cultures and territories mean that Indigenous Peoples must now take steps globally to protect their rights. They must know what is happening with respect to Indigenous rights in every nook of the UN, including its affiliates such as the WTO, WIPO and the World Commission on Protected Areas (WCPA). These are the new fronts for corporate influence and trickery. Nonetheless, few Indigenous Peoples can afford to send delegations abroad due to the shortage of funding available for this type of advocacy. Even fewer can staff foreign offices or appoint permanent international representatives to maintain a presence at bodies such as UNCHR in Geneva. Only a handful of Indigenous Peoples, such as the Maori of New Zealand and Kuna, have taken this step. The rest are doing their best to protect rights on home soil, but usually find their efforts thwarted by being cut off from global policy processes and industry boardrooms.

> **BOX 3.7** | **Skeletons in our closet**
>
> After centuries of crude fascination, we 'cultured' ones still see Indigenous Peoples as freak shows. Museums worldwide continue to house 'stones and bones'. Not until 2002 did France repatriate the pickled genitals of Saartjie Baartman, enslaved in Africa and paraded in Europe as the 'Hottentot Venus' (Associated Press, 2002). Today, tourists in places like Disneyworld are flocking to the 'oddity museums' of *Ripley's Believe It or Not!* 'billion-dollar-a-year empire', which feature shrunken heads of the Jívaro (Mackie, 2002; Ward, 2002).

Issues behind the scenes

Indigenous leaders are aware that corporate allegiance lies with clients and shareholders. Across the various economic sectors, they see tiresome repetition of corporate approaches to their communities (see Chapter 7). As a result, most find the ecotourism industry very predictable. Conventional ecotourism companies have poor accountability to the peoples and communities whom they claim to support.

Many companies find it difficult to adapt their management style to working with Indigenous Peoples. There are a number of 'standard operating procedures' that stand in the way of relationship-building. These include:

- making overtures to individuals or single communities, rather than the collective membership;
- searching for familiar figureheads at the expense of real representation (for example, matriarchal or hereditary systems);
- 'wining and dining' or barbequing towards a deal instead of sincere, long-term oriented relationship-building;
- withholding regular corporate communications such as business plans and annual reports (that show their full portfolio, performance and profits) or offering poor community adaptations;
- limiting opportunities to meet on company turf to just the visible leadership – when Elders, family heads or other customary authorities should be included;
- hosting shareholder meetings for financial investors only, without including the Indigenous People(s) who hold ancestral title;
- taking project consultants more seriously than the involved Indigenous People(s).

Such practices crosscut industries, but are highly visible in ecotourism due to the more immediate role of communities. While any single one can seriously obstruct communal decision-making, companies frequently run through the complete list or a close variation. Containment is a corporate philosophy that permeates all facets of operations. The goal is 'issues management', the issue in this case being a solution for the 'natives'.

Development ideology

The progress fable

It must be questioned just how governments plan to encourage customary practices, as required by the CBD. Development policy has suppressed Indigenous governance systems, languages, family structures and other aspects of 'traditional knowledge' in an effort to mainstream Indigenous Peoples. Only a fundamental shift in economic thinking would move governments and development agencies in a new direction that is supportive, or at least tolerant, of self-determination.

Questions such as what is knowledge and how different paradigms mesh are not new, nor are they confined to debates around traditional knowledge. Noted scholars such as Berman (1988), Capra (1988) and Daly and Cobb (1989) have explored them at depth. Nonetheless, this debate has not attracted significant attention or support at the policy level. The world's Nobel laureates were essentially ignored in 1992 when they issued the *World Scientists' Warning to Humanity*. Rethinking the Industrial Revolution is not a winning proposal in a society enamoured with economic growth, globalization and cheap (in other words, grossly mispriced) consumer kicks.

There has now been three decades of disenchantment with development policy among ground workers (Cernea, 1991). By the late 1970s the notion of 'development' had been reconceptualized, both generally and in relation to tourism (de Kadt, 1979; Schurmann, 1981). Former policy held that development involved 'replacing so-called backward ways – that is, traditional culture, with modern industrial ways' (Loeb and Paredes, 1991, p31). This brought results that were 'quite the reverse of community development', which 'consistently and systematically destroyed existing traditional communities' (Daly and Cobb, 1989, p166). It led to a generation of NGO activists opposing economic globalization. Their work was instrumental in shaping the *Brundtland Report* (WCED, 1987), which in 1987 introduced the concept of sustainable development. However, it did not prompt any appetite in political arenas for the tough social questions about consumer society, such as equity or corporate ethics. Dominant beliefs, attitudes and institutional practices have changed little.

At the second UN Earth Summit in Johannesburg in 2002 all the old concerns about government development policy were raised. There was an awkward revisiting of 'development' failures, including the much publicized but virtually empty promise of community participation. The *Kimberley Declaration* issued by Indigenous Peoples was identical in spirit and content to the Indigenous *Kari-Oca Declaration* of a decade earlier. As such, governments became defensive about international trade regimes, particularly Indigenous Peoples' and NGOs' suggestion that they have simply become more adept at how they override international law.

This debate about 'development' is important background for understanding issues raised by Indigenous Peoples. As industrial society becomes sick from its own 'success' (that is, *our* consumer excess) some of us are reaching deeper for understanding. Indigenous concepts of connectedness and sustainability are being felt. Unfortunately, world governments have swung the other way.

Programme delivery

Biodiversity, and even human rights, are just a small part of the politics enmeshing Indigenous Peoples. One vital change since the debate on 'development' emerged during the 1970s is that distinctions between issues are becoming clear. Indigenous Peoples are speaking out on their own behalf. They are presenting specific grievances and recommendations to world governments concerning their colonial history and their collective rights as peoples. As a result, many activist groups backing Indigenous Peoples' right to self-determination vis-à-vis tourism are becoming sensitized to Indigenous Peoples' core concerns. The Ecumenical Coalition on Tourism issued a statement in January 2002 saying:

> The issues of the Indigenous Peoples are far greater than that of compiling a code of ethics or initiating interventions through agreements or protocols, though this may be seen as a beginning ... The questions of place of the Indigenous Peoples, their land, their identity and political rights are at the centre of tourism expansion
> (Tan, 2002, p7).

Nevertheless, world governments are pressing ahead with an economic agenda that subordinates Indigenous Peoples. Both development agencies and corporations are in delivery mode – delivery of programmes, delivery of services and delivery of props for the consumer lifestyle. Top-down thinking is alive and thriving in tourism. 'We want to develop a handbook for ecotourism to educate communities and NGOs' (The Philippines, 1999). The notion of handbooks has ignited within the WTO-OMT, UNEP, TIES and other broker institutions.

Still, most governments insist that the ecotourism industry is intrinsically 'different', allowing decision-making by communities. This is not most Indigenous Peoples' experience. Facilitated workshops may be offered to solicit community input on programme design. Invariably, though, community feedback is sandwiched between goals and outputs dreamed up elsewhere, in another time zone (that is against the corporate clock). What gets fed back to the local community as a synthesis document or work plan is barely recognizable. Community participation in this type of industry framework is no more than a predetermined exercise of 'connect the dots'.

BOX 3.8 Kuna Chiefs say no to conventional 'development'

We, the Saila Dummagan ... denounce that we have been and continue to be the victims of a development model based on ambition, the plundering of natural resources and contempt for peoples' lives, for peoples and their cultures ... As leaders ... we express our will to continue struggling [for] ... development based on the principles of our culture: respect for people, Mother Earth and dialogue and solidarity among peoples.
(Kuna Nation, Gathering at Ibedi, Panama, 2003)

Indigenous concepts of development

Indigenous knowledge

Governments have expressed frustration with Indigenous Peoples' growing scepticism about ecotourism. Industry is equally puzzled by their misgivings. From a business perspective, ecotourism seems an inclusive vehicle for economic growth; it is inconceivable why communities would rather opt out, or else 'flunk out', on market terms. Yet, values-based decisions are the driving force. Most Indigenous Peoples are saying an emphatic 'NO' to corporate thinking. Illustrating this sentiment is Fiji, where Indigenous Peoples comprise over 80 per cent of the population. 'For Indigenous communities in the Pacific, the idea of business is alien... Some say time is money, but our cultural feeling is that it is exceptionally rude to rush' (Malani, 2003). So the government of Fiji is working with villages to build appropriate concepts for tourism.

Indigenous leaders reiterate in forum after forum, both locally and internationally, the source of their shared discomfort with development policy. Issues such as land rights and intellectual property abuse are raised, with countless testimonies of ongoing misappropriation. Beneath all these disturbing accounts of 'the industrial way' is a strong theme. Worldwide, Indigenous Peoples are cautioning against our commercialization and liquidation of life systems. Ecotourism really is the 'last frontier'. It has seeped into sanctuaries that are *essential to life* – namely, sacred sites, sacred ceremonies and sacred healing knowledge.

Continent to continent, Indigenous Peoples have in common a distinct understanding of sustainability, shaped by their relationship with the land. Their bridge is a spiritual concept of ownership, often described as non-ownership. This is expressed as a relationship carrying both rights and responsibility. Many Indigenous Peoples, such as the Hopi in the US and the Kogi in Colombia,[20] have urged those of us living out of balance (the global consumer class) to heal our chaotic relationships. They compare their sacred knowledge systems to a fulcrum. Ignoring this body of knowledge will take all of humanity over the brink (see Ereira, 2001; Davis, 2004).

While governments are by now used to hearing of Indigenous knowledge about sustainability, it is generally regarded an indulgent and dramatized topic. Following the first UN Earth Summit in 1992, Indigenous knowledge became imbedded in UN talks on seemingly everything: biodiversity, climate change, desertification and wetlands, to name a few. Still, it is difficult for bureaucrats used to corporate timelines and industry-driven budgets to comprehend its value to their work. The attitude is: 'Let's move on to the real stuff now.'

Incorporating Indigenous knowledge in tourism

Much of the ambivalence towards working with Indigenous Peoples for sustainable tourism comes from ignorance about who they are, what their cultures embody and why coping or survival strategies change.

Many professionals assigned to manage programmes allegedly supporting Indigenous knowledge have seen or heard gossip of 'stray' communities. One example often cited is the adoption of practices such as clear-cutting or indiscriminate hunting or fishing. Some encounter these community incidents and find reason for cynicism towards all Indigenous Peoples. They begin to view submissions by Indigenous leadership as pure political posturing, rather than a sincere ethical stand on environmental issues.[21]

Meanwhile, Indigenous Peoples report bias from government and institutional staff. Professionals often listen to Indigenous 'subjects' as a matter of intrigue, but are quite tickled to encounter communities afflicted with environmental dysfunction just like other places. This kind of professional 'objectivity' has soured many a relationship. Usually, community decisions are judged outside of their colonial context. Decisions perceived as culturally inconsistent are construed to validate top-down programming (that is, more 'development' according to donor-led frameworks).

The ecotourism industry is spared similar scrutiny despite its agenda of economic growth, its leading role in climate change and its highly questionable conservation interests. This shows the double talk on biodiversity conservation that permeates bureaucracies and institutions. It is a reminder to be wary of altered realities. Most donor programmes claiming to support Indigenous Peoples reap more from community breakdown and failures (as 'fix it' agents) than from healthy examples of self-determination reflecting customary law.

Although the customs and circumstances of Indigenous Peoples internationally vary widely, patterns of colonialism and responses to it are similar. Few place first priority of tourism profits on conservation because conservation is an *industrial* concept that differs vastly from sacred knowledge of life systems. Some apply their earnings to hospital construction, while others prefer to build schools. These decisions reflect the need to resume self-determination in primary areas. Regaining basic aspects of customary governance undermined by 'development' is pivotal to maintaining culture. Frequently, Indigenous Peoples must imbed this effort in accepted funding streams or donor (that is, government) support will be withheld.

Will we learn to respect cultural concepts of business and profit? Or will we stay tuned for the weak links so that 'rescue remedies' like ecotourism can be imposed?

BOX 3.9 | **Dare to know Nepal**

In our culture we are not taught to exploit our guest; now we hear that the more you can exploit the guest the better you will do... This seed in our children's mind is really damaging ... We should examine the intentions, attitudes and behaviour of tourism. There is no spirit of friendship and brotherhood ... The tourists always believe they have paid all the costs; but to Indigenous Peoples the cost of bringing more tourists is high. (Stella Tamang, South Asia Indigenous Women's Forum, IIFB, Workshop on Tourism, *UN Convention on Biological Diversity*, Malaysia, 2004)

Indigenous tourism initiatives

While many Indigenous Peoples are saying no to tourism, or wish they could, some see tourism as a powerful addition to their toolbox for protecting rights. A recent guidebook on 'community based Indigenous tourism' printed in France describes a range of existing initiatives (see Blangy, 2005/2006). One question remains: does such a guidebook facilitate self-determination? Only if each and every entry is sanctioned in full by the appropriate Elders. Some Indigenous Peoples may wish to avoid indiscriminate 'public' exposure, and the unwanted intrigue and visitation it can bring. Others are wary of thrusting Indigenous Peoples at large further into the open marketplace.

In the tourism sector, one issue causing consternation and significant sarcasm has been the emergence of a casino economy on tribal lands in the US. Tribes like the Seminole and Apache have used casinos to raise money for self-determination, such as the litigation of land rights, buyback of ancestral lands or community economic development (Sahagun, 2003). Many advocates of ecotourism have reacted to this with indignation. It either does not fit their idea of Indigenous Peoples as custodians of the sacred (especially the land) or reinforces racist stereotypes (for example, the 'lazy drunk Indian' interpretation of colonial history). What many critics of such initiatives miss are Indigenous Peoples' own dialogues around the subject.

Ben Sherman of Indian Country Tourism (ICT) has noted that 47 per cent of Native Americans in the US live below the poverty level (Sherman, 2002). He points out the contradiction between economic goals in the corporate world and the native value of not accumulating capital. In his view, the philosophy of free enterprise is 'progressive', and 'the great majority [of Native Americans] in the US are now wanting to merge their economies into the global economy'. To promote this, ICT has partnered with American Express and the World Travel and Tourism Council to help address business capacity issues in Aboriginal communities (Sherman, 2002).

Although the Aboriginal casino economy in the US generates some US$5 billion profit annually (Barlett and Steele, 2002), several tribes in North America like the Navajo and Hopi are voicing discomfort about such mainstream economies and partnerships. While some foresee entering international markets to secure an untainted, independent income, many also envision changing the nature of these markets. They see themselves bringing a more human (often spiritual) face to economic initiatives. It is a fundamentally different view of business, mixing a pragmatic approach to self-determination with cultural principles.

Many small Indigenous hospitality businesses are being conceived as a holistic enterprise, based on communal revenue needs. Decision-making is commonly governed by a community board with representation of families. Elders guide this process. Ultimately, the goal is twofold. The obvious goal is to create a viable business that restores self-reliance for next generations. The secondary goal, often unstated, is to undertake international (cross-cultural) relations for the protection of rights. For Indigenous Peoples, owning a successful tourism business can be an entrée to new types of dialogue helpful to defending ancestral title.[22] Some, such as the Tampuen in Cambodia, are effectively using tourism to affirm their Indigenous identity and rights. Their Yeak Laom project announces who they are and what type of tourism is acceptable (see www.geocities.com/yeak_laom/ecotourism).

This latter type of project promotes self-determination; however, proposals of this nature often meet resistance from government-affiliated funding institutions, or are tempered by the involvement of government donors. Anything too explicit about land rights is taboo, despite the inherent and inalienable link between land rights, sacred knowledge and biodiversity.

The Garífuna of the Honduras have created their own small-scale tourism project to resist government forms of 'development', only to be persecuted (see Chapter 6 discussion on 'The elusive equilibrium'). In 2005 one Garífuna woman had her home raided by Honduras' Criminal Investigative Division and another was sentenced to 'preventative custody'. Rights groups fear 'that repression against Garífuna will increase, under pressure from the international tourism industry to get control of their lands (Flores, 2005).

BOX 3.10   Indigenous Peoples speak out

We want to make it clear that our peoples will not tolerate the 'folklorization' of culture ... many cultural expressions are eminently spiritual and they form part of our peoples' Cosmovision and therefore are sacred... Thus, they are not touristic merchandise that governments can use as promotions of tourist attractions without the consent of the peoples as cultural exchange and under cultural norms. (*Declaration of the Indigenous Peoples Caucus of Latin America, UN Permanent Forum on Indigenous Issues,* New York, 2004)

Conclusion

Fifteen years into the 'eco' tourism boom, Indigenous Peoples find themselves lacking the capacity to evaluate relevant policy forums and programmes. Governments and development agencies have developed a global framework for 'sustainable' tourism, without engaging the very peoples affected. The consequences are being felt on two levels. On the surface is a violation of international law on self-determination, with all the imbalance and discord this brings. Much deeper are profound lessons about human relationships.

We are at a juncture where it is vital to reassess the dialogue on sustainable tourism. There are vast discrepancies in approaches to 'development' between industry and Indigenous Peoples (see Appendix 1). In the corporate/consumer world, governments are sewing up trade regimes, putting peoples and communities in bondage for the sake of economic growth. Among Indigenous Peoples, the bottom line is not money but the sacred contracts sustaining life systems.[23] When these two systems come into dialogue, there is opportunity for empathy, enlightenment and a momentous shift.

Effective cross cultural dialogue will be welcoming of the contentious issues. The process will be non-discriminatory and create safe ground for everyone involved. There will be open brainstorming and consideration of solutions. This means a willingness to grapple with issues such as:

- remedies for racism in the tourism industry;
- principles for building new relationships respectful of Indigenous rights, customary law and cultural protocols;
- review of the rights infringements and culture loss resulting from 'best practice' schemes launched by the public and private sectors;
- policy and financing mechanisms to support Indigenous Peoples' rightful role as entrepreneurs; and
- a proper ombuds body to address Indigenous Peoples' testimony on the *systemic* barriers to sustainable tourism.

It is time to start this listening journey, with sincerity and humility – particularly from major industry players such as the WTO-OMT.

For this type of dialogue process to succeed, there must be built-in provisions for parity. Mutually agreed terms of reference and ground rules for dialogue must be developed between the parties. Indigenous Peoples must be able to represent themselves, hire consultants, exchange information and otherwise be prepared on an equitable basis vis-à-vis government and industry. There must also be full provision for the dissemination of meeting transcripts and audio/video documentation so that Indigenous leaders unable to attend pertinent UN meetings, or related negotiations and consultations, can stay abreast of outcomes.

Currently, the WTO-OMT is the greatest barrier to a breakthrough. Since its induction as a UN-specialized agency in 2003, it has yet to show any commitment to Indigenous rights. The much ballyhooed 1999 *Global Code of Ethics for Tourism* mentions Indigenous Peoples in Article 2(2), but carefully sidesteps collective rights (that is, the right to self-determination). Indigenous Peoples are forced to file disputes to the implementing World Committee on Tourism Ethics (established in 2004) as stakeholders, not rights holders. This tells us that the well-entrenched WTO-OMT Business Council is still light years away from meaningful dialogue on life and death matters.

Recommended reading

- Kajoeramari, R. Chief (1999) Speech delivered at Third Annual Caribbean Tourism Organization Conference on Sustainable Tourism Development, Paramaribo, Suriname, 9–12 April
- *Kari-Oca Declaration and Indigenous Peoples Earth Charter* (1992) Rio de Janeiro, Brazil, 25–30 May
- *Kimberley Declaration* (2002) International Indigenous Peoples Summit on Sustainable Development, Khoi-San Territory, Kimberley, South Africa, 20–23 August
- LAKHUN Foundation, Cordillera Ancestral Development Centre (2002) *An Open Statement on the UNEP Declaration of 2002 as 'International Year of Ecotourism'*, The Philippines. Available from www.tourismrights.org
- *Statement on the Process of the Regional Meeting on Community-based Ecotourism in Southeast Asia* (2002) Chiang Mai, Thailand, 3–7 March
- *World Council of Indigenous Peoples: Declaration of Principles* (1984) Ratified by the Fourth General Assembly of the World Council of Indigenous Peoples, available from the Union of BC Indian Chiefs Resource Centre, www.ubcic.bc.ca

Key resources

- Cultural Survival: www.cs.org
- Indian Law Resource Center: www.indianlaw.org
- International Work Group for Indigenous Affairs: www.iwgia.org
- Land is Life: www.landislife.org
- Native Americas Magazine: www.nativeamericas.org
- Netherlands Centre for Indigenous Peoples: www.nciv.net
- Survival International: www.survival-international.org
- Tebtebba: www.tebtebba.org
- Union of British Columbia Indian Chiefs: www.ubcic.bc.ca

Figure 3.1 **Two visions for 'development': Indigenous or industrial**

Neo-Colonial 'Development' Paradigm	Indigenous 'Wellness' Paradigm
Survival of the fittest within the global market	Survival of intact Indigenous cultures, in balance with other peoples
Objectives and goals 'scientifically' defined	Objectives and goals spiritually defined
Ecological cycles are subject to 'man's' dominion over nature	Ecological cycles understood as the cyclical renewal of 'Mother' Earth
Sectoral and compartmentalized for easy commercialization	Holistic in scope and approach
Facade of professional objectivity	Overt discussion of Indigenous values
Cultural homogeneity (manifesting in our consumer lifestyle)	Cultural diversity (in other words, a celebration of life)
Land and resources perceived as private and 'public' property	Land and resources perceived as the common spiritual heritage of all peoples
People as consumers (that is, material beings)	People as custodians (that is, spiritual beings)
Starting point of lifestyle desires	Starting point of life needs
Individual pursuits and pleasures	Collective responsibility and accountability
Emphasis on investment capital and investor returns	Emphasis on non-monetary benefits, the 'priceless'
Competition between people(s)	Solidarity between people(s)
Philosophy of extraction and accumulation	Based on ceremonies in reciprocity with Mother Earth
Streamlined legal and policy frameworks to facilitate exponential economic growth	Customary laws to preserve ecosystem integrity and balance with Mother Earth
Decisions made within development agencies by alleged proxy	Decisions made within actual communities by protocol
Driven by industrial concepts and seductive (but misleading) promises	Driven by culture and community aspirations

Development by templates, conforming to the corporate world	Strengthening of culture, not assimilation
Programming based on discriminatory policies standards and practices	Programming based on self-analysis of community needs, values and priorities
Management by certified specialists, according to respective fields of expertise	Leadership by Elders and knowledge keepers through customary spiritual practices
Methods/technologies geared to maximum extraction	Methods/technologies geared to sustainable use and regifting
Reliance on specialized, university-educated consultants trained in industrial thinking	Community innovation based on collective values and sacred knowledge systems
Quantifiable indicators with economic bias, to stretch definitions of what is sustainable	Culture-based indicators of living in balance with sacred life systems

Source: Adapted from Johnston 1998

Figure 3.2 **Questions to ask: Discerning the situation of Indigenous peoples**

> *'Yes' indicates higher likelihood of sustainable tourism*
> *'No' indicates a red flag*
>
> - Do the affected Indigenous People(s) know their rights under international law?
> - Can they freely identify and associate as an Indigenous People, without risk of repression?
> - Can they exercise ancestral title, including the inter-generation responsibility now called 'conservation'?
> - Do they understand all applicable law, policy and guidelines concerning tourism? And the implications?
> - Can they do a background check on the various advocates and champions of tourism in their midst?
> - Can they readily obtain information on tourism, eg trends, impacts, successes and failures?
> - Are they conversant with both the ups and downs of certification schemes, including 'fair trade'?
> - Can they communicate freely and regularly with other Indigenous Peoples, government to government?
> - Have they heard first-hand from other Indigenous Peoples on what makes a tourism 'success'?
> - Are they aware of documented abuses of Indigenous Peoples at various 'eco' tourism meccas worldwide?
> - Do they know how air travel and other tourist behaviour impacts climate change?
> - Do they know the heightened climate change effects on certain Indigenous Peoples globally?
> - Is there the freedom to formalize their own internal planning, via a Traditional Use Study or other means?
> - Can they adequately fundraise to press for the recognition and protection of their rights?
> - Are their own governance bodies properly resourced for daily functions and inter-governmental talks?
> - Is there reasonable hope of balanced negotiations with the national government and/or industry?
> - Is there prospect for successful litigation of rights (and wrongs) under the national legal system?
> - Is there prospect for successful litigation of rights (and wrongs) under the national legal system?
> - Can they access international avenues to protect rights, e.g. WGIP, UNPF or CERD?

- Do they have pro bono legal help and other equitable 'professional' or 'technical' cross-cultural assistance?
- Do they have an interpretation budget enabling Elders to participate meaningfully in key dialogues?

Figure 3.3 **How to spot a fake:**
Discerning between tourism facts and fairytales

Before jumping on board to support a tourism 'success', check your facts with a few questions:

- Whose ancestral territory does your holiday or 'eco' trip occur in?
- Do the Indigenous People(s) own any part of the tourism economy?
- Is there visible poverty, cover-ups of poverty or other signs of exploitation?
- Is the 'public' attitude dismissive of Indigenous Peoples and their rights?
- Is there a military presence, police surveillance of Indigenous Peoples or other indication of judicial bias?
- Have groups like Cultural Survival or Survival publicized abuses in the country?
- Is there disagreement between government and Indigenous Peoples over industry presence or its practices?
- Is there a discrepancy between mainstream and alternative media on racial conflicts reported?
- Are there any grassroots campaigns for the 'environment' or human rights, signalling government neglect?
- Can you verify with the affected Indigenous People(s) that your holiday will directly benefit them?

Figure 3.4 **Advertisement of 'exotic' cultures at tourist museum at Melaka, Malaysia**

Figure 3.5 **Flag hung by sacred fire at Aboriginal Tent Embassy in Canberra, Australia: Genocide is a crime**

Chapter 4

Intellectual Property

**New forms of colonization must stop and decolonization
must begin in earnest.**
*(Elders' Declaration: Kindling a Fire, International Indigenous Elders Summit,
2004, Haudenosaunee territory)*

For Indigenous Peoples, the issue of free and prior informed consent (PIC)
stretches far beyond industry access to ancestral lands. Today the corporate
world is attempting to sell culture and even the building blocks of life itself. It
is also using culture to hawk various products throughout the marketplace.[1]
Globally, no single industry is more implicated in commercializing culture
than ecotourism.

Cultural content and cultural interpretation in tourism products is a
major concern among Indigenous Peoples. Ecotourism companies generally
profess to offer something 'authentic'. Few communities, however, recall any
conversation of substance with tour companies operating in their midst. Tour
operators regularly survey satisfaction among clients, without first ensuring
appropriate community consent, evaluation and monitoring.

Worldwide, the ecotourism industry aggressively appropri-
ates and commodifies Indigenous cultures. Land rights are maligned,
ceremonies are mocked, millennial arts are debased and healing practices are pirated. In the name of biodiversity conservation, 'traditional
knowledge' is celebrated, then spirited away to be repackaged for global markets. This plundering has resulted in animated debate on the subject of intellectual property. The ecotourism industry spans multiple sectors, bringing
exponential impact.

The intellectual property rights (IPRs) regime of the World Intellectual
Property Organization (WIPO) offers no solutions for this dilemma in
ecotourism. Its (ab)user pay approach suggests consent and equity, but is

a leading cause of culture loss globally. Sacred elements of culture are being misappropriated whether they qualify for IPRs 'protection' or not. IPRs neither recognize, nor safeguard, 'property' that is collective and spiritual in nature.

This deadlock demands us to be reflective. Tourism is the largest and fastest-growing industry in the world. Projected rates of growth for ecotourism signal increased pressure on isolated Indigenous Peoples, many of whom have little chance of withstanding the ecotourism onslaught, let alone challenging industry practices. Will we bear witness to industry's indiscretions or shirk responsibility?

The transformative power of travel

Through 'lifestyle' marketing to the global consumer class, all remaining boundaries to commercialization have been blurred. Industry to industry, there is a race to offer new possibilities for leisure. First we accepted reconstituted orange juice as the real thing; now there is a flood of pseudo-products. We consumers are swallowing shrink-wrapped mass experiences in the hope of being nourished. Through industrialization and globalization, we have abdicated to corporations the responsibility for maintaining our own quality of life.

Ecotourism is both the culmination and new front of this consumer abandon. After 48 weeks of unbridled consumption, the tourist takes a month-long 'eco-' holiday. This is deemed to counteract the consumer footprint left throughout the rest of the year. Mentally, it functions like a cleanse, regardless of whether funds paid really reach local communities or their stewardship programmes.

Many advocates of ecotourism cite its power to awaken and engage consumers with respect to the 'environment'. For a moment, the enormous boundaries between the visitor and visited may be transcended, giving the tourist a new sense of connection, purpose and worth. Does this make the experience a balanced exchange? Or is it just another form of taking?

Terms of trade are everything in evaluating sustainability. Often, the crux lies in the grey zones of intent and follow-through. Is there an interest within industry, or among us the consumers, in becoming knowledgeable? Do we appreciate what sacred knowledge is or how it is acquired? Will we accept the responsibility that comes with such knowledge? If not, there is no point in packing a suitcase. We would only export more of our own baggage.

Among Indigenous Peoples, transformation has a different meaning than in consumer society. Many Indigenous cultures have stories of the 'Great Transformer'. This transformer being typically takes two forms. It might enter as a force of discipline to mete out the consequences for living outside the Creator's intended balance (for example, turning human to stone when customary laws are broken). Or it could reward faithfulness, bestowing the gift of knowledge through a transformative experience or vision. Both manifestations help to instil values of respect and generosity in critical times of choice. Both give parameters for 'sustainable use'.

In consumer society, economic growth is hailed as the Great Transformer. But instead of raising Indigenous Peoples into healthy communion with the corporate world, it makes them ever more vulnerable to industry agendas. Neo-colonial poverty, dependency and assimilation have grown more acute, especially as customary knowledge or expressions of this knowledge (including 'biodiversity') are further commercialized. Thus, the only transformation is of core beliefs. Many communities lose sight of their own power to dream and to create alternatives. They become reliant upon the supposed ingenuity of industry, though industry feeds off every colonial wound.

Indigenous Peoples' frustration with global IPRs regimes can be understood in this light. Once the corporate clock is heard throughout a community, timelines for intervention – by the Elders or customary leadership – are extremely short. Industry's impact upon Indigenous governance systems, and the sacred ceremonies sustaining them, destabilizes more than meets the eye. Ultimately, life systems and all of humanity are endangered.

Although ecotourism can present an opportunity to tourists for individual learning, the ecotourism industry is a global frontrunner for culture (that is, *knowledge*) loss.[2] This would suggest that we are not learning so much after all. There continue to be gaping holes in our efforts to safeguard cultural diversity. We are a society of fancy answers and solutions, with little humility, prudence or self-honesty.

Culture as commodity

Industry overview

In ecotourism, a destination's draw is measured not only by the extent of biodiversity and the fashion of local species, but by the prevalence of tribal peoples. Whether an eco-tour is purely nature oriented or includes ethnic components, chances are that the local Indigenous culture(s) will be featured in the marketing package and/or trip itinerary without community permission, input or equitable exchange. This unauthorized use of culture for marketing is one of the ethical issues raised time and time again by Indigenous Peoples.

'Intellectual property rights' is a government term referring to the legal framework established nationally and internationally to register and assign ownership of innovations. The most familiar aspect of it is the patent, trademark and copyright system. As consumers, we encounter some form of this daily in our own household purchasing. We tend to assume that such legislative controls ensure a margin of fair exchange. We take it for granted that they have some form of wider ethical backdrop. However, IPRs are designed to facilitate commerce, full stop. They were never intended to protect peoples or communities at risk of exposure to our consumer excess.

In the tourism industry, intellectual property is a towering issue that casts long shadows over communities. This was largely concealed until eco-tourism became a force. Traditionally, developers have regarded Indigenous Peoples as an externality to their business decisions, easily handled through high-level deals making it financially worthwhile for government to assert 'law and order' (in other words, to clear them their ancestral lands). Today, a new league of companies covets the direct profits associated with Indigenous cultures. To them, gala tourist performances are passé if more intense encounters are possible.

Ecotourism is a value-added approach to profit. Anything exuding culture, through either perceived connoisseurship or actual cultural exposure, commands a premium price. As such, 'eco' tour operators are increasingly careful about the mix of so-called pristine backcountry and local content. Several are intent on access not just to Indigenous lands, but also to some form of personalized 'native' ritual. The lack of protection for these elements of culture in IPRs frameworks makes for low business overhead. Companies are able to 'dream up' new products without cumbersome community negotiations or recompense.

Old school hotels and resorts are taking notes. Since international travel markets fell in 2001, a number have added specialty spas to their repertoire. In many places worldwide, the eco-tourist can prepare for or recuperate from seemingly roughing it at a nearby hotel spa, with 'traditional' treatments incorporating Indigenous healing. Hotel architecture and interior design often carry the Indigenous theme, using fabric motifs, such as the Southern Cross or Navajo-looking designs.

While this folkloric marketing is not new, it has taken on a new vigour and depth in the tourism marketplace. In a number of countries and country regions, national promotions, hotel websites and spa brochures all allude to the 'Indigenous' cultural connection. The symbiosis between industry's old standbys, like beaches or destination resorts, and new ecotourism products is growing. Together, the two are drumming up bed nights for a beleaguered industry.

There is now a close relationship between industry's ecotourism hinterland and the prime beach real estate enhanced by fanciful adaptations of Indigenous culture – for example, the so-called 'Polynesian' dance at resorts in Hawai'i (see Trask, 1999) or Kava 'ceremonies' in Fiji. The Outrigger on the Lagoon resort in Fiji offers a nightly menu of events for the 'Culture Vulture'.

Such big chain developments offer much of the infrastructure and services supporting ecotourism. Client referrals from these hotel complexes are the mainstay of many local ecotourism companies.

At few points along this consumer chain is there a sign of anything amiss for local communities. Most tourists fail to see that the culture they are gravitating towards is usually appropriated, whether locals like it or not. To the traveller, these places offer an idyllic suspension of time. Ecotourism simply consummates their experience of local time.

BOX 4.1   Spa tourism: Healing what?

During 2003, *Outside* magazine published a compendium of top 'Adventure Spas for New Age Travellers' (Can West News Services, 2003). The International Spa Association states that more than 90 million people, in the US alone, received spa treatments in 2001 (*Fitness*, 2002). An emerging trend is the 'medical spa' (Ellis, 2003), or spa incorporating Indigenous healing methods. Four Seasons Hotels and Resorts, among others, have recognized that 'the creation of unique spas is one way of evoking the true spirit of a destination' (Malanowski, 2003, p16). Their properties in Arizona (US), Sydney (Australia) and Punta Mita (Mexico) all feature treatments based upon Indigenous healing knowledge (Ebbutt, 2003).[3] Several other luxury companies are following the Indigenous theme, including famous examples in the US, such as Green Valley Spa, Utah, which offers the services of a medicine woman (Linden, 2001); The Spa at the Ritz-Carlton Lodge, Georgia, and Mii Amo Spa, Arizona, which 'have tapped into Native American treatments for their beauty secrets as well as their spiritual qualities' (Henninger, 2002); and the Miraval Life in Balance Resort and Spa, Arizona, which highlights its 'sweat lodge [that] allows you to experience a Native American purification ritual led by a shaman' (Wycoff, 2004). Then there is Maya Spa in Mexico, which boldly uses culture to sell everything from its *Na Lu'um*, or Mother Earth, massage to reflexology (see www.maya-spa. com). Of all the borrowed 'spa' treatments, the hot stone massage is the most copied; numerous spas bill it as their signature service. In most cases, cultural referencing is minimal. Just a few oddball companies like Aveda have broken rank, giving due credit and profits to associated tribes.[4] This raises questions of cultural protocol and royalties. How often is the sacred root of the treatments honoured? Are spas profiting by association or by consent?

Correcting misconceptions

In international policy forums there is a reluctance to meaningfully address the intellectual property issues raised by Indigenous Peoples. The reasons for this are straightforward. Few delegates grasp the real principles at stake beyond the obvious debates on economics. Even fewer are willing to break meeting etiquette and suggest utterly new ground for dialogue to accommodate Indigenous rights. Individuals representing the major institutions that preside over intellectual property have no leave inside their jobs to begin problem-solving with Indigenous Peoples. Venturing forth risks peer censure, demotion or other potential career embarrassment. As such, it is left to Indigenous Peoples themselves – on their meagre budgets – to raise the spectre of cataclysmic culture loss through tourism.

The position of most governments is that ecotourism brings a net sum of positive impacts. Intergovernmental institutions such as the United Nations Environment Programme (UNEP) share this view and have supported the promotion of ecotourism through events like the 2002 International Year of Ecotourism (IYE). Under conventional impact assessment, decisions do lean in favour of ecotourism, particularly when compared with the more stark landscape of extractive industries. It is only with the addition of *cultural* sustainability as a baseline that the social and ecological devastation of ecotourism unequivocally stands out.

While Indigenous Peoples have begun to reject ecotourism due to the cultural impacts, most governments are unreceptive. The US has declared that there are very few instances of tourism causing the erosion of cultural practices.[5] Yet, across the American south-west, tribes have taken steps to protect their cultures. The American Indian Movement (1984) long ago issued its warning: 'We condemn those who seek to profit from Indian Spirituality… We put them on notice that … they continue their disrespect at their own risk.'

In the absence of restraint by governments regarding mass 'eco' tourism, Indigenous Peoples are pondering how to publicize their plight and its spill-over effect. While several studies document industry growth trends and general industry impacts, few trace with accuracy who profits from what in ecotourism. No substantive record exists of the losses incurred by Indigenous Peoples due to industry's appropriation of their land, cultures and cultural practices. We still have blissful ideas of ecotourism.

Most Indigenous Peoples are too removed from these 'expert' dialogues to know what is taking place or how it affects them. The topic of intellectual property is still confusing within communities. More visible issues such as land rights consume their time until an IPRs abuse hits home and becomes personal. Often this takes shape when a visiting Indigenous leader gives personal testimony, sparking recognition of shared issues. Intellectual property tends to lie low as an underground issue and emerges only once one community story is connected with another. Then it is understood within a community what is meant by the term 'intellectual property'.

For now, Indigenous organizations are organizing information forums wherever possible. In 1994, the United Nations Commission on

Human Rights (UNCHR) issued draft *Principles and Guidelines for the Protection of the Heritage of Indigenous Peoples*, giving a rallying point. IPRs abuse was the major topic at workshops on ecotourism held during the 1998 and 1999 United Nations Working Group on Indigenous Populations in Geneva. Participants spoke of the threat to sacred knowledge by industry impacts on language, ceremonies, arts, dance and other customary practices. Today there continue to be rumblings in the UN over protecting culture, but the improvements are negligible.

Reframing impacts

Social impacts of ecotourism

Information is available on the social impacts of tourism; but there is little mention of IPRs abuse. IPRs comprise an area of political dialogue unfolding swiftly in remote government chambers. Neither Indigenous Peoples nor most support workers in their midst can follow or make sense of these proceedings. The subject remains obscure, despite the central role of IPRs in driving the world economy.

This magnitude of information deficit continues because there is no money to be made outside conventional environmental impact assessment. Most governments and development agencies watch their environmental scorecards, but consistently renege on real measures for biodiversity conservation. They commission palatable impact assessments, glaringly void of *cultural* sustainability.

One reason that IPRs abuse is poorly reported is that impact assessment is the domain of paid consultants and researchers, not of affected Indigenous Peoples. Assessment frameworks emphasize empirical findings rather than political or spiritual ones. In this process, ecotourism impacts are broadly categorized as either positive or negative. Deeper levels of inquiry and understanding are rare, given the short time frames and terms of reference for most 'expert' interaction. Few consultants see the irony of their own presence inside a community, let alone the IPRs they may inadvertently seize through their personal work (for example, publications, audiotapes and videos).

News about IPRs abuse in ecotourism is therefore just emerging. It is in the economic interest of industry to keep culture loss a superficial topic. While many Indigenous Peoples are becoming aware of corporate liability for cultural damages, taking action against industry is like catching a tiger by the tail. How can a tribe or community challenge corporate IPRs when world governments create them and thrive by them? Going to the national IPRs office or national heritage protection body will yield no results unless that country's non-compliance becomes an international embarrassment.

Shopping for answers

Shopping, our favourite leisure activity and holiday recreation, is the main IPRs issue examined in standard impact assessments. Money brought into the community economy is tracked. Jobs, cash incomes and household spin-off receive the full analytical treatment. The assumption that we can somehow *consume* our way out of answering for world poverty dictates how costs and benefits are measured.

For Indigenous Peoples, the main question is PIC, not accounting data that conform them to some 'development' statistic or study. PIC means the ability to freely choose whether to accept tourism and on what terms. It is the heart of relationship-building and a prerequisite for sustainable economics – for example, exchanges that are free of IPRs abuse.

Typically, national marketing of ecotourism proceeds without any comprehensive planning, most notably community planning. This approach is an indicator of heavy future impacts on biological and cultural diversity. It removes the basis for PIC by Indigenous Peoples: 'Our costumes are considered beautiful, but it's as if the person wearing it didn't exist' (Rigoberta Menchu, Maya from Guatemala and Nobel Prize laureate, cited in Mastny, 2001, p27).

The crass commercialism of such tourism has disheartened many a community. After industry takes hold 'we are faced with recreating our own identity' (Velasco, 2002). So much is appropriated of culture, either tacitly or for a pittance, that it begins to feel like a shell. In some Indigenous communities, victims of this type of assimilation are called an 'apple': red on the outside with a white interior. It is a painful experience of dislocation which carries significant shame and anger.

Some think that the shopping frenzy of tourism helps to re-instil cultural pride within Indigenous communities. Between 55 and 72 per cent of Europeans travelling to Canada desire some form of Indigenous interaction on their holiday (Williams and Dossa, 1996); in Australia 68 per cent of international visitors express this interest (NTTC, 2005). Many visitors want to take home a souvenir. Twentieth-century artists such as Diego Rivera and Frida Kahlo made collecting 'folklore' a stylish eccentricity. Today, this fashion continues on the pages of *Architectural Digest*, *Vogue* magazine and in design firms like Ralph Lauren. Upscale-home decor stores in European cities such as Munich and The Hague specialize in Indigenous curios. Many tourists like to upstage this by lugging home their own 'finds'. In the Northern Territory of Australia Aus$50 million is spent on Australian art annually (Chlanda, 2000).

Acquisition is a big part of tourism. This is reflected in the advertising of many pricey lifestyle magazines. The UK edition of *Country Living* carries a Land Rover advertisement showing a sacred totem pole (from a North American tribe) erected in someone's driveway.[6] The advertisement asks:

'Been anywhere interesting lately?' Such marketing pits materialism against spirituality in a way that few consumers grasp. So, is shopping redemptive or is it just a sad reflection of our consumer thirst?

In the ecotourism industry, the concept of redemption is inverted. We are encouraged to redeem travel points and then use our credit cards to accumulate more points for the next faraway jaunt. An American Express advertisement presents a conservatively dressed couple being silly in ornate face masks. It says: 'We hope you had fun on your recent trip to Pago Pago … American Express. Use it ritually'.[7] Here, the pun on spirituality is intentional. Indigenous Peoples are frequently used as a prop by industry, whether pushing merchandise or peddling consumer debt. The bulk of travel purchases stay inside the 'plastic' world, in establishments accepting credit cards.[8] Not coincidentally, this is the world where corporate IPRs reign.

BOX 4.2　**'Wanna Be' Indians**

'He's a Wanna Be. He wannabe connected'.
(Grandfather in *Dreamkeeper*, Artisan Entertainment, 2003)

Goods and services

Making good of consumer goods

Before saying that tourist purchases help locally, we need to look at the logic of patching a hole with a drill.

Ecotourism is making 'exotic' purchases accessible to the mass tourist. At Los Uros in Lake Titicaca, tour operators drop off their clients for 15 minutes at the islanders' handicrafts market. Here, the impacts of industry are evident. Many textiles presented for sale have lost their former precision and meaning; some are loosely stitched pieces produced for volume sales. Local art forms (like the famous Kuna *mola* in Panama) have fundamentally changed in design and colour to suit tourists' tastes. Beyond is Taquile Island, where there is a community co-operative to regulate textile production and sales. The co-operative helps to support their continuing textile mastery; but the islanders have sought outside funding to establish a museum since poverty keeps forcing sales of treasured family pieces. Local Quechua and Aymara cultures are at risk simply because the boats keep coming. Residents have little means of regulating terms of visitation land rights are a hushed subject in Peru. Neither quotas nor royalties are an accepted practice.

While such cycles used to be critiqued primarily through an anthropological lens, Indigenous Peoples now voice their own concerns. Across Indigenous cultures worldwide, art is used to document knowledge, history and innovations. For example, many 'songs, proverbs, weavings and other art forms record [a] plant's special relationship [and uses] to each tribe' (Mead, 1995). Others carry the stories and teachings that embody ancestral title (that is, customary law for sustainable use). When methods, materials and symbolism are changed for tourist appeal, and the sacred nature of certain symbols is commercialized, this breaks the transmission of knowledge to next generations. Families, communities and then entire peoples begin to live out of relationship with one another and the land. Indigenous Peoples' footing to exercise their ancestral title is gradually lost, in both a practical and legal sense.

Acculturation speeds up when sales of cultural items and cultural images are under industry control. Occasionally, Indigenous Peoples can create and hold onto distribution channels that work in their favour, such as artisan associations, fair trade networks or websites. However, in most tourist markets they are forced by colonial poverty to liquidate family arts and heirlooms. Maasai women in Kenya, for example, sell beading that they wore as brides and Ndebele women in South Africa sell dolls given to them upon reaching womanhood. In neighbouring market stalls merchants move in with trunks of cheap factory-made knock-offs. Usually, it is not long before manufactured replicas take over (for instance, machine-loomed weavings, mechanically stamped or beaded leatherwork and pre-cast pottery). Often, it is 'landless' Indigenous Peoples who populate the involved sweatshop factories. Or manufacturing is commissioned to offshore sweatshops (such as in Asia), exploiting the poverty of other displaced Indigenous Peoples. At the National Gathering on Aboriginal Cultures and Tourism promoted by Canada in 2003, the welcome bags for delegates were made in Taiwan.

Indigenous insignias on t-shirts, posters, key chains, wallets and other tourist classics are a red hot intellectual property issue. Worldwide, this level of commercialization often goes hand in hand with calculated political contradictions, such as celebrations of multiculturalism amid racial oppression. Any economy of 'Indigenous' goods divorced from its tribe or community of origin should be regarded as a flag, and a reason to look be wary of any claims of authenticity. Government and industry formulas for tourism, especially ecotourism, tend to make generous allowance for cultural theft. 'Copyright detectives ... scouring shopping centres ... have encountered some shocking examples of poor dealing[s]'(Hanstein, 2004).[9]

The 1993 *Mataatua Declaration on Cultural and Intellectual Property Rights of Indigenous Peoples* was an early attempt by Indigenous Peoples to demand resolution. Since then some have found the traditional resource rights (TRRs) concept useful. It clarifies norms and statutory obligations established in the international arena that apply to culture (see Posey and Dutfield, 1996, pp95–96). This provides a roadmap for community-level talks, where many Indigenous

Peoples are foggy about their collective rights. However, corporate govern-ments still treat TRRs and IPRs like a game of snakes and ladders. For the sake of industry profits, they have downplayed the stir over questionable legal-ity. We, the gullible yet demanding consumer class, lap up the ambiguities. We shop en masse at souvenir stores like Jacks in Fiji, buying doubles and triples of imitation 'arts' and 'crafts'.

Today, Indigenous Peoples must find interim ways of reining in com-mercial exploitation of their cultures. In some regions, certificates of origin, such as the '*toi iho*' trademark of the Maori (www.toiiho.com), are used to verify that items are made by Indigenous artists. In others, communities have preempted manufacturers by utilizing new media to create economies of their own. Some San communities in South Africa who traditionally have placed their designs on bone or ostrich shell are now block-printing textiles (Archer, 1999). In North America, designs traditionally painted on deerskin drums or rock walls have been transposed onto stained glass. Meanwhile, Aboriginal artists in Australia have transferred their painting style onto canvas. These departures enable Indigenous Peoples to tap into the tourist's aesthetic taste while keeping their art form intact. It is a way of reaching out to share with healthy and genuine reciprocity.

Moving from disservice to service

It has been a long accepted racist joke at universities for students to say that they are taking a 'basket weaving' course; today, these very types of artisan skills are sought after as more people of the consumer fold seek to reconnect with their hands, their 'insides' and their life purpose. Many ecotourism pack-ages feature some form of hands-on exposure to arts or crafts production. Examples include the weaving lessons available to tourists in certain towns and villages in the Mayan highlands of Guatemala and the 'dot painting' work-shops sometimes offered through Anangu Tours in Australia. Such vocations often have a meditative effect, helping to restore balance physically, mentally, emotionally and spiritually.

Most tourists are unaware of the full depth of life experiences driving them to seek out such exchanges with Indigenous Peoples. Nevertheless, those open to this form of interaction often connect with something sacred in the process. While art in tourist societies is largely removed from everyday living – and considered self-indulgent, irrelevant or even financially reckless – it is valued much differently in the Indigenous world. Among Indigenous Peoples worldwide, art is a vital part of sacred rites such as puberty, marriage, birth and death. It spans time and space, connecting the living to their ancestors, as well as to the children yet to come.

The history of basketry illustrates the sacred aspect of Indigenous arts. Among the Cahuilla in the US it is 'believed that before the Moon Maiden went up into the sky, she gave them a gift: she taught them how to weave baskets' (Bradley, 2001, p1). Although most tourists having the opportunity to give such traditional art forms a try on a commercial basis would have revealed to them only its surface meaning, there is still considerable depth to this exchange. Within many Indigenous art forms, the 'Creation' made by hand is quite literally meant to mirror what the creator has provided. Many customary arts hold the sacred knowledge necessary for both cultural and physical survival. Therefore, any influence of tourism on this creative process is significant.

In the case of basketry, colonization in some regions abruptly put an end to this customary practice, as 'development' (namely, seized lands, fenced 'properties' and invasive species) took over. In the US, traditional gathering spots for food, medicine and the wild grasses or roots necessary for basketry were lost. Shortly thereafter during the 1900s, assimilation into European lace- making (crocheting) and knitting were encouraged by that generation's wave of colonial 'do gooders' (Bradley, 2001). Basketry would not make a comeback until organizations such as *Nex'wetem*, the Southern California Indian Basketweaver Association, recently emerged to reclaim this aspect of cultural heritage. Artisan collectives like *Nex'wetem* are now increasingly savvy about marketing their creations to tourists, usually with an educational twist.

Creating a visible resurgence of art forms like basketry is one of the most powerful means for Indigenous Peoples to negate IPRs. Dealers in 'antiquities' lose their corner on the tourist market when Indigenous Peoples start telling their own stories again. Peddlers of denigrating 'made in China' tourist wares also lose their lustre. Without the false mystique, there is less financial incentive to exploit.

Often, it is Indigenous women whose experience is most transformed by this shift in the tourism marketplace. Among Indigenous Peoples, women are widely regarded as the knowledge keepers. Globally, colonialism has methodically struck down Indigenous women's social stature (Etienne and Leacock, 1980), dealing a heavy blow to their self-esteem, their income-earning ability in colonial society and their preservation of sacred knowledge through traditional art forms. Now, women are resuming their roles as custodians and teachers. Many have achieved this through their own economies of choice. The BEADS for Education project of Maasai women in Isinya, Kenya (see www.beadsforeducation.org), is a heartening example.

Individual travellers can make a difference to Indigenous Peoples' repatriation efforts if their heart is open and they make the necessary enquiries to find out how. It is all about making the time to care. In our over-clocked consumer world, we seldom read the fine print or investigate industry labels.

Common fire-fighting issues

Photography

The most basic and pervasive of intellectual property issues in tourism to Indigenous territories continues to be photography and film-making. Tourists visiting Indigenous communities tend to aggressively pursue 'character' shots. Thus, the debate on whether tourists should pay for a photo is now familiar and continues to raise indignation from tourists.

A secondary, more serious problem is that most wrongly believe that purchased photos imply PIC. Many photos leaving any given Indigenous community take a trail never envisioned by the person(s) posing. Whether an image is captured without any consent, or traded for spare change, its subsequent commercial use is an abuse of confidence and privilege. It is, nevertheless, commonplace. An Indigenous 'connection' is profitable; in fact, it is astronomically more profitable than actually being Indigenous. One photojournalist travelled for four years to compile *Broken Spears* (Gilbert, 2003), a book revealing 'the secret ceremonies and most important rituals of the Maasai'.

Meanwhile, thousands of backpackers have sold photos in the neighbourhood café back home to fund their next ecotourism trip. Usually no more than US$1 (deemed 'generous') is paid locally for the opportunity to sell a framed print at US$100–$250 (the equivalent of a month or two of an Indigenous person's average monthly wage). Enterprising backpackers have also extended their trips by reproducing images en route. 'We've seen dodgy didges [didgeridoos] and bogus boomerangs manufactured by European backpackers hitting the tourist shops as "authentic Aboriginal art"' (O'Shane, 2003).

Similar to this is the photographer who abuses her professional presence in an Indigenous community. Individuals working on site for a specific agreed purpose often breach this arrangement. They end up using images from the trip for their personal business portfolio. A variation of this is the plethora of non-governmental organizations (NGOs) claiming to work with Indigenous Peoples who use obtained photographs for their own fundraising.

Nevertheless, the most recognized IPRs abuse is the unauthorized use of cultural images for industry marketing or for the production of souvenir merchandise. Pictures of Indigenous Peoples are regularly featured in ecotourism brochures and travel posters. The people in question have no means of knowing the extent to which they are depicted, nor can they track the associated impacts (for example, whose travel plans they now fit into) or compounding revenue theft in the international marketplace.

National Geographic's decision to sell its famous images commercially in 1995, and to commence online sales from its photo collection in 2002, warns of an alarming culture grab. IPRs abuse becomes an exponential problem when journalistic archives such as these are opened for resale. Photos by roaming freelance photographers re-enter the public domain. Intimate shots achieved through limited consent or powerful zoom lenses are re-circulated out of context. Often the secondary applications are demeaning and offensive.[10]

A Maori woman from New Zealand tells the story of a grandmother whose face appears on thousands of postcards but has no income for her senior years (Sinclair, 1998). She comments that it could be her granny next: on a used tea towel. This example raises multiple layers of serious issues in international law, from individual human rights to collective self-determination.

Recently, new areas of vigilance have emerged. One imminent threat is the proliferation of 'virtual tours' over the internet. Using software like RealPlayer, pseudo trips are being manufactured, billed as an immersion experience. This technology opens the way for catastrophic abuse of Indigenous Peoples by visitors capturing private moments of community life on video or audio tape. There is high risk of exposure for ceremonies and other aspects of sacred knowledge, which are deemed exotic and thus profitable.[11] We will see more and more ethno-paparazzi.

Responses to these common problems have come from all quarters and include:

- an Indigenous leader requesting a makeshift contract on the side of a remote rainforest runway – to curb an NGO photographer who snapped a succession of shots while disembarking, before introductions or even hello;
- an eco-lodge company supplying cameras to its community partner for community members to take photos of what they wish to share (Schulz, 1999);
- an NGO photographing tourists at popular markets to study their reaction to the camera lens being reversed; and
- a consultant suggesting an Indigenous-owned and operated photo bank.

These instinctive reactions offer more comfort than protection due to the corporate bias of the IPRs regime. More and more communities merely ban cameras. The Hopi, as a tribe, insist on such etiquette. The Hopi Office of Cultural Preservation stresses: 'Visiting Hopi is a wonderful time to use your mind and heart to record what you are privileged to see' (www.hopi.nsn.us).

Ceremonies

One particularly intrusive IPRs abuse in the ecotourism industry is access to Indigenous Peoples' ceremonies. Ceremonies are generally considered a 'must see' event. Many tourists become pushy about observance, to the point of clambering into a tree or down an embankment to see a community burial. In other cases, it is a ceremonial 'object' generating the mayhem. Industry's focus on tracking jaguars in Latin America is a sensitive issue due to the ceremonial significance of this animal.[12]

Our standard consumer attitude is: 'We've paid, you deliver.' Most tourists have bought a pricey air ticket or perhaps a tour package. These big ticket purchases are seen as licence for full acquaintance with their destination. Generally, the further from home, the more the brazen behaviour. At the Omaere ethno-botanical garden in Ecuador, one European visitor thought it appropriate to ask a guide how 'natives' in the Amazon have sex.

Alongside this voyeurism there tends to be an abandon of other decorum as well. Many tourists associate times of celebration, especially on holidays, with revelry including alcohol or drugs. As a result, their desire to enter ceremonial events is increasingly discouraged. At events like powwows in North America, protocol calls for not just zero consumption on site, but also arriving without a polluted body. At other cultural ceremonies where medicinal or sacred plants are used, most visitors of the tourist mindset misinterpret plants these as mere hallucinogens. Some want to try this 'high', especially when cultural prohibitions exist.

Desecration becomes an intellectual property issue when industry associates its product with an Indigenous cultural image. Affiliating in this way builds expectation in the marketplace of ceremonial type encounters. Many tourists are drawn to a specific company, locale or product for a taste of their pet stereotypes. The majority partake in conventional ecotourism, where these stereotypes go largely unchallenged.

> **BOX 4.3 Illicit highs and lows**
>
> It has become a booming business, that peyote high. Enterprising *mestizos* in search of cash will arrange trips to the desert so that the city kids can build a bonfire and take peyote... As more and more people suffer from comfortable but empty lives, the Native American mind–body panacea of peyote may loom as a kind of Holy Grail or last-ditch cure. What therapy cannot solve, peyote will.
> (Salak, 2002, p94)

Industry capitalization on 'quaint' and 'exotic' image-making is not new – but has substantially accelerated. It also has become more shrewd, taking a countermove to mainstream lifestyle marketing. There are now tours where the economic over-achievers of the world are offered the ultimate reprieve. They are sold a complete body/soul recovery experience. One version of this are the 'Go Native' retreats, where weary business managers trade their suits for feather head-dresses and loincloths for a weekend of mock tribalism.[13] Another variation is the lecture programme available at some secluded 'eco' spas. Canyon Ranch Health Resort (US), for instance, offers speakers on 'mysticism, Southwestern culture and even dream interpretation' (Russell, 2004, p34). Red Mountain Spa (US) offers Native American 'medicine cards' (Urbani, 2003). Such products dovetail with a new breed of consultants called 'corporate shamans', retained by Fortune 500 companies like Boeing and Xerox (Scripps Howard, 2002).[14]

This market niche of ecotourism targets rising consumer concern with health and healing. On one end of the spectrum are affluent consumers seeking an enhanced version of the personal trainer and life coach, who patronize emerging 'total body' spas featuring ethnic remedies. At the other end lie those who have already searched and sampled the gamut of self-improvement products available commercially, and now want complete immersion – for example, cleansing. Many in this latter group have a fascination with the use of sacred plants known to Indigenous Peoples, such as peyote or ayahuasca. Others will pay to enter a 'sweat lodge' ceremony where other forms of spiritual medicine are dispensed. They believe that seeking such treatments on a commercial basis as a tourist is comparable to the real thing. Magazines like *National Geographic Adventure* help them to get there.[15]

Target markets are thus increasingly well defined in ecotourism. Illustrating this is the abundance of 'shamanic' experience trips for tourists. Numerous enterprises have sprung up catering to curious and experimental travellers – for example:[16]

- Magical Mystery Tour of Kenya, offering a chance to 'learn the spiritual and healing practices of the elders of the Kikuyu, Mganga, Samburu and Maasai traditions' (Helliwell, 2003);
- Tibetan Shamanism, offering travel/study programmes in Nepal (see www.tibetanshaman.com);
- Sacha Runa Productions, offering 'sacred journeys to Peru and Bolivia with master shamans' (see www.sacharuna.com);
- Brazilian Adventures, offering 'intensive ayahuasca retreats' (see www.daime.net);
- Expeditions Mondial, offering 'spiritual trails' that 'unwrap the cultures, myths and ceremonies of the southern hemisphere's forgotten peoples' (see www.expeditions-mondial.net).

While some trips raise funds for community projects, such as fighting unwanted oil exploration, they still leave the question of what is for sale and by whom. Is the sacred for sale?

Questions need to be asked at several levels about this type of enterprise. Individuals working as volunteers, staff or consultants with Indigenous Peoples know that it takes a long, slow time to be fully embraced and accepted in communities – for example, invited to ceremonies or other traditional gatherings. Tourism facilitating a quick dip into culture is missing out on this aspect of relationship-building, which encourages self-knowledge and being fully present and engaged as a spiritual human being. Companies that play the role of provocateur with eco-tourists often meddle far deeper in community affairs than any pocketbook can compensate. They begin to undermine the very cultural protocols that govern sustainability.

BOX 4.4 Protection of ceremonies

On Turtle Island, the problem of abuse and exploitation of spiritual ceremonies has come to a head. In May 2003 spiritual leaders of the Lakota Nation in the US made the difficult decision to close all Lakota ceremonies to non-native persons. These seven Sacred Rites had been shared across the continent to help others find their spiritual way. But through prayer and heavy dialogue, the decision would be reversed – for the survival of not just the Lakota, but also all humanity in this time.

Since the 1970s, there has been a seasonal caravan of white 'wannabe Indians' to many native communities.[17] In 1993, Joseph Bruchac reported: 'self-styled shamans [are] found offering sweat lodges … not only in North America, but even in Europe. *Tipis* and *inipis* can be found each year along the Rhine… *The European Journal of Native Studies* now has a regular feature called "The plastic medicine man watch".' Today, there continues to be a profusion of ceremonial perversions. Ceremonies are being commercialized, diluted with New Age beliefs and tainted by alcohol or drugs. There is no shortage of alleged 'medicine wo[men]' and 'shamans', willing to doctor for a price. Asian tourists pay top dollar to pretend they are undertaking a pampered vision quest, or *han-ble-c̓i-ya*.[18] The men's movement has made the sweat lodge, *inipi*, its own precinct.[19] New Age women are holding 'goddess' sweats and 'virgin' sweats (Red Cherries, 2002). Meanwhile, 'every spring, about 5000 Germans descend on a small town called Radebeul just outside Dresden, to play Indians at the Karl May Festival' (CBC, 2005).

Chief Arvol Looking Horse, 19th-generation Keeper of the Sacred White Buffalo Calf Pipe, has instructed natives and non-natives alike to stop the sale of ceremonies and sacred pipes.[20] Pure mind and clean heart are required under the Sacred Rites. This is the protocol (see Giago, 2003). Will the ecotourism industry take this lesson to heart? Or will it dig deeper into its repertoire, continuing debauched product offerings of 'ceremony'?

Some Indigenous Peoples aware of these dynamics, such as the Lakota in the US, have chosen to block third-party commercialization of their ceremonies, banning non-natives from ceremonies. Others such as the Quechua in Ecuador have decided to launch their own tourism programmes, offering healing sessions with medicinal plants that are free of industry fluff. For the great majority, however, control over ceremonies already exposed to visitation is near impossible. At places like Chichicastenango in Guatemala the tourists keep arriving, convinced by *Lonely Planet* and other guidebooks that they will have front row seats to a 'chicken sacrifice' or other worthwhile local drama.

Medicinal plants

Another worrisome intellectual property issue is the appropriation of Indigenous Peoples' knowledge of medicinal plants through ecotourism. This was the sleeper issue at the World Ecotourism Summit (WES) in 2002. The government of Fiji called the practices in question 'a theft of knowledge and violation of heritage' (Malani, 2002). Klaus Toepfer, executive director of UNEP, later conceded in a private meeting that 'Indigenous knowledge is a main asset of today's globalized world' (Toepfer, 2002).

Specifics of IPRs abuse within the ecotourism industry are still lacking. Most community-level organizations lack the finances to document cases sufficiently to protect themselves from corporate libel suits or other harassment. Nonetheless, it is known that ecotourism is used as a guise by pharmaceuticals companies 'bio-prospecting' in Indigenous territories worldwide (Pleumarom, 1999; Malani, 2002; *The Dominion Post*, 2003). This has severe side effects on biodiversity in countries such as South Africa[21] and Sri Lanka (BBC, 2004).

There are two main forces behind this bio-prospecting:

1   *The pharmaceuticals race*: the pharmaceuticals industry is shaped by a dozen or so multinational companies who hold the world monopoly on patented medicines for disease treatment. These companies are in a race to identify plant compounds with medicinal applications from the world's fast disappearing biodiversity. They are particularly interested in medicinal plants used by Indigenous Peoples because traditional use 'means pre-tested or pre-screened' for toxicity and contraindications (Harry, 2000).[22] By piggy-backing on Indigenous knowledge, they have built a US$200 billion-plus annual market share (Macquarie University, 2004).

2   *The nutriceuticals boutique*: the nutriceuticals niche of the pharmaceuticals industry markets immune boosters to

health-conscious 'yuppies' worldwide.[23] This herbal market is estimated at UK£11 billion in North America and Europe alone (BBC, 2004). Companies are competing to 'discover' the combination of nutriceutical elements used by Indigenous Peoples in order to market lifestyle products to this consumer group (Wills, 2000). Big-box merchandising by Wal-Mart and crew is the corollary since most herbal products cannot be patented. Popularized remedies 'borrowed' from Indigenous Peoples include kava for stress and maca for male fertility.

Under the protection of IPRs, these two pharmaceuticals markets represent the biggest of big business. Patents and brand trademarks confer huge profits on corporations. Thus, one score by a company can fix its financial statements for years to come. Many companies are prepared to take unusual (that is, unethical) measures to gain a shortcut to profits via 'traditional' knowledge.

In target communities, Indigenous Peoples are seldom privy to the corporations' agenda or rules of play. Villagers in Laos were offered US$1 by a 'low-profile' visitor for each plant pointed out that has anti-inflammatory properties (Wills, 2000). Clandestine one-time payment deals such as this are the norm, if any compensation is offered.[24] The involved tribe rarely receives royalties or knows the secondary uses of a sample (for example, patent applications, cosmetics formulations or other benefits accruing to the research patron) (Harry, 2000). Several companies are known to have taken medicines from the Maori of New Zealand without consultation or benefit-sharing (*The Dominion Post*, 2003). The UK company Phytopharm claimed to have discovered the Hoodia cactus, long used medicinally by the San (also known as the 'Bushmen') of South Africa (GRAIN, 2004).

The pharmaceuticals industry is not alone in making dubious advances to obtain plant samples from Indigenous Peoples. Some respected conservation NGOs have secured profitable research opportunities concerning plant genetic resources in Indigenous territories. Government scientists have also been known to offhandedly propose medicinal plants research to Indigenous Peoples.[25] Frequently, this bio-prospecting takes place under the cover of 'protected areas' or other biodiversity programming, through projects intermingling ecotourism. Trip diaries divulging associated ceremonial information are often openly published, much to the consternation of affected tribes.[26]

> **BOX 4.5** **The Indiana Jones brigade**
>
> Today, pharmaceuticals companies send Indiana Jones-styled re-searchers into rainforests around the world to cajole their secrets out of tribal medicine men and scout out new plants that might be proved as remedies and profitably mass marketed.
> (Greenwald, 1998, p51)

Bio-piracy is a common occurrence that raises serious questions. When is a tourist actually a researcher operating by stealth? When is an anthropologist, ethno-botanist or community volunteer simply a glorified tourist? When is an archaeologist really a scout for the ecotourism industry?[27] Organizations like Earthwatch[28] and Greenforce,[29] which match volunteers with a myriad of biodiversity research projects globally, traverse some bumpy ground in this regard. So, too, does the Smithsonian Institution through its intrepid Smithsonian Study Tours 'designed to reflect' the magnate's own 'vision, interests and concerns'.[30] 'Development' tourism is a rising trend with a poor record of disclosure.

Thus far, only a minority of Indigenous Peoples have been alerted to the link between the ecotourism industry and bio-piracy. Some communities still openly display their traditional knowledge of plants. In Kenya, one remote Maasai village features an interpretive trail showing tourists their mainstays for curing, each plant and shrub labelled and described on a decorative stone tablet. In Peru, the Ese'eja offer ethno-botanical walks at *Posada Amazonas*, their joint-venture eco-lodge (Singer, 2003, p86).[31] Many ecotourism companies now advertise bio-prospecting as a trip activity. The Africa Adventure Company in Botswana, for example, offers a luxurious overnight stay adjacent to Bushmen camps, where tourists will 'search for medicinal plants' (Blakesley, 2003, p47).

Where the silence on bio-piracy has been broken, Indigenous Peoples are exceptionally guarded. Many communities are keeping knowledge about plant combinations private. They are circumscribed in their acceptance of tourism:

> What is asked by our Peoples is to be able to design our own terms of visitation. Maybe people find this too radical. But 'investigative' tourism is a real issue and so it is necessary for us to see who comes in (Schultes, 1999).

The Nlaka'pamux in Canada have set their terms by manufacturing a line of attractive 'herbal' soaps for sale to tourists under the label Siska Traditions.

These soaps, and brochures describing their basic medicinal properties, are an assertive self-introduction.

Strategies of protection adopted by Indigenous Peoples include:

- telling stories with 'inside' humour to deter or confuse unscrupulous visitors;
- declaring a patent-free zone within their ancestral territory to prevent profiteering;
- strengthening mechanisms for collective control so that individual persons or families (or single communities) cannot be exploited;
- establishing their or single communties own ethno-botanical zones for culturally controlled 'eco' tourism;[32]
- developing their own wellness centres for visitors – that is, a holistic clinic environment where medicinal plants can be used in the proper sacred context.

Languages

The most startling intellectual property issue of all is the abuse of Indigenous languages. The ecotourism industry's bread and butter come from Indigenous territories; but proper place names are seldom used. Moreover, business is rarely conducted in the language of the people. There is a thorough linguistic recoding of all interactions, forcing cultural makeovers of new magnitude. Yet, we hear little of language loss or its heavy toll. Instead, language classes (usually in English) are considered a lubricant for 'development' and business.

Ecotourism has a ratio of six or so dominant consumer cultures and languages to the several hundreds of distinct Indigenous cultures targeted. This makes it a potent vehicle for language loss. Communities must acquire new language skills in order to secure respectful terms of trade, to minimize reliance on third parties for tasks like research and fundraising, and to liaise with other tourism-impacted Indigenous Peoples. Without these skills they risk being sold out or falsely represented by 'do-gooders' and unscrupulous dealmakers.

Rapid language loss, and language humiliation, abounds in global ecotourism destinations. The Anangu of Australia are one of the few peoples to have preserved their own language as the means of exchange (see www.anangutours.com.au). This is a serious concern given that Indigenous languages encode much of the ecosystem knowledge passed down generation to generation over millennia. It is all the more serious when we realize the place of Indigenous languages in sacred ceremonies.

Indigenous Elders warn that ceremonies vital to recalibrating life relationships – that is, to guiding humanity's survival and healing – can only be conducted in their original language. This admonishment has been issued numerous times. It is echoed in the biosphere around us. As we push the industrial economy onto remote communities, this supposed marvel of an economy is cutting off our life support systems on Earth. Are we too far removed from the sanctity of life to listen?

Reconnaissance at the frontline

Economics: From the head or heart?

Sustainable economies are based on relationship-building. Where there is genuine interchange, duplicity or other deceit is unusual. Nonetheless, there are sociopaths in all realms, including economics.[33]

Investors, entrepreneurs or business agents merely pretending to create a good relationship with Indigenous Peoples have sociopathic traits. They lack feelings, care and conscience when issues such as individual human rights or collective ancestral rights are brought to their attention. Their goal is to 'make the money and get out'. In such cases, business practices are often tinged by racism.

Indigenous Peoples' encounters with this business mentality are not infrequent. Nevertheless, affected communities typically do not know what they are entangled in until the transgression is either undoable or complete. The economic manipulation is well camouflaged, couched in legitimate-sounding promises of consultation or partnership. The proponent's ready access to corporate lawyers is often the clincher.

There are several variations of such underhanded economics. In the ecotourism industry, the abuse happens at every level. It ranges from the 'tourist' snapping a picture with the intent of personal profit, to the front person who resolves to make a deal and then let background investors take over. When profits accrue down the chain, the end retailer is implicated. Most wholesalers and retailers know the nature of globalized deal-making. Their arithmetic would not jive if industry pricing and labour standards suddenly shifted into line with international human rights benchmarks.

Most IPRs abuse in the tourism sector has gone this troubled course. The extent of abuse is still little known, even by those directly affected. Indigenous Peoples seldom circulate in the global economy where the sales and infractions are made, due to their extreme poverty and, increasingly, out of personal choice.

Legislation: Refuge or robber?

In IPRs regimes, registered property is governed by the 'fair-use doctrine'. Under this provision, material can be used for limited purposes without the consent of its artist or author (Phillips, 2000). The uses must be non-commercial or they are not exempt. However, in the hospitality industry, fairness is highly subjective. Rules are continually bent in industry's spirit of 'hosting' (that is, attracting a perpetual stream of tourists).

The *Agreement on Trade Related Aspects of Intellectual Property Rights* (TRIPS) has a major influence on ecotourism. This agreement, enacted by the World Trade Organization (WTO) at its inception in 1995, was designed to accelerate economic globalization. It obliged Southern WTO members to make harmonized investment protection available by 2005 through either patents or an alternative *sui generis* system.

Little protection exists for Indigenous Peoples under international IPRs regimes. WIPO admitted this at its Roundtable on Intellectual Property and Indigenous Peoples in Geneva in July 1998. At this closed event, WIPO staff fielded questions from a small group of Indigenous delegates. WIPO confirmed that the IPRs regulatory framework offers few safeguards to Indigenous Peoples in key areas relevant to tourism, including:

- the use of cultural images in industry marketing – for example, brochures, posters, videos and travel magazines;
- the staging of performances for tourists – for example, dance, storytelling and artisan demonstrations;
- the maintenance of collective property – for example, cultural knowledge or traditional cultural expressions (TCEs).

Mechanisms such as the *Performances and Phonograms Treaty* exist but are not widely known to Indigenous Peoples or are not accessible in practical terms.

In October 2000, the WIPO General Assembly established the Intergovernmental Committee on Genetic Resources, Traditional Knowledge and Folklore (IGC), with a mandate to discuss intellectual property issues relating to 'traditional' knowledge' (TK) and TCEs. Its work extended into 2005 without achieving any safeguards for Indigenous Peoples or cultural diversity. Reasons for the stalemate include:

- *Stretching the truth*: WIPO member governments, especially Northern nation states, have no intention of safeguarding TK or TCEs. Their debate on TCEs started during the mid-1970s without tangible results since 'folklore' is considered public domain (GRAIN, 2004, p14). Round two on TK commenced in 1998 in order to resolve messy policy debates hampering commerce. 'There is no win–win solution to this conflict because at the roots it is about the control over the world economy' (GRAIN, 2004, p16).

- *Confusing issues*: WIPO is playing with language to obscure its goals. In July 1999 Indigenous observers to WIPO called for a *sui generis* system that recognizes customary law – that is, not an Indigenous version of IPRs but a tool originating from customary law. By 2003, the IGC had formed an expert panel to review *sui generis* mechanisms for TK protection. However, customary law is not admissible to WIPO since colonial nation states still reject the peoplehood (sovereignty) of Indigenous Peoples.

- *Evasiveness of concerning international law*: the IGC is prolific in its documentation and careful about diplomacy, in order to convey an impression of due diligence. Its adherence to the letter of international law on Indigenous Peoples, nonetheless, is purely allegorical. Documents speak of 'protection' for TK and TCEs; but this infers protection under the predatory IPRs system. They must be read with this duality in mind. 'IPRs are private monopoly rights and therefore incompatible with the protection of TK' (GRAIN, 2004, p16).

- *Fast-tracking the industry agenda*: although WIPO long refused funding for Indigenous Peoples to monitor its proceedings in Geneva, in 2004 it finally announced 'full and effective participation of TK holders' in decision-making concerning TK. The informal consultative forum for Indigenous Peoples in advance of the IGC sessions during 2004–2005 seemed commendable. However, it was designed to help fast track work on TK for corporate confidence.[34] Globally, consultation is used to facilitate corporate expansion into Indigenous territories and culture repositories (see Chapter 8).

- *Parroting back concerns*: WIPO poses as a good listener, feeding back Indigenous Peoples' own submissions. In 2004, it issued case studies, authored by an Indigenous lawyer from Australia (Janke, 2004). WIPO (2004) asked: are IPRs part of the problem or part of the solution? All the while, WIPO members plotted public relations. Australia seemed a role model for transparency despite a long string of judicial rulings exposing its own IPRs abuses towards Aboriginal artists – for example, *Milpurrurru* versus *Indofurn Pty Ltd* (1995) 30 IPR 209.

- *Give the dog a bone approach*: in 2004, WIPO produced an impressive list of principles for the protection of TK. This included the principle of recognizing TK rights holders, the principle of prior informed consent, and the principle of equity and benefit-sharing. The list may placate some critics of the IGC, but belies any good faith toward Indigenous Peoples. WIPO is a consort of the

WTO and is frank about its ambition to 'create a world patent system with WIPO at the helm' (GRAIN, 2003, p12).

WIPO (2004) notes Indigenous Peoples' warning that maintaining diversity 'in the face of globalization is a critical need'; but it is the last body desirous or capable of safeguarding cultural diversity. WIPO itself knows this. It freely admits that 'cultural materials are considered under intellectual property law to be in the public domain when, in fact, customary law or spiritual restrictions on its use may well still apply' (WIPO, 2003). So let's stop pretending that the IGC is principled.[35] When WIPO announces that it welcomes the recognition of Indigenous Peoples' rights (WIPO, 2004), there is reason to be suspicious.

In 2003, the United Nations Educational, Scientific and Cultural Organization (UNESCO) adopted the *International Convention for the Safeguarding of the Intangible Cultural Heritage*. Its debut was timed to take some heat off WIPO. At the UN, lofty commitments get made when the corporate hand gets caught double dipping (that is, profiting from rights violations). As industry closes in on TK and TCEs, all kinds of moves suggesting safeguards will happen. But everything remains for sale. The same nation states that signed onto the *UN Convention on Biological Diversity* (CBD) and its wider family of international agreements also make up WIPO, WTO and the WTO-OMT.

BOX 4.6 Cultural sustainability

After all the speech-making by world governments on cultural diversity, Indigenous Peoples still lack the government support necessary to take their rightful place in policy debates. Funds are particularly scarce for Indigenous guidance on sustainable use in tourism. Why? Because ecotourism is an all-encapsulating issue, offering the perfect platform for Indigenous Peoples to publicize common breaches of international law. An Indigenous compendium of IPRs abuse and other rights violations in the ecotourism industry would considerably shift the scales of dialogue on sustainable economics.

Conclusion

The industrial model for globalization of the 'common good' is corrupt and unapologetic. It hurts people and promotes commercial genocide. If we do not reclaim economics as an intensely personal issue, we shall be our own undoing.

While some countries capitalizing on ecotourism have poor records with human rights organizations, and continue to obtain Indigenous cultural property by force or deceit, many more are simply party to the polite looting facilitated by industrial property law concepts and by international trade agreements. It is accepted practice to privatize Indigenous Peoples' heritage, citing job creation or some other 'common good' justification.

IPRs offer industry a nucleus of legal mechanisms to deflect attention when routine practices are criticized. Most cultural critiques of ecotourism, however, never get beyond hearsay. Under legal doctrine, few of industry's most destructive practices are found reprehensible. Bare bones impact assessment, – with only bland commentary on cultural sustainability – ensures a wide margin for corporate self-promotion.

It goes without saying that no significant remedy is in sight, either from a legal perspective or through policy. The mandates of WIPO and the WTO absolutely counter Indigenous Peoples' rights and the principle of cultural sustainability. Justice cannot be found within the very international bodies infringing upon rights, or inside colonial courts entrusted to uphold IPRs. Nor can it be facilitated by alternative dispute mechanisms such as mediation or arbitration, often delivered by corporate thinkers retiring or seeking mid-career redemption.[36]

Change will come through our own individual conscience maturing. There are several initiatives under way by Indigenous Peoples to repatriate their heritage. Sacred belongings are being returned to the care of medicine people; sacred sites are being made operational again; and colonial history is being retold. Through these efforts, we are seeing the true dynamic of who nurtures biodiversity versus who is selling it off. No one has a monopoly on life, though industry does try to convince us otherwise.

While we have allowed IPRs abuse to reach unfathomable extremes, there is still a gentler road that beckons. Getting our needs straight is a personal journey, inside our own self. It does not take some iconoclast to come along and rearrange our thinking. Within our own sacred experience of life we are each called upon to grow. We can grow like a plant towards light, or keep turning on the artificial lights for visibility amid the darkness of our consumer addictions. Which will it be?

It is possible for each of us living the industrial way to initiate change by endeavouring to:

- disband our dangerous intellectualism, which is destroying cultural diversity;
- admit our misguided sense of consumer entitlement, which is consuming life systems;
- reject impassive economics, which permit human rights violations and other systematic oppression;
- shun IPRs abuses, which disguise fraudulent transactions and 'culture' rackets;

- transfigure our own *personal* economy, which means 'invest with a more spiritual or elevated character'.[37]

Recommended reading

- *Collective Statement of Indigenous Peoples on the Protection of Indigenous Knowledge* (2004) Agenda Item 4(e): 'Culture', United Nations Permanent Forum on Indigenous Issues, May
- Dutfield, G. (2002) *Protecting Traditional Knowledge and Folklore: A Review of Progress in Diplomacy and Policy Formulation,* International Centre for Trade and Sustainable Development, Geneva
- Gaia Foundation and GRAIN (Genetic Resources Action International) (1998) 'Global trade and biodiversity in conflict', *Seedling,* April
- GRAIN (Genetic Resources Action International) (2004) 'The great protection racket: Imposing IPRs on traditional knowledge', *Seedling,* Barcelona, January, pp13–17
- Indigenous Peoples Council on Biocolonialism, www.ipcb.org
- Posey, D. A. and Dutfield, G. (1996) *Beyond Intellectual Property: Toward Traditional Resource Rights for Indigenous Peoples and Local Communities,* International Development Research Centre. Ottawa, Canada
- Tourism Investigation and Monitoring Team (2001) *Dossier on Ecotourism and Biopiracy,* Prepared for the Third World Network Seminar on Biodiversity and Intellectual Property Rights, Kuala Lumpur, Malaysia, 31 January–4 February 2001, available from www.twnside.org.sg/tour.htm

Figure 4.1 **'House of Visual Knowledge' in Maasai village, Kenya, for the repatriation of history**

Figure 4.2 **Quichua tribe presents its own cultural offerings, Ecuador**

Chapter 5

Sacred Sites

**At birth our umbilical cords are buried on the land to
symbolize our tie to the land.**
(Sovereign Dineh Nation, 1998)

In the consumer world, travel is imbedded in our consciousness as a right.
The integration of corporate marketing with frequent flier programmes has
entirely confused our sense of rights and privileges. High consumption is being rewarded through travel, as Visa and other credit card companies woo us
for market share. Airline points are now so common that they can be traded
like currency.

On world travel markets, industry's renditions of paradise have long
been sold. This has created a financial incentive for companies to source out
more obscure products. More and more companies are turning to commercial
opportunities described as New Age, promising some form of cosmic grit.
Many people distanced by consumerism from their own connection to the
sacred will pay to have even a small vestige of it back.

Marketing firms welcome this tension between consumerism and the
sacred. It creates value on the mass market for experiences that are considered
priceless. This is fertile ground for tourism, especially 'eco' or cultural tourism
that promises to stir body and soul. Many consumers want to feel more alive
and in touch with primal needs. Through sophisticated marketing, they are
manipulated by their own sense of something missing.

During recent years, a number of credit card companies have capitalized on this trend. Their ad campaigns equate travel with freedom. The
message: it is worth going into debt to buy your freedom. Here, two spiritual
poles are juxtaposed in order to ensnare the consumer. Sentimentality is used
to create a yearning for simpler times and slower moments. Through tourism,
you can buy a bundle of days where time is seemingly suspended.

Spiritual angst within the corporate/consumer world is pushing tourism sales in new directions. One repercussion is the commercialization of sacred places. Tourists follow magazine editorials into commercialized aesthetic experiences. 'You'd be surprised how many guests we got from a single mention in a magazine on spas' (Gooch, 2001, p164).

For the ecotourism industry, travel to Indigenous Peoples' sacred sites is prosperous. From a financial perspective, Indigenous 'heart' lands and ceremonial centres make superb product for a soul-depleted consumer world. What does this mean? Why the fuss over access to these areas?

The sacred in every day

Urbanization of the sacred

Among tourists, sacred places are the refuges carved out on a personal basis to recover from the priorities and pace of consumer society. These are places where time is said to stand still. They provide sanctuary when daily living becomes hectic. Going there is an attempt to buy time.

Most people identifying themselves as eco-tourists have their primary residence in a city, suburb or town. The majority are tied intimately by lifestyle to urban services and factory thinking. They purchase food plants at a nursery rather than saving seeds and they pour household chemicals down drainpipes. Only a few have struck out from this lifestyle, initiating movements such as guerrilla gardening,[1] community gardens or farmers' markets. For many, travel is sought out as balance to a daily life lacking conscious connection.

Today's understanding of 'sacred' is shaped largely by world cities. According to the UN 50 per cent of the world population is now urban.[2] Most of us highly competent consumers walk on pavement and breathe fumes almost daily. Nearly all of us set our schedules by the corporate clock. These kinds of ordinary events are what either heighten or dull our appreciation of the sacred. They condition our thinking about life systems, which some Indigenous Peoples refer to as the 'Web of Life'.

In urban areas worldwide, there are two main streams of people. There are those who reside there by choice – because they are sufficiently wired into its economy to live 'well', fed by corporations' executive trough. They usually live in the pricier green, leafy neighbourhoods that are gentler on both their own souls and the imaginations of their children. In more barren neighbourhoods, individuals are drawn more by circumstance; their yards are landscaped with consumer compensations. Their families have, at some point, migrated to urban life in search of jobs or job security. Many long for some form of 'roots', but find this ever more elusive.

The breakdown of family and community in these urban environments is driving the phenomenon of travel. Individualism is expected and accepted. The meaning of 'neighbour' continues to narrow. It is an increasingly unnatural environment, where media billboards promise innumerable forms of consumer release. Subtle variations of this consumer lifestyle are sold by television worldwide. Why? Our discontent fuels spending; it is good for economic growth.

Tourism offers us the ultimate break: a holiday where we can leapfrog into another lifestyle, one even more lavish than our own. Millions have joined the middle-class market of mass travel, including mass 'eco' travel; but for *billions* the economic entrapment of cities is a one-way ticket to landlessness and poverty. Internationally, there is only a small tourist class: the world minority who can afford travel. We are the beneficiaries of the Industrial Revolution and economic globalization; yet through our holidays, we seek a quieter place and time.

BOX 5.1 Shangri-la

Asia has long been the leader in marketing spirituality. Bodh Gaya in India is teeming with tourists, all eager to sit under the bodhi tree where Buddha attained enlightenment. Its throngs are deemed a success, despite a growing gap between the sacred and consumer kitsch.[3] In 2004, India began pitching the 'forgotten holy destinations' of Buddhism. It told foreign tour operators 'Our goal should be Nirvana' (AFP, 2004, pB8).

Today, Asian countries are using spirituality to market 'eco' tourism. It has proven seductive like elsewhere. Bhutan, legendary for its circumspect approach to tourism, hosted just 7535 tourists in 2000 in order to maintain cultural integrity (*The Province*, 2002). In 2002, the United Nations International Year of Ecotourism (IYE), Bhutan announced that visitation permits would double. Will the so-called 'last Shangri-la' withstand this?

In 2002, China launched its own *Shangri-la Ecological Tourist Zone* to compete for market share. It anticipated 'loads of tourists' on top of the 1.2 million visitors already visiting the region in 2001. To kick start this, Sichuan Province alone laid out plans to invest Cdn$960 million (Anthony, 2002). The new infrastructure laid the way for mass pilgrimage.

This is the backdrop to tourism encircling Indigenous Peoples' sacred sites. Industry is fully poised to profit off the spiritual void in our consumer world. Yoga tours are sold in conjunction with Machu Picchu and 'authentic Andean ceremonies' (see, for example, www.sacredearthjourneys.ca). Yoga is also offered in combination with luxury spa services at resorts boasting a sacred site connection (for example, www.sanctuaryoncamelback.com).

Industry attentiveness

Many people now travel within their own cities to escape the personal costs of today's disconnected consumer lifestyle. For some, the destination is a bar or billiards hall; others retreat to a coffee house, neighbourhood gym or day spa. These are the sacred sites of our consumer society. This is where we go to salvage some harmony when we feel too footloose.

Increasingly, patrons of these types of establishments are choosing to take the experience home. Rising concern over world security has caused people to spend more on nesting. This means more weekend outings to lifestyle stores like IKEA. There are 24-hour 'super' stores such as Home Depot for those wanting to hammer nails at midnight. In cityscapes where the lights of commerce govern and birds no longer can navigate the night sky, we too are reaching for new bearings.

These consumer trends are being watched by industry. New lairs are conceptualized daily to tap into the expanding leisure market. Gated communities and exclusive recreation clubs are multiplying. 'Comfort' food and 'slow' food have resurfaced in restaurants. And yoga is now common vocabulary in upscale households. There is an unprecedented commercialization of quiet spaces and so-called 'inner' places.

The tourism industry is paying attention to the consumer thirst for simplicity. Many hotels and resorts are trying to look and feel like a pampered version of home. Their bath products are labelled as aromatherapy. Fireplaces and even granite-encased cook stoves are found in some luxury rooms. Views out of the bedroom window have taken on new meaning.

Harnessing our discontent is easy for the corporate world. Marketing is about fashion and it thrives off manipulated cycles and counter-cycles. Before any industry loses the pulse of its clients, it tests out new consumer milieus. The government of Australia, worried over its wartime image, is pumping up tourism sales by associating 'Brand Australia' with spirituality (Muqbil, 2004, p3). The new women's magazine *Travelgirl* has an arts and spirituality editor.

Healing through travel

In the rush between home, work and leisure, consumers are daydreaming about healing travel. As depression, anxiety and sleep disorders grip consumer society, we are self-medicating. There is a new wave of therapeutic retreats for 'men and women ... running on empty because of busy careers and schedules' (Koontz, 1998; Kadane, 2004). Exhausted women are being drawn to 'gal exclusive getaways' like annual spa weekends with a cultural twist, advertised by luxury resorts adjacent to sacred sites. Groups of men are river rafting through Mayan ceremonial caves. Most are unaware of considerations such as local customary law, or else feel that they are immaterial.

Various alter egos of ecotourism claim to have discovered 'Indian time'. Ironically, 'embarking on an ascetic journey has become just another variation on America's extreme-sports craze – extreme spirit, if you will' (Gooch, 2001, p166). Although some travellers are content to 'try to discover the richness of everyday activities in another culture' (McCarthy, 2001, p26), consumer intensity usually is slow to lift. Few visitors to Indigenous sacred sites arrive through cultural protocol. Most rush in on corporate time – booking massages, joining facilitated meditation groups or taking expensive healing workshops at ceremonial centres without developing any relationship with the Indigenous custodians.

During 2000, the new millennium intensified interest in sacred sites of Indigenous Peoples. Tourists choosing to commemorate this event became more interested in the power of place. Travel agencies pandered to them with images of sunrise over some mythical landscape. Since then, the market for sacred sites visitation has broadened. Many people now recognize that certain 'sites have been set apart because a certain energy or power emanates from them, which people can access and utilize for spiritual strengthening or healing' (Seventh Generation Fund, 2001). Some of us living by the Gregorian calendar are specifically drawn to sacred sites for their apparent timelessness.

What does this sudden consumer 'appreciation' of sacred sites mean? Industry presence at sacred sites goes hand in hand with national permitting. Before long, Indigenous Peoples must request permission, too. This may seem fair – an improvement over languishing outside appropriated sites or posing as tourists in order to conduct prayers (Associated Press, 2000). But today, there frequently is just lip service to accommodation of rights. Denial of ceremonial access is still common. The more revenues combed off a sacred site or its tourism and recreation spin-off, the greater likelihood of government acquiescence to consumer 'user' groups.

If we measure impacts conventionally, it is evident that popular sacred sites are visibly marred within 15 to 20 years – like any other ecotourism industry destination. However, desecration happens within the first moment of commercialization. The unseen energetic changes threaten the ceremonies that sustain sacred knowledge of life systems.

Unauthorized industry activities on ancestral lands speak to a deep sickness within consumer society that we must collectively heal. We are so addicted to personal gratification that we feel fine about bowling over 'disposable' places and peoples. We are totally desensitized to systemic abuse.

BOX 5.2 | **Mythical New Mexico**

In 2001, New Mexico launched a new tourism campaign that targets people seeking spiritual well-being. One advertisement showed an Anasazi pueblo with the message: 'These ruins are more than a doorway to the past, they're a monument to mankind's enduring human spirit' (see www.newmexico.org). Its double entendre was clearly unintentional. Surrounding communities still endure the indignities of colonization. No one knowing the colonial history of America would be attracted to it on the basis of spirituality. Genocide remains an open wound.

Later advertising proclaims: 'The myths and legends of New Mexico spring from its very soil'. Ads like this are placed in lifestyle magazines such as *Organic Style* to target the spiritually curious consumer.[4] They whet the appetite for cultural encounters and ceremony. How much does this drive unwanted tourism to sacred sites? Lots. Most visitors go via conventional industry, not through Indigenous Peoples' own protocol.

During 2004, local Indigenous Peoples' concerns about desecration led to a Summit on Consultation Protocols for Protecting Native American Sacred Places in Albuquerque, New Mexico. Today, the Sacred Lands Protection Coalition (US) and other networks help keep the pressure on government for change.

New cross-cultural issues in tourism

Ecotourism: Using nature to nurture

Our need for spiritual antidotes to consumerism has pushed travel deeper into fabled 'new frontiers'. Indigenous Peoples' cultural landscapes and sacred sites are the new meeting place for the corporate world and its most globalized citizens: eco-tourists. Communities ask: 'Why are all and sundry permitted to enter and plunder [our] sacred sites' (DeTerville, 2002)? But to people of the consumer mindset, cultural protocol restricting entry to designated people – or requiring a ceremonial cleanse before entry – seems affected and overdone.

Increasingly, all-inclusive resorts are locating next to known sacred sites[5] or are perched on the edge of raw nature experiences associated with spiritual reconnection. Waterfalls, pounding storm waves and even hair-raising wildlife calls are the new design consideration for architects. Eco-lodges bring an experience of the outdoors inside while making the outdoors romantic and inviting. They give visual holiday form to the nature music associated by many consumers with spas and other urban hideaways.

The demand for these types of mediated experiences with 'nature' is taking travel companies into remote terrain, where neither corporate culture nor business practices are a natural fit. Many ecotourism companies have found themselves embroiled in disputes with Indigenous customary authorities over access to sacred sites. Others operating in backcountry areas worshipped by city folks as 'wilderness' are baffled to encounter community protest. They wonder how tourism in these seemingly vacant spaces could generate such flack. But while their clients lap up solitude, local Indigenous People(s) experience the grief of lost custodianship, lost access and lost privacy.

BOX 5.3 Sacred sites: Navel of the Earth

Worldwide, a number of Indigenous Peoples refer to sacred sites as the Earth navel. The Meitei in Manipur regard Kangla Pungmayol as the 'centre of the Earth'; the Arumanen from the Philippines call Savang te Sinimburan 'the navel of Mother Earth, the beginning and the end of the universe'; for some Aztec/Maya peoples, Hueco Tanks in the US 'is the navel of the continent, the connection of North and South' (Yachay Wasi, 2002). Similarly, the Kogi in Colombia call the Sierra de Santa Marta the heart of the world (Ereira, 2001).

This echo is not contradictory. Among Indigenous Peoples, each sacred site is understood as a portal between our physical world and other spiritual realms. Each has a guardian obligated to maintain the ceremonies for spiritual connection. Indigenous Peoples have been steadfast in this responsibility, despite racist harassment. Many have managed to safeguard sacred knowledge so that humanity can still choose to reconnect.

Today, several Elders are speaking in plain language about the purpose of sacred sites, in order to balance and discipline our consumer recklessness. Through ceremonies, the knowledge of prohibitions and limitations is sustained; 'elders pass on to grandchildren the system of moral values that is based on respect of … Mother-Earth' (RAIPON, 2004). This knowledge is vital to restoring life systems on Earth. Many Elders say the time for amends is short.

The concept of natural sacred sites – such as volcanoes, rocks, rivers, caves or trees – is foreign to most of us, despite their role in world religions.[6] Even more incomprehensible is the assertion that the land itself is sacred. Events such as the United Nations Educational, Scientific and Cultural Organization's (UNESCO's) International Symposium on Natural Sacred Sites, Cultural Diversity and Biological Diversity in Paris during 1998 and UNESCO's conference on sacred mountains in Wakayama, Japan in 2001 have made no dent in our consumer ego. In the corporate/consumer world little is considered out of bounds. 'Biodiversity' has become synonymous with the corporate race to locate and exploit diminishing and scarce resources. We now decorate our homes with plasticized biodiversity.

A recent controversy in Canada illustrates the misconception about natural sacred sites. In December 2000, a family spa enterprise applied for a permit to mine mineral mud from Spotted Lake in the territory of the Okanagan in British Columbia. Twenty years earlier, the same family had proposed a health spa on site. The lake in question has been used by the Okanagan People since time immemorial for healing and ceremonies and is therefore ruled off limits for commercial enterprise. In both instances, the Okanagan had to undertake legal and political interventions to prevent defilement.[7]

In Hawai'i, the advent of ecotourism has presented opportunity for industry reflection. Recent marketing highlights the 'mystical' attributes of Hawai'i. Yet, local artists and activists urge us 'to understand our complicity in the decimation of Hawai'i's land and people' (www.downwindproductions. com). On the back roads, ancestral Hawai'ians have erected signs announcing 'Love this Land'. Similar signs at the Aboriginal Tent Embassy in Australia say: 'Listen to the Earth'. When will we twig that spirituality and our relationship with the land are indivisible?

The main cross-cultural barrier to relationship building with Indigenous Peoples is the understanding of what is sacred. Indigenous leaders say that industry is accustomed to going where it pleases, at any cost. Whereas in consumer society, there is a perception that 'a tribe sees a site it wants, then invents a sacred element on which to base a claim' (Genzlinger, 2001). What kind of emotion do these accusations carry? Are we motivated by concern for humanity's course or by competition and personal acquisition?

BOX 5.4 Akoo-Yet (Mount Shasta)

In the old lessons, and according to the old laws, to ascend this mountain with a pure heart and a real purpose, and to communicate with all of the lights and all of the darkness of the universe, is to place your spirit in a direct line from the songs of Mis Misa to the heart of the universe. Few people are able to accomplish this. To do so, a person must be born for the making and maintaining the 'connection' between his/her nation and all that there is – and for no other purpose. This is one way Nature has of ensuring the health of the whole Earth.

(Daryl Wilson, member of A-juma and Atsuge tribes, sharing his grandfather's story; Wilson, 2000, p12)

Protecting Indigenous sacred sites

The correspondence between sacred sites and the growth of ecotourism is subtle. As a result, the issue of sacred sites only peripherally enters tourism policy. Yet, industry practice at sacred sites is the most overlooked, underrated but reliable indicator and determinant of sustainable tourism. Close attention should be paid to how sacred sites are characterized in national ecotourism plans and corporate marketing.

The level of awareness about sacred sites is a wonderful diagnostic for sustainability. Where the link between sacred sites and biodiversity conservation is understood, there is good footing for sustainable tourism. Where it is overlooked, downplayed or ignored, there is sure to be a poor charade of sustainability.

In international forums on the 'environment', a number of cross-cultural clashes are evident concerning sustainable use. The incorporation of so-called 'traditional' knowledge (that is, sanitized sacred knowledge) into intergovernmental debates since the UN's Rio Earth Summit in 1992 has not lessened the friction. Basic premises of these policy forums are closed to review. Consequently, all discussions circle back to private-sector 'sustainability' and 'leadership'. Policy affordability is measured in economic terms, as if we can afford to continue industrial binging and splurging.

This explains the vast divide between what governments are prepared to call sacred sites, and Indigenous Peoples' understanding of sacred lands. World governments (corporate nation states) and Indigenous nations (autochthonous peoples[8]) hold two distinctly different relationships with the land. For Indigenous Peoples, 'sacred places include land (surface and subsurface), water and air' (Shown Harjo, 2002). But most countries see the land as a composite of resources to be marshalled for industry, not a sacred and inviolable whole.

While it is now generally accepted in world policy forums that Indigenous sacred sites have a role in biodiversity conservation, identified sites are, in effect, cordoned off. They are categorized by world governments as a separate entity rather than as part of any whole. Conservation non-governmental organizations (NGOs) advocating protected areas status for Indigenous lands, such as Conservation International's (CI's) Sacred Land project in China,[9] can have the same effect. Vital connectivity gets suppressed regardless of which conservation banner flies. Conservation ultimately serves industry, while sacred knowledge guards the integrity of life systems (see Chapter 6).

Sacred sites do exist among all Indigenous Peoples; they are called sacred because of the function they serve in exercising ancestral title. In Indigenous cultures, sacred sites are like the water that carries oxygen through the bloodstream. There is no blood or life without the water. Together, ceremonies, sacred knowledge and the conjoined territory embody and support life. The film *In the Light of Reverence*[10] names this relationship. Sacred areas are a place of connection, where 'larger than life' relationships are understood. Burial grounds, battlefields and massacre sites are all sacred since life knowledge comes through the ancestors.

Problems arise because the term 'sacred site' has been put inside a colonial box. To most world governments, a sacred site is akin to a reserve. It is interpreted and handled as site specific rather than on a territorial basis. This may lead to legislation recognizing a single confined site. However, safeguards are hard to secure since colonial courts belittle Indigenous Peoples' oral testimony on ancestral title. In the government realm, sacred site functions receive no real recognition or support. Anthropologist and archaeologist 'expert' opinions are overriding Indigenous Peoples' own oral history as to whether a reported sacred site is actually sacred (Kluger, 2003). Neither industrial science nor the government league of experts gives any credence to knowledge systems sustained by spiritual ceremony.

Co-managing 'heritage'

Sacred sites legislation is equivalent to other colonial law-making. National recognition often just reconfigures unlawful annexation, displacement and resettlement. For example, a sacred site may be named a national treasure. This creates a false impression of reconciliation. Once land is apportioned, cultural authorities cannot legally assert customary law on sustainable use. Instead, they are encouraged to apply 'settler' laws, which give virtual amnesty to government misdeeds.[11]

Through sacred sites legislation, governments are able to localize and control Indigenous Peoples and their economic influence. If conflict mitigation measures such as co-management exist, customary law never supersedes colonial law on jurisdictional questions. Enforcement is left to nation state discretion and adjudication. So, what happens if government is chronically, criminally negligent, or if tribal Elders order the spearing of a grossly abusive tour operator? Who gets jailed?

On world heritage registries, each sacred site stands alone – singled out for qualities valued by the national government. This usually spotlights the kind of uniqueness or scarcity which is valuable on world markets, as opposed to the truly priceless. It brings serious consequences when there is a national aspiration of tourism. In the name of heritage conservation, commercial opportunities are advanced. Ecotourism companies scanning the *World Heritage List* for product ideas soon target newly inscribed Indigenous sacred sites or Indigenous cultural landscapes.

Indigenous Peoples have expressed alarm at this concealed desecration of their sacred sites. Sometimes they speak out on a fire-fighting basis when customary access is threatened or prevented by tourism. Usually, however, concerns are framed in a wider spiritual context linking people and land. Most Indigenous leaders hesitate to discuss sacred sites outside the reality of broader relationships which influence sustainable use – such as ancestral title, colonialism and corporate conservation ideology.

In Brazil, for instance, the Waura would not consider their territory properly demarcated without Kamukuaka's cavern, central to their story of Creation. When government zoned the Upper Xingu region, it left this territorial marker outside the Waura's domain. In 2002, regional tourism plans pointed to the cavern as a prime attraction, prompting the Waura to press for correction. 'These sites are like umbilical cords linking us to our spirituality' (Taukane, 2002).

Among Indigenous Peoples internationally the issue remains *sacred lands*, not sacred sites. 'We have our territory marked spiritually' (Edeli and Hurwitz, 2000). Some sites are especially sacred because of the energy and prayers centred there. But once all 'belongs' to industry or sits in other private hands, humanity's sacred bearings are lost. The Kogi in Colombia warn us of this confusion (Ereira, 2001). They are trying to regain access to their full stretch of ancestral lands (corridors linking the mountains to sea) so that vital ceremonies can be restored, in order to salvage balance before it is too late.

BOX 5.5   World heritage or sacred unity?

The *Convention Concerning the Protection of the World Natural and Cultural Heritage* was jointly drafted by UNESCO and the World Conservation Union (IUCN). Since 1972, over 170 countries have signed on.[12]

Countries can nominate cultural 'properties' to the *World Heritage List* if they 'are of outstanding universal value from … ethnological or anthropological points of view' or meet other criteria (Pedersen, 2002, p16). Natural 'properties' are selected on the basis of their aesthetic or scientific value – essentially 'from the point of view of science or conservation'. In 1992, cultural landscapes became a new category, reflecting the *UN Convention on Biological Diversity* (CBD) Article 8(j), which concerns 'traditional knowledge'.

The World Heritage Centre (WHC) supports the *International Cultural Tourism Charter* guidelines.[13] Unfortunately, the WHC manual, *Managing Tourism at World Heritage Sites*, does not conform to these principles (see Pedersen, 2002). It is stakeholder driven and recommends many methodologies and practices which would infringe upon Indigenous Peoples' ancestral title and rights. User groups take precedence over ancestral guardians.[14]

Many Indigenous Peoples optimistic about the *World Heritage List* get caught in its financial crosswinds. 'World Heritage Sites are prime attractors of tourists' (UNESCO, 2003) and often boost visitation rates (Pedersen, 2002, p11). But impoverished local communities bear the costs of such tourism. As such, national tourism receipts tallying 'benefits' are deceiving.

The World Heritage regime caters to nation state economic interests and therefore can shelter few Indigenous Peoples. Countries want marketable samples of heritage, not integral systems bridging sacred knowledge and governance. Today, we prioritize the sacred as if it can be toyed with.

Collisions of conscience

Business sanctity

Government ogling of 'exotic' sacred sites is the cause of serious rights violations against Indigenous Peoples. However, the gravity of such violations tends to be downplayed due to lingering prejudices towards Indigenous spirituality.[15] Religious intolerance is linked to the mass promotion of sacred sites tourism (Samuel, 2002). Typically, Indigenous Peoples' appeals for support receive little empathy. Few businesses or aid agencies are deterred from investing in a country because of a disputed sacred site.

Today, there is a brutally eloquent continuation of colonial policies and practices. Worldwide, many Indigenous sacred sites are depicted as 'archaeology' and ceremonial items found there are described as 'artefacts'. They are cast as 'heritage' of mankind, rather than active centres of ceremony and spiritual connection. This is a linguistic coup with far-reaching implications.

Such language is a potent form of extinguishment. It symbolically erases not just land rights, but also Indigenous Peoples. Calling this process 'culture loss' instead of genocide is part of the problem.[16] Few countries are confronted on their deliberate bid to quell Indigenous cultures, due to our ongoing casual acceptance and use of colonial terms. In diplomatic arenas, there is considerable linguistic finessing to avoid scrutiny. Within our own homes, the seat of so-called 'democracy', we guffaw at the suggestion of involvement.

The adoption of Indigenous sacred sites as national patrimony is about profit, not any real affinity. Countries such as Peru and Thailand have built thriving tourism economies by romanticizing 'their' ethnic heritage. This is a branding strategy geared to swaying outside perceptions. It depicts multiculturalism and harmony where none exists. Eco-tourists themselves are branded. We are led to see ourselves as discerning and 'cultured' when, in fact, our consumer purchases finance repressive governments both at home and abroad.

Many sacred sites that have been stylized for tourism become a magnet for other commercial propositions as well. They are a prized backdrop for high-end advertising campaigns. Sacred sites in the US frame ads for gas-guzzling sport utility vehicles. Easter Island's famed stone carvings appear in credit union and bank advertisements. Machu Picchu in Peru was the set for a beer commercial, resulting in damage to the *Inti Watana* sundial, its 'most important shrine' (Salazar, 2000).[17] This says just how parched we consumers are.

In most cases, Indigenous Peoples lack the political stature and financial wherewithal to initiate talks with government or the tourism industry over sacred sites misappropriation. Although examples exist in

New Zealand of Maori tribes modifying protocol to allow industry access to certain sites (Hinch, 1999), few Indigenous Peoples worldwide have been able to assert their right to free and prior informed consent. Groups like the Sacred Land Defense Team, launched by the Earth Island Institute, thus play a vital support role – provided they follow the guidance and instruction of Indigenous leaders.

Countries regularly sidestep applicable international law, using national legislation to deflect Indigenous rights. This legalized contempt of law, the old standby trick of global trade, is endangering us all. Even so, when Indigenous Peoples take steps to safeguard sacred sites, sacred knowledge and sustainable use – which are *indivisible* – they risk more social ostracization and criminal charges. There is still a pall of racism over dialogues on sustainability. We give a nod of importance to sacred sites while disparaging their function.

Financial utility

The global ecotourism industry is swarming at some Indigenous sacred sites, thanks to national incentives. In many world regions, Indigenous sacred sites have become an industry emblem. They offer a sensational focal point for industry to build its itineraries on. Venezuela, for example, showcases Angel Falls – a natural sacred site in the ancestral territory of the Pemón.[18] South Africa is known for Table Mountain, sacred site of the San.

Sometimes this tourism has a noxious underside, capitalizing on colonial invasion routes and colonial massacre sites. In the US, South Dakota was boycotted for its tourism campaign commemorating the 200th anniversary of the Lewis and Clark Expedition; some Lakota blockaded the re-enactment. Their protest was over not just picnics and outhouses atop burial sites, but the glorification of genocide. Nonetheless, millions of travellers were expected along the Lewis and Clark Trail, including eco-tourists retracing the historic voyage on the Missouri River (see www.lewisandclark200.org).

Today, a number of businesses specialize in guiding tours to sacred sites. While the majority of tour operators are on the same bandwagon, repackaging hot products, others are trying to shake affiliation with the ecotourism masses. Mystical Journeys Inc. (US) declares that 'It's the difference between being a tourist and a pilgrim.' However, their client testimonies still speak of trips and travel. Most distinctions are more about a company's market niche than the tourist's reality.

Power Trips, a magazine billed as 'the travel guide to Mother Earth's sacred places', gives an indication of emerging 'sacred' travel markets and their size. Several similar news groups and websites feature advertising for shamanic ceremonies and healing 'on site'. While they may present themselves as authoritative on sacred sites, there is little mention of connected Indigenous Peoples or cultural protocol for visitation. Nor are advertisers' promise of affiliation with 'real' Indigenous people normally verified. Companies regularly divest themselves of their own claims of cultural sensitivity.

Isolated mountain areas, revered as *apus*[19] in South America, are a stronghold of the ecotourism industry. Sacred mountains such as Kilimanjaro in Tanzania have become pilgrimage destinations.[20] Outfitters such as Myths and Mountains (www.mythsandmountains.com) give tourists the confidence to go. The Mountain Institute, meanwhile, is educating travellers on the cultural and spiritual significance of mountains (see www.mountain.org/sacred-mountains). Even so, protocol transgressions are common. Cable cars traverse Table Mountain and were nearly installed at Machu Picchu. Mato Tipila (known as Devil's Tower National Monument, US) and De-ek Wadapush (known as Cave Rock, US) are international rock-climbing destinations, despite Lakota and Washoe declarations that recreational use is sacrilegious. 'Weekend warriors' have become as problematic for Indigenous Peoples as traditional tourists.

Petroglyphs and pictographs are another mainstay of the ecotourism industry. Industry has put them within reach of consumer masses. Though sensationalized as 'primitive', they fascinate visitors whose own rites of passage have degenerated into teenage graffiti or rebellious hair dye. Sacred places once restricted to initiations or vision quests are now flagged in travel websites, guidebooks and park hiking maps. At known sites such as Dauphin River (the Bechechilokono of Saint Lucia), Ukhahlamba Drakensberg Park (the San of South Africa) and Stein Valley (the Nlaka'pamux of Canada), uninvited visitation has led to ongoing desecration.

Place to place, tourists' calling cards are similar; chewing gum and film canisters are left behind. In the Tohono O'odham territory in the US, 'Someone has traced around the petroglyphs with chalk. They've shot at them, spray-painted them' (Norrell, 2004). In Southern Africa, tourists 'have been caught splashing soft drinks or urinating on the fragile images to enhance them for photographs' (*The Vancouver Sun*, 2001). At Ngaut Aboriginal Site in Australia, 'People used to carve out the [petroglyphs]... They once found one in luggage on the way to Europe. The guy got a US$20 fine' (Paekal, 2003). Petroglyphs and pictographs are marketed as 'a monument to the ancient people' and 'spiritually moving' (KZN Wildlife, 2003); but casual visitors are not connecting.

Deadly ironies

In consumer society, we are linear and goal-oriented, thoroughly conditioned by advertising media. We want to go to our destination, see it and move on. Industry uptake on our idiosyncrasies is quick. Since we like to graze, trips are tailored for a short attention span. But there is always a unifying theme. This is what provides the emotional trigger to purchase.

Among consumers, there is an obsession with youth, played upon industry to industry. We isolate our elderly and buy concoctions or holidays said to restore our own vigour. The ecotourism industry has tapped into this discomfort with mortality, plying images of healthy, youthful people as world 'explorers'.

So why the psychosis on trips? Why do tourists traipse through tombs, look at bones, gasp at mummies and buy 'relics'? Is it okay for us to look if no one is watching? We are obviously okay with certain people being dead. If we examine why, it might send a shiver of denial through us.[21] There is perhaps more than a tinge of racism.

Ecotourism styled after *National Geographic* magazine is into burials.[22] At Sacsayhuaman in Peru, tours enter caves of the dead. In Hiwanaru (colonized as Saint Lucia), a recent proposal for tourism development was said to include the exhibition of 'remains'. Intrusions such as this lead to the looting of funerary items. The Tutchone in Canada have had to post a sign to keep tour buses out of their graveyard. 'Tourists will hop over the fence for a photo beside the totem pole; they will pocket a rock from the burial caves' (Henwood, 1999).

While Indigenous Peoples mobilize to restrict access to burial grounds, energetic tourists can now sign up for archaeological digs under the wing of enterprising researchers. This politically correct form of gawking is not censured. Some scientists are still fortifying the collections and prestige of well-endowed famous institutions. Others are seeking cell samples from Indigenous populations for high-stakes medical research (see www.ipcb.org).

Protection is a moot subject despite international law on human rights and intellectual property. In each case, the living family of the deceased must fight social convention in order to regain care for their ancestors. Although repatriation pressures are increasing, some countries still use museum exhibits to promote tourism. Peru's continuing advertising gimmick for Machu Picchu is Inka burial items.[23] Puerto Rico (actually Borike) persists with the public display of ancestral remains in 'cultural' and 'ceremonial' centres, while officially denying the existence of present-day Indigenous Peoples (United Confederation of Taíno People 2002). In July 2005, when Taíno leaders occupied the Caguana Ceremonial Centre at the state run 'archeological park' in Utuado, police ordered their arrest and barred their lawyer from entering.

Ironically, while the ecotourism industry parades the dead, death is knocking all around us. Consumer crudity is now snapping back in an ominous backlash. Worldwide, water, air, soil and newborn human babies are all contaminated. Still, we disassociate from past evidence of extinctions and from own ancestors' survival knowledge (for example, organic farming of heritage stock). Just when corporate 'experts' and industrial science have hit their most obnoxious plateau, profiting off today's industrial chaos, we are zoning out. How long will we travel to distract ourselves from the current mayhem?

Sacred site sensations

Machu Picchu: Rites of profit

Machu Picchu in Peru offers a quick lesson on the industry of ecotourism. This sacred site of Quechua-speaking peoples receives an estimated 2.5 million tourists annually (*Los Angeles Times*, 2001), including 'some 500,000 foreign visitors a year' (Vargas, 2002). Peru has unilaterally proclaimed it an 'archaeological' site. Its management strategy shapes market images of Machu Picchu worldwide as a 'ruin' open for exploration.

Machu Picchu was named a World Heritage Site in 1983 as outstanding cultural and natural heritage. Since then, Peru has set the pace for nations marketing the 'remains' of Indigenous cultures. Nearly every major ecotourism company internationally now includes Machu Picchu on its menu of five or so 'must see' global destinations. Trip brochures hail the 'lost' Inka civilization, alongside degrading cultural clichés of today's so-called primitive and colourful 'Indians'. It is a fable worth US$6 million in yearly gate receipts (UN Foundation, 2004), plus 'a US$1 billion-a-year tourism industry' for Peru (*The Economist*, 2001).

A recent Visa card advertisement of the Canadian Imperial Bank of Commerce powerfully tells the story.[24] It features a woman walking alone across Machu Picchu, experiencing a mystical quiet. The caption reads: 'Susan went to Peru for the people. Specifically, the ones that have been dead for 500 years.' Worldwide, this type of market uptake sanctifies and normalizes ongoing transgressions of Indigenous rights. It suggest that the real custodians of Machu Picchu are gone, not merely shut out.

For local Indigenous Peoples, the appropriation of Machu Picchu by the globalized tourism industry is a threat to survival, both culturally and in practical terms. For centuries they had kept silent on Machu Picchu to protect it (Samuel, 2002). Now they cannot afford the US$20 entrance fee for access.[25] Nor can they work there as guides or sell anything within or around the park. Unofficially, public washrooms in the vicinity are off-limits for their use. Due to such racial discrimination, there is no regulation of visitor conduct in keeping with cultural protocol. At the *Intipunku* ceremonial site, companies regularly unpack tables and table cloths for a meal. At another altar, tourists pour Coca Cola down a channel where offerings of *chicha* were once made.

On the Inca Trail leading to Machu Picchu, the dynamics of the ecotourism industry are particularly graphic. Companies charge tourists up to US$250 or more per day, while paying substantially less to Quechua porters monthly.[26] On this four-day trip up and down steep inclines, the sandalled and sometimes bloody feet of porters contrast sharply with visitors' sturdy hiking boots. Some local eco-tour operators provide anaemic white bread as a porter food staple.

The impacts upon Quechua children working as porters are most telling. One boy of 12 accompanies a 40-something European woman, buckling under a load that her own son would never be allowed to carry. Another young boy has a hole dug into his back by a leaking kerosene can, but is told that the company's first aid kit is reserved for tourists. Children, universally held sacred, are getting caught in the profit equations of the ecotourism industry.

These operational standards at Machu Picchu are not isolated.[27] There is a tendency among ecotourism companies to operate in several world regions annually. Thus, corporate practices in one locale influence ground operations elsewhere. Customer expectations of service also get shaped from vacation to vacation. There can be incremental change, or cross fertilization of racial and class prejudices.

Blunders at Machu Picchu epitomize the ecotourism industry. Neither world governments nor industry have meted out any peer sanctions. In June 2004, Peru launched a national process to establish guidelines for Machu Picchu. This was more about appeasing critics than saving face. It worked. A month later the World Heritage Committee failed to place Machu Picchu on UNESCO's endangered list, although the International Council on Monuments and Sites had called for emergency intervention. Globally, corporate governance is in full swing.

BOX 5.6 The Machu Picchu mess

Machu Picchu has become an industry whirl. In 1999 Orient-Express Hotels Ltd struck a joint venture with Lima-based Peru Hotel South America; together, these two companies now dominate the tourism trade to Machu Picchu. They purchased the Hotel Plaza de Armas and Hotel Monasterio del Cusco, as well as the Machu Picchu Sanctuary Lodge and Machu Picchu Inn, from the Peruvian government. They also acquired the tourist train between Cusco and Machu Picchu in a government auction, with plans to invest US$20 million in upgrades. While their separate 25-year concession for a cable car was defeated, the clout of this partnership remains undisputed. 'We have a lot of money invested in Machu Picchu. We're not going to let it fall apart' (Luxner, 2000, p5).

Indigenous Peoples in Peru have been unable to lobby for rights or even minimal safeguards, due to the political violence during 1980–2000, which primarily targeted Quechua communities. A Truth and Reconciliation Commission was established by the transition government in July 2001, probing political assassinations and disappearances. However, that same month President Toledo hosted a swearing-in ceremony at Machu Picchu, aiming to boost national tourism – again, on the backs of Indigenous Peoples. Machu Picchu tourism now grows at 6 per cent annually (Laville, 2004).

Condé Nast Traveler magazine joked in 1999 about Starbucks' inevitable debut at Machu Picchu, saying 'Homogenization marches on'.

While Peru is plainly culpable, the situation is more complex than one maverick government. Industry, as a whole, shares responsibility for the wanton marketing and desecration of Machu Picchu. The UK company Orient-Express Hotels Ltd is particularly implicated due to its heavy investment in tourism throughout the Sacred Valley. However, our neighbourhood travel agency is just as involved. So are we, once we buy the US$416 train ticket for the morning ride to Machu Picchu, or pocket the savings from a more 'plebeian' route (Cembalest, 2004).

Uluru: Test of conscience

At Uluru in Australia, we can see the softer side of the global ecotourism industry. Uluru is the sacred site of the Anangu and lies in Uluru-Kata Tjuta National Park. This area has been inhabited by the Anangu for some 60,000 years. Today it is registered as part of the national estate of Australia and recognized as a World Heritage Area cultural landscape. Its global status rivals Machu Picchu; but due to its isolated geography visitation stood at 400,000 in 2002 and by 2005 approached 450,000. With Australia now branded and marketed as a 'spiritual' tourism destination, visitation may spike.

Uluru became famous as a jointly managed park. In 1985, it was handed back to the Anangu in exchange for a 99-year lease to Australia's director of national parks. Though both parties say this relationship 'is still in its pioneering years', there is little public commentary on outstanding colonial issues. Eight of 12 members on the governing board are nominated by the Anangu, suggesting local control in accordance with customary law, called *Tjukurpa* (see www.deh.gov.au/parks/uluru/). However, in the eyes of Australia, this World Heritage Area falls under the *Environment Protection and Biodiversity Conservation Act* (1999) and other companion legislation. During 2004, Australia assured the world that this legislation provides certainty for industry investment.[28]

Co-management agreements of this nature have come into disrepute (Stevenson, 2004); nonetheless, gains were made by the Anangu through their arrangement with Australia. They receive 25 per cent of park revenue and conduct their own commercial activities in the park. Park management follows the principle of *Tjukurpa Katutja Ngarantja*, or *Tjukurpa* above all else. Still, Uluru is considered public property by the global ecotourism industry. Globus, 'the worldwide leader in escorted travel', has used the image of Uluru to peddle its tours.[29] Condé Nast has promoted its Amazing Destinations television programme on the Travel Channel using Uluru.[30]

Industry's sense of entitlement at Uluru is producing tensions locally (see www.eniar.org). In 2002 Anangu from the base community, Mutitjulu, filed a number of racial discrimination complaints against the nearby resort town of Yulara. The Anangu were encountering restricted access to shops and facilities, including the Yulara swimming pool (a treat for children when temperatures rise to 40–50°C). By 2003 the conflict involved Voyages Hotels and Resorts, which operates the Ayers Rock Resort and Longitude 131°. Voyages Resort was found guilty in Federal Court of promoting 'exclusive' tours to an area called Yulara Pulka without the necessary permit from the Anangu. A year later *National Geographic* Magazine and *Conservation International* (CI) swept these not so small details under the desert sand. Their 2004 World Legacy awards for 'excellence' recognized both Anangu Tours and Voyages. The Australian Tourist Commission commended Voyages for 'improving the future of local Indigenous communities'. Clearly, Australia is still groping for legitimacy.

Today, the pressing question with respect to Uluru is how its runaway commercialization affects Indigenous Peoples worldwide. The tourism industry leans heavily on Uluru and Machu Picchu for mystique. These two sacred sites are used interchangeably to foment global 'eco' tourism growth. On the one hand, industry images of Uluru spur rights abuses against Indigenous Peoples internationally. But the Anangu themselves seem to show 'that Aboriginal culture is strong and alive'. Only recently have news reports indicated otherwise: 'the great red rock of Uluru hides a shameful secret that Australia's tourism promoters would rather the world did not see... Just a few hundred yards from the giant monolith lies an impoverished desert settlement in which Aborigines are slowly poisoning themselves to death by sniffing gasoline' (Squires, 2005).

The debate over climbing Uluru is what we should watch. For spiritual reasons, the Anangu request that tourists *not* climb. Nevertheless, 60 per cent of visitors remain focused on climbing. Only 50,000 or so visitors opt for non-climbing tours with Aboriginal-owned Anangu Tours (that is, 11 per cent). In the heart of the Mother Tree *iwara*, or track, most guests are throwing respect to the wind. After the Anangu closed Uluru to climbers for an unprecedented ten days due to an Elder's death in 2001, industry '[feared] that future abrupt shutdowns could result in litigation from tourists who have travelled thousands of miles just to add an Uluru summit to their life lists' (Callan, 2002).

The Anangu have sent a powerful message through their '*No Climb*' request (see www.anangutours.com.au). The Uluru website states: 'Anangu have not closed the climb. They prefer that you – out of education and understanding – choose to respect their law and culture by not climbing.' This is the most sacred of requests. It reminds us that we each have free will. The same teaching reverberates across a great many spiritual traditions and world religions. Through our life choices, we determine whether today holds healing or hurt, harmony or discord, material or spiritual growth.

Consumer consciousness: Oxymoron or global shift?

There is a profound message emanating from Machu Picchu and Uluru. Through industrial ecotourism, the ultimate desecration is happening at these two sacred sites. It is significant that both sites hold powerful teachings about the value of respect.

In Aboriginal lore, Uluru is the place where the spirit of Mother Earth entered. This sacred site exemplifies the body of knowledge known as sacred law – also called harmonic law or natural law. Indigenous Peoples worldwide hold this system of law in common. Today, many are attempting to reach us to warn that materialism and economic growth have put natural systems out of balance. This message is being pigeon-holed by world governments as 'traditional knowledge'. It is viewed as something incidental, which will be filtered out through stakeholder dialogue (in other words, commercial interests).

Surrounding Machu Picchu, there is repeated symbolism of *pachakuti*, the cyclical time of renewal. This era is described by Indigenous Peoples across Turtle Island (that is, the Americas) as a form of cosmic reordering, marked by the potential for great psychological and spiritual shifts within humanity. The nature of change experienced depends upon whether people embrace the principles of respect and balance, or turn away from sacred law. Today, we are on the latter path, descending into ever more chaos.

These stories of Creation at Uluru and Machu Picchu exist continents apart, but convey the same message. They establish principles for interdependence and co-existence – the sacred relationships that embody sustainability. They also indicate a time of critical choice. On more than one level, each is a gateway to higher consciousness about how we treat one another and the Earth. Comprehending this and abiding by explanatory customary law will be fundamental to our social learning.

Graham Calma, a spokesperson for Mutitjulu, says 'many traditional owners feel their culture is weak because people climb Uluru' (ABC News, 2003). Culture loss of this magnitude will be catastrophic, unless we are jolted into remembering that life hinges on responsibility. The great shaking of consumer society is now underway. In Peru the Quechua guardians of the Qoyllur Rit'i ice-cutting ceremony, the *ukukus*, watch knowingly as their sacred glacier melts due to climate change. They warn us that 'when the snow disappears from the tops of the mountains, it will herald the end of the world' (Regalado, 2005). How do we digest such 'traditional knowledge'? For now, tourists are jetting in to see the festival, not far from Machu Picchu – foggy like the aeroplane contrails behind them.

Mass ecotourism, mainstreamed into our affluent consumer ethic, is out of control at both Uluru and Machu Picchu. Even so, these two sacred sites remain flagships for the so-called 'eco' tourism industry. Under these emblems, ecotourism is racing forward as a star performer for the globalized corporate economy. At the same time, key biodiversity indicators are alerting us to serious biosphere imbalances globally. Fire retardants applied to airline seats and polychlorinated biphenyls (PCBs) used in electronics manufacturing in Asia are showing up in the bodies of Arctic wildlife.

Lessons from these two sacred sites should frame current government dialogues on sustainability. Are world leaders prepared to accept messages from the Elders? Or will our current cycle of distorted and materialistic decision-making have to play itself out?

BOX 5.7 | **The Dineh teachings**

The Dineh holy people long ago warned against destruction of the natural world. Certain sacred places, they told us, must never be disturbed. These places, and certain elements, are interconnected and interdependent through reciprocal relationships that are a model for humans to follow. Life, they said, cannot exist out of balance.

(Valerie Taliman, member of the Navajo nation, US; Taliman, 2002, p36)

Conclusion

In consumer society there is an epidemic of moneyed people gasping for a living, breathing holiday connection. Our psyche is buzzing with things to do, places to go and wish lists to buy. The tourism industry simply turns these impulses on us. We have come to equate travel with quiet and clarity. Holidays are the time to get perspective back.

Some tourists are drawn to sacred sites because they seem timeless and enduring. Natural sacred sites like mountains offer healing from our industrialized lives. We may not understand a site's full significance; however, we welcome the respite from corporate bombardment. Such experiences go beyond lolling about and being entertained. However, many other tourists visit 'historic' sacred sites merely out of curiosity about other times and lives.

Although sacred sites travel is booming, our consumer self-awareness is tenuous. Even the most authentic of holiday transformations in outlook or attitude can fade. We return from vacation feeling quite centred about our choices, but then return to the consumer fray. Moments that touched us and encounters that shifted our experience become memories. Promises made soon slide off our 'to do' lists.

So much of culture is about time. How do we see the time between birth and death? What do we do with our own given lifetime? How do we remember our ancestors? Where do dreams fit in? These are the kinds of questions that cut across cultures. They knock on our door again, again and again. If we don't take the time to know our own self intimately, our ability to connect with others is impaired.

Consumerism competes for our life attention. We may travel to certain sacred sites to heal. But when the money clock strikes 12, the travel budget is spent and it is time to go home. We seldom really go home, though, in a spiritual sense. Industry's experiences of sacred sites are designed to tantalize, not to bring closure. Companies want you back. If they took you to Machu Picchu this year, they tempt you with Kilimanjaro next. It can become a rolling, snowballing relationship which remains detached from people, place and soul.

Indigenous Peoples whose sacred sites are subject to industry profiteering know the real significance of these areas. There is usually a certain time in life to go and a long process to prepare. When this cultural protocol is followed, then it is possible to call on a sacred site. There are no shortcuts and there is no entrance fee. Nor is there some mythical place that can do it for you. It is about connecting to the sacred within your own self, wherever you happen to be.

Few of us living the consumer lifestyle can relate when Indigenous Peoples say the land beneath our own feet is sacred, because we have forgotten how the land feeds and sustains us. Few of us see industrial impacts on life cycles, because we all revolve around consumer goods. So long as Earth systems limp along under the strain of industrial development, most still say 'all is well'. Our own communities may buckle and our own spirit may ache, but we are sold on the consumer status quo.

It is time to get clear about what is real, innate and ours from birth, versus what is fabricated for the sake of corporate profit. We need to rethink how we 'spend' our time. And we must have another look at the saying: 'time heals all'. There are steps we can all take to become more discerning:

- *Step away from corporate time*: decide that you have time to be scrupulous. Consumerism is a mood disorder. Unless we inoculate ourselves against corporate manipulation, we become party to industrial abuse.
- *Disengage from project time*: refuse to compartmentalize life, life systems or people. If we live, work and play with an understanding that all is connected, we will rediscover healthy relationships.
- *Commit to a lifetime of service*: know your life calling. When we work for the love of fellow humanity, we become gentle on the rituals and places that nurture them. We can experience our own sacred spaces in a sacred way.

- *Embrace this time of prophecy*: learn the universal teachings. Industry's metronome is not keeping natural time nor other sacred contracts. Yet, all around us there are signs indicating which direction to turn for restored balance.

Once we reorient ourselves, it is evident that the sacred is within us, around us and beneath us each moment. We no longer need to fly around the world to visit someone else's sacred site.

Recommended reading

- Ayres, E. (2004) 'Have a good life: Just charge it on your Citibank card', *World Watch*, January/February, pp3–4
- Ereira, A. (2001) 'Back to the heart of lightness', *The Ecologist*, vol 31, no 6, July/August, pp34–38
- Taliman, V. (2002) 'Sacred landscapes', *Sierra*, Sierra Club, vol 87, no 6, November/December, pp36–43, 73
- Wilson, D. (2000) 'Grandfather's story', *The Ecologist*, Special issue on the Cosmic Covenant, vol 30, no 1, January/February, pp12–14

Figure 5.1 **Aboriginal peoples call for humility and connection, Aboriginal Tent Embassy, Australia**

Figure 5.2 **The Tutchore protect their burial ground, Canada**

Chapter 6

Protected Areas

**The environmental assessments and following studies were not complete
and honest. The process was structured so that the corporation would
gain approval and [so] that Native people would once again be sacrificed,
at all cost.**

(Rosalin Sam, St'at'imc, 2004)

The concept of protected areas continues to generate lively debate; but is it
necessarily alive? Inside governing institutions the emphasis is on dispassionate
analysis. Such analysis is called objective when, in fact, it generally serves the
status quo. There is a protectionism framing the debate which has little to do
with biodiversity or the emotional ties we like to associate with biodiversity.

It remains to be proven that protected areas, or tourism in protected
areas, deliver any real or lasting benefits. Many questions still need to be addressed first-hand by affected Indigenous Peoples via their Elders, in the context of sacred knowledge. Otherwise, we live inside a destructive intellectualism. We quibble over jobs or ownership, while life systems buckle. There is no
consensus or reliable insight on mutual benefiting.

Today, this unfinished business threatens the credibility of protected
areas, causing tension over legislation and policy development. Governments
are showcasing protected areas within their biodiversity portfolios. Meanwhile,
Indigenous Peoples say that free and prior informed consent (PIC) is an outstanding legal requirement. The disagreement is over more than legality and
political process; it touches every aspect of our humanity and how we choose
to interrelate.

One would assume that the common ground in this seeming standoff
is biodiversity. But this very point is a source of contention. Is biodiversity
primarily an economic term or is it a reminder to cultivate healthy, balanced
relationships? Can economics be brought back inside the sacred circle of life?
Who among us can fundamentally and passionately speak for *life*, in light of
corporate globalization and how it desensitizes one and all?

To embrace the core questions we need a place for dialogue with equilibrium. There must be room to venture beyond economically sanctioned debate, without peer censure. This means choosing tolerance over protectionism. It means magnanimity instead of partisan positions. Government processes on sustainability are structured as debate; but taking sides is no way to sustain life.

BOX 6.1   **Conservation logic**

Globally, a potent 'new' form of industry commercialization called ecotourism is being advanced hand in hand with protected areas. Although this industry is known for its reprehensible track record vis-à-vis the 'environment' and human rights, governments are looking to that same model of ecotourism as an incentive for biodiversity conservation and benefit-sharing.

'There are currently some 60,000 protected areas in the world, the majority of which have been established on Indigenous Peoples' lands without their consent' (Colchester, 2003). The world's most profitable ecotourism destinations are affixed to these ancestral lands. Although corporate governments say it is a symbiotic relationship, most target communities see a parasite and close cousin to other industries.

Behind the veil

Conservation optics

A persuasive argument has been made for protected areas under the precept of sustainable development. In global policy talks concerning the 'environment', protected areas are a key binding agent. They are a Palatable international norm, offering enough political grease and 'wriggle room' to keep players on board. When debates heat up over equity issues, governments can congratulate themselves on meeting this one imperative.

In international policy forums, our collective will is to believe in the benefits of protected areas. The consensus is that protected areas represent an ideal. While they are ascribed a number of qualities that have often proven elusive (such as community benefits and conservation), they remain a touchstone in dialogues on sustainability. Around them there is an overwhelming expectation of social buy-in.

Protected areas hold this hallowed place in 'environment' talks because they appeal to our nostalgia and common sense. The more that various industries visibly mar or debilitate ecosystems, the more protected areas come across as solution-oriented. In just a few decades, they have shifted from an icon of 'wilderness' into a lauded tool for 'conservation'. They have moved out of picture books into science texts and governance manuals. 'Salvation' politics remain strong.

To most proponents of protected areas, it has been a surprise when Indigenous Peoples object in principle to this mode of 'conservation'. At the surface, there seems a natural crossover between the objectives of protected areas and the perceived values of Indigenous Peoples. However, an increasing number of Indigenous leaders are dismayed by what they see as the false pretences accompanying protected areas. They know that protected areas, like their own ancestral lands, are ultimately viewed as real estate.[1]

Ethical opportunities

Conceptually, protected areas are a product of the Industrial Revolution and its legacy of perceived trade-offs (namely, development versus conservation). If industrial-style economics were not gripping global society and scarring the human landscape, there would be no need for this type of problem-solving. Nor would there be value in showcasing such an alter ego of the corporate world, something that offsets our consumer excess. We would be mainstreaming the ethic of sustainable use rather than brandishing linear planning models.

Industrial logic has led us to assume that setting aside 12 per cent of our national lands and waterways in protected areas will anchor the conservation of biological diversity. However, the real moral force behind protected area networks is not the accepted 12 per cent target, but the 88 per cent reserve of 'productive' lands. This residual 'resource' base is the bottom line in government decision-making. Protected areas have a public relations function in securing maximum commercial access to merchantable lands.

Governments submit to the yoke of protected areas because this conservation formula leaves investment opportunities intact. Outside protected areas, companies retain full latitude of operations; poor environmental practices, exploitative labour standards and unprincipled legal manoeuvring are still the global standard (Bakan, 2003). Inside protected areas, there is often no intrinsic difference. Development restrictions may be lifted when corporate arguments outweigh alleged conservation goals.

Many protected areas are disembowelled as the world looks on. There have been a number of financial indiscretions – including uranium mining in Kakadu National Park, Australia; oil exploration in Yasuni National Park, Ecuador, and Lorentz National Park, West Papua; illegal timber trade in the Philippines and countless other tropical countries; and now widespread mass 'eco' tourism. Bordering parks, similar patterns prevail; chemical-drenched golf courses are being developed on the edge of some parks (McNeely, 1999).

Protected areas are a strictly voluntary initiative that suits our corporate-minded world. They enable governments to conduct a show of hands in favour of biodiversity, without any reckoning for mismanagement or corporate excess. We consumers can feel good, too, rationalizing our Wal-Mart[2] influenced overindulgence despite the grim costs. Yet, there is neither true reprieve from global loss of biodiversity, nor good faith towards those vulnerable to corporate globalization. The high casualties of economic growth continue.

Protected areas are a decoy, leading us away from real dialogue on sustainable use. Neither airways nor subsurface areas fall within the rubric of protected areas. This is because the world economy is driven by oil.[3] Together, global industries, automobiles and households consume some 83.2 million barrels of oil a day (*The Province*, 2004). Oil pumped from the ground for consumer conveniences such as plastics and toiletries has become a toxic, choking Earth envelope. So, if we were to actually correct anything, we would have to begin by cordoning off above and below as sacrosanct. We would have to protect ourselves from our own selves. Now that the World Conservation Union (IUCN) has partnered with the oil industry via the Energy and Biodiversity Initiative of Conservation International (CI), the chances of this happening are ever more remote.

Worldwide, Indigenous leaders know that protected areas cannot be a catalyst for profound social change. They are realistic about why protected areas exist and how they play out as a bargaining chip in negotiations on access and use of 'resources'. This pragmatism has led some Indigenous Peoples to completely shy away from endorsing protected areas, and others to use the concept to further their own guardianship responsibility. During 2003, Adivasis evicted from the Wayanad Wildlife Sanctuary in India exercised their ancestral land title, only to be brutally suppressed.[4] But the Cofán of Ecuador, who secured co-management of the Bermejo Cofán Ecological Reserve in 2002 – as well as the lower reaches and buffer zone of the Cayambe-Coca Reserve in 2003 – have used this leverage to influence the evolution of national 'conservation' policies.

Economic master plan

The elusive equilibrium

Protected areas are a model for land use and land valuation that is increasingly called into question at the community level. Even so, they remain of high stature internationally. They are enshrined in the *UN Convention on Biological Diversity* (CBD) as a recommended tool for biodiversity conservation. Disputes over protected areas are therefore spreading, although governments, corporate non-governmental organizations (NGOs) and private-sector consultants advocating them often downplay grassroots dissatisfaction and concerns.

Today, protected areas hold considerable political value for world governments. They are a means of gaining social licence for the ambitious economic agenda known as globalization (previously called colonization). Usually, their introduction is timed, their location is calculated and their beauty is commemorative. Like the city park bench, they are a civic gesture designed to win support. Symbolically, protected areas stand for principled commerce – even if this seldom plays out.

Ecotourism is providing new impetus for protected areas. Parks *per se* often have not satisfied either local communities' sustenance needs, or governments' desire for economic growth. Governments are proclaiming these to be convergent interests and proffering ecotourism as a win–win solution.[5] In their eyes, the ecotourism industry brokers a palatable compromise between economics, 'conservation' and 'development'. This is the ultimate combination under the ideology of sustainable development, which blesses economic growth.

Behind this hype, the match between ecotourism and protected areas is strained. Most affected communities are barely on the bandwagon; many would rather make their own symbolic backpack or canoe. So, is the ecotourism industry heaven sent or hell bent? Many Indigenous Peoples and grassroots-minded NGOs steadfastly maintain the latter. They say that this top-down corporate matchmaking is tipping threatened peoples and ecosystems onto the endangered list. According to the Bhotia in India, their ancestral lands were classified as part of the Nanda Devi Biosphere Reserve, without any consultation; their displacement and subsequent 'mountain tourism' has caused 'a colossal loss of traditional skills and knowledge' (Rana, 2003, p2). The Garífuna of Honduras give equally grim news:

> We, the Indigenous and black people of Central America are subject to a process of appropriation of our territories, due to the imposition of protected areas... The lack of respect from the investors, tour operators and the travelers regarding our territorial rights, is a condemnation to the survival of our peoples ... [tourism projects] are turning into a menace to our future, that is the case of Plan Puebla Panama, that is including a so-called ecotourism component... The privatization of the natural resources that has been proposed by the World Bank, though the creation of several national parks that will be run by private foundations ... [causes us] great concern about the lack of recognition of our ancestral territories' (Flores, 2002).

This is where we need to pay attention. Community-based leaders and advocacy organizations are telling us that the ecotourism industry is prone to ethnocentric bungles and botches. Many oppose institutional partnerships with government which link protected areas and industrial ecotourism. They are wary of conservation conglomerates that appear to navigate more by their annual reports than by slowly built community relationships. This has not fundamentally slowed groups such as Conservation International (CI), The Nature Conservancy (TNC) and the World Wide Fund for Nature (WWF-International), which preside over most protected areas tourism.

Worldwide, there is sharply divided opinion on the efficacy of protected areas, and the appropriateness of industry or corporate-style NGOs styling tourism for parks. Even so, the argument of economic growth has trounced the so-called 'precautionary approach', supposedly a core principle of the CBD. Governments are keen to partner with the ecotourism industry and its allies. Since the first Ministerial Roundtable on Tourism and Biodiversity in Bratislava, Slovakia, in 1998, this handshake has been firm.

Today, institutions that have helped along the global ecotourism industry, and smoothed its access to protected areas, are walking a poetic political line. The International Ecotourism Society (TIES) has encouraged the return of 'protected lands' to Indigenous Peoples (Epler Wood, 1999). The IUCN and the Ford Foundation were front and centre at the Ceremony on the Sacred Dimension on Protected Areas at the World Parks Congress in 2003. The World Bank has undertaken work on the cultural and spiritual values of biodiversity, despite undermining these very values (Survival International, 2002, p13; Colchester, 2003, pp104–106). And CI has promoted the World Legacy Awards together with advertising-rich *National Geographic Traveler* magazine, giving the 2004 Heritage Tourism Award to Anangu Tours at Uluru. Amid the hoopla, few spot the inherent contradictions.

In most government and institutional analysis on protected areas, the creed is 'we can agree to disagree'. This form of 'balanced' dialogue means that issues are heard out, but action remains discretionary. Outside official meeting rooms the stonewalling can be quite direct. In many a corridor discussion, Indigenous Peoples' documentation of rights violations and ecosystem abuses gets summarized by the deal brokers as 'all that crap'. This phrase, and variations of it, are imbedded in the universal language of impact assessment. It is toxic communication, which leads to toxic outcomes.

When 'dissent' (a government word for sacred knowledge) is suppressed like this our decision-making lacks equilibrium. The effects radiate system wide, touching all aspects of life. We can see this today in the Earth's contaminated waterways, chemical-laden air and poisoned soil. It is even more poignant in the exploitation of peoples, now fuelling corporate globalization. Our relentless materialism is going unchecked. Consumer confidence is dubbed as good, despite its obvious devastation to life relationships.

Now that the ecotourism industry is aiding in the commercialization of alleged conservation lands, we must ask: *how can 'eco' tourism possibly differ with the same industry gatekeeper?* The lessons, like the problem, are multilayered and reach deep into our consumer psyche.

BOX 6.2 **Blue Book blues**

In 2000, the World Commission on Protected Areas (WCPA) issued guidelines on *Indigenous and Traditional Peoples and Protected Areas* (Beltrán, 2000). How reliable are these 'Blue Book' guidelines?

> When you pick it up and hold the book, it has no heart, no feeling. My arms feel cold holding that book. They have real gall to write about our places and our knowledge. They know nothing of what we know, yet it is presented as *the* way. Have they lived with us? Have they eaten with us to share? Before they start writing about us they need to think about where they got their information. People who write about us should live with us so that what they write is true.
> (Ruby Dunstan, Nlaka'pamux, Elder and lifetime chair of the Stein Valley Nlaka'pamux Heritage Park, British Columbia, Canada)

Results-based safeguards

Many fiscally conservative governments are using 'results-based management' as their mantra for achieving sustainability. This term suggests an overarching empirical method. It is meant to instil confidence in government programming and accountability. However, there is little dialogue on what gets measured or how, outside consumer confidence. Even less clarity surrounds the question of who can evaluate success. Left undefined or unchallenged, the default is conventional impact assessment. Public- and private-sector appointed experts continue to wield a formidable power over Indigenous Peoples, their cultures and ancestral territories.

Applying results-based management to protected areas reinforces colonial relationships. It ties biodiversity assessment to abstractions like balance sheets, graphs and computer simulations. This is the domain of high-priced consultants, where Indigenous Peoples are eclipsed by government budgets and corporate pockets. As such, there is no democratic debate on points and counterpoints with respect to the purported benefits of protected areas. Gross national product (GNP) governs the discussion agenda. In this type of process, Indigenous expertise is inadmissible from the start. Sacred knowledge never graces the table.

In protected areas, tourism is much more than a management prescription whose results can be cleanly monitored by GNP accounting. Through the ecotourism industry, 'development' ideology is thriving. Isolated Indigenous Peoples are being drawn further into the national economy. Some governments are quite smug about this 'benefit' of ecotourism. It brings previously flat economic zones into the fold. Brazil, for example, borrowed US$11 million from the Inter-American Development Bank in 2002 to promote ecotourism to Amazonian parks.

Although the ecotourism industry ostensibly finances conservation, its financial windfall is seen primarily in company earnings and government taxation, not by local communities. Local pressures on the land may ease as meagre tourism jobs become available; however, demands from affluent outsiders increase. The situation of the Orang Asli in Malaysia is typical; their 500 or so members living within Taman Negara National Park are inundated by 15,000 tourists a year (Telfer, 2003). For Indigenous Peoples, this results in new magnitudes of impact. Government 'conservation' policy caters increasingly to business needs.

. The ecotourism industry results in a number of severe impacts upon Indigenous Peoples in and around protected areas. These include:

- cultural impacts (for example, repackaged forms of economic assimilation);
- psychological impacts (for example, false promises of good faith);
- health impacts (for example, continued denial of human rights);
- spiritual impacts (for example, desecration of culturally significant areas).

When such impacts are tallied, the benefits picture is not pretty. Everything seemingly provided by industrial ecotourism is taken away through a back door, via other mechanics of the global economy. Only a small minority of Indigenous Peoples report any exceptions; in these rare cases, the enterprise is culturally defined and community led.

We seldom hear of the 'externalities' to ecotourism profits in protected areas. Governments may acknowledge them but do not follow through with financial support for appropriate analysis or problem-solving. Research into industry's impacts – by Indigenous Peoples – is conspicuously underfunded. The best that government or industry normally will do is to invite further 'consultation'. This shifts the burden of proof further onto Indigenous Peoples. It also channels Indigenous feedback through third-party (for instance,

---

BOX 6.3   'Ego' tourism to Indigenous lands

In 1990, the Kogi in Colombia issued *The Elder Brother's Warning*, then closed the gates to their high mountain territory. The gates were closed so that the ceremonies could be safeguarded, allowing the *Mamas* to fulfil their sacred obligation to care for this world. Since then, tourism has been a constant threat; there has been a steady stream of 'backpackers and New Age tourists inspired by the film and its message... For some reason, the part of the message that says: "Stay away – we do not want you here" seems to be beyond the comprehension of many Europeans and Americans' (Ereira, 2001, p36).

bureaucratic or interest group) reporting, distorting highlighted issues. Often the process gets arrested by 'experts', some of them Indigenous and playing the race card for influence (see Chapter 8). Discreetly, oppression is layered on top of oppression.

Protectionism unmasked

The new government trend is to merge protected areas and tourism into one offering. The understanding is: 'Without an agreement, there is no financial package.' Reading between the lines, this means that jurisdiction (that is, surrender of ancestral lands) and economics (such as funding for community economic development) are tied. It also implies a template approach to tourism development. The goal is to create an inviting investment climate by priming Indigenous Peoples for future cooperation with the private sector.

To advance this agenda, governments have brought on board a number of implementation agencies. The United Nations Environment Programme (UNEP) has undertaken case studies on 'best practices' to advise CBD signatories on national strategies for sustainable tourism. CI, TNC and WWF-International are all moving in synchrony with one another and with UNEP, enshrining institutionally defined best practices which seem mindful of Indigenous Peoples. However, all sway to the marketplace and have limited personal engagement with representative Indigenous leadership. Their terminology and modes of business reflect this. They have in common a *rights-evasive approach* (which is hardly precautionary).

Proponents of protected areas are moving ahead with their blueprints for 'conservation', some with good intentions but many making calculated trade-offs. This implementation schedule is proving to be a wake-up call for Indigenous Peoples. We have reached the end of the era where lands will be set aside under the instrument of protected areas.[6] New park designations are slowing down, apart from politically expedient cases. Thus, the focus is shifting from land selection to land management. Protected areas tourism is part of this repositioning and is still revving up.

The politics of conservation are escalating. Maps produced by WWF-International and Terralingua (see www.terralingua.org) show that most remaining world 'resources' lie within Indigenous Peoples' territories. Another map reveals the serious impacts of economic globalization upon Indigenous Peoples (IFG, 2003). Forest Trends, meanwhile, has issued a report confirming that forests thrive when Indigenous Peoples have secure land rights (Houlder, 2004). However, when governments capitulate and bar extractive industries, protection is seldom the final word. Protected areas are still expected to perform. Through tourism, countries can recuperate the 'costs' of conservation. Involved NGOs, companies or consultants can draw sizeable management fees and research budgets.

On the world stage there are glossy reports of conservation accomplishments by the various powers that be. Co-management has been showcased for a while, but with a less convincing sales pitch over time. Indigenous Peoples are treated like park mascots, involved only to the extent that is politically convenient. Countries such as Canada and Australia, which swap notes on Aboriginal containment yet export their supposed co-management expertise, have had their cover blown.[7] Neither the Uluru-Kata Tjuta National Park agreement, nor its contemporaries, are a badge of Aboriginal approval for the colonial economic agenda or for corporate conservation, its close cousin. As Stevenson (2004) notes: 'It would be difficult to conceive of a more insidious form of cultural assimilation than co-management as currently practised in northern Canada.'

BOX 6.4 **Community conservation areas: Safety valve for whom?**

Collaboration between conservationists and Indigenous Peoples remains sketchy. At the 2003 World Parks Congress a small group of professionals operating under the banner of the IUCN Theme on Indigenous and Local Communities, Equity and Protected Areas (TILCEPA)[8] took up the issue of rights, pressing for recognition of community conservation areas (CCAs).[9] The concept took hold more than the process to define it. While there had been animated debate within TILCEPA on implications for ancestral title and rights, this question was never properly put to Indigenous Peoples' leadership internationally – especially on the ground where consent really matters. Instead, TILCEPA turned to the International Indian Treaty Council (a single organization headquartered in San Francisco, US) to help pass a resolution on CCAs at the 2004 World Conservation Union (IUCN) Congress. Talks were rushed for the sake of showing a 'success'.

What are the risks as the terminology of CCAs becomes mainstreamed by the IUCN and the World Commission on Protected Areas (WCPA)?:

- CCAs are one more bureaucratic fixture leading us to talk more in terms of communities than peoples, as if collective rights (such as self-determination) are secondary.
- CCAs will become part of the institutional paper trail (at the UN and nationally) cumulatively extinguishing Indigenous rights.
- CCAs could cause harm where different tiers of rights existing under international law are manipulated for corporate gain.
- CCAs may prove an encumbrance to Indigenous Peoples as more pursue avenues in the international arena to assert or safeguard their ancestral title and rights.

The latest concept to be embraced by inter-government institutions like the World Conservation Union (IUCN), and taken up within the CBD, is community conserved areas (CCAs). This concept adheres to accepted political lingo and works well within the protected areas framework since governments are much more inclined to engage Indigenous *communities* than Indigenous Peoples (who have explicit collective rights under international law) in 'conservation' and 'development'. It may have particular applicability in Asia and Africa, where the notion of 'Indigenous Peoples' is repressed. Nonetheless, in many countries the CCAs concept will be used by government for Kodak moments – to recognize certain 'activist' centres at the expense of others.

Indigenous Peoples break queue

Voices of the Millennial Peoples

Most Indigenous Peoples have watched the protected areas concept with caution. It is does not inherently line up with the principle of ancestral title (that is, sacred knowledge of sustainable use), nor do associated debt-for-nature swaps or biodiversity research stations. These are all tools of the biodiversity trade that carry layers of intent and controversy. They come from a European worldview that pits industrial science and money against 'God' (see Berman, 1988). Between them, mixed intentions are the common link demanding our scrutiny.

Many Indigenous Peoples comment upon the obvious irony of protected areas. Indigenous Peoples view the land in its totality as sacred, with no part to be regarded less integral than any other (see Chapter 2). Today, the very lands nurtured by them over *millennia* are being placed under government management regimes that move by the corporate clock – for 'protection'. With few exceptions, this has led to progressive sequestration of Indigenous territories. It also has abetted dangerous trends such as bio-piracy. In Surin Islands National Park, Thailand, the United Nations Educational, Scientific and Cultural Organization (UNESCO) has supported government documentation of Moken ethno-botanical knowledge.

Numerous Indigenous Peoples' declarations on self-determination, land rights and intellectual property identify protected areas as a concern.[10] These were reiterated at the Fifth World Parks Congress in 2003, a once-in-a-decade event. Protected areas can be highly problematic from the perspective of Indigenous rights. They suggest action on biodiversity conservation, without tackling the underlying corporate causes of biodiversity loss. Government negligence, industry appetite and our own consumer apathy remain uncorrected.

The protected areas movement is a colonial offshoot. Many Indigenous leaders view protected areas not as a conservation tool, but as another economic assault on their people's territory and/or that of other tribes. They see parks as part of the process for territorial alienation. Under domestic park agreements, there is ultimately less control over end uses of the land than if jurisdiction and stewardship had remained contested under international law.

Internationally, several Indigenous Peoples have asserted their sovereignty vis-à-vis parks. In Guyana, 'While communities see that national parks may be better than [mining or logging] concessions, they state that they are no different in the sense that they interfere with and negate Indigenous land rights' (Forest Peoples Programme, 1998). In the Philippines, the Tagbanwa chose to 'stick with their rights based approach to resource management rather than accepting an uncertain participatory approach' (Ferrari and de Vera, 2003).

This casts long shadows over today's celebrated cases of land demarcation of ancestral territory (often called a parallel to protected areas) and of joint management in designated parks. When countries such as Australia recognize Aboriginal 'traditional landowners', they are speaking in a certain political context. Cabinet decisions, legislation and policy can all be reversed if public safety or national security are broadly interpreted. The Arctic National Wildlife Refuge in the US, for instance, was targeted for oil (due to the war over oil). Any threat to economic growth be removed; if Indigenous People get in the way, there may be mock 'compensation' – for example, ecotourism.

BOX 6.5 **Coercive conservation**

During 2003, the International Human Rights Advocacy Centre issued its report *Coercive Conservation Practices in Sub Saharan Africa* (Hebert and Healey, 2003). It documents the unflattering side of the ecotourism industry: forced evictions from ancestral lands (by abuse, torture and murder) in order to groom serene parks for tourism.

Today, parks stained with the blood and trauma of Indigenous Peoples are prime candidates for an 'eco' tourism makeover, under the wing of a corporate (and, thus, well-marketed) non-governmental organization (NGO). Giving jobs to the supposedly 'landless' blurs and discredits their stand on land rights. It also keeps them off profitable 'conservation' lands.

Protected areas managers generally implement the 'conservation' policy set by policy-makers above without many qualms. Their job is to keep protected areas financially afloat and functional in corporate terms. Many, therefore, see protected areas as a catalyst for the ecotourism industry to return to its conceptual building blocks: the funding of so-called conservation. The argument is that if protected areas do not draw adequate numbers of tourists, they may lose their ecological integrity (McNeely 1999).

In ecotourism, there is a trend towards takeovers and new parent companies prescribing 'proven' corporate formulas for growth (Epler Wood, 2002). One concern this raises among Indigenous Peoples is how property regimes may change. Some multinational forest giants prefer private land ownership to licences or other forms of tenure because this means less red tape. There is a growing suspicion that tourism companies will follow suit, using privately held ecotourism reserves as a means of cashing out on today's second wave of mass ecotourism. Already, governments are providing tax incentives for the creation of private reserves.

The privatization of protected areas and the devolution of protected areas management are major grievances raised by Indigenous Peoples. Both infer lawful extinguishment of ancestral title. This disregards applicable international law. It makes lawbreakers of Indigenous Peoples in colonial courts should they implement their own customary law to safeguard lands. Indigenous leaders opposing government-sanctioned mass tourism may be economically sanctioned (for example, by having their funding withdrawn), penalized with harsh resettlement conditions or face other intimidation and death threats.

Internationally, Indigenous Peoples are having to become creative about how they publicize their plight. The *Breath of Life* exhibition, featuring the poetry of Kevin Gilbert (Wiradjuri, Australia), alongside photographs of the Aboriginal struggle within colonial Australia, has been a powerful communications tool.

BOX 6.6   **Privatization of peoples**

Globally, the trend is towards privatizing national parks. The World Bank and groups such as Conservation International (CI) have been on this track for over a decade.[11] Today, transactions are accelerating due to government emphasis on tourism. The move by a Dutch financier to take over a string of parks across five African countries has caused particular alarm. Sakwiba Sikota, member of parliament in Zambia, calls this bid by the private African Parks Management and Finance Company the crime of the century: 'He should have consulted with the people and their representatives' (TIM Team, 2003). The proposal included elite eco-lodges with concessions of 20 to 35 years.

Infringement of rights

At this juncture in talks on biodiversity, it would be careless to assume that protected areas overlapping with Indigenous territories benefit the people or safeguard life systems on Earth. Impact assessments using conventional measures are not adequate to discern the truth about government 'conservation' efforts. Four areas of possible rights infringement need to be examined:

1   *Protected areas may serve as an extinguishment tool.* Protected areas
provide governments with a politically correct way of negating
Indigenous Peoples' land title for the purpose of economics.
They enhance a country's marketability to the tourism industry,
as well as to an array of funding agencies in the business
of conservation. Behind the scenes, some are used for cross
purposes, too; they shield industries from regular permitting
procedures, enabling government to make direct awards of
extractive rights. In both cases, ancestral title is buried under
national interest ('development'). The land is, in essence,
privatized.

2   *Protected areas may be wielded as a bargaining chip.* Governments
use protected areas to curb 'bleeding heart' opposition to their
economic agenda. Successful agreements are often more a
concession than precedent. Once a park is announced, it may
benefit the local Indigenous People; however, it also fills the
regional conservation quota, increasing the commercial exposure
of other Indigenous Peoples and their territories. Subsequent
parks proposals are rejected on the basis of 'affordability'. This
is particularly true in joint management scenarios. For example,
the famous 1994 *Clayoquot Sound Agreement* and the 1996 *Clayoquot
Sound Interim Measures Extension Agreement* between the Nuu-chah-
nulth and Canada is deemed a one-time deal.[12]

3   *Protected areas may double as a trade barrier.* Protected areas tend
to limit livelihood options for Indigenous Peoples. Often,
management agencies put forward such convincing conservation
arguments that customary activities are restricted or even
prohibited – including Indigenous Peoples' long histories of
trade. Communities lose their hunting grounds, medicine
gathering spots and other traditional-use areas. This creates the
need for a monetary economy and thereby assists with economic
assimilation. It also breaks continuous occupancy and use of
the land, jeopardizing the defence of ancestral title and rights in
colonial courts.

4   *Protected areas may function as a morale breaker.* Indigenous Peoples'
aspirations around protected areas are seldom realized. Many
supporting protected area initiatives later find their hands
tied in exercising ancestral title (that is, guardianship), due to
surrendered authority. They discover that protected areas are just
as legally restrictive as other forms of colonial jurisdiction.

Outside protected areas, Indigenous Peoples encounter plenty of barriers to self-determination on ancestral lands. They cannot readily access fee simple 'private' lands because they are priced out of the market, nor do they normally wish to (unless for emotional reasons) because their ancestral lands often were never ceded. They cannot access 'public' lands because of the steep licence fees; nor would most want to (unless for legal challenge) due to unsustainable licence terms: high volume and high revenue targets. Customary law requires conscientious objection.

Inside protected areas, the options can be just as repugnant. Indigenous Peoples are constrained in where and when they can pursue customary activities. They may have to apply for permits or abide by park codes to carry on activities which have been their sustenance for millennia. Many choose to forgo such administrative requirements for reasons of principle. They end up criminalized under parks legislation for 'poaching', root gathering, bark stripping, cutting poles for shelter or meeting other survival needs.

The new Night Safari Park in Chiang Mai, Thailand is one of the more tasteless and misguided 'innovations' in parks marketing. It converts national park land and adjacent areas into a grotesque show of 'biodiversity' – mingling in wildlife imported from Kenya and Australia for supposed 'eco' tourism. International protests have centred on the illicit trade of wildlife (including endangered species), Thailand's shabby zoo standards and other issues of animal welfare (see www.ecoterra.org). But what of local tribes? The Thai Public Relations Department says that the park is 'a world class destination, based on the traditional cosmology'. At the opening ceremony in July 2005, project director Dr Plodprasop Suraswadi, environment minister Yongyuth Tiyapairat and their entourage all dressed up as Native American Chiefs (see Figure 6.1). 'Folk culture' was then splashed across the government itinerary. The ugly twist to this is that Suraswadi himself has orchestrated recent expulsions of Indigenous Peoples from Thai protected areas (see www.twnside.org.sg/tour.htm).

BOX 6.7 **Amazon outrage**

We have historically and presently been the main and best contributors to conservation. For this reason, we reject positions that accuse of us being predators or of opposing development. (Coordinating Body of Indigenous Organizations of the Amazon Basin, or COICA, First Latin American Parks Congress, 1997)

Conservation reconsidered

The doctrine of conservation suggests that someone is looking out for future generations. We are coasting on this false sense of comfort. Most of us engage in the world economy daily. Through our everyday transactions, we consent to its shape and form.[13] While this has put corporations in the driver's seat, each of us has the capacity to sense whether the steering wheel is out of alignment. We need to use our own judgement, or industry think tanks will continue to take us where they please.

Increasingly, it is not just Indigenous Peoples who doubt protected areas and related tools for conservation. There is a diverse community of others worldwide expressing similar concerns. This is evident in the anti-globalization protests against bodies such as the World Trade Organization (WTO). The question in common is: protection from what? From government deception? Many grassroots activists see industrial 'eco' tourism as a principal threat.[14]

If the combination of protected areas and 'eco' tourism is the best governments have to offer, but Indigenous Peoples are urging caution, the issue warrants more attention. Indigenous Peoples' guardedness towards protected areas is a strong indicator of potential biodiversity loss. It is based upon their long horizon of living within the concerned ecosystem(s) and the onerous responsibility of guardianship that defines ancestral title.

When issues polarize, we need to watch the deployment of ideology. In the dialogue on protected areas, it is common for government and industry to speak in terms of roles rather than authority. For example, negotiations might include provisions for community participation. This is a corporate language unto itself, which gets very pedantic. Usually, the result is a very genteel but equally ruthless type of 'resource' appropriation.

In most forums on conservation there is tremendous 'peer pressure' put on Indigenous Peoples. This is the case whether government, the private sector or NGOs fund and chair the process, or seemingly co-chair it with Indigenous leaders. The thrust is that Indigenous Peoples should accept the offering because 'this is as good as it gets'. If they don't seize the goodies (that is, a protected area designation or parks/tourism package), both the goodies and the tray carrying them (in other words, the negotiations or consultation process) will be removed.

This approach to dialogue is offensive. It is identical to techniques sometimes used to socialize children. The same food is put in front of the 'child' (in this case, Indigenous Peoples) again and again, until the so-called obstinacy is corrected and hunger (namely, poverty) drives the decision to eat. This presumes that Indigenous Peoples will:

- relinquish their customary guardianship (sovereignty), which is considered a sacred responsibility;
- waive their right to free and prior informed consent in favour of consensus with predatory third parties;

- submit to the authority of a known abuser (the corporate governance regime);
- believe against the odds in negotiated benefits from tourism (such as equitable royalties).

Against this backdrop, it is hard to imagine that governments could sustain support for protected areas among many Indigenous Peoples. Protected areas and joint management agreements create yet another repatriation challenge for Indigenous Peoples. They are sure to remain a contested topic internationally, especially with the ecotourism industry hovering over Indigenous territories now deemed national 'conservation' zones.

BOX 6.8   The final parks depravity

In recent generations, our consumer sensibilities towards life and beauty have changed. Globally, the landscape has taken a monotone corporate direction. Protected areas are fast becoming an anachronism. Now scientists are recommending designer ecosystems instead of natural life systems. A report funded by US charitable foundations and government agencies says: '"unprecedented partnerships" must be forged between scientists, politicians, communities and corporations to decide which aspect of the natural world should be kept and which sacrificed for the sake of progress' (Staples, 2004, pA1). In one brushstroke, Indigenous Peoples, natural ecosystems and ancient Earth cycles are being made obsolete.

Government protection or perversion?

Life and death decisions

Sacred contracts for land guardianship exist across Indigenous cultures, uniquely in each. One commonality spoken of today is the obligation to uphold sacred relationships. From birth, there is instruction from the Elders regarding correct associations and interactions. Children learn how to feed themselves from the land, with respect for both what it gives and does not give through the course of days. Gratitude is instilled. Sharing is expected. This is the basis of connection; prayer and ceremony are the remembrance.

What frightens governments is the tenacity of Indigenous Peoples. When they see communities marked by extreme poverty suddenly saying 'no' to industrial-style development, there is alarm. Worldwide, colonial poverty has been introduced like a disease. If the people emerge intact – with spiritual health, life gratitude and a heart set upon protecting sacred lands – this presents a dilemma. The oppressor may have to come out from behind its mask. It is time to buy out, smoke out or extinguish the competition.

Globally, there are numerous cases of Indigenous Peoples risking their lives to safeguard supposedly 'protected' areas, or to demand protection status for endangered lands. The Indonesian military has killed members of local tribes in retaliation for their resistance to oil drilling inside Lorentz National Park (The *Ecologist*, 2002, p19). The Ecuadorian military has been just as ruthless, helping oil companies to access 'unprotected' ancestral lands (Amazon Alliance, 1999). Other governments let unemployed forest workers or miners do the dirty work.

Brutality for the sake of industrial access is common in both 'protected' areas and other vulnerable ancestral lands. The violence does not disappear for the sake of squeamish tourists. It just morphs into something harder to detect: coercive conservation. For years, world governments have traded human rights for GNP. In many world regions, 'eco' tourism is synonymous with the repression of Indigenous Peoples. A few 'Indian' sightings are good for business; but many tourists still think pristine parks are theirs to discover.

Governments call coercive conservation an anomaly, but it springs from the lap of international finance – an industrial net binding us all. Countries such as Kenya, Tanzania, South Africa, Namibia, Botswana and Zimbabwe all service their foreign debt with staged 'wildlife' tourism. Through re-colonization, budgets of the industrialized nations are balanced.

In countries where the government relationship with Indigenous Peoples over conservation seems more amicable, similar politics persist. In Canada, two neighbouring Indigenous nations, the Nlaka'pamux and St'at'imc, have had to carefully choose their respective paths for safeguarding ancestral lands. When the women determined that the people must rally, it was clearly about defending the sacred at the risk of dying.

The Stein Valley Nlaka'pamux Heritage Park

Through the Stein Valley in British Columbia, Canada, the territories of the Nlaka'pamux and St'at'imc became world renowned. When Canada issued logging rights to Fletcher Challenge during the mid-1980s, this initially split their communities. Many families living in destitute colonial poverty were hopeful for jobs. But *Stagyn*, as the Stein is known to its peoples, would not be logged. It is a spiritual watershed of the Nlaka'pamux and St'at'imc, where body, mind, soul and spirit are one; where the ancestors sing; and where ceremonies known since Creation hold balance for the peoples. The Elders called for it to stay untouched, lest the sacred teachings be forgotten.

The journey of the Nlaka'pamux and St'at'imc to safeguard the Stein was as rough as it gets. Both had been threatened with incarceration as Canada grabbed their lands, corralled them into reserves and whisked away their children. Now avarice descended again. There were death threats;

logging trucks that tried to knock Indigenous leaders from the road; burned cars; and outlandish bribes. Canada has no treaty with the Nlaka'pamux or St'at'imc, no lawful claim to their territories or to revenues from there. So it blocked Chief Ruby Dunstan from speaking at the Rio Earth Summit in Brazil in 1992, fearing a tarnished international reputation.

The world still found out about the Stein. As Canada pursued its back-door politics in the international arena (see Johnston, 2001), and huddled with its lawyers, the Nlaka'pamux and St'at'imc developed their own strategy. They hosted a music festival that drew the likes of John Denver. They enlisted the help of Maori in New Zealand. And they finally got a two-minute audience with Fletcher Challenge's president. But what swung their struggle was the voice of the Elders. 'There was a lot of hurt that came with the Stein, games that hurt people' (Dunstan, 2003a). When feelings were raw and families became divided, the Elders spoke what they saw.

At this critical point, 50 or more Elders called Chief Ruby Dunstan to the community hall. They told her in their own language what she must do, as chief, to keep the *Stagyn* from corporations. That was the 'old way' of receiving instructions. The Elders asked that the people take care of the *Stagyn* and keep it as pristine as possible. 'I would do it all again, because of the words they said' (Dunstan, 2003a).

In 1987, the *Stein Declaration* was issued, with considerable shock effect. This declaration was signed together by the Nlaka'pamux and St'at'imc, in recognition of shared traditional use areas. It announced: 'We will maintain the Stein Valley as a wilderness in perpetuity for the enjoyment and enlight-enment of all peoples and the enhancement of the slender life thread on this planet.' During this time, environmental groups came forward to support the Nlaka'pamux and St'at'imc. It was at times a tenuous relationship, requiring a tight rein when these groups did not understand cultural protocols. Although their inspiration differed, and some environmentalists were eager for demon-strations or recognition, they learned to wait until asked.

By the time negotiations for parks status began in 1993, the St'at'imc had withdrawn, feeling that a 'protected areas designation would come close to a relinquishment of sovereignty' (John, 2003). However, the consultant brought in by the St'at'imc stayed on, mostly on a shoestring. John McCandless was an experienced negotiator who knew how to frame the Nlaka'pamux message so that it would be received. He also had the instinct that comes from heart. Ruby, now appointed as lead negotiator, worked with his backup to secure an agreement.

Over 18 months of negotiations, the Nlaka'pamux were bounced about by the British Columbia government. Provincial negotiators kept chang-ing until the Nlaka'pamux threatened to renew the *Stagyn* fight with new vig-our. By then, the provincial government wanted a framed agreement to hang on the wall, because province-wide tension over treaties was mounting. It tabled a template agreement which essentially said: 'The park belongs to us.'

When Ruby Dunstan insisted that Nlaka'pamux title must be accommodated, the provincial government flatly refused. Ruby walked out and the province asked the new Chief and council to replace her as negotiator. The draft agreement was then presented with only a slight variation, but on stationery with a 'native' design. On the eve of the signing ceremony, Ruby still had to fight for recognition of the Nlaka'pamux as a people, and for insertion of the word 'Nlaka'pamux'. 'They said: "Ruby, you drive a hard bargain here." I told them the *Stagyn* is not for bargaining' (Dunstan, 2003). The co-management agreement for the Stein Valley Nlaka'pamux Heritage Park was signed on 25 November 1995 (Dunstan, 2003b, p9). Several environmental groups complained about its heavy 'native content'. The victory for the Nlaka'pamux is that the park carries their name and its provisions are without prejudice to their ancestral title. The liability is that the tourism sub-agreement added in 1996 specifies the international potential for tourism development. The province has some discretionary room to promote tourism.

Today, the Nlaka'pamux live with the comfort that the *Stagyn* is safe for now, but with pragmatism about the province's sagging level of good faith. There is sadness that tourism to the famous 'Stein' is mounting. The Nlaka'pamux, like the Anangu of Uluru in Australia, see an opportunity to teach respect. However, most visitors are disregarding cultural protocol and enter without asking permission. Some who attended the music festivals feel entitled because they helped to 'save' the Stein. Others have heard about the Stein and want to see it for themselves. 'If they go in with that attitude, they won't be able to see what is there' (Dunstan, 2003a).

While Ruby Dunstan is alive, her voice carries the memory of the Nlaka'pamux Elders' instructions; she was named by the Elders as lifetime caretaker and mother of the *Stagyn*. Her concern is that anyone named to the Stein co-management board always has a heart for the *Stagyn*: 'Make sure they have a heart for the *Stagyn*' (Dunstan, 2003a).

The 2010 Olympics and St'at'imc title

Canada's hosting of the 2010 winter Olympics puts the St'at'imc territory on the world stage for a second time. Some of the St'at'imc Chiefs say that this timing is destined. As with the *Stagyn*, there is a message to humanity.

In British Columbia, mass tourism is on the upswing, following plunges in commercial forestry and fisheries. The provincial government wants to double tourism by 2010 (Nichiporuk, 2004). The Cariboo Chilcotin tourism region, where the St'at'imc live, is considered underdeveloped. It is seen as having a unique image, summed up as the 'cowboy spirit' (Nichiporuk, 2004).

The 'cowboy spirit' is an accurate characterization of the area.

Canada has yet to abandon its Comprehensive Claims Policy or misleading treaty negotiations process, designed to extinguish Aboriginal title and rights[15] and thereby attain economic certainty. The province's agenda, meanwhile, is to privatize both 'working forests' and so-called 'protected areas.'

The 2010 Olympics support this frontier agenda. The Olympic Bid Corporation[16] was established in 1989 but did not address the St'at'imc Chiefs until December 2002, just three weeks before the bid reached the International Olympic Committee (IOC). Its economic plan for the hinterland was hatched and incubated in city boardrooms. The committee then approached a single St'at'imc community (of 11), Lil'wat, with incentives (Ramsey, 2003). This secured an appearance of Aboriginal buy-in and benefit, but at the price of Canada contravening international law.[17] An appeal for human rights vigilance towards Canada was made to the IOC by the St'at'imc Chiefs and from within Lil'wat itself.

The real issue, nonetheless, is not the 2010 Olympics, but its aftermath. British Columbia 'wants to turn a 17-day sporting event into 17 years of economic opportunity' (Tait, 2002). The Olympics are regarded as a springboard for backcountry tourism. Promised 'benefits' include infrastructure that would open the St'at'imc territory to the global ecotourism industry. Isolated St'at'imc communities easily could become the 15-year ecotourism statistic, destitute due to culture loss. 'Aboriginal tourism is viewed as the *premier* market-ready product' regionally, alongside history/heritage, the Stein 'wilderness' and ecotourism (Denbak, 2004).

Fortunately, this tourism issue is not falling upon inexperienced hands. A decade after the *Stagyn* conflict, the St'at'imc would mobilize to protect sacred areas in the scenic Duffey Lake road corridor from logging.[18] Soon after, the threat of mass tourism rallied them as a nation. Canada's Indian 'radicals' have not gone away.

During 2000, the St'at'imc established a protection camp named *Sutikalh* after the province approved the Cayoosh Resort without due consultation. The *Sutikalh* ('Winter Spirit') area is the last untouched watershed in St'at'imc territory and traditionally has been a destination for medicine people. It was declared a 'no go' zone, meaning: 'No commercial development … absolutely different than what a protected area entails' (John, 2003). This sparked resistance. In 2001, an armed gang arrived in trucks stripped of licence plates to destroy the camp; in 2004, another incognito visitor put a gun to the camp keeper's head. The sentiment is: 'If those damned Indians think they're going to run roughshod over everyone, we'll go out there and tune them up.'

Recent adversity has proven healing for the St'at'imc. During the *Stagyn* fight, they had developed their own tribal police force, parallel to Canada's national police. This time, the St'at'imc Chiefs Council became operational. During 2000, the St'at'imc Chiefs, from all 11 communities, including Lil'wat, signed a declaration opposing the proposed 14,186-bed Cayoosh Resort. In 2001, the German Bundestag issued a letter of support on the matter to the prime minister of Canada, urging immediate accommodation of ancestral title.[19] In 2003, the United Nations Special Rapporteur for Human Rights and Fundamental Freedoms visited to lend support.

So, what does the future of tourism hold for the St'at'imc territory? Much of this depends upon an honest reckoning with history. Today, the central town of Lillooet features the *Gold Rush Days* festival. This claim to fame has not been healing for race relations.[20] Lillooet was the largest centre north of Chicago during the 1860s and beckoned countless miners from California, where 'California Indians were hunted to near extinction during the Gold Rush', thanks to a murder bounty and open racism (Associated Press, 2002). In some respects, this mentality has lingered on. If it is mainstreamed into government ecotourism promotion, under a 'cowboy spirit' theme, there will be continued tension. Unemployed settlers in search of the next boom, and protective native communities are not a good mix.[21] During 2005, some St'at'ime communities have developed their own cultural tourism offerings to create a healthier track for dialogue.

For now, debates on the 2010 Winter Olympics continue. Lil'wat families are mired in poverty, though nearby Whistler is the largest ski resort in North America. Canada has banked on Lil'wat's economic vulnerability,[22] involving them in order to give the Olympics a cultural spin and to reap big bucks from cultural tourism.[23] It maintains that the Olympic legacy will benefit Lil'wat, though precedent says otherwise. In 2004, the Olympic Bid Committee reeled in an unspecified multimillion dollar deal with Visa to promote travel to the area, plus a Cdn$200 million sponsorship from Bell Canada telecommunications. Who benefits?

In the larger picture, Canada's reassurances are not comforting. Canada funded the 2004 *Akwe:kon Guidelines* under the *UN Convention on Biological Diversity*, which dilute impact assessments on Indigenous Peoples' lands into a mere community affair, rather than a process of *peoples* bound by applicable international law. Thanks to Canada, prior informed consent was removed as a principle of international law from the 2004 CBD guidelines on tourism (see Chapter 10, 'Prior informed consent defeated'). These moves at the UN to evade Indigenous rights give Canada relief vis-à-vis the 2010 Olympics.

The 2000 Olympic Games in Australia give an indication of things to come. Isabelle Coe, Elder and caretaker of the sacred fire at the Aboriginal Tent Embassy in Canberra, established an offshoot of the embassy in Sydney 'to inform visitors and the media about the suppression of Indigenous rights by past and present governments' (VPTE, 2000). Elder Kevin Buzzacott carried the fire ceremony over 2500km to Sydney.

The St'at'imc, like other Indigenous Peoples, are turning to the ancestors for guidance. The St'at'imc Chiefs Council is founded on the 1911 *Declaration of the Lillooet Tribe* and operates by the *St'at'imc Tribal Code*. It listened to the women when 'they said legal and political approaches alone would not be enough to stop the destruction of the land' (John, 2003). The spiritual fires are now lit, to safeguard what neither colonial governments nor their protected areas will honour. Will we take the time to understand these sacred fires?

Reprogramming for dialogue

Building depth perception

In today's globalized economy, it is hard to disassociate from ugly profit tactics. Just when we think our conscience is clean we have to look again. The U'wa of Columbia ask: 'Who made the metal that constructed each feather that covers the big bird? Who made the fuel that feeds the big bird?' (The U'wa, 2000). We cannot support one industry without supporting a handful of others. Industrial tourism goes hand in hand with oil exploration, mining, road-building and logging. Looking at this, the easiest rationalization is to ride ecotourism's shirt-tails by choosing among the flaunted schemes for partnership, certification or poverty relief. But we should challenge ourselves to see further, and to understand industry's overall impact upon peoples, their lands and life systems on Earth.

'Eco' tourism in protected areas is not an easy read; but once we understand industry's repertoire it is not so complicated. Whether a country is a direct perpetrator of industrial abuse, or is associated by investment and trade, its tactics will be similar. Most governments use strategic legislation, policy or pilot projects as backlighting in order to obscure their economic manoeuvring. Many hide behind the CBD and its growing array of instruments and offshoots. The CBD, once a promising tool for biodiversity conservation, is fast losing credibility.

Indigenous leaders concerned about the long-term impacts of protected areas tourism on their peoples' ancestral title and rights, cultural survival and daily sustenance are taking steps to counteract misinformation. Many have notified agencies overseeing protected areas of the great harm caused by routine policy, programmes and activities. At the Fifth World Parks Congress in 2003, a formal statement from Chiefs cautioned the Tourism Task Force of the WCPA against treading in areas pertaining to rights, culture and international law which it does not understand (Gavidi et al 2003). 'We would respectfully notify the WCPA Task Force on Tourism and Protected Areas that we cannot accept their current work.'[24]

We can listen to such messages, or write them off as inflammatory and biased. Before reacting, we should make sure we understand the workings of our own lifestyle and life compass.

BOX 6.9 U'wa wake-up call

... like the birds make long journeys without any rest, we will also continue to guard our small corner of the Earth against the *riowa* (whites). We will continue to sing to sustain the equilibrium of the Earth, not only for ourselves and our children, but also for the white people, because they also need it. In the hearts of the U'wa, we are worried for the future of the children of the white people, as well as for our own, because we know that when the last Indians and the last jungles have fallen, the destiny of their children and ours will be the same.
(Letter from the U'wa, Colombia, to the World, 2000)

Reaching out for understanding

In our globalized society, consumerism is promoted like a cult, at the expense of healthy relationships with ourself and others. The psychology of substitutes takes hold. The more we release our own conscience, the more reliant we become upon pacifiers like shopping. We become ever more vulnerable to corporate marketing. What breaks the spell is someone knocking on our door at the moment we feel thirsty, who knows to give water and not a substitute.

Today, Indigenous Peoples hold the glass of water for consumer society. They are telling us that protected areas cannot compensate for what 'development' destroys. They are reminding us that there is no replacement for life systems. The Elders are redrawing our forgotten family tree. But we disown our thirst and push back the glass of water. We resist seeing protected areas as the hallmark of a lost society.

The lesson here is that relationships are sacred. This holds true in ecology and physics, just as it applies to our human relationships, now skewed by industrialization and corporate globalization. We are part of one another's life quilt, no matter how the pieces are shuffled. We are all related in the 'Web of Life'.

Relationships are always a part of our landscape, whether healthy or dysfunctional. But effective relationship-building happens between equals, when each chooses to work on being whole. In the consumer world, we start to mend when we see beyond material seduction – that is, individualism. For Indigenous Peoples, the turnaround comes when culture is used to heal economic assimilation (in other words, chronic colonialism). New relationships are possible when the two decide to meet on this journey. It is a spiritual decision, moved by mutual recognition.

For meaningful cross-cultural dialogue on sustainable economics, we must reframe the question of conservation. We need to ask what is worthy of protection. This question needs to be posed with candour (see Appendix 3). What would we grieve the loss of? For some it might be spotting migratory birds; for others, it is knowing the garden calendar. All of these rhythms of life and place are now rapidly changing due to our industrial economy – through disturbances like climate change. This is evident across continents, though we claim not to be entwined or responsible.

When we remember who we really are, and understand this in the context of daily relationships (for example, our consumer purchases), we can see others and respond compassionately. From this place of introspection we are able to bring a heart and spirit to topics like sustainability. There emerges an entirely different shade of human potential and human will for working together.

Conclusion

There is a distinct dark side to protected areas. The ecotourism industry is no more forthright. Yet, both are considered tools for biodiversity conservation as if there was no history of disrepute. And both are peddled to Indigenous Peoples without hesitation. This could mean that the toolbox mismatches the task; however, there is good reason to go further and speculate on the task itself.

Today, the ideological foundation of protected areas is reason for alarm. Protected areas provide no assurance of sustainable use, if sustainability is understood as healthy behaviour. They are developed in the context of economic growth – that is, 'resource' consumption. Revenue objectives of government will still be met and industry priorities will still be catered to. It is scandalous to suggest that this safeguards anything.

National strategies for biodiversity conservation evolve in step with the global consumer class. This is an uncomfortable thought, but is vital if we are to reach an understanding of sustainable relationships. There are a number of points we need to ponder:

- *Industry and parks are of one ideological flesh*: internationally, the same economic organism governs both commerce and conservation. The government principle of 'sustainable use' is tethered to industrial economics.
- *Protected areas sit inside the national economic pie*: the allocation formula for protected areas facilitates economic growth. It disregards any precautionary approach toward life systems.
- *Protected areas confuse the notion of individual versus collective property*:

representative landscapes and contiguous habitat are set aside for the fabled 'common good', yet there is no onus on economic players to respect ancestral title (in other words, the connected whole).

- *Immunity is a governing principle of protected areas*: protected area networks are designed to compensate for abuses in the private property system, not to redress them. This presumes that rights can exist separately from responsibility.
- *The protected areas concept is primarily of the mind*: 'conservation' is driven by economic pragmatism. Budgets and financial statements rule, though a shadow of heart (including an appearance of profound care and concern) appears in parks marketing to mask their true purpose.
- *The ecotourism industry supports protected areas logic:* that is, the economic status quo. It routinely oversteps individual human rights, Indigenous rights and life thresholds on Earth – affecting us all.
- *Indigenous models for sustainable tourism are economically unattractive*: initiatives that are culturally sustainable do not satisfy government and industry ambitions, or give revenues (such as high taxation) towards supporting the consumer lifestyle.

In the end, we need to talk about protecting our own individual integrity, not conservation or biodiversity. No moralizing or code of conduct has proven transcendent enough to rein in corporate globalization or devastating industry impacts. The ethics of professionalism and objectivity have failed us. All that we can count on for a gentler, kinder future is personal inventory. One by one, we can unearth our own humanity from the faceless heap of consumerism, to understand the chain of cause and effect between world markets (our consumer demands) and exploitative relationships (industry abuse).

Recommended reading

- *Cultural Survival Quarterly* (2004) Special issue on 'Indigenous Lands or National Parks?', spring
- Ecumenical Coalition on Tourism and World Council of Churches (2002) *Statement of Indigenous Peoples' Interfaith Dialogue on Globalization and Tourism*, Chiang Rai, Thailand, 14–18 January 2002
- Forest Peoples Programme website, www.forestpeoples.org
- Hebert, L. and Healey, S. (2003) *Coercive Conservation Practices in Sub-Saharan Africa*, International Human Rights Advocacy Center, Denver, US
- *Indigenous Peoples' Declaration to the Fifth World Parks Congress* (2003) Durban, South Africa
- Sam, R. (2004) *Here is Our Story on Sutikalh*, available from the author by writing to sutikalh2003@telus.net
- The U'wa (2003) 'Letter from the U'wa to the World', reprinted in *Oilwatch Network Bulletin*, no 36, March 2003

Figure 6.1 **Chang Mai Night Safari, Thailand: Dignitaries and park staff dress up as North American 'Indian Chiefs' for opening ceremony**

Figure 6.2 **Billboard protesting uranium mining in Kakadu National Park, Australia**

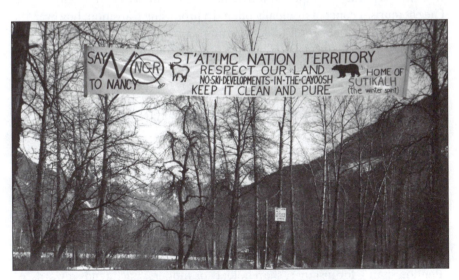

Figure 6.3 **Sutikalh Protection Area, St'at'imc Territory, Canada: Banner opposing industrial-style development**

Chapter 7

Partnerships

We have proved that the problems of the Indigenous and Tribal Peoples are similar in Africa, Asia and the Americas; that the same ecocide and ethnocide carries on regardless; and that those responsible are united and coordinated at the international policy-making level.
(Charter of the Indigenous and Tribal Peoples of the Tropical Forests, Penang, Malaysia, 15 February 1992)

Our need for balanced economies has long pointed past community involvement in corporate schemes, towards more community-centred aspirations. The ecotourism concept originally offered a promising transition; however, the pitch for communities soon took on a market meaning. Ecotourism became an industry, with a conspicuous absence of prior informed consent (PIC) from those targeted as 'destinations'.

International agencies promoting 'eco' tourism have yet to grapple with the industry's broken promises to Indigenous Peoples. By mandate or perceived necessity, most work with industry, directly or indirectly utilizing conventional modes of business. This means that Indigenous Peoples are viewed in project terms. They are seen to offer 'social capital' and 'biodiversity' (Toepfer, 2002), or 'cultural resources'. It is a dehumanizing approach, without any substrate for real relationships.

The principle of partnering, although supposedly central to ecotourism, has not resonated in many boardrooms of any shade. To corporations and conservation groups alike, Indigenous Peoples represent either a means to an end or an impediment. Both normally answer to constituencies with a short attention span – for instance, shareholders or funders. Each tends towards 'A-type' project thinking. In this type of institutional structure, it is common for Indigenous Peoples to be surreptitiously factored into 'done' deals.

There are examples internationally of seeming breakthroughs in cross-cultural business relations with Indigenous Peoples.[1] In tourism these include private-sector collaborations; non-governmental organization (NGO) technical support arrangements; and joint management protocols for protected areas. Yet, few such agreements ease the apprehension of involved communities.[2] The majority are standard agreements aimed at business certainty (such as avoiding conflict) or business proficiency (for example, imparting management systems or administrative skills).

The dialogue on partnerships urgently needs to be reframed, if we are to reach any understanding of 'sustainability'. We need to have a candid look at life relationships together with Indigenous Peoples. This means learning how to relate, rather than hiding behind some professional, institutional or other tourist perspective. It means taking a walk in their world as opposed to compressing them into ours. In this way we can come to know not just the land through its peoples, but also our own selves through fellow humanity.

Industry psychology

Community employer

Industry's typical entry point for dialogue with Indigenous Peoples is benefits. The overture is not about whether tourism is fundamentally desired, but about how many jobs will be provided. Job offerings are normally predetermined, conceived with local poverty in mind. Colonial poverty is acute among Indigenous communities and many companies are savvy about capitalizing on this, continent to continent.

In tourism, like other economic sectors, corporations consider their benefits package complete. They are used to approaching communities as a service provider (that is, an employer). Their vision is 'one for all and all for one'. When this fails to win over Indigenous Peoples, many executives are dumbfounded. They have a benefactor mindset and expect communities to be self-effacing, accommodating and compliant.

Most travel wholesalers think that hiring a local guide or two will dispel any front-end opposition in a community or subsequent misgivings. Unconcerned about liability over Indigenous rights, they leave other details of community liaison to subcontracted tour operators. Both tiers of management in this dynamic realize that they are skimming the surface of community relations. However, ecotourism markets have veered towards conglomerates, making tailored solutions to local grievances ever more unlikely.

Profit margins were never high in ecotourism; today's slimmer industry profits can make for ruthless accounting. During a depressed business cycle, or other industry-sung blues, there is little compliance with advertised or legislated ideals. The majority of companies slip into a cavalier partnership mode. When Indigenous self-determination is foreclosed like this, there is no prospect of true partnering.

Community trainer

Industry tells Indigenous Peoples that they cannot make it alone in tourism. Looking through an industry lens, this would appear to be true. While many communities are strong on product design, most lack independent avenues for marketing. Several have abandoned or lost promising projects due to poor market access. These cases indicate the dearth of culturally relevant systems for 'development' support. But they have been indexed as failures unto themselves, and are cited as a reason for private sector-led partnerships.

The assumption is that communities need a taste of industrial style success in order to appreciate the wisdom of so-called 'development'. Industry has taken on a trainer persona to whet this appetite and NGOs are offering 'community' capacity-building. For both, the focus is usually on industry shadowing. In Mexico, for example, the Adventure and Eco Tourism Association helps communities to train guides and understand business plans. A few Mexican groups, such as Balám, have spoken against such industry bias.[3]

Most training offered flows from industry needs, rather than from community ability and potential. Such 'big brother' interventions are a far cry from any kind of 'sister community' principle. Partnering can under these conditions can be oppressive, with helpful-looking agreements becoming a front for cultural assimilation.

At the World Ecotourism Summit (WES) in 2002, there was broad support for conventional corporate training. One industry delegate said bluntly that community groups should stick to enterprises that complement existing infrastructure; for instance, if there is already an eco-lodge, they should offer day trips for the lodge clients. His message was: 'If you compete with the private sector you will never achieve a good relationship with them.' Ironically, the private sector itself is based upon competition. Ecotourism companies are still racing into isolated areas, where the big payoff is to encounter 'uncontacted' Indigenous Peoples. To many, success means being first to sweeten a sour deal. It is about bringing these 'exotic' communities on board – on industry's terms.

Only a small band of ecotourism companies acknowledge that Indigenous Peoples urgently need shelter from industry 'development'. They, too, were outspoken at the WES. One observed: 'Indigenous Peoples need to be treated as peers and partners if they are to be successful in tourism' (Seltzer, 2002). However, the *Cairns Charter on Partnerships for Ecotourism* – produced following the WES – is a roadmap by and for industry. Reading it, one must bear in mind the *Oaxaca Declaration on Indigenous Tourism* (available from www.touris-mrights.org) and its stern message to industry.

While there are lessons for Indigenous Peoples from the corporate world, now that the economy (and therefore defence of rights) has been further globalized, the need for learning goes both ways. Industry still looks at business proficiency in terms of economics only. Economy wide, the attitude towards 'competitors' is to outmanoeuvre, swamp or absorb them. Retired air force pilots and professional athletes are thus coaching business executives on corporate game plan. And Indigenous Peoples are mirroring back the ominous results of this thinking, appealing for dialogue. Today, their role goes well beyond guardianship of ancestral land (or so-called 'biodiversity'). Thanks to industry transgressions across our biosphere, they have become the global gatekeepers for life systems.

Governments and global institutions pushing corporate models of partnership for 'environment' or 'development' must take note and rethink the presumed hierarchy of innovation and training. To industry, Indigenous Peoples and their ancestral territories are product. There is little hesitation about selling a people or the land that is their identity, lifeblood and survival; or co-opting them into 'self-governing' versions of the same act (see Box 8.1). Today, this type of transaction puts *every* living child on Earth as collateral. So, who is in need of teaching? What can we teach each other?

Partnership etiquette

Industry scorecard

In consumer society, most of us collect possessions and experiences. Some of us go further and become a collector of corporate adrenalin. This has become our common consumer blood type; when we feel low or empty it is a material infusion that lifts us.

In the ecotourism industry, like elsewhere in the global economy, investment can turn to sport. If a community is not for tourism 'development', it is often presumed against it. To many companies, opposition merely signals to push harder. The principle of good faith is abandoned, especially when a community has vastly lesser financial means, yet effectively resists. Corporate testosterone, professional ego and personal pride kick in.

In the ecotourism industry, corporate policies for relations with Indigenous Peoples are on par with other industries, save for a few truly outstanding exceptions. Industry marketing scribes work hard to cover up this likeness. However, it is evident in daily operations, from product research to product delivery. The ecotourism industry is known to take shortcuts at the expense of target communities – for example:

- pursuing product development by stealth, without invitation;
- taking refuge in substandard national legislation – for instance, with respect to environment or human rights;
- moving slowly on remedial measures – for instance, ancestral veto on 'development' plans;
- concealing performance, such as its treatment of Indigenous Peoples and lands elsewhere in the world.

It is a rare company that walks its 'ecotourism' talk, practising respect. Two industry role models are Elzinga Adventure in Canada, which used to donate 3 per cent of its pre-tax profits to the Indigenous NGO Cultural Survival Canada, and Wildland Adventures in the US, which supports Maasai self-determination.

Non-disclosure remains the standard, accepted practice in the corporate world, especially relative to Indigenous Peoples. It is common for a company to initiate a business deal involving an Indigenous People on one continent, while already profiting elsewhere from first- or second-hand abuse of Indigenous Peoples.[4] The ecotourism industry is particularly duplicitous, given its cultivation of a 'community friendly' and 'respectful' market image.

While the ecotourism industry draws ire for such inconsistencies, it must be emphasized that its shortcomings are symptomatic of an *economy-wide problem*. There is no dysfunction in this industry that we have not already seen in others. The question is: how do we talk about ethical partnering when we are enmeshed alternately as consumers, shareholders, students and admirers (that is, lifestyle converts) of industrial commerce?

Corporate audits

True partnerships cannot grow amid speculation. When a community discovers that it has been bandied about as part of a business plan, trust is shot.

It is incumbent upon ecotourism companies to undertake early and direct dialogue with Indigenous Peoples. Some businesses feel that they have taken exemplary steps in this direction. However, feedback from target communities suggests that there is a great distance to go in corporate learning. Most companies still develop terms of reference for dialogue before any introduction or appropriate discussion with Indigenous leadership.

Projects shaped in seclusion like this miss the essence of partnership. There may be an outward appearance of cooperation; but company overtures seldom elicit any real consent or capacity locally. In fact, many advances are highly offensive. Companies routinely:

- offer a token of 'friendship' (such as a short wave radio) in order to expedite a deal at minimal cost;
- hire a communications specialist, often a woman, to soften community resistance;[5]
- create an impressive but dead-end initiative for involvement, such as a community advisory board or other 'in-vogue' showpiece, rather than a genuine mechanism for joint problem-solving;
- deflect communications to junior staff who lack the discretionary authority necessary to advance dialogue;
- parachute in a troubleshooter – for example, a consultant – to avert conflict rather than maintain familiar faces;
- utilize consultant reports to deflect attention away from harmful practices;
- avoid providing funds for balanced talks, such as equivalent access to lawyers and other topical expertise;
- withhold information on profits or other anticipated points of conflict.

The International Ecotourism Society (TIES), an industry association, has acknowledged: 'We need to incorporate the needs of the community' (Epler Wood, 1999). Most needs assessments are now more formalized and claim a degree of community consultation. Nonetheless, companies tend to use these diagnostics to plot their community courtship instead of making a more concerted effort at direct ethical dialogue. Aboriginal relations are a hard sell within corporations. Departments or staff who are delegated this portfolio often have to fight for their own existence.

Many 'new' approaches to partnering are replicating past efforts, but offer important lessons. One lesson is that rapid assessment should not apply to community work with Indigenous Peoples. Evaluations that scan community needs do not begin to touch the complex situation of Indigenous Peoples (that is, legal, political and historical issues pertaining to Indigenous rights), let alone applicable cultural protocol, sacred knowledge or spirituality.

We need to move beyond doing things in the name of Indigenous Peoples towards an open, empathetic and honest ethic of interaction. Only on this footing can relationships foster mutual benefit and understanding.

Figure 7.1 **Building new corporate relationships**

Real partnerships are characterized by partnership building. In the ecotourism industry more homework is required before calling a proposal or existing business arrangement with Indigenous Peoples a partnership. There are seven key points for companies to contemplate:

1 *Commitment*: Companies should ask themselves if they are really prepared to learn. Conventional business has devastated successive generations of Indigenous Peoples.

2 *Heart*: Companies should search their motivation. Do they have the ability to understand, support and abide by cultural concepts of business? Mutual benefits will not occur otherwise.

3 *Personality*: Companies should examine their willingness to listen. In local communities the people may want to talk about life and life values before moving onto business. Without this frank exchange there is no ground to determine compatibility.

4 *Courtesy*: Companies should be honest about how far they will stretch corporate etiquette. Most will learn foreign customs, providing that business sticks to conventional timelines and procedures. This ritual is not enough in Indigenous territories because it is just a shallow makeover to strike a deal.

5 *Sincerity*: Companies should evaluate their stamina for relationship-building. Whereas corporate culture focuses on creating memorable moments – perhaps a cross-cultural workshop or fieldtrip – most Indigenous communities watch for a natural flow, arising from the sincerity of those involved.

6 *Character*: Companies should be up front about the limitations of their economic agenda. The average CEO is now on board for only two to three years. If this leadership or other 'people' pillars of a partnership proposal are unstable, relationship-building will be compromised.

7 *Justice*: Companies should decide at the outset if they will finance real capacity-building. The first training priority of most Indigenous Peoples is how to satisfy prior informed consent. They must be able to know and defend their individual and collective rights or there is no basis for partnership.

Fundamentals for change

Wrestling the corporate way

Understanding the grip of corporations on our thinking is vital to any discussion on sustainable relationships.

Within global industry belts, most of us have been socialized to some degree in the same world view, whether from North or South, colonizer or colonized. This is a powerful determinant of how we will envision or handle change. Regardless of how we define ourselves – or which sustainability club we might identify with – there is significant overlap of assumptions (for example, jobs), expectations (for example, lifestyle) and habits (for example, consumerism). How this manifests depends upon how close we sit to the corporate/consumer inner circle.

The corporate way infuses nearly all types and levels of economic partnership. All of the major international institutions allegedly promoting sustainable development – for instance, the United Nations (UN), the World Conservation Union (IUCN) and the World Commission on Protected Areas (WCPA) – function on business principles. Most development agencies and NGOs interacting with Indigenous Peoples also repeat corporate behaviour daily. Even many community-initiated models for partnership show glimmers of the same cross-fertilization. Through economic imperialism and colonialism, the ideology of 'progress' has travelled far.

Acculturation is one of the most overlooked aspects of partnership. It means that few communities will object initially to standard arrangements. However, it also puts many programmes for sustainability on a collision course. While some say 'biodiversity offers an opportunity to establish new partnerships and promote new approaches to old problems' (McNeely, 1999), little is so new after all. In the global economy, biodiversity is considered a *resource* as opposed to a life building block. Most biodiversity partnerships, including ecotourism, are geared to commercial access (not safeguarding life systems).

Many donors are using partnerships to export corporate 'development'. In the ecotourism industry, mass marketing remains the prescription for economic doldrums. Governments are plugging remote communities into global markets through tiered incentives for partnering. There is great financial pressure to conform – namely, colonial poverty. The book *Dumbing Us Down* (Taylor Gatto, 2002),[6] which looks at how state education serves industry, gives vital perspective on this trend. Cosmetic changes, like talk of 'capacity-building', are proving wafer thin.

Globally, we have been educated into a dangerous sleep. The corporate mind is so invasive in our lives – and so revered (especially through malls, television and tourism) – that we suppress our natural, instinctive, biological response to *crisis*. Instead of fundamentally redirecting the world economy and our core life relationships (first and foremost, consumerism), we are rationalizing the loss of bio-cultural diversity and accepting more 'management' models.

Addressing the corporate legacy

As the *UN Convention on Biological Diversity* (CBD) is 'implemented', the emphasis is on private-sector partnerships, or partnerships stylized after the private sector. This follows the partnership path laid out at the Rio Earth Summit in 1992 through *Agenda 21*, plus the Partnership in Action theme of the UN International Decade of the World's Indigenous People (1995–2004). It is a stakeholder framework that benefits industry.

Groups enlisted by government to oversee biodiversity 'partnerships' with Indigenous Peoples fit the existing economy, as do their ground partners. They care about recognition in the financial world. Thus, projects must turn a profit in order to be regarded a success. This forces funded Indigenous Peoples to become globally competitive, accepting a long list of industry practices which contravene customary law. With corporate grooming, some become party to the spoils – for example, the climate change, disrupted hydrology and contaminated life elements now evident worldwide.

The institutional concept of partnership is ultimately about *taking*, not giving. It is about convincing Indigenous Peoples to bring about their own demise by copycatting industry and becoming consumers. This dynamic is difficult to explain in our corporate system, where colonialism is viewed as a hiccup along the way to 'progress'. However, it raises a contentious point frequently discussed by Indigenous leadership.

Worldwide, Indigenous Peoples forced from their ancestral territory for the sake of industrial commerce watch the steady stream of 'resources' taken, and the accompanying onset of poverty and environmental degradation. Revenues enrich the involved governments, companies and investors. Crumbs from the profit (or 'generous' posthumous bequeathments) are then used to finance so-called sustainable development. It is an ongoing mirage, known today as development assistance, poverty alleviation and philanthropy.[7]

Today's philanthropists are often yesterday's industrialists, seeking penance. Some have amassed a fortune in so-called artefacts that are 'given back' to society as collections.[8] Others are setting up private 'eco' reserves or financing parks management. Frequently, the 'giving' is as riddled with problems as the original taking; the collective cultural property of Indigenous Peoples is still privatized. In the documentary film *The Corporation*, one former CEO bluntly says that the day is near when 'people like me will be in jail'. For now, though, the corporate way persists. We consumers pad the pockets that finance chronic colonialism.

This continuum frames the current dialogue on partnerships.

Indigenous Peoples are being asked to partner with 'donors' who are players in, or distinct product of, colonialism. They are expected to solicit handouts from destructive and exploitative forms of trade, rather than demand royalties from consensual economic enterprise. 'Development' as such is a hypnotic dance around Indigenous land rights. The latest affront is the World Bank Grants Facility for Indigenous Peoples, announced in 2003 to allay long-standing criticism from Indigenous leaders of bank projects (Lucas, 2001; Deen, 2003). This US$700,000 programme for development 'partnerships' earmarks the equivalent of one or two executive salaries for 350 million Indigenous Peoples worldwide.

At the 2004 World Social Forum in India, Southern tourism NGOs denounced 'donor-led' ecotourism. They called for a social review of tourism – including the role of broker NGOs in promoting forms of 'sustainable' tourism that harm impoverished peoples.

BOX 7.1 Indian giving

When funding and other corporate 'giving' stems from industrial activities which capitalize on colonialism or damage life systems, it is inaccurate and misleading to call this philanthropy, corporate citizenship or corporate social responsibility. It is *takers* who do such 'giving'.

Retooling pilot projects

International talk of partnerships has sparked a queue of proposals in the tourism sector. Consultants serving governments and UN agencies are recommending collaborations with communities to identify 'best practices'. Some NGOs have promoted similar pilot projects, citing past liaison work as proof of their supposed affinity with communities. Since both camps are more akin to the corporate world than to Indigenous cultures, there is mounting friction. The focal point is 'biodiversity' investments with Indigenous Peoples as a strategic add-on.

Many Indigenous Peoples see value in pilot projects for sustainable tourism. Nonetheless, feedback on classic pilot projects is telling. 'We have a hard time understanding NGOs and companies' ways. Most of the time, we really don't relate to the proposed projects' (Hernandez, 2002). Some institutions insist that they have listened and are now looking to support existing community initiatives rather than start their own (Hillel, 1999). But the majority either underestimate the significance of relationship-building or are absorbed with their own ideas.

When differences arise with Indigenous Peoples, it often is over approach (that is, best practices). In Tanzania, a Maasai employee of government has suggested that 'development agencies should act as brokers between rural communities and the business sector' (Ole Sikar, 2002). However, since roles and responsibilities are usually shaped by donors, top-down scenarios predominate. South Africa's strategy of 'anchor' projects for ecotourism allocated US$10 million to strengthening existing enterprises, such as hotel infrastructure (Kotzé, 1999).

Most government pilot projects are value-added initiatives, designed to squeeze additional revenue from established tourism attractions. Data is collated primarily for industry growth rather than for modelling sustainable tourism. Partnership guidelines and funding criteria reflect this. There is persistent, systemic bias against Indigenous (community-crafted) proposals, to the extent that groups such as the World Wide Fund for Nature (WWF-International) admit their reluctance to directly fund Indigenous Peoples (Oviedo, 1998). This has led to the privatization of not just development, but also privatized, opportunistic advocacy of 'Indigenous' interests by third parties.

Internationally, a handful of mega-NGOs are in active partnership mode, securing concessions for ecotourism from governments. Conservation International (CI), The Nature Conservancy (TNC) and WWF-International all partner locally for international distribution of their own 'community' concepts. It can be profitable for such organizations to peddle their management and training services. Many a government is looking for someone to solve its frontier headaches, especially the 'development' quandary. Becoming known as a reliable trainer of feisty communities is the ticket to influence. So the 'Big Three' continue to put their respective signatures on global conservation, long after park boundaries are drawn.

Many Indigenous leaders are aware of the aggressive marketing of services by certain NGOs and know the cronyism that goes with it. NGOs large and small are capturing the bulk of funding available for 'community' innovation in tourism. Most advocate conservation but disregard cultural protocol and Indigenous land rights. Several profit by association, fundraising for their own cause in the name of Indigenous Peoples or ancestral territories. Indigenous rights are undercut on a number of levels as these groups ingratiate themselves with governments and other donors. Their 'non-profit' persona speaks more to a personal identity crisis than any identity or existence (for example, funding independence) outside industry or industrial philanthropy.

To verify that pilot projects naming Indigenous Peoples are legitimate, we need to know the relationship-building track record of the proponents, plus any silent partners. Gradually, Indigenous Peoples are gaining the means to tell this story, despite subtle intimidation from funders. Disclosures must be publicized widely to discourage future hedging; otherwise the attitude 'make hay while the sun shines' takes hold and communities get used.

Consultants: The identity crisis

Industry terms of reference

Consultants (or consulting NGOs) are often the first tier of deal brokers enlisted to involve Indigenous Peoples in ecotourism. Governments rely heavily upon consultants to promote national ecotourism plans at the community level. They usually enlist consultants accomplished in multi-stakeholder situations. These professionals have an uncanny ability to structure a deal in favour of industry growth.

For a number of reasons, Indigenous leaders have objected to the public and private sectors' reliance upon consultants. Foremost, consultancy on 'biodiversity' and 'Indigenous issues' has become a lucrative business. This can fetter professional judgement. Consultants are prone to validate their own work, pushing concepts that protect client interests. Indigenous Peoples and Indigenous communities become secondary to personal business (or budgetary) pursuits.

Among Indigenous Peoples, distrust of outside consultants is near universal. Few consultants fronting new programmes or pilot projects receive a warm community reception. Much of this wariness stems from the disconnection between government policy and Indigenous Peoples' rights and needs. However, it can also be a more personal reaction. Some professionals find an underhanded glamour in working with Indigenous Peoples. Others become cocky in their role as a 'community guru' for hire.

In the ecotourism industry, the credibility of consultants is especially shaky. No other global industry has billed itself as a perfect match for Indigenous Peoples of the world. While some communities are keen to check out the advertised advantages of ecotourism, many Indigenous leaders see this industry as the ultimate deception. The industry looks good but cuts to the core of Indigenous rights, making self-determination all the more paramount. Initiatives such as Ecotourism Exchange in the Amazon (backed by CI, the World Bank and partners) seem to support community reflection (Rome, 2003); however, stakeholder forums are hardly the place for a private exchange of views between Indigenous Peoples. Funders are clearly hesitant to turn Indigenous Peoples loose to do their own inquiry. So, on live consultants, the 'independent' glue for much doubletalk.

During preparations for the 2003 World Parks Congress, this particular quandary came to life. One senior advisor on tourism to the WCPA – who brandishes her position on a jointly managed park board, plus other 'Indigenous-friendly' credentials – suggested that veteran Indigenous leaders could not prepare analyses of adequate calibre for publication. This kind of 'back room' talk is detrimental to relationship-building. It is unacceptable that such ethnocentric remarks are still made by the inner circle of policy-makers.

Any consultant attempting to parley industry growing pains or community anxieties into a consultation, pilot project or best practices contract should rethink their role. Often, client terms of reference (that is, government or institutional goals) are at odds with international law on Indigenous Peoples' rights. In this situation, should industry consultants close their eyes and hope for the best? Should they attempt to educate themselves and their client, while fulfilling the contract? Or should they notify all parties involved or affected that the project is compromised?

Personal breakthroughs

At this stage of the ecotourism trajectory, many tourism professionals are aware of Indigenous Peoples' negative experiences with tourism, as well as their ongoing letdowns with consultants. Nevertheless, most lack tools for relationship-building beyond the rhetoric of community participation. They have little frame of reference for the core issues – for example, Indigenous spirituality or land rights. Nor do they have professional grounding in situations where these issues come to life, such as the front line of blockades. Few break through this experiential divide. Their outlook remains one of deal brokering (politely called 'facilitation' or 'conflict resolution').

Even among those consultants working for Indigenous Peoples, either through direct hire or placement by development agency, there is a vacuum of experience. Their mentors are primarily from the corporate/consumer world. Thus, the transition to working in actual communities is not easy. The roles of adviser or troubleshooter are usually tried. But few sit alongside Indigenous leaders, Elders and women long enough to learn the protocol, humility or other dimensions of Indigenous customs for dialogue and decision-making.

Often, Indigenous Peoples hold their own consultants at the same arm's length as outside emissaries. Most have seen hired help or self-nominated consultants (for example, NGOs or ecotourism companies espousing 'partnership') breeze in and out. Much of the apprehension is simply cross-cultural; there are different time horizons and different material motivations at play. Even when professionals offer their services on a *pro bono* basis, the motivations are sometimes murky.[9]

In most instances, the prospect of relationship-building through consultants is limited. Cultivating relationships takes more than an ability to move fluidly between worlds. Raw humanity and heart are necessary to traverse the cross-cultural divide. Communities want to know your values and are, by now, quick to read sincerity levels.

Individuals who are successful in a consulting capacity with Indigenous Peoples understand the difference between deal brokering and relationship-building, whether on their own behalf or a client's. They avoid assignments with industry where they would be used simply to finesse a deal for conventional economic growth. They are mindful of the 'expert' syndrome: the temptation to grandstand on the backs of communities. Instead of pushing conventional ecotourism, they seek ways to support Indigenous Peoples in their own cultural analysis and decision-making on sustainable tourism. This prepares the ground for real partnerships, where two pillars of knowledge support the effort. Sacred knowledge is given proper space.

Consultants who go this uncommon route typically share many of the following traits:

- strive to remain aware of character in everyday life (for example, reflect on lifestyle choices and investment decisions);
- identify on a soul level with their work (for example, have a sense of life calling and life purpose);
- conduct themselves with humility (for example, extend respect to *all* regardless of race, culture, gender or perceived class);
- consciously ground and reground themselves to stay alive to their work potential;
- listen to Indigenous leadership, Elders and communities regardless of competing timetables;
- stay open to correction by Indigenous leadership, Elders and community members; and
- find the courage to come from the heart in their role as a 'professional'.

NGOs: Ethics in action

Partners or pirates?

A handful of NGOs have been pivotal to Indigenous Peoples' quest for their rightful place in government dialogues on sustainability. They include Cultural Survival in the US; the International Work Group for Indigenous Affairs in Denmark; The Netherlands Centre for Indigenous Peoples in Amsterdam and Survival International in the UK. Their tenacity in playing a support role to Indigenous Peoples and Indigenous NGOs is a refreshing contrast to some of the NGOs engaging in 'turf infighting' today. The strength of their respective efforts is that they continue to recognize their own learning curve with respect to roles and responsibilities.

Many other NGOs with a conservation and/or social justice scope have campaigns that are compatible, to an extent, with Indigenous Peoples' own goals for the protection of rights. Some, for example, play a vital role in challenging industrial-style economics. Since 1999, several have staged effective anti-globalization protests outside ministerial trade meetings in Seattle,

Genoa and Kananaskis amongst a number of places. Others are watchdogs in major environment forums, such as UN negotiations on biodiversity or sustainable development. World governments have attempted to muzzle them. In meeting rooms, they get co-opted as 'friends of the chair'. On the street, tear gas, batons and criminal charges are being used to 'police' them.

It is a chilling commentary on our times that NGOs dedicated to environment or human rights work are appeased, infiltrated or persecuted. This should rouse our curiosity about what is really going on and why. What do we need to know? In 2001, NGOs were singled out as a global threat by the US, protector of the 'American dream'.[10] If these groups have such power to subvert corporate governments, they must be telling some shatteringly *simple* truths. No wonder some countries and government agencies like the World Tourism Organization (WTO-OMT) and the CBD Secretariat have tried to rock relationships between NGOs and Indigenous Peoples.[11]

In practice, most conservation NGOs are stronger on lobbying world governments than on supporting Indigenous Peoples. While NGOs active in biodiversity arenas have been sensitized to Indigenous Peoples' circumstances, or may even represent Indigenous Peoples at arm's length (as an Indigenous NGO), most are so wrapped up in a single agenda that they forfeit relationship-building. Many pursue invitations to Indigenous communities, only to peddle their own programme. They hear Indigenous leaders speak but are more focused on their own airtime. Thus, the meaning of ancestral title eludes them. Several well-promoted 'capacity-building' programmes suffer from this NGO myopia.[12]

A great many NGOs, including some self-made 'Indigenous' NGOs, have no compunction about influencing government programming for Indigenous lands, or usurping the voice of Indigenous leadership on this front. Politically, this poses a challenge for Indigenous Peoples. Since the 2002 UN Earth Summit in Johannesburg, NGOs have gained leverage. Parterships were a main theme of dialogue at the summit. Some conservation NGOs now feel new relevancy in the eyes of international institutions and funders, as conduits to communities and 'go-betweens' for community participation. Quick networking on their part has sealed the fate of many development assistance and capacity-building programmes, especially in burgeoning funding areas like sustainable tourism.

Many conservation NGOs have yet to recognize the inappropriateness and danger of developing platforms, or pursuing partnerships, without the prior informed consent of the affected Indigenous People(s). Often, they unwittingly push programmes that cause culture loss. This happens where conservation and tourism are paired, utilizing conventional industrial ecotourism or a close 'community-based' facsimile. Governments and development agencies may call it a partnership to add some elegance to the exchange;

but Indigenous rights and cultural protocols are nevertheless overstepped. Currently, one high-risk area of NGOs' work is the emphasis on third-party certification over ancestral title and rights (discussed in Chapter 9).

A few NGOs are brainstorming for ways to build new relationships. Crooked Trails in the US is facilitating cross-cultural exchanges with a view to tourists mingling over shared 'work and play' (see www.crookedtrails.com). The Sacred Earth Network facilitates Indigenous Peoples' travel, enabling Indigenous leaders from Siberia to visit Indigenous nations in the US for talks on spiritual restoration (see www.sacredearthnetwork.org). These efforts are meaningful because they help dissolve the barriers to reconnection.

BOX 7.2 The partnership hot seat

Conservation International (CI), The Nature Conservancy (TNC) and the World Wide Fund for Nature (WWF-International) all have catchy campaigns to market their brand of conservation. CI champions biodiversity hotspots, TNC trumpets the world's 'last great places' and WWF-International has its 'Global 200' set of priority conservation areas. 'Eco' tourism is pushed by each. This has led to a mixed verdict for Indigenous Peoples. What if their ancestral territory is not a *cause celèbre*? What if it is? With mega non-governmental organizations (NGOs) presiding over 'conservation' the principle of self-determination is lost. Corporate assimilation and, therefore, culture loss become a given.

Macro-problems

A major barrier to community relations, especially among larger conservation NGOs, is their tendency to step forward as counter 'experts' to industry on the environment. Organizations such as CI, TNC and WWF-International have been so effective in marketing their expertise on biodiversity matters that they usually are taken more seriously by government than the affected Indigenous Peoples, whose ancestral territory is under discussion. Many know their Rolodex better than the long ripple of affected peoples globally. While this can prove handy, on occasion, for those communities linked in as project 'partner', it alienates NGOs from the broader Indigenous constituency they often claim to have.

One issue this raises is the murky definition of what makes an NGO. During 1999, TIES entered the UN dialogue on sustainable tourism under the NGO banner.[13] This caused an uproar among participating tourism NGOs since TIES is perceived as an industry body. Indigenous delegates voiced even greater indignation, due to the implied commonality of interests with Indigenous Peoples and Indigenous communities. Since then, similar concerns have been expressed about entities like CI. TIES and CI are both viewed by many grassroots organizations as conservation consultancy businesses that bill themselves as NGOs.

International tourism NGOs are all relatively small in size and generally identify with target communities. As a group, they tend to think of themselves as scrupulous in their interactions with Indigenous Peoples. Many do attempt a supportive role, though with limited opportunity for frontline ground interaction. Most of those active at the UN are challenging world governments and corporate NGOs on their ethic of partnering. They have called for an end to industry-slanted community engineering. This peer review has been scoffed at by some powers that be, including the WTO-OMT (see Chapter 8), but is a serious indicator of trouble in tourism 'paradise'. Its occasionally self-righteous delivery should not deter us from listening.

During the International NGOs' Workshop on Tourism and Biological Diversity in Berlin, in 2000, there was heated exchange over approaches to partnership. At this meeting, CI was reprimanded for its attitude. Other workshop participants found CI condescending and standoffish, particularly towards Indigenous Peoples. Some noted with concern that CI, TNC and WWF-International have a monopoly on 'development' funds for so-called sustainable tourism, citing WWF-International's entwinement with the World Bank (for example, the World Bank–WWF-International Forest Alliance). Others cringed at the in-house financial clout of such groups, derived from their pro-industry stance. 'The large NGOs will support undemocratic process which smaller people-centred NGOs with constituencies must morally object to' (Rao, 2000). They may look 'hands on' with Indigenous Peoples, but tend to lean on intermediaries whose representation (that is, cultural mandate) or cross-cultural relationships lack depth.

Indigenous leadership is outspoken internationally on these same issues; however, their rapport with NGOs is complex. Cross-cultural differences are pronounced with big and small NGOs alike (see discussions on stakeholder consultation in Chapter 8).

BOX 7.3 | **World Wide Fund for Nature (WWF-International) says whoops!**

In 2004, the World Wide Fund for Nature (WWF-International) warned that we are 'plundering the planet at a pace that outstrips its capacity to support life'. Yet, WWF-International itself has promoted mass 'eco' tourism. In Nepal's Annapurna Conservation Area Project, financed by WWF-International, visitation jumped from 14,300 in 1980 to 63,000 in 2001. The numbers alone were appalling, in terms of impacts; but the bitter pill for WWF-International was admitting that the tourism was exploitative (Bookbinder et al, 1998). Today, this lesson seems distant; WWF-International membership travel is alive and well, patronizing conventional tour operators.

Micro-challenges

Indigenous Peoples' concerns over the business of advocacy extend to many smaller NGOs as well. A number of these NGOs are continually shape-shifting in order to tap into biodiversity-related funding. Indigenous leaders watching this trend have expressed dismay at such tactics. Their questions tend to be relationship-oriented: who came together to create this new entity? Who are you, really?

There is intense competition among NGOs for advocacy niches. Some seek to amplify a 'sexy' regional issue, such as the protection of a threatened species or a high-profile watershed. Others are known to troll UN forums for the next big issue, when advocacy work itself becomes seductive. For both these groups, ecotourism is the most potent elixir to emerge in some time. It uniquely combines the ecological and social aspects of biodiversity – namely, the concept of a conservation economy.

Product differentiation among NGOs is taking a new twist, in response to recent attention to cultural diversity in biodiversity arenas. It is now fashionable to partner with Indigenous Peoples. In the tourism sector, as elsewhere, several smaller NGOs are attempting to associate themselves with Indigenous causes in order to preserve their advocacy domain. Playing a broker role between governments or development agencies and Indigenous Peoples can bring useful publicity, if not substantial 'project management' fees.

The renewed intrusiveness of NGOs into conservation within Indigenous Peoples' ancestral territories is hindering relationship-building. NGOs' brazen air of moral authority – whether for or against ecotourism – is increasingly unwelcome inside Indigenous communities. Few of the more fundamentalist NGOs can see their own paternalism or other corporate-influenced behaviours. Many support the going industrial concepts of 'sustainable' use or 'protected' areas (which presume commercial access or negotiated trade-offs) instead of ancestral title.

It is only a small circle of Indigenous leaders that has international exposure to this positioning of NGOs with respect to biodiversity. Those who witness the jostling are quick to pick up on NGO indiscretions. Some tourism NGOs and NGO representatives have posed as if they were historically active in the CBD process, or claimed to be working with Indigenous Peoples. Appearances were made at the United Nations Working Group on Indigenous Populations in Geneva in 1998. Project literature, some of it plagiarized, looked convincing. This proved a winning strategy, rewarded with funding, contracts and influential consultancies on sustainable tourism.

NGOs who go astray like this often avoid being chastised by peers because the issues themselves are so demanding that others choose to focus on the work. Nonetheless, their conduct does affect how NGOs at large are received by Indigenous Peoples. NGOs often manifest the very values that they are ostensibly against – individualism, aggression and primacy of economics; even in venues such as the United Nations Commission on Human Rights (UNCHR).

It is time for NGOs to work for reconnection, rather than the disunity ordained by funding structures. This means a humbling look at *internal* affairs. NGOs can begin the clean-up by:

- maturing – demanding order in their own house;
- moving together – rejecting funding structures that breed competition, betrayal and short sightedness;
- making amends – working with an open mind and spirit to help Indigenous Peoples combat untruths;
- meeting Elders – requesting teaching from Indigenous Peoples on appropriate protocol, priorities and practices.

Relationship-centred advocacy

Across the spectrum of NGOs interested in biodiversity, there is an urgent need to retune the relationship-building compass. NGOs whose mission impacts Indigenous Peoples and their ancestral territories should work on the basis of an invitation from Indigenous leadership, rather than search for a solo problem-solving role. Their basis of work should be not only transparent but also in clear view for other Indigenous Peoples (which means reaching further than the internet). Southern NGOs are generally much more attuned to these nuances. Many understand first hand that conventional 'conservation' partnerships are exploitative.

There is a small handful of NGOs worldwide who follow Indigenous Peoples' experiences with tourism in earnest; these include the Ecumenical Coalition on Tourism in Hong Kong, Equations in India and the Tourism Investigation and Monitoring Team (TIM Team) in Thailand. All of these organizations play an invaluable role in collecting and disseminating information critically needed by Indigenous Peoples. However, due to funding constraints (in other words, deliberate government barriers) for this type of service, none has the wherewithal to properly synthesize and deliver information fast or far enough. Few funders have supported any degree of 'early warning' system on ecotourism for Indigenous Peoples.

Alongside these tourism NGOs working in solidarity with Indigenous Peoples, there are a few parallel NGOs who identify themselves as Indigenous. The most widely known of these is Indigenous Tourism Rights International (ITRI), formerly known as the Rethinking Tourism Project (US). Such groups face a mammoth task, for most Indigenous communities lack even basic information on the ecotourism industry. Since the NGO construct is foreign to Indigenous Peoples, these groups often have to work just as hard as any other

NGO to convey the relevance of their work. They may face similar challenges in establishing community partnerships. For instance, some have boards or staff comprised largely of university graduates, professionals and/or academics, who tend to be geographically (or even culturally) removed from the issues they deal with. This can lead to programming that misses the mark with Indigenous Peoples and their communities.

The greatest setback for some Indigenous NGOs is that they are just as divorced from Indigenous leadership as others in the advocacy realm. They may develop their own mandate instead of working through a protocol process. Furthermore, if working on a single issue like tourism, they may be unfamiliar with the breadth and depth of issues around ancestral title and rights. This can impair both their programming and their efficacy on Indigenous rights issues. Their radar on relationship-building often differs from that of customary leadership or Elders.

Some Indigenous leaders will correct NGOs, including Indigenous NGOs, when cultural protocol concerning representation is disregarded. Well-intended groups who think they know what they are doing can inflict damage if not properly mandated and guided or accompanied as per custom

---

BOX 7.4 Real partnerships

During 2001, Survival International set out to enlighten European tourists on Botswana. 'In order to protest the Botswana government's inhuman treatment of the Bushmen, [it held] a weekly vigil … during the summer tourist season – directly opposite the Botswana High Commission in London' (*Shaman's Drum*, 2001, p15). In 2004 Survival launched a Botswana boycott at the ITB World Tourism Fair in Berlin. This helped the Bushmen to become visible, but did not at all endear Survival to government or industry.

Survival's campaign (2004) stated:

> … the government seeks to assimilate the Bushmen in the same way that devastated so many peoples in Australia and North America. It actually denies the existence of the Bushmen as distinct peoples … arguing that to distinguish between peoples is racist. This is a convenient view: for if a people never existed then their destruction never happened.

Needless to say, Survival is still not considered partnership material by the 'key players' in so-called sustainable tourism. In 2005 'Botswana's President Mogae … said that he decided to deport Australian Professor Ken Good as a "threat to national security" over his links with Survival International' (see www.survival-international.org). The San themselves are, in effect, persona non grata among world governments and their corporate 'conservation' allies.

by Elders. They may consent to something that they do not understand in its complete historical context. For example, they might enter a dialogue process or partnership without understanding its full ramifications on Indigenous rights (see Box 8.5). It is not uncommon for Indigenous NGOs with an 'experts board' to pursue or be manipulated into unproductive partnerships. Among Indigenous Peoples, 'experts' are not synonymous with leaders. Many 'experts' lauded nationally or internationally are essentially government made.

NGOs can help to unravel the procedural mess by ascertaining cultural protocol before jumping into any advocacy whirlwind or biodiversity partnerships.

Internal deal brokers

Fractured identities

It takes courage to look objectively at partnerships in order to assess where they thrive versus where they teeter or fall from grace. Analysis of partnerships between industry interests and Indigenous Peoples can be particularly taxing. As in any relationship, there are always two or more perspectives to consider. But there is also the aftermath of colonialism to digest:

> As colonized people, we are colonized to the extent that we are unaware of our oppression. When awareness begins, then so too does de-colonization (Trask, 2000).

In the corporate world, the tendency is to look for an internal deal broker, then exploit this community contact. However, internal deal brokers are not just those coaxed by industry; eventually some also emerge locally, looking for a share of profit. This dynamic fed the slavery trade in Africa and continues to mark global commerce, still at the expense of fellow humanity.[14] It can be a short distance from being an interpreter or entrepreneur to selling the sacred.

In the ecotourism industry, the meaning of partnership is easily blurred. Companies seek high-impact, believable cultural contact with Indigenous Peoples. Often, this is achieved via the back door, by hooking up with the 'right' individual locally. They look for someone who is receptive and then present financial incentives. This kind of partnership is defined by money passing hands, rather than by any meaningful rites of relationship. It is built by encouraging community members to covet (that is, to desire colonial 'trinkets and beads').

The bottom line is that poverty is persuasive. It is poverty that enables the ecotourism industry to access many of its prized destinations. Most Indigenous Peoples either cannot afford to mount a legal defence (on the basis of land rights), or cannot maintain unity under the grinding stress of poverty to negotiate for what they need. In these conditions, it is possible for a company to pay an individual community or community member for access to not just ancestral lands, but also to collectively held ceremonies, sacred sites or cultural knowledge. These are all spiritual trusts that under customary law – and free of duress – ordinarily would not be sold.

Payoffs like this are foreboding. The ecotourism industry is now active in areas that are culturally and ecologically sensitive. It also is treading on ceremonial ground that it does not understand. This interruption of customary practices puts Indigenous cultures at high risk. Distancing Indigenous Peoples from their ancestral territory, and from their spiritual connections to the land, is a lethal form of acculturation. Before long, more community members are willing to cut down their own symbolic life tree – for a fee. This type of commercialization, masked as partnership, is destabilizing life systems on Earth.

Rebuilding trust

The ecotourism industry must break its cycle of abuse in order to salvage credibility with Indigenous Peoples. When a company urges someone 'inside' to run ahead of cultural protocol, cooking a deal before mandated Indigenous leadership satisfies the protection of rights, it is divisive. The approached deal broker might promise introductions, and even attempt conflict resolution, but often underestimates his people's strength.

Many Indigenous leaders speak openly about this dynamic, which is common when industry seeks access to ancestral lands through partnership. Often, leaders find themselves at odds with their own college-educated youth, who are handpicked by industry to serve as intermediaries. 'The invaders have bastardized our education process, interfering with our very ability to think and be Aboriginal. They have been successful in creating "white thinking" Aborigines' (Anderson, 2000).

The issue of internal deal brokers is a delicate one, reminiscent of other 'divide and conquer' scenes over the span of colonialism (see Chapter 8 for more detail). From the perspective of partnerships, it simply is important to note the damage of such relationship shortcuts. Typically, racism is fanned in all directions.

Most partnership proposals to Indigenous Peoples are an attempt to crack the nut. They are built on racist stereotypes and attitudes about what Indigenous Peoples deserve or where their breaking point lies. Communities understandably react with bitterness, especially when their own kin become embroiled. Sometimes, reactive second-hand racism emerges – especially if there has been prolonged, systemic oppression. Once this takes hold, even respectful and sincere overtures will grate on community nerves. Anyone associated becomes suspect.

Some of these dynamics of partnership are hard to digest, regardless of where we sit. For consumers, complicity in industry's abuses is unthinkable; it takes a searing inversion of our own worldview to see the links. Among Indigenous Peoples, the issue of internal colonialism is painful. However, change starts with empathy and compassion. There is humanity to be found in looking at our own personal inconsistencies.

Kahlil Gibran, author of *The Prophet*, speaks beautifully of the qualities of healthy partnership in his treatise 'On Marriage'. He speaks of the two pillars in a partnership each being whole. 'Give your hearts, but not into each other's keeping ... the oak tree and the cypress grow not in each other's shadow' (Gibran, 1985, p22).

Mundo Maya: Behind the mask

La Ruta Maya: **The preview**

Internationally, the tourism programme that stands out as the looking glass on conservation partnerships is *Mundo Maya*, a collaboration between Mexico, Guatemala, El Salvador, Honduras and Belize. This programme, originally known as *La Ruta Maya*, offers a quick synopsis of the global ecotourism industry.

La Ruta Maya was a tourism circuit designed to make Mesoamerica into an all-season destination. It never had any equity in store for the Maya.[15] All along, it was a partnership concept played out at another level (Johnston, 1994). The name was concocted before intellectual property entered the daily language of Indigenous rights.

La Ruta Maya was a hybrid of the tourism industry, conservation movement and development community. The concept emerged during the 1960s; but it was the 1980s debt crisis that motivated cooperation. Wilbur Garrett, past editor of *National Geographic* magazine, saw this window. In 1988, his La Ruta Maya Conservation Foundation joined Partners for Livable Places in the US to resuscitate the proposal. They convinced regional governments to allot needed 'conservation' lands. An ecotourism mega-project was born.

La Ruta Maya was part of the economic plan hatched for a streamlined regional economy. One parallel was the *Paseo Pantera* conservation and ecotourism project – spearheaded by Wildlife Conservation International, the New York Zoological Society and the Caribbean Conservation Organization. Another was CI's Rainforest Imperative initiative. In the background were funding agencies such as the US Agency for International Development (USAID) and the United Nations Development Programme (UNDP), which funnelled aid through various NGOs, often without coordination (Ashton, 1992b). In the innermost recesses lurked the International Monetary Fund

(IMF) and the World Bank, overseeing economic growth on behalf of international corporate interests.

The Maya, if mentioned, appeared as recipients of 'trickle down' rather than active agents in their own 'development'. This same development model had already caused the displacement, acculturation and impoverishment of Indigenous Peoples elsewhere in Latin America and worldwide. But proponents of *La Ruta Maya* deflected criticism of the plan on the basis of its alleged participatory component.

Mundo Maya: Its debut

Prior to the launching of *La Ruta Maya* in 1989, discussion of a related programme called *Mundo Maya* had begun. *Mundo Maya* incorporated the same concepts; however, it addressed the social issues ignored under its close twin and was specifically referred to as 'alternative' tourism (SECTUR, 1993).

The conceptual document for *Mundo Maya* was written by Guatemalan anthropologist Alberto Rivera. He approached *Mundo Maya* as a tool for socioeconomic development and was the first to identify community participation as an essential component. Initially, regional governments were taken aback by Rivera's inclusive vision for *Mundo Maya* (Toriello, 1992). But they were quick to recognize its public relations value and become acquainted with the buzzwords (OMM, 1992a, 1992b).

In 1990, regional tourism ministries agreed to transform *La Ruta Maya* into *Mundo Maya*. This shift was motivated by branding. Industry recognized that the region's uniqueness rests not just upon 'archaeology', but also upon the distinct traditions and lifestyle of the living Maya (SECTUR, 1992). 'The intention … is to offer visitors an integral vision of Mayan history and culture' (SECTUR, 1991). Tourists interested in culture stay twice as long (SECTUR, 1990) and visit more places than traditional tourists (OMM, 1992a).

From the beginning, *Mundo Maya* was described as a 'low-impact' tourism programme (OMM, 1991), shunning mass tourists (OMM, 1992b). 'We want people that respect the culture of our ethnic groups and the nature of our parks' (Leibman, 1993, p11). But in 1990, the same year that *Mundo Maya* was launched, Mexico declared: 'Our short-term goal is to double the annual number of foreign visitors and tourist expenditures … by 1994' (SECTUR, 1990). Through *Mundo Maya*, the whole region was slated for a surge in visitation.

Despite the contradictions, all the rhetoric of ecotourism accompanied *Mundo Maya*. Member countries maintained that the overall thrust would be tourism paying for archaeological restoration and ecological conservation (SECTUR, 1991, 1992). Their sales pitch cast the Maya as partners.[16] What went unsaid was governments' desire to buy peace, or portray it, in zones rich in 'resources' – for example, the Petén and Lacandón.

Mexico's status as a 'mega-diversity' country attracted immediate support for *Mundo Maya*, as did the elaborate promises of community participation. In 1989, the European Economic Community (EEC) provided the initial feasibility study; it then committed US$1 million for a second phase of feasibility studies during 1991–1992. Further marketing guidance came from the World Tourism Organization (WTO-OMT). Thus, marketing for *Mundo Maya* was in full gear shortly after it had been endorsed.[17] Problems common in other 'eco' destinations such as the Amazon (Harrington, 1991) soon surfaced. Mass ecotourism took hold, anchored by private mega-projects.[18]

During this period, government partnerships blended a cocktail of international corporate interests. *Mundo Maya* implementation was supposed to be accomplished via the national ecotourism councils (NECs) established under Paseo Pantera (Ashton, 1992a). These stakeholder bodies were largely funded largely by USAID, under its Regional Project for the Management of Natural Resources. However, during 1992 the WTO-OMT announced a separate set of NECs, under its own Conservation Strategy for Central America. In this mêlée, implementation fell directly to the private sector, as intended (OMM, 1991; SECTUR, 1992).

Environmental groups assumed a lead role in *Mundo Maya* by making land available for it. NGOs perceived as 'local', like Friends of the Forest and Defenders of Nature, called for a major expansion of Guatemala's parks. Their campaign coincided with efforts by CI in the US and its global peers to arrange 'debt for nature' swaps.[19] Before long, international NGOs were prominent in the management of regional parks. WWF-International and TNC both became involved in Guatemala's National Council for Protected Areas; TNC won the contract to prioritize conservation sites for Guatemala (Weinberg, 1991).

Funders large and small played a role in *Mundo Maya* straying from its conceptual foundation. A number of programme 'partners' such as USAID, the Inter-American Foundation and the Rodale Institute claimed to have Maya participation at their 'eco-development' sites.[20] But only 3 of 23 such projects in regional protected areas were found to effectively involve communities. Overall, programming and recommendations tended to be self-referencing.[21] Many NGOs guiding the NECs were too stuck on conservation ideology to serve local communities (Ashton, 1992b).

During *Mundo Maya* consultations, neither Maya customary authorities nor targeted Maya communities had a voice (Faust, 1993). No influential NGOs put their clout to supporting the Maya. This was a foreboding start for a programme allegedly committed to community participation. Brochures presenting the 'colourful and friendly' people (INGUAT, 1991) clashed with the daily brutality of regional human rights abuses. Maya protests at archaeological attractions such as Cobá more than hinted that things were amiss (Daltabuit and Pi-Sunyer, 1990).

> **BOX 7.5** **Reason to blush**
>
> One of the deepest ironies … in the ecotourism discussion is the simultaneous romanticization and devastation of Mayan Indian culture. As with conventional tourism … the Indians are seen as a major asset… Yet, these same people are the targets of a consistent policy of ethnocide… It's rather surreal to talk about ecotourism in a country where the people … are essentially in a state of permanent enslavement.
>
> (Gardner, 1991, p30)

The *Mundo Maya* encore

In January 2003, the Mundo Maya Sustainable Tourism Programme was re-launched at the headquarters of the Inter-American Development Bank (IADB) in Washington, DC. It had the same marketing spiel: preserving and showcasing the Mayan heritage. But it came with a bigger swirl of players. In a globalized economy, it is the players who should be watched. Place to place, their programme stamp becomes noticeable.

Like its predecessor, this reborn *Mundo Maya* is pushed largely by American interests. During 2002, the IADB and two neighbouring NGOs – CI and Counterpart International – made a joint presentation to the *Organización Mundo Maya* (OMM). Their sales pitch, reminiscent of Wilbur Garrett's 1988 proposal, stressed the global significance of regional biodiversity. But once again, it coincided with far-reaching, contradictory plans for industrialization of the Petén and Lacandón. Again, it came on the heels of incompatible human rights embarrassments, such as the failed 2001 *Indian Rights Law* of Mexico. In 2003, the year that the IADB announced its US$150 million investment plan for 'eco' tourism and 'conservation' in *Mundo Maya*, Indigenous leaders from Latin America protested outside the IADB headquarters.

Counterpart International (2004) describes *Mundo Maya* as a precedent-setting 'new and innovative sustainable tourism development project'. However, the refurbished version looks remarkably unchanged. This time, *guarantees* for the participation of the Maya were added, including micro-enterprise. But the new Mundo Maya Alliance elevates the role of NGOs, *not* of the namesake Indigenous Peoples. *Mundo Maya* design and implementation is being guided by a trio of influential NGOs from Washington, DC.[22]

Mundo Maya is like a clock; its value is not the face but the workings behind. In 2001, Mexico resurrected its mega-resorts approach to tourism development, targeting pristine beaches. In 2003, the US hosted preliminary talks on the *Central American Free Trade Agreement*. A decade earlier, *Mundo Maya* had identical goalposts: mass tourism and trade liberalization were the real goals. So who are the silent partners? Why do they do such shady business?

It turns out that the IADB is dabbling in *Mundo Maya* while hurrying along grander industrial schemes. In 2001, the IADB and partners directed US$4 billion toward *Plan Puebla Panama* (PPP): a blueprint of 'arteries for global trade and development' (Weinberg, 2003). Although it provides for 300 'bio-reserves' and loans to 'Indigenous ecotourism projects', the Maya were not party to the decisions. Many observers say that PPP will turn the region into 'a corporate extraction paradise' (Zinn, 2002), causing vast displacement of Maya communities (see www.acerca.org) and further violent repression (Kinane, 2002). In October 2002, there were Indigenous demonstrations against PPP across Mexico and Central America (Brosnan, 2002). The Garífunas in Honduras spoke out against 'eco' tourism in solidarity with the Maya (Flores, 2002). In 2005 the Garífunas issued a statement singling out the IADB and World Bank for their role in perpetuating poverty through such schemes; and for their practice of buying off select Indigenous 'leaders' for the sake of this 'economic globalization' (Flores, 2005).

Next of kin to PPP is the Mesoamerican Biological Corridor (MBC), launched in 1997. This initiative, a US$6 billion project of the World Bank and its public/private 'partners', has made promises comparable to and complementing *Mundo Maya*. Its stated goals include the protection of cultural patrimony and traditional knowledge. While some efforts at community participation were made with the assistance of WWF-International (Rivera et al, 2002), the Maya were not properly informed or engaged in any decisions. Most 'have no idea that they're part of a bio-corridor' (Weinberg, 2003, p49). Ground 'partnerships' and 'co-management' exercises are dominated by conservation NGOs. In the aftermath, Mayan groups are denouncing ecotourism (Weiner, 2003).

To many, *Mundo Maya*, PPP and the MBC are partners in crime. Although researchers know that remaining pristine areas in the region lie primarily within Maya ancestral territories and forced resettlement lands (Rivera et al, 2002), displacement and bloodshed are still openly accepted. More than ever, there is an aggressive, strategic interest in regional oil. Corporate bioprospecting is also proceeding unchecked. Several blistering exposés have publicized who is behind the transgressions and how ecotourism plays into resource acquisition. CI, for example, is accused of supporting 'militarized conservation' (Weinberg, 2003, p51), brokering paltry 'benefit-sharing' agreements with Indigenous Peoples and turning Indigenous Peoples against one another (Choudry, 2003, p19).

Now that Mexico and its Central American partners have turned to ecotourism for protected areas financing (CCAD, 2003, p34), the cover-up of associated Indigenous rights violations is thickening. The United Nations Environment Programme (UNEP) is partnering with the United Nations Educational, Scientific and Cultural Organization's (UNESCO's) World

Heritage Centre to link biodiversity conservation and 'sustainable tourism'; three of their six global sites are in *Mundo Maya*. UNESCO, meanwhile, has made OMM a partner in its World Heritage Tourism Programme, alongside the National Geographic Society. Some observers say that these recent partnerships are 'draping business in the blue flag of the UN, adding the blue dye to green washing' (Iyer, 2004, p10).

The UN's choice to enter these industry partnerships, despite Mundo Maya's historical disrepute, is reinforcing 'business as usual'. While Maya-owned tourism programmes such as *Maya Ik* and *Maya Lu'um* have evolved to counter *Mundo Maya* exploitation, corporate-style NGOs (based in the US) and like-minded 'conservationists' continue to grip regional ecotourism:

- CI (2003) reports that its Washington DC team of NGOs developed the regional sustainable tourism strategy.
- TNC completed the tourism management plan for Sierra del Lacandón National Park in Guatemala.
- RARE Center for Tropical Conservation (US) developed the Mesoamerican Ecotourism Alliance to partner conservationists and eco-tour companies.
- Archaeologist Richard Hansen of the University of California at Los Angeles (UCLA) has promoted Mirador Basin National Monument, proposing infrastructure for 80,000 visitors a year (Buettner, 2003).

Ironically, as RARE develops promotional materials for nature destinations 'seldom seen by most tourists' (see www.rarecenter.org) and The National

---

BOX 7.6 Proper protocol

As a coalition, Indigenous Peoples of Latin America have begun to address some of the serious issues around 'partnerships'. Their message to non-governmental organizations (NGOs) attending the Brundtland Commission hearings was:

> We are concerned about the 'debt for nature swaps' which put your organizations in a position of negotiating with our governments for the future of our homelands... While we appreciate your efforts on our behalf, we want to make it clear that we never delegated any power of representation to the environmental community or organization within that community... We propose that you work directly with our organizations on all your programmes and campaigns which affect our homelands.
> (*Cultural Survival Quarterly*, 1991, p28)

Geographic Society scouts for new archaeological destinations to commercialize (Berman, 2003), other NGOs and private consultancies are being called upon to mitigate the impacts of rapid tourism expansion in Mundo Maya (see www.coralcay.org).

Amid this organized chaos, the business partners of *Mundo Maya* remain faithful to the idea of ecotourism covering both its own blemishes, as well as the indiscretions of other industries. Its pivotal partners are now promoting similar 'pro-poor' industrial ecotourism in other Indigenous territories worldwide. Who made them the global authority on 'development' and 'conservation'? What gives them permission to put Indigenous Peoples, life systems and all of us in further jeopardy for the sake of economic growth?

Conclusion

It is time to release the idea that 'eco' tourism involves any flavour of personal bond between industry groups and community. This is a marketing gimmick, with no foundation except those rare, visionary cases of matchmaking where a truly special connection happens. Most conservation economics is about wringing profit from endangered life systems and heritage, not salvaging an intact future while we still can.

While the vocabulary of industry constantly changes, business practices remain steady. The ecotourism industry illustrates this better than any other. Apathy towards Indigenous Peoples remains strong despite all the partnership rhetoric. Partnership champions are prone to micro-managing their own interests. Most sway to the economics of hobnobbing, showcasing and the middle ground, guarding their spot at the funding trough.

Through the ecotourism industry, we get a full view of industrial-style 'sustainability'. After decades of fancy talk about ecotourism, there is still no sign of any industry (or consumer society) decision to eschew exploitation – be it social, cultural, ecological or spiritual. The majority of partnering is attempted in the midst of market-condoned exploitation. Partnerships conceived in this dialogue climate *hurt* people.

Behind these serious inequities of ecotourism there are lessons. While industry interests are ruled by economic sustainability, most Indigenous economies are distinctly organic in how they move. Traditional Indigenous economies have heart, embrace the welfare of others and are self-correcting. This sounds a little flaky to those of us whose first language is industrial-style economics (in other words, 'every man for himself'). Especially if sacred knowledge is brought into the picture. However, we should dig deeper for understanding.

Today, the reality is that both the ecotourism industry and Indigenous Peoples are experiencing a crisis in how to reconcile their identity with economics. Companies, NGOs and consultants like to think of partnerships with Indigenous Peoples as a form of prior informed consent, not conventional deal brokering. Indigenous Peoples, meanwhile, find it painful to see consumerism uprooting many of their own communities. In dialogue, the two might spring apart if not for the heavy marketing of partnership itself.

Unfortunately, most critiques of partnership stop here, giving the impression that a group retreat, mediated negotiations or role playing might help to bring common ground. But the impediment to creating real partnerships is not structural or procedural. It is inside *you and me*, those whom governments brainwash into being 'consumers'. Ultimately, we provide the consent for business standards, industry to industry.

The challenge is to become more disciplined, not as just consumers but as guardians of our own destiny. Whether a professional, tradesperson, activist or homemaker, we have in common many social filters. It is us (not industry) who makes a pact with target communities, setting global terms of trade. So, when we say 'don't pass the buck', are we avoiding liability or embracing integrity? Spiritually, these night and day choices differ greatly.

To reach peace in our own self, we need to re-evaluate our level of thinking. Any dialogue that becomes polarized (for example, self-centred, competitive, protective or judgemental) blinds us to our shared life umbilical cord. Today, we consumers live in this polarity, mesmerized by the latest colonial lifestyle perks. From this place the path towards relationship-building and legitimate partnerships demands introspection. It is time to:

- *Contemplate the true meaning of a service economy.* Are we in service to ourselves or others? Serving others means being entrusted and staying trustworthy. It is a relationship based upon full disclosure and mutual consent, free of ego and malice.
- *Find our real common ground.* Today, we are so enmeshed in defining relationships economically that we live in a state of divorce. We no longer know how we are connected to each other, spiritually or within life systems.
- *Open ourselves to more expansive possibilities.* In this era, many Indigenous leaders worldwide are working for unity. In spiritual terms, unity means respect for the knowledge of connection. Each life and life decision has a great ripple of impact.
- *Choose generosity over greed.* Each of us has the power to create beauty and call people home. Partnerships that are healthy for the people involved will be good for the Earth and a spiritual ladder for all humanity.

Recommended reading

- Chapin, M. (2004) 'A Challenge to conservationists', *World Watch*, vol 17, no 6, November/December, pp17–31
- Choudry, A. (2003) 'Privatizing nature, plundering biodiversity', *Seedling*, Journal of Genetic Resources Action International (GRAIN), Barcelona, October, pp17–21
- Iyer, S. R. (2004) 'Global compact: Summit and counter-summit', *Third World Resurgence*, vol 167/168, July/August, pp9–13
- Ottaway, D. B. and Stephens, J. (2003) 'Inside The Nature Conservancy: Non profit land bank amasses billions', *Washington Post*, 4 May, pA1
- Weinberg, B. (2003) 'The battle for Montes Azules: Conservation as counterinsurgency in the Chiapas rainforest', *Native Americas*, spring, pp40–53

Figure 7.2 **The 'Wooden Indian' who shows up in tourist quarters world wide to meet and greet tourists (here in Dominican Republic)**

Figure 7.3 **Brawny 'Indian Chief' welcomes tourists to the Amsterdam flower market, The Netherlands**

Chapter 8

Accommodating Indigenous Rights

**Genocide includes the laws, policies and practices designed
to eliminate our cultures.**

*(Eli Mandamin, International Institute for Peace Through Tourism
(IIPT) Conference, Scotland, 1999)*

Indigenous rights are alien to the corporate world. Their collective and spiritual nature fundamentally counters industrial economics. Given this, industry tends to shrug off Indigenous Peoples' communiqués as antiquated, unrealistic or radical thinking. This has far-reaching consequences for our immediate 'biodiversity crisis'. It is difficult to forge bridges of communication on sustainability when one 'side' sees no reason, need or basis for connection. Industry will litigate for its own short-term interests, though we all sit on the same life team.

Globally, government and industry have resisted appeals for the accommodation of Indigenous rights. Even so, Indigenous Peoples' revived political and economic presence is affecting commerce. They are now vocal across the United Nations (UN) and at the World Trade Organization (WTO). Their persistent lobbying of international bodies and their articulate submissions on sustainability have created an impetus for dialogue. Even in countries where human rights violations are endemic, business interests detect this change.

Consultation of Indigenous Peoples is increasing, though rarely as a voluntary practice. It is undertaken when government or industry feel cornered and need a public relations makeover. While many countries have ignored or directly perpetrated commercial violations of Indigenous rights, less political cover exists today. Globalization is biting back at the corporate world. As our consumer markets flood with excess, there is a corresponding depletion of life systems. If corporate media fail to warn us of the brewing chaos, information seeps in on the air currents. The Inuit in the Arctic, for example, are experiencing the worst of industrial toxins and climate change.[1] Industry infringement of human rights and collective ancestral rights is visible in the biosphere – if not by the lack of simple decency between peoples.

Negotiations with Indigenous Peoples, recently unthinkable to colonial regimes and their trade partners, are becoming a feature of the global economy.[2] Every industry has its own cases of community engagement; each is grasping for ways to limit local entanglement. But the new etiquette of global trade requires an appearance of reconciliation.[3] Internationally and nationally, public policy is addressing Indigenous Peoples. It is a sign that the financial stakes of biodiversity are high; the goal is to ward off conflict so that business is unimpeded.

In the tourism industry, like other economic sectors, we are stuck in unproductive patterns of communication about what is sustainable. We need to pull out of this now. No dialectic will restore balance if we continue to neglect relationship-building. It is relationships, and daily economic transactions comprising these relationships, that define our humanity and success. So, are we sincere about learning how to restructure the economy for balance and respectful interchange? Or are consultation and negotiations simply our way of convincing Indigenous Peoples to forsake their cultures, sacred knowledge, ancestral territories and Mother Earth?

BOX 8.1   The self-government mirage

Self-government and self-determination are worlds apart. Self-determination is the fundamental right of Indigenous Peoples under international law. However, most governments like to shift the dialogue to self-government instead in order to preserve economic sovereignty. Self-government means consenting to become the Indigenous figurehead of an essentially colonial programme.

Consultation

Indigenous Peoples' experiences of consultation

In both governance and business, there is a vast difference between calling the shots and making decisions. Calling the shots is what happens in a situation of exploitation. It can take place behind all sorts of façades, including consultation. You simply design a consultation process that follows the rules of business (for example, industry timelines; a written paper trail, not oral record-keeping; predominance of lawyers and 'experts'). This enables selective intake of critiques from Indigenous Peoples. Submissions that fall outside established mandates and procedures can be discreetly set aside.

Globally, Indigenous Peoples' experiences with consultation have been negative. Whether consultations focus on economy, environment and/or heritage,
the methodology is essentially one and the same. All are fixed on corporate
interests – namely, on investment certainty and economic growth. For this reason, government and industry portrayals of consultation seldom bear resem-
blance to locally reported impacts of consultation on Indigenous rights. While
governments promote consultation as something progressive, many Indigenous
leaders regard it as a tool for the *extinguishment* of rights. Why? Because governments are known to deliberately confuse rights and interests (Tenckhoff, 1999).
Obligations to Indigenous Peoples are dodged by elaborating new laws and
policies, which are subtle yet forceful in effect.

Today, there is a proliferation of public- and private-sector consultations offering funded participation to select Indigenous Peoples. Often the
funding is billed as capacity-building in order to secure buy-in. However, its
purpose is to channel Indigenous Peoples into the corporate/consumer fold.
When Indigenous Peoples try to create latitude within such a process, they
normally find it stacked against them. Like the lottery and casino, there will
be occasional 'wins'; but this is merely tactical – designed to keep everyone at
the table. In time, most Indigenous participants come to see consultation as a
silencing exercise rather than as platform for dialogue: 'We go blue in the face
repeating ourselves.'

Many Indigenous leaders watching the historical rounds of 'Indian'
policy see consultation as a continuum. First, religion and alcohol were used
by world economic powers to make their communities pliant; now money is
the dominant force (Leach, 2003). Government architects of consultation,
of course, react with indignation at this comparison. But most consultation
serves to divide, conquer and impoverish, just like previous colonial handouts. The only difference with money added to the equation is that the impoverishment is spiritual. As before, government intent is to smooth the way
for industrialization.

For these reasons, consultation has stirred anxiety among many
Indigenous elders. Several personally remember the course of colonial genocide
or heard their grandparents' stories. To them, it is offensive to see Indigenous
rights framed as interests or demands and forced through a process of 'claims'.
Consultation is just another colonial policy developed by government word-
smiths. One old matriarch has instructed Indigenous leadership: 'Don't take
any money; it's chicken feed for chickens' (Smith, 1975). Internationally, more
and more Elders are encouraging leaders to directly exercise their Peoples'
ancestral title on the land, and to demonstrate the sacred connection between
rights and responsibilities.

Nevertheless, some Indigenous leaders find consultation to be a difficult form of economic integration to resist. Internally, they face extreme

post-colonial poverty in their communities. Externally, they bump into the democratic ideals (and pressure) associated with consultation, which persist in public opinion regardless of how unlawful policies towards Indigenous Peoples become. Neither are easy histories to resolve. The real darkness of colonialism, especially the extent of genocide (*millions upon millions* exterminated for the sake of colonial fortunes), has been hidden for so long that many think those with a memory are just sore losers, or griping instead of getting industrious. But it is another sick twist to suggest that 'getting even' financially will heal.

There are long outstanding questions for us all to ponder with respect to industrial-style economics, colonialism and development ideology. How far are we willing to ply consumerism today? When will we, the citizens, decide to act in good faith? What will it take for us to get an accurate world picture?

BOX 8.2 False consultation

False consultation is like an abusive relationship. The abuser decides to host a forum to discuss grievances. Out of this arise principles for reparations (for example, sustainable development). Arrangements are then made by the abuser to compensate the victim through more of the same (namely, economic growth). In the closing act, the victim is supposed to seek feedback (for instance, technical support) so that they can become an abuser. Anyone objecting to this process is told that the scars (including poverty) are their own fault. They are told that if only they would cooperate, the benefits of the dysfunction would be theirs. This is how the abuser obtains licence for more of the same. It is a powerful psychological process mingling honeymoon moments (such as consultation) with extreme forms of control. Indigenous Peoples call this 'business as usual'.

Tourism industry consultation

Tourism disasters such as the Banaue Rice Terraces in the Philippines have become a convincing reason for consultation. Most Ifugao face increased hardship despite the usual promises of poverty relief (Malanes, 1999). Culture loss has been particularly devastating. Looking at Banaue and Machu Picchu in Peru alone – both United Nations Educational, Scientific and Cultural Organization (UNESCO) World Heritage Sites – it is clear that industry must do its best to look contrite.

The tourism industry is a relative newcomer to consultation in Indigenous territories. This can be an opportunity or liability. If the industry chooses an ethic of relationship-building, there may be ground for timely learning; if it carries on ignoring Indigenous rights or pursuing false consultation, there will be unprecedented conflict. Indigenous Elders have already seen the gamut of industrial consultation. Patience is wearing thin, especially now that ecotourism puts culture itself up for tender.

Thus far, consultations with Indigenous Peoples in the tourism industry are indistinguishable in format and results from other industries (for example, forests, petroleum, mining, hydroelectric, agriculture, fisheries or pharmaceuticals). Ecotourism is no exception. Industry wide, marketing usually still precedes appropriate local consent and community planning. Governments are at the front and centre of this market development. Many have a tourism ministry equipped with full-scale promotional machinery, which sets the pace. As such, most initial consultations have damaged trust.

The tourism industry, now embarking on standards and certification, should take a good look at ethics for the consultation of Indigenous Peoples. The mere existence of consultation does not signal a departure from exploitative practices; nor does a new industry brand like 'ecotourism' or policy talks on 'sustainable' tourism. Neither do critiques of consultation performed by industry connected groups which are known to perpetrate self-serving consultation.[4] Either there is a collective shift in economic practice or system-wide restructuring is still required.

Indigenous Peoples are providing consistent feedback to the various global industries on consultations with respect to sustainable use. The tourism industry, the world's largest and fastest growing industry, should take these warnings to heart. Consultation as we know it puts us all at unacceptable risk, because there are no reliable filters on economic growth. Sacred life systems are caving in because our governments have abbreviated life as 'biodiversity', open for commercial consultation and sale.

Community participation in ecotourism

Community participation is a basic premise of ecotourism. Little has advanced in the discourse on participation since the 1980s. Normally, those articulating community needs with the most sincerity and resolve receive the least institutional support.

Community participation is understood by government and development agencies as diligence towards target communities. It is a 'catch-all' term applied to poverty and environment programming, which primarily takes the form of reporting. When community submissions are invited, the forms of input welcome are so intellectually constrained that most Indigenous cultural contributions are lost on involved professionals, 'experts' and business interests. There is no space for sacred knowledge in policy, programmes or activities. Following such consultations, participating Indigenous Peoples are no closer to considering themselves constituency or partner. The proposed 'development' normally marches forward anyhow, showcased as another stakeholder 'success'.

In the ecotourism industry countries, corporations and non-governmental organizations (NGOs) alike are mastering the lingo of community participation. Community participation can be a golden key to funding or licensing. Some destination countries and regions, such as Mundo Maya in Central America, have successfully featured Indigenous Peoples in their applications for development assistance. Many companies and NGOs, meanwhile, have won government concessions because they offer to get communities on side. Yet, little programming, product development or national branding ever originates from or serves the target communities. Tribal authorities are usually consulted *after* the germinal analysis and decision-making.

Recently, there have been calls to redress this shortcoming of industry. At the World Ecotourism Summit (WES) in 2002, many regional reports on ecotourism (for example, Africa and South Asia, where Indigenous rights are still openly dismissed) identified the need to better address local community needs and to ensure real community participation. They revealed an ongoing lack of meaningful consultation. NGOs such as Indigenous Tourism Rights International (ITRI) and the Ecumenical Coalition on Tourism (ECOT) brought this to life with clear examples. Indigenous delegates, though sparse, emphasized the rarity of prior informed consent (PIC) worldwide.

Identification of such problems will test policy-makers to the core. The notion of community participation is another colonial offshoot. Where industry markets Indigenous territories, Indigenous Peoples are circumstantially involved from day one. Most are seeking to exercise their ancestral title (that is, their rights and responsibilities) – including the right, and perhaps responsibility, to say 'no' to tourism. Community participation is thus a misnomer. Although promising, it is simply a clever addition to development ideology. International law on the rights of Peoples speaks to *self-determination*, not automatic integration in the global economy community by community.

Today there is intense debate over consultation, which some see as growing pains with respect to 'process' and which others see as strategic stalling (Johnston, 2000). A number of biodiversity professionals now maintain that 'To ensure full participation in decision-making, we need to vest locals with decision-making authority' (McNeely, 1999). However, Indigenous Peoples *already* hold authority under their own customary law, which is recognized under international law. Governments cannot give back authority which Indigenous Peoples never relinquished. They can only accommodate what exists: ancestral title and its notion of sacred guardianship.

We need to do more than acknowledge the gap between the theory and practice of ecotourism. It is time to expose where ecotourism theory is fundamentally misguided vis-à-vis Indigenous Peoples. We must be willing to say exactly how ecotourism theory is abused to circumvent international law on Indigenous rights.

> **BOX 8.3** **Perspective from 'paradise'**
>
> Tourism is deeply rooted in a history of colonization and unequal relations between people and regions… [Its] supposed benefits … have not 'trickled down' or benefited Indigenous Peoples. The destructiveness … has brought great harm to many Indigenous Peoples and communities around the world. We have heard of many government bodies, international environmental treaties and other policies as they are made about 'sustainable tourism'; yet, Indigenous Peoples have not been invited to participate effectively in these policies which will have negative consequences for the rest of time.
>
> (Siosiua Po'oi Pohiv, Human Rights and Democracy Movement, Tonga, International Indigenous Forum on Biodiversity, Workshop on Tourism, *UN Convention on Biological Diversity*, Malaysia, 2004)

The stakeholder approach

Background

Consultation is usually associated with a stakeholder process. It initially became widespread as a form of environmental impact assessment. The first step for a project proponent is to advertise its intentions. Community receptivity is then tested through vehicles such as development plans, open houses and public forums. Typically, the review period lasts from six weeks to a few months. Over this time frame, domestic (in other words, colonial) legal requirements for project planning are satisfied. Often, this is considered enough to assuage or sideline 'detractors'.

Consultation would be described more aptly as a phase of marketing than as dialogue. Impressive reports, presentations and road shows are prepared. Public relations are finessed. The task is to convert doubters into believers. Casting potential opponents as 'stakeholders' is an integral part of this product packaging. Indigenous Peoples are told all the reasons why they supposedly need the proposed industry development. They are pressed to cash in their allotted meal ticket, as if feeding themselves is not an option.

Stakeholder consultation is a highly contentious topic between world governments and Indigenous Peoples. A stakeholder approach negates not only Indigenous land rights, but by extension Indigenous Peoples' broader footing in international law. While this is an obvious impediment to dialogue, governments rarely concede any negligence or breach of trust. Instead, there has been a concerted effort to make stakeholder consultation the international standard for dialogue with Indigenous Peoples.

In international deliberations on sustainable development, including 'sustainable' tourism, many countries, inter-government institutions and allied groups are collaborating to push stakeholder processes. Some of the involved countries know full well the damage this will do to Indigenous Peoples worldwide. Nonetheless, there is an economic pact to sow stakeholder consultation. The United Nations Environment Programme's (UNEP's) Biodiversity Planning Support Programme has promoted national stakeholder plans. Both The International Ecotourism Society (TIES) and Conservation International (CI) facilitate stakeholder-driven national ecotourism plans, country to country. As well, stakeholder consultation is now being streamlined into protected areas via the Tour Operators Initiative of UNEP, UNESCO and the World Tourism Organization (WTO-OMT).

In the larger picture, stakeholder consultation is a barrier to learning about sustainable use. Its ground rules lead to stunted dialogue with Indigenous Peoples. When will the 'key players' in the ecotourism industry wake up to the damage caused?[5] When will it be recognized that stakeholder approaches muzzle Indigenous Peoples, limit their self-determination and diminish cultural diversity?

Application to biodiversity

The emphasis on stakeholder consultation is increasing now that biodiversity is big business. In 2000, the World Wide Fund for Nature (WWF-International) issued its famous map showing the concentration of global biodiversity in Indigenous Peoples' ancestral territories. Governments are well aware of this spatial distribution of 'natural capital'. According to Canada, Indigenous Peoples hold the bulk of remaining world resources inside their territories (Chandler, 2003). Governments are eager to secure access with minimal red tape (that is, 'Indian' interference).

Increasingly, the public and private sectors are uniting to preserve free enterprise in Indigenous territories. Capitalism is defined in the *Oxford Dictionary* as business entities organizing and producing 'for their own profit'. In a colonial context, 'free' enterprise means doing business without properly negotiated conditions, such as cultural sustainability or equitable payment of royalties to Indigenous Peoples. But now, free trade politics require a modicum of lip service to local participation. Stakeholder consultation provides industry with the social licence for economic growth.

Under the *UN Convention on Biological Diversity* (CBD), governments have invited the private sector on board for implementation. Higher in the UN there is the Global Compact Initiative, welcoming the major world corporations (see Iyer, 2004). These alliances between the public and private sectors are causing unease among many Indigenous leaders, who equate it to the 'fox in the henhouse'. Nonetheless, most policy consultations on sustainability are being shaped according to industry imperatives. Through consultation, industry itself is determining what are 'affordable' local costs and benefits.

In government forums on biodiversity, stakeholder consultation is the accepted mode of problem-solving. Scientists and other 'managers' within environment bureaucracies are promoting stakeholder dialogue as if it is non-partisan. The general view is: 'We need to identify the stimulus for bringing together all the various stakeholders' (McNeely, 1999). Among involved professionals, this often distils down to immense peer pressure. Submissions must be sufficiently non-offensive, non-controversial and non-threatening or invitations to contribute will be withheld or revoked.

Indigenous Peoples are far from dispassionate (the corporate world would say 'professional') about stakeholder consultation and its effect on their cultures, traditional governance systems and ancestral territories. Many Indigenous leaders see participation in a stakeholder process as tantamount to denouncing their Peoples' rights. In order to understand why, we must look at the basic premises of the stakeholder approach.

Stakeholder dialogue is open to invited or self-identified 'interest' groups. In theory, all of these groups enter on level footing – that is, with equal opportunity to be heard. However, this levelling is problematic in the context of Indigenous rights. It presumes that Indigenous Peoples (millennial custodians holding ancestral title) can be slotted into land-use consultations alongside those who want to reap (some say rape) profits from their territory. Would anyone holding fee simple 'private' land title accept this arrangement if the table was turned? Under the present system, groups such as Consumers International (advocating for *consumers*) are intervening in CBD talks on 'traditional knowledge'.

Indigenous leaders have seen their Peoples' rights and responsibilities compromised in a number of consultation scenarios. Consultation can rapidly destroy bio-cultural diversity if it:

- facilitates industrial access or development in a culturally or ecologically sensitive area (for example, 'protected' areas);
- commences without invitation by, or consensus with, the affected Indigenous People(s);
- occurs under the auspices of a stakeholder, such as an NGO, who subjugates rights holders;
- lumps together rights holders with stakeholders (for instance, with industry, development agencies, NGOs and/or consultants);
- accords certain stakeholders or 'experts' a special consultative or advisory status over and above Indigenous People(s);
- allows industry or its agent (including government) to appoint the chairperson, adjudicator or rapporteur;

- sports a token Indigenous 'co-chair' rather than a rights-based protocol agreement on the dialogue process;
- involves consultants hired unilaterally without the full involvement and agreement of Indigenous People(s);
- rushes ahead without first resolving capacity imbalances that could impair the legitimacy of consultations;
- creates a paper trail suggesting due diligence, where meaningful consultation has yet to occur.

All of these scenarios are a sign of conflict of interest, and likely industry bias, in consultations.

BOX 8.4 | **Consultation Shortcuts**

Government and industry like to get on with business. They typically fund a few select organizations and individuals for consultations, essentially predetermining the outcomes. This is common at the United Nations (UN). Certain people are touted as 'experts', while Indigenous leaders at large must vie for an opportunity to simply attend. When participation is based on quotas and 'handouts' instead of rights, the consultation is staged. There are no safeguards for cultural diversity.

Consultation with integrity

Some uncomfortable truths

Many a consultation with Indigenous Peoples goes off track in its process. There are two main reasons why these processes go sideways. The first is that consulting agencies and institutions exclude Indigenous Peoples (especially mandated or customary Indigenous leadership) from process design. The second is that consultation itself has become an industry. It is not just government, industry or NGO consultants (for example, 'experts' and lawyers) who profit from consultation, but also individuals within advocacy groups who learn how to play the system.

Among some NGOs, including Indigenous organizations, there are individuals who are savvy about tapping into the financial benefits of consultation. These individuals often feed off others who do 'hands-on' community work in order to create an air of expertise. They then market themselves to consultation agencies as 'go-betweens', community representatives or Indigenous authorities. Some end up holding the purse strings for consultation or for Indigenous Peoples' involvement in consultations.

NGO representatives with interests aligned to the consultations can be particularly susceptible to impropriety. Governments, development agencies and industry like to turn to NGOs for 'one-stop' consultation or as a shortcut to Indigenous outreach. While some consulted individuals ignorantly tread into unproductive roles with respect to Indigenous representation, others are looking to wield influence.

Indigenous NGOs often face the most demands regarding consultation. Pressure is put on them to be something they are not. They are approached by government and industry as a proxy for formal Indigenous leadership. This opens room for misjudgement among inexperienced NGO staff. Some agree to provide technical input in political forums, not realizing that their role becomes political and, thus, undermines Indigenous rights.

Nevertheless, Indigenous Peoples are not immune to misconduct by individuals. Some recognized Indigenous leaders have commented on the opportunism by some so-called Indigenous 'representatives' and its damage to rights.[6] Individual abuses have included:

- criticizing yet personally benefiting from stakeholder processes;
- creating a monopoly on consultation by plugging information on key international processes concerning 'biodiversity';
- forming cliques that reinforce personal roles as Indigenous 'representatives' or Indigenous 'experts';
- capitalizing on the hierarchy of knowledge and science in government consultations on sustainable use.

Often, there is a reluctance among witness Indigenous organizations to denounce peer behaviour because of their dependency upon some alleged 'leaders' for funding and for introductions. While consulting agencies say that such disputes are internal matters for Indigenous Peoples to resolve, most in fact cultivate this individualism.

Some Indigenous spokespersons argue that 'full and effective participation comes down to dollars' (Fortier, 1998) – that is, larger consultation budgets. Others go further and say the funding must reach *mandated* representatives: Indigenous leadership recognized under cultural protocols. However, most agree that consultation of Indigenous Peoples is crippled before it even gets started. Sadly, false consultation has become the norm (see Box 8.2).

Today, most consultation of Indigenous Peoples is an elevated form of programme delivery. This differs fundamentally from consultation that allows dialogue and mutual learning. Our task ahead is to regain humility. Without respect and tolerance for sacred knowledge, there is no such thing as real consultation, let alone integrated management.

It must be realized by government, industry and their 'partner' NGOs that current methods of consultation do not serve any of us in the long term. Ultimately, we all live in the same house and are sustained by the same life-lines. We therefore need to look at consultation itself as a sustainability issue. If current processes do not deliver or reasonably promise truly sustainable use, plus healthy (and healing) relationships, it is time to retool.

BOX 8.5 Manipulation through NGOs

Colonial governments have encouraged Indigenous Peoples and persons of Indigenous heritage to organize as non-governmental organizations (NGOs) in order to create a non-threatening platform for Indigenous participation. This is expedited through funding mechanisms. It has led to rampant abuse of NGO status in government forums on sustainability. Organizations that are quali-fied to give technical input only are being recruited for political functions (that is, 'Indigenous' representation). The result is a misleading pool of policy, pro-grammes and activities – with an appearance of Indigenous Peoples' consulta-tion and support. Government and institutional partnerships often showcase these 'successes' in order to reinforce the gains. Before long there is a formida-ble paper trail for Indigenous leaders to undo.

Housekeeping matters

The ambiguity existing between NGOs and Indigenous Peoples needs to be cleared. Government policy slotting Indigenous Peoples as non-government entities – and funders' strictures on granting or lending to Indigenous Peoples (for example, their non-recognition of ancestral land rights) – have led to a crop of Indigenous NGOs. The NGO designation can be highly problematic with respect to Indigenous rights. It is time to look at this more literally, in the context of governance, and to understand how it plays into false consulta-tion. In some world regions, especially Africa and Asia, Indigenous Peoples may need to adopt NGO status to avoid government persecution. In others, Indigenous community groups legitimately need a vehicle to fundraise. But here the discussion is on misuse.

Many NGOs push positions and programmes that are damaging to Indigenous Peoples, especially to proper Indigenous representation. This raises the question of when an organization is merely an NGO, versus when it represents Indigenous Peoples or has authority to speak concerning ances-tral lands. There are NGOs (and NGO spokespersons) serving in the name of Indigenous Peoples as policy advisers on biodiversity, protected areas, tra-ditional knowledge, sacred sites – and other 'sustainability' issues – who are not mandated by cultural protocol to do so. They do not report anywhere other than to colleagues enmeshed in the same mode of work. UN rosters and governments call lists are full of them: those whose inexperience is exploited, as well as those who know enough to step down but choose to stay.

The task of clarifying the line between NGOs and Indigenous Peoples is a shared one. NGOs need to address this housekeeping matter as a community, to curb the widespread abuse of Indigenous 'association' and the misappropriation of funds available for Indigenous capacity-building. Misconduct by organizations known as Indigenous NGOs, however, is more complex and should be referred directly to Indigenous Peoples' mandated leadership. The challenge here is that breaches of protocol occurring nationally or internationally (such as at the UN or affiliated agencies) may continue for some time due to the isolation of affected Indigenous Peoples. This underlines the need to vocally identify the problems and let protocol take its course. The whispering needs to stop.

At the Seventh Conference of the Parties (COP7) to the CBD in Kuala Lumpur, there was a stir concerning Indigenous representation after the tourism dialogue. A strong statement there from Indigenous Peoples, spurred by guidance from Chiefs (see Gavidi et al, 1993), brought government chagrin and caused some Indigenous Caucus members to scatter. In the background, one Indigenous representative, a long-time observer who legitimately represents Indigenous leadership back home, commented on the discord. He noted that many within the Indigenous Caucus (also known as the International Indigenous Forum on Biodiversity, or IIFB) lack any mandate to be there, speaking on behalf of a particular tribe, let alone for Indigenous Peoples of the world. This is an open secret of the CBD that few are willing to go on record about.[7] Few want to talk of the trade-offs behind Article 8(j) on traditional knowledge.

It is incumbent upon governments, development agencies and policy institutions to stop running false consultations, and to embrace dialogue for mutual benefit and understanding. Today, mutual benefit is not an economic concept; it means ensuring adequate shelter for the world's children from the ecological upheaval which we are fast entering. Industrial impacts are so advanced now that even an outright retreat from 'business as usual' would not register in the Earth biosphere for some time. If we do not take an immediate precautionary approach on all fronts, beginning with conscientious dialogue, industry will hand us bleak leftovers for *this* generation of youth. The signs of trials to come are already in the sky. So, let's look up at those airplanes, the pollution and the changing climate with the wonder of a child.

> ### BOX 8.6   Peoples versus communities
>
> In international law, Indigenous Peoples hold collective rights as peoples, not as communities or community groups. 'Peoplehood' is self-defined by their ancestral territory, language and governance system. Forming a non-governmental organization (NGO) – that is, a 'non-government' body – in effect renounces this peoplehood. It helps colonial governments to confuse issues by referring to Indigenous Peoples as communities, ethnic minorities or interest groups – as opposed to collective *rights holders* whose rights must lawfully be accommodated.

Getting there

Releasing old habits

Worldwide, Indigenous leaders concerned about the serious impacts of economic growth, and the tourism industry's lead role, are watching the trend of consultation. It is evident that the next big wave of industry consultations among Indigenous Peoples will concern tourism development. Consultation approaches in policy arenas and other economic sectors foreshadow the path that this is likely to take.

With all the attention accorded to global trade and trade agreements at this point in history, we have a conscious choice now about how future economics unfold. It is especially important to remember this with respect to tourism. The ecotourism industry is about to launch more extensive and more elaborate consultations on 'sustainable use' – that is, industrial access – than ever seen. These consultations will not reflect social issues (for example, recolonization through economic globalization) or ecological constraints (such as Earth thresholds) any better than previous efforts unless there is a principled overhaul of industrial logic.

There are a number of consultation practices to avoid if governments, the tourism industry, individual ecotourism companies or their respective partners and agents (for instance, NGOs) are to have credible dialogue with Indigenous Peoples. These practices, commonplace across all global industries, essentially neutralize consultation. They are techniques for distance and disengagement.

The following consultation practices must cease if cultural and biological diversity are to be safeguarded:

- *Misallocation of consultation funds*: Government, industry and affiliated institutions argue that consultation is proceeding in the best way given budget constraints. However, means and ends are often manipulated. Small consultation budgets are a product of allocation decisions and thus reflect fiscal priorities. Normally, these scant funds are earmarked for Indigenous groups perceived to have an 'objective' grasp of the issues. They go to individuals who will participate without raising too many caveats, such as 'without prejudice' clauses. This practice results in:

- dangerous 'yes' dialogue;
- unfounded consultation 'successes';
- mistrust of the process among Indigenous Peoples;
- predominance of NGOs rather than mandated Indigenous leadership.

- *Courtship of moderates*: linked to the above, there is a tendency in consultation to groom Indigenous figureheads. These individuals are valued for their seeming discretion.[8] Some Indigenous leaders have denounced such 'artificial government paid leadership' and are challenging consultation agencies on their selection criteria (Anderson, 2000). Others are publicizing the 'buyouts'.[9] The practice of hand-picking Indigenous representatives or being otherwise complacent about Indigenous representation results in:

  - race-based as opposed to culture-based (that is, leadership) representation;
  - a false economy, with those endorsing the process rewarded with a salary or repeat contracts;
  - lost capacity, because the same clique is invited to all the different consultation venues;
  - a process that is disconnected from ancestral title, peoplehood and sacred knowledge.

- *Disregard of Indigenous peoplehood and territoriality*: consulting agencies often attempt to involve just one Indigenous individual, group or people in a consultation process. Often, issue-specific NGOs are invited instead of actual Indigenous Peoples because this is more expedient. Or consultations proceed with one-dimensional Indigenous representation, instead of respecting territorial overlaps or all relevant Indigenous governance structures. This practice is illustrated by some political appointments, where named Indigenous 'representatives' speak more on their own personal behalf than for any constituents or informed membership. In these situations of 'one window' consultation, there is no meaningful attempt at due diligence. The results are:

- limited problem-solving potential;
- layers upon layers of work (such as, policy, programmes and activities) lacking foundation;
- deals that break apart once real tribal authorities and constituencies emerge;
- weak precedents for relationship-building.

- *Jumbling of political and technical representation*: the 'fill the slots' approach to consultation gives a wide margin for abuse. Some invited or self-nominated Indigenous 'representatives' are freelancers or NGO technicians who lack any mandate from their own Elders or people.[10] Often, this goes unseen for quite some time at home and among peers due to the long distances and excessive travel involved. Industry and NGOs may be indifferent because 'business as usual' is efficient and profitable. The result is:

  - illegitimate consent for development programmes or specific policy agreements;
  - prolonged self-regulation by industry and its agents;
  - abandonment of the precautionary principle;
  - irretrievable loss of trust once the process is unmasked to representative leadership.

- *Imposition of methodologies*: most industry consultations of Indigenous Peoples take place in boardrooms, hotel rooms, conference halls or community settings made over to simulate corporate environments. Funding agencies have reinforced this meeting pattern by giving preference to Indigenous proposals featuring workshops, conferences, and other training often in urban centres. Through capacity-building programmes, Indigenous Peoples are encouraged to shift into business dialects. These practices result in:

  - assimilation of Indigenous Peoples into conventional economic pursuits;
  - loss of confidence in existing cultural knowledge, due to the new syndrome of 'training';
  - crippling of cultural initiative because everyone is 'programmed';
  - repetition of industry impacts in Indigenous communities and ancestral territories.

> **BOX 8.7** **Shake the shackles**
>
> At the United Nations Working Group on Indigenous Populations in 1999, the Sovereign Union of First Peoples in Australia urged Indigenous organizations to rethink their basis of participation in the much romanticized UN system. Increasingly, Indigenous Peoples utilizing the UN to promote an ethic of stewardship are realizing that 'There is a fine line to walk between playing the system and being played' (Alfred, 1999, p79).

Risking new approaches

Although generalizations can be unreliable, they become a necessary checkpoint in times of crisis. If they stand out in crisis moments, we are in trouble. Today we are in crisis. Today the business practices described above are rife in our industrial economy.[11] And we are in total denial of the urgency for change.

The ecoto ecotourism industry, like others, wants a template for involving Indigenous Peoples. Indigenous Peoples encounter the same challenges with tourism companies on their doorstep as in industry-wide consultations or cross-cutting policy talks between industries. This is what happens in a globalized economy: micro- and macro-processes mirror one another. As a result, no consensus exists on the subject of consultation – at any level. Government and industry envision different means and ends than Indigenous Peoples. Meanwhile, the consultation boat we have put our faith in is going in circles. One oar of the boat is too long. How do we steady the decision-making?

Indigenous leaders have called for far-reaching changes in consultation practices. Frequently, they are accused of wanting to quash a process simply because they feel disenfranchised. The assumption within industry is that participation is a monetary event – for example, payday or other compensation. However, the issues run far deeper. Most Indigenous Peoples are unaware of the wide range of consultations affecting them, particularly internationally in venues such as the UN and World Trade Organization (WTO). Others tread water trying to keep up. Few end up swimming down any consultation stream for long; the trickle of promised 'benefits' is too costly once culture and rights start to wash away.

When these issues are aired, government and industry purveyors of consultation usually try to internalize the problem-solving. Their philosophy is to navigate the rocks as opposed to fundamentally re-route. Recently, one prominent multinational company quipped: 'Without good working relationships, a very good process will fail. With good working relationships, even a poor process can work. More important than designing a new process, we are trying to create a new way of behaving within the process.' Window dressing is usually the goal.

In this quest for a congenial-looking status quo, government bodies such as the UN, World Intellectual Property Organization (WIPO) and the World Conservation Union (IUCN) have become fields for careful diplomacy. Governments speak ambiguously of 'traditional knowledge holders' instead of *peoples* with distinct collective rights. Meanwhile, conservationists push the concept of community conservation areas (CCAs) (see Chapter 6) rather than support underlying ancestral title, which is the bedrock of Indigenous rights. There is a gradual corruption of language that creeps up on Indigenous Peoples. Before long, it is hard for 'participants' to differentiate compromise from catastrophe. Indigenous Peoples' own proposals, such as the World Heritage Indigenous Peoples' Council of Experts (WHIPCOE) and the project known as Call of the Earth, begin to reinforce the language of 'experts'. And informal groups such as the IIFB become an advisory body to nation states (unbeknownst to most Indigenous Peoples worldwide). Protocol can fall aside amid the promise of breakthroughs.

When dialogue gets watered down like this, precious time is lost. Flawed consultations are patched and polished to expedite 'results', deflect criticism and 'court-proof' the outcomes. We are left with consultation look-alikes, which are short on leadership, spiritual principles (particularly sacred knowledge) and common sense. These solutions – called affordable – serve the industrial economy, not humanity or life systems. They fast-track corporate globalization, while numbering our days of intact air, water and soil. Still, we consent to play the role of naive 'consumer'.

The first test for sustainability within a policy forum or other consultation is whether the *process itself* infringes on rights (or thwarts responsibility). If a process involves or affects Indigenous Peoples, yet prejudices or violates Indigenous rights, it should be rejected. Any consultation negating collective rights, confusing individual and collective rights or recognizing only individual human rights may expedite culture loss and even contribute to genocide. Principled consultation will correct these political distortions and be rights compliant instead of rights evasive.

Negotiations

A sister process

Most negotiations with Indigenous Peoples on ecotourism are abridged, similar to consultation. Few business or conservation interests view Indigenous Peoples as a rightful player in economic development. As such, the negotiations agenda seldom provides for self-determination. It focuses, instead, upon hypothetical benefits. Usually, this means a 'jobs for Indians' attitude. Commercial access to Indigenous ancestral territories is presumed and fiscal management imposed. The Maasai report: 'biodiversity and ecotourism projects funded by … agencies such as the European Union, US Agency for International Development (USAID) and others' simply open their lands to big investors (Ole Sakuda, 2004).

The ecotourism industry is rooted in corporate culture, where economics are racially tinged and it is acceptable to short-change Indigenous Peoples. Local compensation, pay scales, working conditions and other human rights abuses tell this story. There is usually no special bond between company and community, unless profitability or other advantage dictates otherwise. Ecotourism companies, like others, tend to:

- locate where their monetary investment gets most yield;
- establish business with minimal entanglement with 'bleeding heart' community- or rights-related issues;
- seek 'soft' solutions (for example, job training) to any grievances that arise;
- revert to national (that is, colonial) laws when tired of relationship-building exercises;
- pursue standard conflict resolution (such as courts, arbitration and mediation) rather than applicable cultural ways.

Many conservation groups promoting ecotourism share these same traits.

In industry negotiations, cost-cutting is the main drive. The involvement of Indigenous Peoples, whose communities are subjected to extreme poverty, does not change this fundamental nature of negotiations. In fact, it may accentuate any underhandedness. Most negotiations proceed in spite of highly unequal negotiating capacity. As with consultation, built-in provisions for capacity-building tend to lack substance.

In many locales, this skewed arrangement means that target communities never quite get organized. Communities find themselves fire-fighting instead of taking proactive or unified positions. Under the pressure to respond, customary systems for communication may be bypassed. Decisions are made on incomplete information. Rumours can take hold, dividing families and neighbours. It is not uncommon for corporate agreements to be reached in the heat of such turmoil.

At some point, this kind of corporate negotiation strategy boomerangs back in a profound way. This may happen in the short term, when mandated Indigenous leadership is sought out by their people to resolve concerns or internal conflict about a negotiated agreement. Or it can manifest over generations, once the ecological debt and spiritual dimensions of a deal become apparent.

Today, it is getting harder for industry (including corporate NGOs) to deflect criticism of conventional negotiation practices. While corporations spurn Indigenous feedback on economics as emotive and unsubstantiated, they cannot so easily dismiss scientific findings, such as those reported in *New Scientist* in 2004 (see Honey, 2004) and the *Millennium Assessment* of 2005 (MEAB, 2005). Ecological anomalies now confirm an imbalance in industrial economics and 'development' relationships. From now on, claims of participation, partnership, conservation and poverty alleviation will need more mettle.

Bargaining

Negotiations often are referred to as bargaining. While some bargains carry fair terms of agreement, others have the connotation of being cheap or unfair. In the corporate world, there are clear geographic and societal (for example, class or caste) divides in the type of bargain struck. When negotiations are among peers – for instance, between Northern business interests and their 'elite' Southern counterparts – there is parity or at least mutually acceptable risk. But when negotiations involve people living in colonial poverty, the outcomes are usually exploitative.

In our globalized economy, where most corporations operate or trade across North and South, many negotiations have two tiers. There is the tier of benefits enjoyed by the deal-makers and then a second tier of less savoury impacts, hitting local communities or disadvantaged (that is, oppressed) segments of these communities. Typical impacts include sweatshops, child labour and indentured 'ghetto' jobs. Displacement of local enterprise by multinational companies is also common. While the tourism industry harbours some of the most serious cases of this skewed commerce, few ecotourism companies understand or admit their part in perpetuating it.

In corporate negotiations involving Indigenous Peoples, the same bargaining ethics apply. Most companies offer so-called 'entry-level' jobs, topped off with a few premium positions to reward community brokers. This practice gets moralized through Darwinian arguments of economic growth, contending that the economically fit will prevail and provide. But most affected Peoples and communities call it economic bullying or bribery.

In the world of corporate bargaining, there is little room for delivery of benefits from ecotourism to Indigenous Peoples. Some of the impediments to relationship-building are structural. Indigenous Peoples, forcibly removed from ancestral lands (in the eyes of industry, their 'equity' – but now appropriated as 'real estate'), sit at the bottom of the negotiations hierarchy. Nonetheless, the greatest barriers currently are procedural and are imbedded in our attitudes.

Traditional corporate bargaining revolves around safeguards. Nothing proceeds without legal checks and balances protecting corporate interests. Legal efforts have been particularly sharp recently, following Indigenous

Peoples' newfound assertiveness internationally. As Indigenous leaders share information on industry practices among themselves, corporate policy on Indigenous Peoples is becoming more defined. The baseline for negotiations is typically twofold:

1   *Companies like to minimize encumbrances.* They seek to contain community expectations, especially financial aspirations.
2   *Companies try to steer clear of profit-sharing.* They like to avoid this subject, for fear of setting a company or industry precedent.

Increasingly, Indigenous Peoples are demanding public clarification of corporate policy. At the World Parks Congress (WPC) in 2003, Indigenous delegates said that conservation conglomerates such as CI and The Nature Conservancy (TNC) should proclaim a formal policy on Indigenous Peoples in order to demystify their means, ends and the many dangerous contradictions in between.

Some corporations have sought to avoid suspicion and conflict by trying new methods of dialogue. In Kenya, Jade Sea Safaris held mediated discussions with Elders of the Turkana tribe over the proposed Lobolo Ecolodge, which would charge tourists US$300 per night (Singer, 2003, p90). Does an independent mediator level the playing field? Not if tribal leaders lack the means to cross-check industry proposals against cultural impacts elsewhere. Mutual *readiness* for negotiations is a must. Within communities, this includes knowing how partnerships have played out for Indigenous Peoples in other 'eco' tourism meccas globally. Prior to entering any negotiations, Indigenous Peoples must be able to undertake private, self-directed research and thorough deliberation of rights-related issues. Otherwise, it remains unclear whether tourism is truly desirable and what to accomplish in negotiations.

In pilot projects where corporate baselines seem to be transcended, most Indigenous Peoples remain on guard. One situation where community vigilance is required is in joint ventures such as eco-lodges, where the profit-sharing agreement calls for ownership transfer within a certain time frame, usually 15 to 20 years or longer.[12] Most communities would have no means of knowing relevant statistics on industry performance – for example, that most ecotourism destinations worldwide are irreversibly damaged within 15 years (Ashton, 1999). Mutual benefits will not occur unless the involved Indigenous People and their leaders are aware of industry trends, can anticipate short-sighted actions by their business partner, and secure advance consensus on an effective dispute-resolution mechanism.

> ## BOX 8.8 Invitation to the Corporate Box
>
> Governments are seeking new ways of fighting Indigenous Peoples' resistance to corporate assimilation. Some have invested in talk shops, supporting events like the 2003 World Summit of Indigenous Entrepreneurs. Others pitch in with industry to fund 'Indigenous' tourism expos. At these talk fests, handpicked 'achievers' are brought together to help pump out the message that being 'industrious' is good. There is usually good music and good food to create an atmosphere of 'prosperity'.

Interest-based negotiation

The main technique for accomplishing corporate objectives is interest-based negotiation. This model of bargaining, made famous by the Harvard University publication *Getting to Yes* (Fisher et al, 1991), has influenced negotiations worldwide. It is characterized as win–win and has been used to propagate the ideology of sustainable development (in other words, economic growth). The method is now so universally accepted within industry that governments and development agencies incorporate it within community capacity-building via training modules on negotiations. It is the underlying framework for multi-stakeholder dialogue (including consultation).

The dilemma is that interest-based negotiation is at odds with rights-centred questions. Indigenous rights cannot lawfully be negotiated away – that is, extinguished. Lumping together rights and interests will create cross-cultural conflict, especially when economic interests override all else. It is not just the exclusivity of benefits that offends, Indigenous Peoples but the concept of exponential economic growth or profit. Spiritually, this concept is a mismatch with ancestral title, where responsibility is an inherent *prerequisite* of any rights. Thus, in most industry or government negotiations with Indigenous Peoples, there is only a short-term illusion of dialogue and common ground. The bubble bursts when rights are circumnavigated to facilitate corporate goals.

Today there is growing tension over interest-based negotiation due to renewed commercial interest in Indigenous cultures and lands. The public and private sectors have rallied with a new generation of public-relations tools. These range from broad agreements such as the CBD to project-oriented protocol agreements with communities, such as a memorandum of understanding stipulating terms for negotiations, research or investment. In very few cases do these agreements build trust. Their contents are largely predetermined. Economic baselines will be adjusted only so far in favour of so-called 'sustainable use'.

The tendency within government and industry is to make seemingly progressive agreements safe through meticulous drafting. This process is vetted by privately retained or in-house lawyers and their 'expert teams' (for example, accountants, economists and anthropologists). Most bystanders to the process, and even many participants, are oblivious to the full extent of legal finagling and backtracking. Indigenous leaders, accustomed to watching these economic exercises and their predictable outcomes, are often the lone voice of dissent. While it is very difficult for most to maintain sufficient vigilance,[13] they know the gist of it all and frequently are heard saying that all concessions are taken away in the details.[14]

There is an expression in the colonial world called 'Indian giving'. The origin of this term is the widespread cultural teaching among Indigenous Peoples that all belongs to the Creator. By custom, it means that nothing can be owned or accumulated; that there is a responsibility to use gifts unselfishly; and that in daily life the individual should generously 're-gift' to others. But the term itself is derogatory, implying that gifts may be taken back out of caprice (self-interest). Ironically, this very principle governs most government and industry negotiations with Indigenous Peoples. Negotiated policy and implementation measures water down legislation on Indigenous rights. Negotiated funding agreements limit Indigenous self-determination.

Economic interests rule in interest-based negotiations. This stands out in the ecotourism industry, due to the large gap between rhetoric and practice. It is not getting any easier to inject a pure principle of 'sustainable' use in industry negotiations. Many development agencies, international institutions, NGOs and their consultants now have just as much economic interest in maintaining an economy of scale in the tourism sector as government and industry. While they may advance policy language that sounds prudent, agreed principles are hardly ever shored up or implemented. It is more profitable to have an industry in disarray than one that is tuned into Indigenous rights, human rights or other biosphere feedback (for example, cultural sustainability).

This offers some insight to why Indigenous leaders may respond with seemingly non-compromise positions in negotiations. Within Indigenous cultures worldwide, prosperity is measured according to mental, physical, emotional and spiritual integrity. When Indigenous leaders see all integrity compromised for the sake of profit, they are guided by their own customary law to take action to restore balance. This can mean distancing or abstaining from established dialogues on 'sustainability' if the process itself is unbalanced.

There has been a conspicuous absence of representative Indigenous leaders in forums such as the CBD and the 2002 World Ecotourism Summit (WES), as well as bodies like the Tourism Task Force of the WCPA.

Relationship-building

Negotiation of interests, litigation of rights

Negotiations on Native title in Australia tell a largely global story. Land claims are characterized by government as Native title *interests*, not rights. So, when the Northern Territory government discovered with alarm in 2002 that all parks and reserves declared during 1978–2000 were legally invalid, it launched negotiations accordingly. Chief Minister Clare Martin professed win–win joint management; however, she also:

> ... warned [that] her government would tie up the [Aboriginal] land councils in decades of litigation unless they agreed to these principles:

- that parks remain accessible to visitor on a no fee, no permit basis;
- that Aborigines immediately lease back all parks for a minimum of 99 years;
- that parks maintain business as usual while negotiations are completed;
- that mining and exploration leases and tourism operator concessions are guaranteed;
- that resolution be by negotiation rather than litigation (Toohey, 2002).

The Northern and Central Aboriginal Land Councils accepted, though the terms blatantly block self-determination. With Australia's *Native Title Act* 'failing Aboriginal claimants', litigation is a cost that few Aboriginal nations can sustain (ABC Network News, 2002). Even presiding judges admit that 'the deck is stacked against Native title holders' (ABC Network News, 2002).

Globally, colonial nation states and their corporate-minded brethren still believe that policy can overrule law. Most countries have turned their back to international law on the rights of Indigenous Peoples, including related norms such as traditional resource rights (TRRs) (see Posey and Dutfield, 1996). While the United Nations Permanent Forum on Indigenous Issues (UNPF) in New York City seems a fresh outlet for dialogue, many Indigenous leaders feel that it abets the offenders. Some say: 'We are now, whether we like it or want it or not, forced to play this game in the field we have agreed upon, by the rules we have acquiesced to, so we have to play it well or never show up' (Laifungbam, 2003). Others look to more direct, bilateral means of redress with government instead of conventional consultation or negotiations.

Indigenous Peoples, better networked now than ever, are identifying new international avenues for campaigns. During 2004, the UK was sued on two fronts. The Sovereign Union of Aboriginal Peoples commenced action against the British Crown for allowing Australian laws that harm Aborigines. Simultaneously, tribes from Papua New Guinea filed a UK£25 million suit against the UK for backing a project that destroyed ancestral lands (Barnett, 2004). Similar cases have been filed in the US using the *Alien Tort Claims Act* (Stein, 2003).

Increasingly, Indigenous Peoples are using such instruments to confront multinational corporations as well. At the 2003 session of the UNPF, delegates demanded 'that multinational corporations accept legal responsibility for policies that destroy Indigenous lands and lifestyles' (Rizvi, 2003). Tourists and the tourism industry will soon feel the heat. Tuvalu, a Pacific nation disappearing due to global warming, is taking legal action in the World Court against the US and Australia, 'the leading per capita sources of greenhouse gases' (Price, 2002, pT3).

The precautionary approach

The precautionary approach referenced in the CBD takes on new meaning in light of trends discussed above. Before we can say that this principle exists or guides us, it must first be exercised in government, corporate and institutional boardrooms. It needs to be operational in all phases of decision-making, including the design of consultation and negotiations processes. Otherwise we forfeit everything that we say we are trying to protect.

Most reviews of consultation and negotiations practice adhere to corporate convention. While government or industry might concede to flaws, neither is necessarily committed to a better process. Both lean towards legalistic solutions that recycle the same offerings. New frameworks for dialogue essentially function like the old. And once one process adjustment is made, another gets ever more remote, due to claims of 'affordability'.

We have now had a long trial run of stakeholder dialogue following the *Brundtland Report* (WCED, 1987) and recent UN Earth Summits (1992 and 2002), yet hurtle down the same economic path. Feedback from Indigenous Peoples discredits the much ballyhooed progress. Internationally, Indigenous leaders continue to advise governments of systemic violations of both individual and collective rights, and associated environmental degradation. This foreshadows further rapid loss of cultures, biodiversity and, ultimately, human spirit.

Currently, there is no precautionary approach to speak of. At the WPC in 2003, famed scientist Richard Leakey complained about the 'Indigenization' of conservation, calling it a political move. He merely verbalized what many feel. Today, most of us hearing the debates on conservation think of 'traditional' knowledge as a poker card. It is alright for Indigenous Peoples to lay it on the table; but the kings and queens of the deck still rule.

While it is possible for government and industry to engineer or purchase consent through consultation or negotiations, we should be careful what we bargain for. When legalities are manipulated to protect and promote industrial interests, there is no chance of a win–win outcome. At some point in the trajectory, natural (sacred) law takes over. As social systems break down (now manifested by our rapid consumerism), so do Earth systems. This is the price of moral inertia. In time we are all made to listen.

A truly precautionary approach will depart boldly from the corporate/consumer way. It will take us towards new relationships based upon mutual respect, understanding and care (Figure 8.1). We can begin by:

Figure 8.1 **Relationship building: Sacred principles for reconnection**

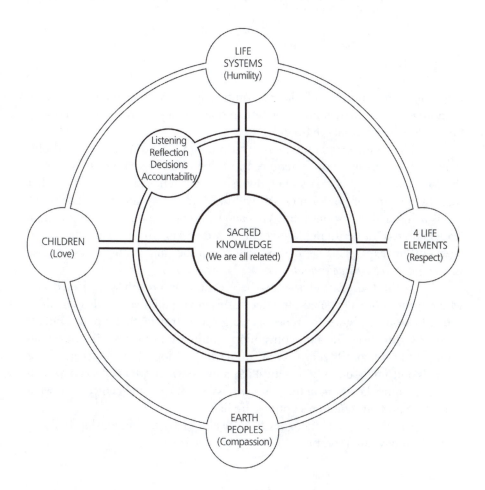

- setting aside what is *non-negotiable* (sacred life systems);
- reconnecting rights and responsibilities, starting at the personal level;
- approaching dialogue as a process for relationship-building, not pushing private interests;
- agreeing that consultation and negotiations must not violate, evade or prejudice Indigenous rights (or individual human rights);
- harmonizing international law and national law with customary law for the safeguarding of bio-cultural diversity;
- implementing interim measures for cultural sustainability to prevent oversights, cover-ups and repeat mistakes;
- discussing cross-cultural training with Indigenous leaders, and implementing appropriate programmes from the executive/ professional level 'down'.

Conclusion

It is time to shift our level of dialogue on sustainability. Indigenous leaders are spending an inordinate amount of time requesting a just process – as industry hurtles forward, happily self-regulated.

The deadlock will not be broken through legal or political stand-offs. A unified leadership effort is required to bring about precautions. What will this look like? It will be marked by diversity, irreverence and creativity, rather than by bullying or conformity. We will heed ancestral title: the teaching of rights being tied to responsibility. We each will reflect upon our own potential leadership role rather than hiding behind or deferring to 'government,' 'management' or 'experts'. Together, we will remember and remind one another that *sacred knowledge cradles us all*.

In the tourism industry – where economic growth is projected and where most performance audits cater to this goal – the need for leadership is acute. Ecotourism is, for the most part, a growth strategy built upon standard economic directives. It takes conventional industry to places which are culturally and ecologically sensitive. Without intervention, this will accelerate us towards bottoming out as a society. That may be where we need to go for collective learning; however, in this moment, we still have some choice as to what our future and our children's options are like.

To advance our dialogues from deal-making to relationship-building we need to pay attention to:

- *Governance*: it is time to look to our Elders for guidance on how to sit together and address the pressing issues. In today's consumer society, the Elderly have become 'disposable;' whereas among Indigenous Peoples, Elders are the historians and keepers of customary law. Facing today's crises in life systems, we cannot shut out those in our own midst with a memory of more compassionate and giving times. We must invite the Elders to sit in our centre circle. We must let them direct us and help the youth, also abandoned today. We need a 'greying', not greening, of the globalized economy.

- *Leadership*: it is critical that we understand what makes a leader. In the business world, we value the executive, the entrepreneur and the broker. Through corporate mass media, this brand of leadership has eclipsed all others. Despite this, there remain several small pockets of leadership in unassuming places, where the great qualities of humanity remain integrated. Some cultures retain their customs of recognizing leaders in connection with spirituality (that is, sacred knowledge). Some families teach their children to practice gratitude and respect. These are the visionary types of leaders needed today. These are the leaders who can heal broken channels of communication. We need to elevate them while recognizing our own potential.

- *Integrity*: in order to create a future for today's children we must put own inner compass to use. Each of us is born with the ability to discern a good path and to interact with care, concern and gentleness. Individually, professionally and interpersonally, we must choose respect. We must learn how to responsibly exercise our free will so that there is intact air, soil and water to sustain those around us and behind us.

- *Grounding*: when we engage in those parts of our life that we think define us – such as our jobs, professions, careers and bargain-hunting – we need to remember what anchors us. We need to know some ritual other than consumerism. We need to be able to find our own inner quiet. If we can remember this internal place, we will safeguard our own sacred selves, as well as the sacred life experience of others. We will be able to enter dialogues and make decisions without abandoning our humanity.

Recommended reading

- Alfred, T. (1999) *Peace, Power, Righteousness: An Indigenous Manifesto*, Oxford University Press, Toronto, Canada
- Braddock, J. (2004) 'New Zealand Labour government cuts off Maori claims to the foreshore', 10 June, Distributed via the Protecting Knowledge List Server of the Union of British Columbia Indian Chiefs, Canada
- Johnston, A. (2001) 'Oh Canada: Your home on Native land – The struggle for recognition of Aboriginal Title and Rights in British Columbia', *Native Americas*, fall/winter, pp74–79
- Olol-Dapash, M. (2001) 'Maasai autonomy and sovereignty in Kenya and Tanzania', Cultural Survival Quarterly, issue 25, vol 1, 30 April, available at www.culturalsurvival.org/publications/csq

Figure 8.2 **Sign beckoning tourists to commercialized 'kava ceremony' in Nadi, Fiji**

Figure 8.3 **Bare breasted statue lures tourists to souvenir shop on Coral Coast, Fiji**

Chapter 9

Sustainable Tourism

As we consumers lose our own culture, we become gluttonous on others.
(Leah McIntosh, 2004)

In 1982, the United Nations (UN) asserted that tourism can 'provide the energy for moral and intellectual understanding' (Brown, 1999). Today we hear from the UN that tourism will spur poverty relief. There is talk of 'sustainable tourism', though the ecotourism industry itself has operated with impunity for three decades. We are now at a crossroad where our moral ambiguity must stop. Will we continue to rely upon the false lifelines thrown to us, or sincerely ask what would sustain life systems?

The question of what makes sustainable or ethical tourism is an old one. A whole generation of professionals and academics has greyed without advancement in key areas. We have formulas, guidelines and pilot projects, but no deference to international law on human rights or Indigenous rights. Despite this, during the World Ecotourism Summit (WES) in 2002, many industry delegates remarked on the 'progressive' work under way – especially certification.

Countless studies have shown the correlation between human rights, Indigenous rights and biodiversity conservation. Reference to 'traditional' knowledge in the *UN Convention on Biological Diversity* (CBD) reflects this. *Resolution 1926* of the Organization of American States (OAS) reaffirms the relationship. Even so, Indigenous rights remain a taboo subject in most policy forums – branded as 'too political' by the politically inclined. Easing global terms of trade with Indigenous Peoples is simply *not* on the economic agenda.

Ecotourism is far from politically neutral. Inside the industry, performance audits abound, dutifully exploring both positive and negative impacts – including the perceived effects on Indigenous Peoples. Nonetheless, there has been a persistent omission of true cost accounting. Much of the data used comes from industry bodies such as The International Ecotourism Society (TIES), the World Tourism Organization (WTO-OMT) and/or the World Travel and Tourism Council (WTTC). Submissions from Indigenous Peoples themselves on rights infringement are seldom welcome or accommodated in impact assessment.

A number of groups and personalities presiding over the domain of impact assessments have publicly supported Indigenous Peoples while discretely blocking Indigenous self-determination. Some world 'authorities' on sustainable tourism walk this fence. A recent case involved the Tourism Task Force of the World Commission on Protected Areas (WCPA) (see Box 10.4). Within most policy institutions internationally, the vocabulary is suggestive of rights but serves industry interests.

We must ask why resistance to dialogue on Indigenous rights is accepted in the echelons of impact assessment. For a time, skirting the issues raised by Indigenous Peoples can be regarded as an oversight; but soon there is a graduation from being preoccupied to being negligent. Somewhere in the human psyche it becomes permissible to ignore warning signs of abuse and to support the status quo. How can we discuss this? How do we retrieve our humanity?

Taking action in support of fundamental human rights is a highly personal decision, stirred by our innermost self. In consumer society, the conviction is often momentary. But we each have a choice of how to proceed once empowered with information. We can plead ignorance, walk a middle road or eschew economies that violate the rights of Indigenous Peoples. After two decades of redundant debate on ecotourism as supposedly 'sustainable' tourism, it is appropriate to ask ourselves exactly where we stand.

BOX 9.1 **Tacky tourism: Whose idea is it, anyway?**

The ecotourism industry still coasts on its 'superhero' image. One observer notes: 'The ambitious claims made for ecotourism stretch credulity: If eco-tourists are bridging cultural divides, saving the planet and eliminating poverty on their vacations, what superhuman feats are they performing when they're at work?' (Theroux, 2001, p62). This is where the truth comes out. Most of us are just working in order to *consume*.

Nothing revs up the consumer treadmill more than the expectation of trips and travel. Corporations know this because they invented it. Holiday time is a legislated 'right' in the North. Tourism is the new opiate of the consumer masses.

Biodiversity

Projections

TIES continues to define ecotourism as 'responsible travel to natural areas that conserves the environment and improves the welfare of local people' (Bien, 2003). This presumes that we are informed and compassionate consumers, knowledgeable of what our dollars sustain. Sadly, most of us know little of our own global impact. Ecotourism is a trail-blazing industry that brings the commercial process right into a myriad of communities, often in isolated areas or in the most sensitive of ecosystems. It has more 'sprawl' than any other economic sector.

Today, ecotourism has an intensity reminiscent of the fur trade and rubber boom. It is one of the last hurrahs of primary industry. Whereas other economic sectors are scrambling to compensate for over-harvesting – for example, diversifying into biotechnology – the tourism industry directly markets species loss. Ecotourism companies are racing into the heart of remaining stands of biodiversity. According to Ray Ashton, a long-time international consultant on sustainable tourism, 'It is a mess out there' (Ashton, 2003).

In 1999, the United Nations Commission on Sustainable Development (CSD) urged world governments to 'take strong and appropriate action … against any kind of illegal, abusive or exploitative tourist activity'. Many governments are now rallying at the UN for sustainable tourism in vulnerable ecosystems. The *CBD Guidelines on Tourism* are an international effort to codify and encourage good practice. However, the premise of these guidelines is industry access. Vulnerability is not qualified, nor are its underlying causes named. The guidelines vindicate current industry standards more than they challenge industrial ways. So, will future research deal in truth or profit?

All around us the costs of industrial-style development are stacking up (Broswimmer, 2002). Climate is swinging with dangerous momentum;[1] animal mating and migrations are out of rhythm; plant cycles are off; genetic diversity is plummeting.[2] At the Global Biodiversity Forum in 1999, World Conservation Union (IUCN) chief scientist Jeff McNeely noted: 'We need to ask what will be the result under different scenarios, the what ifs' (McNeely, 1999). During the Fifth World Parks Congress (WPC) in 2003, the IUCN still speculated on the various possibilities (see IUCN, 2003). But protesters of economic globalization are emphasizing the importance of looking at just the current scenario and understanding where it leads.

Culture loss, like environmental mayhem, has been profitable for the tourism industry. Worldwide, companies solicit reclusive Indigenous Peoples for 'native' shows: a peak event for tourists. Impoverished families must decide whether to share intimate customs or vestiges of culture. 'Participating' can instil pride; but it also takes a toll on identity and self-esteem. The poverty grinds on, illuminated by tourist encounters. No other industry so flagrantly prospers off colonialism. None penetrates and threatens Indigenous cultures so deeply.

At Indigenous Peoples' workshops on tourism held concurrent to UN meetings during 1997–2004, there were comments about Columbus being the first tourist. Humour was used to raise the issue of genocide. Why? It is difficult for us to appreciate genocide in *any* context, let alone in relation to biodiversity loss. Most of us look at subjects like 'alien invasive species' with blinkers on. We can grasp phenomena such as non-native grasses overtaking endemic flora, but not whole cultures and populations being culled or subdued by colonial policy.

Today, tourism embodies another kind of death's door. In tourism, like other industries, we are still taking more than we give back. Tourism's impacts upon cultural diversity alone are devastating. But during the last decade, the Earth, too, has sent us a neon message about its immune system. Yet, jets are soaring, hot hotel water is running in drought areas and resort chemicals are leaching into the groundwater.[3] Global tourism, especially so-called 'eco' tourism, is forecast to grow. 'Our children are growing up with the assumption that their lives will incorporate extensive travel' (Malanowski, 2003, p16).

There are major intercultural differences in problem-solving between the corporate/consumer world and Indigenous Peoples. However, answers will not come through any duel of 'experts', or even a chummy joint group of 'experts'. Breakthroughs lie in understanding the simple truths, such as cause and effect, inside our own selves. We are all capable of this and should not be fooling ourselves that someone else can do the soul searching for us. Self-knowledge is required for real dialogue.

BOX 9.2 | **Corporations: Our concierge for the final journey**

In 2004, the US Department of Defense and Arctic Council both issued red alerts on climate change. The World Wide Fund for Nature's (WWF-International's) *Living Planet Report 2004* states: 'the human race is plundering the planet at a pace that outstrips its capacity to support life' (WWF-International, 2004b). Still, we sign onto waiting lists for the latest consumer gizmo. Consume the Earth to heal it, corporations say. See the polar bear and fabled 'Eskimo' (actually, the Inuit) before they disappear. This is the morbid face of 'eco' tourism. It is like one last binge in our spiral of consumer addiction.

Efforts to incorporate biodiversity

Countries are trying to figure out where to place biodiversity in their policies. This can be a perplexing and vexing question within bureaucracy, due to the competing economic mandates. While most public agencies report favourably on steps taken to conserve biodiversity, few like taking the heat of external evaluations. Governments and institutions named in grievances at bodies such as the United Nations Working Group on Indigenous Populations (WGIP) in Geneva or the United Nations Permanent Forum on Indigenous Issues (UNPF) in New York generally duck transparent reporting. Most give small soundbites of information instead. Industry is equally evasive; only 6 per cent of top companies are reporting known environmental and social risks (UNEP et al, 2004).

Between government and industry, there is a tacit agreement that biodiversity should be partitioned off for private access and profit. Some enabling legislation and policy is shaped nationally via public consultations. However, much of it evolves in the course of bilateral trade missions or in concert with world trade bodies such as the Asia Pacific Economic Cooperation Forum (APEC) and the World Trade Organization (WTO). These supra-organizations have taken to conducting business behind barricades, following mass protests by anti-globalization groups. Their resolutions contravene not only the CBD, but also common sense about 'sustainable use'.

According to the United Nations Environment Programme (UNEP), a major barrier to biodiversity conservation is the lack of methodologies (Higuero, 1999). In response, UNEP launched its Biodiversity Planning Support Programme to harmonize planning between sectors; the World Bank created a Biodiversity Overlay Programme to address issues by sector; and the IUCN has recommended 'strategic environmental assessment' to create a biodiversity filter on all programming under biodiversity-related conventions, such as the *World Heritage Convention*. Nevertheless, the political machinery for maximizing biodiversity *revenues* is intact. The WTO Committee on Trade and Environment has wrestled over extending observer status to UNEP and its various secretariats. Countries are moving as a pack to maintain investor confidence – juggling commitments, counter commitments and appearances.

Biodiversity programming has three main levels, none of which has matured with a view to the long term:

1   *Cultural shell*: biodiversity conservation is defined relative to cultural diversity, but is practised as cultural assimilation. On the surface, CBD programming supports traditional knowledge. But off record, Indigenous Peoples are told: 'You've got to become competitive in our world.' Tourism is pushed onto communities as a survival suit, along with other market prescriptions.

2   *Environmental streams*: biodiversity is regarded as a component of integrated 'resource' management. The goal is to incorporate it into economics. This mindset of separateness misses the intrinsic law of connection. It lets the 'eco' tourism industry disown its

overall impacts and stage misleading biodiversity rescues, often aided by conservation groups with their own narrow agendas. Indigenous Peoples have asked for holistic reconnection instead.

3   *Economic core*: biodiversity is not considered 'critical capital' (Higuero, 1999). In fact, most biodiversity loss is regarded as an 'externality' by economists (McNeeley, 1999). This characterization has enabled governments to rework definitions of 'eco' tourism, saying that tourism revenues will give legitimacy to biodiversity. Realistically, however, prosperity thinking just trudges on – as if current economic growth is sustainable.[4]

Most attempts to mobilize industry in favour of sustainable tourism emphasize how Earth changes will affect sector earnings. In the midst of system-wide alerts, economic arguments are still the dominant psychology of persuasion. We are banking on financial wizardry to patch up the life web.[5] Space tourism is the latest market niche,[6] magnifying ethical questions such as what are the *prerequisites* for commercial 'rights' (really, privileges).

Success of conservation programmes, many experts say, rests upon whether government and industry are economically motivated. This logic guides the World Bank: 'We need to show how biodiversity underlies the productivity of economic sectors like tourism. In other words, we need to instill the fear of God regarding lost revenues' (MacKinnon, 1999). In 2000, the IUCN and Conservation International (CI) convened a meeting with the private sector on biodiversity. Economy wide, institutions said to be responsible for biodiversity are reassuring the private sector. There is now a business case for biodiversity reminiscent of the original ecotourism singsong (see WBCSD, 2004). The United Nations Tour Operators Initiative (www.toinitiative.org) is being showcased, although it completely overlooks cultural sustainability.

Pursuing biodiversity 'solutions' that are revenue focused rather than relationship centred is a materialistic path characteristic of our time. Proposals benefiting the private sector are supported with serious government spending; meanwhile, rabble-rousing protests are contained and concealed. 'Pro-poor' tourism marketing has buoyed this agenda, facilitating industry growth while covering its impacts. Only through Tourism Concern's SWEATSHOPS Campaign and other watchdog efforts are some of the truths seeping out. Currently, we reflect little upon entwined issues such as international debt, economic globalization, poverty and our consumer lifestyle – or their real spiritual dimensions. But when something is manipulated for unreasonable personal gain a social toxicity develops, manifesting as 'impacts'.

Can we retrieve our memory and sense of sacred life boundaries? Or are all boundaries negotiable once profit is tasted?

| BOX 9.3 | Biodiversity conservation: 'Eco' imperialism in Indigenous territories |

Many non-governmental organizations (NGOs) are pressuring Northern countries to bear the 'cost' of conservation, saying: 'It's immoral and impractical to expect the poor to pay' (Kirby, 2003). This has us headed for backlash. No country perceives adequate 'disposable' income without economic growth. Many have responded by pushing mass 'eco' tourism for parks. Indigenous Peoples are the casualty of this conservation logic – the proverbial canary in the mine.

Cross-cultural viewpoints

Today we consumers benefit from a global travel market where it is standard practice to liquidate, slash and blowout product, especially airline seats. Megan Epler Wood, founder of TIES, states that our 'green purchasing habits appear to be on the decline' (Epler Wood, 2003, p5). We fly our food halfway across the world, while filling our homes with luxury items mass produced for a pittance in global poverty belts seemingly a world away. Then we criss-cross the globe again on holiday. As we stash our air miles and other 'loyalty' points, we look for more deals. Our holiday savings from all the 'cheap' flights and 'free' tickets (which have incalculable costs, not least of which are culture loss and climate change) are pocketed rather than amassed for the good of target communities or supposed conservation.

Whereas consumer society is programmed to take, Indigenous generations typically are taught restraint, in order to care for the grandchildren of grandchildren. Governments fear the power of this cultural teaching. It has proven resilient over the course of colonialism despite aggressive, and frequently violent, policies of economic domination and cultural assimilation. More and more Indigenous leaders are vocally challenging economic growth and globalization on moral, ethical and spiritual grounds.

Many governments are upping monetary tactics to smooth industrial access to Indigenous territories. Some have incorporated nominal partnership provisions within tourism-related development plans, consultations and agreements. Others piggyback corporate-style capacity-building onto community economic development. Involved communities resent the manipulation but feel cornered. Most have lived the aftermath of 'development' several times over. Industrial impacts upon culture always last longer than the local business cycle; they are essentially *interchangeable*, whether ecotourism or another industry.

At a community level, the seasons of government programming are known. Elders watching the undulations of government policy know the pattern. They caution Indigenous leadership against being mesmerized by a programme term like 'biodiversity', which has such obvious economic undertones.

A great number are concerned that Indigenous Peoples are being encouraged to develop their own economic arguments for industrial-style 'conservation'. They see this as the ultimate assimilation tactic. If governments succeed, the language of commerce overtakes that of Creator, Mother Earth and customary law. For this reason, a number of Indigenous Peoples are living in voluntary isolation – asking to be left alone.

Many Indigenous leaders feel that Indigenous Peoples have a teaching role in this phase of humanity's societal and spiritual development. The picture they paint is like an upside-down hammock. If we put biodiversity inside this hammock, it will tumble out into disarray, but turn the hammock around and life will be cradled. In other words, if we take care of sacred relationships first, the rest will follow. Balanced economies *can* happen.

Impact assessment

Abundance

Impact assessment has been normalized to the point that basic methodologies are known and change little between economic sectors. Methodologies taught ten years ago are largely the same ones taught today. For all the talk of innovation, there is still one ubiquitous formula. This goes 'hand in glove' with global trade.

Impact assessment concerns relationships and how they are defined. Scientists have described natural systems in different ways – from bioregions, ecosystems and watersheds down to riparian zones. Events like volcanic eruptions, which happen intermittently but affect world climate with force, have shown how intricately these systems are linked globally. Nevertheless, we have yet to correlate this to even a single ongoing mass tourism activity such as air travel. Air tickets are not priced at anywhere near cost, nor is the average 'eco-' tour experience or (more importantly) tourist lifestyle.

The sobering concept of 'full-fare' tourism, coined by Canadian Professor Peter Williams (1991), is not factored into biodiversity programming. In air travel alone, industry's supply-and-demand arithmetic is causing ecological anomalies at warp speed.[7] We are in a high flux climate situation, yet still travelling at whim. There are now an estimated 1.7 billion members of the global consumer class (WRI, 2004); nearly 1 billion are airborne for a trip each year (TNC, 2003, p3). And thanks to our expanding consumer waistlines, it now takes extra jet fuel to thrust one of us over a continent (*Vancouver Sun*, 2004).

Most impact assessment centres on the question of abundance, in its narrowest of meanings. Decisions are made by one measuring stick: revenue.[8] Data are processed to see how the perceived supply can meet economic demand;

eventually, scarcity is marketed at a premium. This has led to fisheries, forests and fossil 'fuels' being viewed in corporate terms instead of as life essentials or part of the Earth equilibrium. Today, 'eco' tourism is taking over as the runaway enterprise in many threatened and endangered ecosystems.[9] It is a double-dipping economy, primping diverse Indigenous cultures into a cliché 'Indian' commodity alongside stylized 'nature'.

While systems for impact assessment are supposed to be comprehensive and impartial, they are more an instrument for the status quo than social learning. Most indicators for 'sustainable use' adhere to headline categories identified in the CBD. As the name suggests, they are oriented towards *usage* and generally come into effect during the operations stage of a project. They seldom apply to initial community contact such as consultation, negotiations or other early aspects of relationship-building – which set the corporate tone on local issues. This pre-emptive winnowing of issues rules out free and prior informed consent (PIC) by affected Indigenous Peoples.

In ecotourism, there is a coarse filter on impact assessment because the economic stakes are high.[10] This loose screening of impacts is justified as 'results based'. All kinds of companies are reporting their alleged good deeds to help prove industry responsibility. Industry's celebratory approach presumes that biodiversity is ultimately:

- proprietary (not tied to ancestral title);
- subservient to business (not sacred);
- negotiable (not a delicate balance);
- immune to economic (that is, *societal*) dysfunction.

Herein lies the divide between the paradigm of consumerism (economic growth and industrial 'conservation') versus the principle of ancestral

---

BOX 9.4 **The ecotourism industry: Gasping for air**

In the March 2004 issue of *New Scientist*, research confirmed a myriad of impacts on wildlife from so-called 'eco' tourism (Ananthaswamy, 2004). The International Ecotourism Society (TIES) conceded: 'These findings undermine the premise that ecotourism is an ecologically sustainable activity' (Honey, 2004). However, it was quick to develop a public relations spin. Other industry advocates chimed in, defending ecotourism as 'the lesser of two evils' for Indigenous communities (Petropoulos, 2004).[11] But observers caution that 'attempts to shift to other euphemistic terms and come up with new "feel-good, can-do" concepts to invoke "acceptable tourism" ... have no chance to succeed in the long run' (Pleumarom, 2004, p2).

title (balanced living). Ancestral title provides a very different perspective on impact assessment: abundance lies in healthy relationships, reached from the inside out.

Best available science

The novelty of the *UN Convention on Biological Diversity* (CBD) is that governments are obligated to apply both conventional science and 'traditional knowledge'. Although traditional knowledge features prominently in the CBD text and negotiations, Indigenous Peoples' advances in the process are not as extensive as world governments would have us believe.[12] Collective rights receive superficial treatment only (see Chapter 10).[13]

In biodiversity decision-making, the creed of best available science is a myth. TIES has noted that 'We need to speak of limits of acceptable change, not carrying capacity' (Lash, 1999). However, there is little practical support for Indigenous Peoples to influence, much less oversee, impact assessment from the standpoint of cultural sustainability. Industry still answers to the hospitality maxim: 'The customer is always right.' This standard underpins most consultant–client relationships for impact assessment.

Indicators of this closed shop surround us. World think-tanks are talking about 'sustainable intensification' to meet market demands. World industries are flocking to 'nature identical' biotechnology. Amid this intellectual chaos, governments are negotiating life trade-offs that none can actually underwrite. In Australia, there is a state permit aptly called 'Consent to Destroy'. Equivalent permitting in Peru led to extensive damage of the sacred centre of Machu Picchu, the *Inti Watana* sun dial. How often do we understand what we are about to destroy?

In tourism, there is a particularly urgent need to harmonize knowledge systems. The ecotourism industry is creating destinations out of Indigenous sacred sites, ceremonial centres and village courtyards. Most of us lack a personal reference point for what this means. We cannot comprehend or construe the impact upon target communities, much less biodiversity or life systems. As members of the global consumer class, we are usually numb to the devastation of others even when it signals our own.

Current dialogue on sustainability is divisive. There is often more energy directed to being right than to being cautious or just. This has led to increasingly rigid role playing – for example:

- Industry views Indigenous Peoples and NGOs as sheltered from real world realities (that is, economics).
- NGOs see industry and Indigenous Peoples as single-issue advocates, ignoring the larger conservation picture.

- Southern and Northern groups clash on the question of leadership (for example, economic competence and moral authority).

Indigenous Peoples, on the other hand, find 'biodiversity' interest groups too linear to realize the connection within Creation, between Peoples and among issues. Many Indigenous leaders say that the gift Indigenous Peoples hold is the knowledge of our connectedness.

Adaptive management

In impact assessment, we have adopted standardized analysis. Most expert studies conform to industrial frameworks for 'sustainable' development. Thus, business acumen is a requisite skill. Adjustments may be made to reflect political context – for instance, a recent election or new policy initiatives; however, the decision-making process typically satisfies client(s), peers and public opinion (in other words, consumers) over Indigenous rights.

This brand of professionalism, called 'playing it safe', can lead down a dangerous path. It means a routine programme of work with familiar components. Some see such replication as a hallmark of good science but to others it signifies conformity and control. In history, we have many examples of master decision-makers denying that things are out of control. Today we need to revisit this history. Scientists such as David Suzuki (Suzuki, 2003, 2004) and Terje Traavik (Traavik, 2002) are echoing the 1992 *World Scientists' Warning to Humanity* (see Union of Concerned Scientists, 1992). Traavik has warned that 95 per cent of scientists are working on the side of industry; only 5 per cent at best are truly independent. Such admonishments are still not registering on most nation state governments.

Discussions on sustainable tourism have gone a conventional course. Today we are at the stage of best practice studies. At the 14th Global Biodiversity Forum in 1999, the IUCN announced that case studies would be an important way of integrating biodiversity – meaning, to capture and communicate the lessons. During 2000, the CBD Secretariat invited case studies on tourism and biodiversity, under the topic of sustainable use. This was applauded widely except by vigilant tourism NGOs.[14] These groups wanted to see some basic *preconditions* for analysis, safeguarding Indigenous rights. Otherwise, third-party analysis of 'best practices' on ancestral lands would prevail, giving an incomplete picture of industry and its interactions with Indigenous Peoples.

All along, the government consensus was that too much attention was being given to the negative impacts of 'eco' tourism.[15] As a result, no fund was established alongside the CBD to ensure direct, representative or proportionate case studies from Indigenous Peoples. Not until the World Parks Congress in 2003 was there any meaningful support for Indigenous Peoples to inject their own analysis into the debate.[16] At the WPC, a double session was dedicated to examining whether tourism can deliver benefits to Indigenous Peoples. But by this stage the *CBD Guidelines on Tourism* were virtually a done deal. The reprimand issued by Indigenous leaders concerning good faith and due diligence in such institutional processes therefore perturbed those marshalling the debate (Gavidi et al, 2003; see also Box 10.4).

International institutions coordinating policy development have chosen a bland tract of inquiry, in a tumultuous time. Most undertake studies that profoundly impact Indigenous Peoples without first investigating whether this work would infringe on Indigenous rights. The practice has been to commission consultancy reports or stakeholder consultations synthesized by a consultant. 'Experts' working in this staid environment generally adhere to its conventions. Thus, most institutional research is entirely out of synch with Indigenous concepts of conservation, development and sustainability – though it may appear otherwise.

This institutional detachment from Indigenous rights is the accepted *modus operandi*, despite recent rhetoric at the United Nations (UN) on 'traditional knowledge' and cultural diversity. Some groups have shown glimmers of trying to turn around their relationship with Indigenous Peoples. In 1999, WWF-International issued guidelines on equitable biodiversity research, including prior informed consent (Laird, 1999). During 2003, TIES released *Rights and Responsibilities*, a compilation of codes of conduct, with support from Indigenous Tourism Rights International (ITRI). However, such products are usually the brainchild of professionals, rather than a result of appropriate protocol talks with Indigenous Peoples. Most are part of the same stock in that they are handed down amid conflicting institutional goals and programmes. The IUCN is frequently singled out in this regard. Its handbook *Business and Biodiversity* was funded by Novartis and Rio Tinto, two companies notorious amongst Indigenous Peoples, as well as a consortium of petroleum and chemical corporations (IUCN et al, 2002).

Attitudes within 'conservation' and 'development' agencies are the *real* capacity-building question of our day. Some of the better relationships incorporate cross-cultural training; however, there is a need to go much further

---

BOX 9.5   The industrial way: 'Progress' through social decay

Industrial fisheries, like industrial ecotourism, 'grind away' local ecology within 15 years (Ashton, 1999; Nierenberg, 2003). The numbers don't get any better in the forest or mining sectors (see Ayres, 2004). Industry to industry, there is, essentially, one profit model. We are now so desensitized that even the brash marketing and sale of *oppressed peoples*, via 'eco' tourism, is accepted.

and to ensure a system-wide 'train the trainer' process for institutions themselves. Institutions with this degree of influence over peoples, humanity and life systems must look at their own role in oppression and corporate pillaging. Otherwise, the institutions themselves are blatantly unsustainable.

Standard-setting

We need to ask why principles for sustainable tourism are so elusive. If principles are said to exist but are not widely defended or implemented, then in practice there are none. What we have, instead, are peer agreements. Industry sectors create their respective 'sustainability' (that is, access) plans; consultants, intermediary agencies and corporate 'conservation' groups jostle alongside, competing for the inner sanctum. Grassroots organizations get limited access in the name of democracy, but are expected to offer manageable rebuttals, not complete alternatives.

Policy talks are proceeding as if the same industrial paradigm that got us into trouble can somehow get us out (see Berman, 1988, pp188–189). Many 'experts' still extol *free* market economies (which means absolved of true costs and liabilities), despite the known risks and untold dangers. These are the experts endorsed by most nation states. In their wake, there is little attention towards cautionary messages. Standard-setting issues raised by Indigenous Peoples at the WGIP and UNPF, for example, are poorly integrated within other UN norms.[17]

World governments may concede to a human rights framework for environmental protection (see www.earthjustice.org), since individual rights have proved navigable for global corporations. However, most steer clear of the *collective rights* of Indigenous Peoples, which could rein in industry at large insofar as 'biodiversity' is concerned. Ancestral title is therefore thoroughly wrung out in the human rights wash. For this reason the WGIP (housed within the UN Commission on Human Rights) is corrupt in the eyes of many Indigenous leaders. 'There is *no* government who can sit in this room with us and honestly say that they would/will protect our rights' (Anderson, 1999).

The doubletalk infests CBD talks. In 1999, Canada, true to its 'give then take' form, recommended that tourism assessment 'include the cultural and spiritual impacts of tourism' (see Box 10.5).[18] The US – a political ally on 'Indian' policy – objected, saying that this would be 'neither technical nor scientific'. Their exchange played on UN terminology, which speaks to the so-called 'intangible' heritage of Indigenous Peoples: a thoroughly trivializing and deprecating concept. It underscored how lightly governments take matters of sacred knowledge. To Indigenous Peoples, spirituality is the reliable signpost; it is our material world of *consumerism* that is illusory.

Standard-setting in global arenas is more theatre than dialogue. Some say that 'policy-making lies often in the hands of people with limited field experience' (Mader, 2002). Others believe there is inadequate accountability. Both, of course, are true. This is where corporate governance differs from ancestral title and customary law. Indigenous governance systems are personalized at the culture and ecosystem level.

There is an immense responsibility, today of all days, to get policy right. How prepared are we? Some of the tough questions are outlined below for personal thought and contemplation.

Government contributions

To what higher ground can government mandate (that is, consumer democracy) lead us? Most environment ministries are responsible for partitioning resources, not stewardship *per se*. Standard practice includes:

- planning on election timelines for political longevity;
- building consultations around investor confidence, rather than pressing sustainability issues;
- bowing to commercial influence in the design of indicators for sustainable use;
- servicing industry, not target communities (especially exploited ones), through national ecotourism plans.

As a remedy, it has been suggested that national policy should 'define the roles and relationships of ecotourism partners' (Ole Sikar, 2002). However, policy alone is insufficient since many national governments are implicated in the infringement of Indigenous rights. Indicators for sustainable tourism must apply to the policy process itself. Furthermore, all indicators must be consistent with international law on the individual and collective rights of Indigenous Peoples (see Appendices 1–4).

Institutional contributions

How much should we invest in institutional problem-solving? Institutional projects and partnerships are the mainstay of sustainable tourism programming. In 2002, UNEP, WTO-OMT and the IUCN jointly published a guide for tourism in protected areas (Eagles et al, 2002). Simultaneously, CI developed biodiversity indicators for protected areas and WWF-International spearheaded its 'ecoregion approach'. WWF-International's efforts included guidelines for Arctic tourism, later evaluated by the Sami Council (Baer, 1999). These endeavours all convey a sense of purpose and transparency, but whose purpose and how transparent? Few affected Indigenous Peoples are aware of such programmes in their formative stage, though they primarily target Indigenous territories. It is a full on colonial relationship – from the moment of 'introduction', they have little leeway to avoid the institutionalization of ancestral lands. There usually is *no prior informed consent* for either institutional presence or applied corporate methodologies.

Consultant contributions

Can we restore trust in consultancy reports? Conflict over biodiversity is profitable. It leads to all kinds of contracts, from social modelling (for example, management plans) to social interventions (such as mediation). Career consultants steer the course of 'innovation'. This tight-knit group includes:

- multinational consulting firms which offer 'one stop' shopping;
- independent consultants providing boutique services;
- academics who double as consultants;
- consultancies masquerading as NGOs;
- community 'representatives' practising internal colonialism.

While there are several programmes to develop standards for 'eco' tourism, Indigenous Peoples rarely benefit at the front end (for instance, through equitable advisory fees) or from deliverables (including recommendations). To consultants, Indigenous Peoples are a subject representing billable hours. Now they also signify competition, due to recent international attention to 'traditional knowledge' and Indigenous self-determination.[19] Many consultants on the cusp of new policy trends are looking to protect their market share.

Professional contributions

Will professionals acknowledge their own blind spots? For many it is difficult to separate fact from fantasy when working outside their own social realm in impoverished rural areas. Often professionals are just as moved in their reactions as tourists in such areas, because they have more in common with them (namely, life experience) than with locals. There is usually a strong sense that ecotourism must be good for communities. This leads to project terms of reference, and further project proposals that compromise Indigenous rights. The process and content of most projects lack cultural relevancy.

Academic contributions

Will academics study their own kind? In today's expert-dependent society, academics are looked upon as impartial arbitrators of issues such as ethics, equity and progress. Within academia, opinions generally count if they reference peers and pass peer review. Often, there is scepticism towards other knowledge systems, especially customary law. This has prompted some editorial boards to resist publishing analyses of sustainable tourism that primarily reference

Indigenous Peoples themselves. It has resulted in a stream of discourse that is short on questions and perspectives of critical priority to Indigenous Peoples.

Advocacy group contributions

Will NGOs scrutinize their own shortcomings? Several NGOs concerned about 'sustainable' tourism have doggedly followed policy development, while themselves mired in conventional problem-solving. At the 1999 International Workshop on Sustainable Tourism and Biological Diversity in Vilm, Germany, most NGOs were quiet once discussion turned to developing sample indicators. Similar inertia struck the 2000 follow-up meeting of international NGOs in Berlin, Germany. Deliberations were again more reactive than visionary, and stuck in critiques. Many NGOs neglect the ground relationships vital for real insight and legitimacy – in particular, proper protocol with Indigenous Peoples.

Indigenous peoples' contributions

Can capacity-building be reframed? Governments tell Indigenous Peoples that they need training. This programme delivery has an overwhelmingly corporate format. While some programmes dovetail with certain needs – for example, skills for self-determination – most groom 'participants' for limited industry roles. Indigenous Peoples must then use assessment criteria determined by funding agencies. In light of this, the most important training for Indigenous Peoples concerning the tourism industry is how to protect rights, especially in relation to national ecotourism plans. Their own *internal and independent* evaluations of private, public and, allegedly, 'non-profit' sector initiatives in their communities' midst are paramount for cultural sustainability.

BOX 9.6   Air travel: Altitude sickness for one and all

In the mid-1990s, Herb Kelleher, CEO of Southwest Airlines, commented: 'What's under way is the Wal-Martization of the airlines business' (Reguly, 2001). Since then there have been cost-cutting mergers, such as the Air France takeover of KLM Royal Dutch Airlines (Jones, 2003). One travel agent witnessing industry adjustments says: 'It's a giveaway, really. This is a wacky business and it's getting worse by the hour' (Bellett, 2003). The cost of air tickets, never based on real cost accounting, is increasingly disassociated from industry's impacts upon the biosphere and humanity. According to British experts, 'permitting the predicted growth in air travel from 180 million passengers a year to 500 million would destroy plans to tackle global warming' (Clover, 2002).

Tourist contributions

Will we travellers reclaim our life compass? The UN has studied consumer behaviour, with the tourism industry peering on.[20] However, both are content to let us consume so that economic growth sizzles on. Consumer profiling has merely helped companies to hone their product placement. While many of us are horrified by the thought of being so manipulated, few recite anything different than today's media (that is, mainly corporate) images of the 'good life'.[21]

Institutional and professional frameworks

Doctrine of objectivity

Many of us assume that the core tenet of sustainability is 'Do no harm'.[22] Yet, one of the most *harmful* ground rules of our time is objective dialogue. Respected world leaders maintain that: 'We need to speak to really effective things, not to emotions' (Toepfer, 2002). In more balanced times this might serve well; but today it suppresses ethical debate. Some issues and values deserve a passionate defence. Otherwise we enter a barren landscape of dialogue across world economic sectors on what is sustainable.

The ideology of corporate objectivity, especially scientific objectivity, is filtered down to communities through institutional programming and funding. As more Indigenous Peoples revalue their own culture and cultural knowledge, this is being questioned. In one community workshop in Peru, the facilitator stopped midway to pull aside the host NGO to clarify goals. Why? Because there was no emotion around the table for community 'conservation' issues. Indigenous Elders usually teach the youth to share their knowledge with emotion intact: with *heart*. But in this case the real 'hands on' people were missing; invited local professionals (albeit Indigenous) were attending in their place. So the workshop was not a community event after all.

Neither professionals, nor any other specialists or interest groups, should presume to say for Indigenous Peoples what is sustainable. Those of us immersed in the professions, lifestyles or other economic benefits of the corporate/consumer world need to understand issues like complicity before any real open mindedness can exist. It is hard to bring objectivity to cross-cultural work if one's own contradictions remain unexplored.

Particular care is due with regard to cultural sustainability. It may be appropriate to contribute technical support to cross-cultural dialogues if Indigenous leaders issue an invitation. However, the dialogue process, project methodology and/or evaluation tools should all be vetted broadly by affected Indigenous Peoples first – especially by those not typically on the government call list or institutional roster. If such cross-checks are thwarted by lack of government funding or other bureaucratic barriers, it is time to demand a dialogue process that is sustainable. This means insisting that Indigenous leaders have appropriate access to information and technical support in order to represent their peoples effectively – otherwise, Indigenous rights may be skirted through 'democratic' procedures.

Expert analysis

Being an authority on 'sustainable' or 'eco' tourism does not imply high community regard. Appointed experts usually do what is economically expedient. Few insist that standard-setting conforms to the inherent and inalienable rights of Indigenous Peoples. This raises the question of who is the client. Is it the agency paying the bill, or those whose lives, cultures and ancestral lands are immediately on the line?

Most Indigenous Peoples have ongoing challenges with 'experts' sent into their midst. Those parachuted in by government or industry are usually biased against customary systems and are therefore unprepared for cross-cultural work. Those working for development agencies or NGOs, meanwhile, often become overconfident; they consider themselves sensitized to community and cultural issues but can be just as impaired by 'expert' thinking.

Indigenous leaders have voiced particular concern about experts working in an overview capacity, who advise on policy and programmes for sustainability. With biodiversity so topical, many such experts now feel compelled to comment superficially on Indigenous Peoples. Mere *mention* of 'Indigenous issues' has become a form of professional due diligence.

In recent years there have been irresponsible commentaries on Indigenous rights by individuals who do not work daily in the realm of rights. One noted tourism scholar has said that the rights of Indigenous Peoples are 'often oversimplified and romanticized' (Bushell, 2000, p99). While culture or cultural traits can be romanticized, *rights* cannot. Rights are a technical issue involving customary law, international law and a thorough grasp of what colonial law entails. Is compliance with international law a romantic aspiration?

Often, professionals who are considered well rounded and objective are recruited onto government teams for policy development. For example, 'moderate' NGO representatives were called upon to help push through the controversial *CBD Guidelines on Tourism*. One also acted as a sounding board on the problematic sub-guidelines concerning Indigenous territories. In both cases, the involved individuals proceeded even after being informed (by fellow NGOs) that the process and frameworks utilized would severely undermine Indigenous rights (see Chapter 10, 'Surviving the "Indigenous" guidelines').

Individuals working in the field of sustainable tourism need to understand that their work impacts Indigenous Peoples and must adopt a personal code of conduct for themselves, reflecting on the following:

- Neglect of Indigenous rights (that is, ancestral title and the right to self-determination) is unacceptable.
- Advisory services are not appropriate if the client seeks to minimize due diligence called for in international law.
- Dabbling in issues concerning Indigenous rights, culture and governance can seriously harm Indigenous Peoples.
- Templates and other consulting standbys undermine both Indigenous rights and cultural diversity.
- Work that impacts Indigenous Peoples carries a responsibility first and foremost to the people, via their Elders.
- Good intentions do not release one from respecting cultural protocol, such as proper avenues for prior informed consent.
- Understanding comes by listening openly to Indigenous Peoples, not applying our corporate/consumer logic.

The ecosystem approach

Governments have committed through the CBD to an ecosystem approach to conserve biodiversity. However, the ecosystem approach is now obsolete. Our globalized consumer economy has already raised the ante. We are dealing with endangered *life systems*.

Ecotourism is a pronounced form of consumerism. Impacts in destination ecosystems, though often high, do not reflect the true cost of travel. We need to look at the multiple ecosystems damaged in the course of tourists' home job, hobbies and investments. 'People [who] are of the tourist nature spend 95 per cent of their time in the system that is destroying it all' (Leach, 1999). Our ability to travel comes from this broader consumer lifestyle.

The systems theory called 'biodiversity', which drives the ecosystem approach, is fractured. It enables us to view tourism costs at destinations such as Machu Picchu and Uluru as anomalies, rather than as a sign of toxic societal trends. We travel without realizing that our holidays refresh and prime us to be productive workers and, thus, good consumers. We visit Indigenous territories without understanding the irony that most Indigenous Peoples themselves do not travel.[23] While we jet around, they scramble just to reach the UN.

We are at a juncture in consumer society where self-knowledge needs to balance out hierarchical thinking. Reminders to reconnect have come from a number of quarters. Provocative books such as *The Cultural Creatives* (Ray and Anderson, 2000) and *Spiritual Perspectives on Globalization* (Rifkin, 2003) are emerging. They echo teachings such as the ancient Hopi prophecies about the path of materialism versus the path of heart. Where we travel in life is a highly individual choice, though advertising constantly tries to sway us.

A real life-systems approach will bring human behaviour into synchrony with sacred principles. We do not need to get fancy about indicators for sustainability. The four life elements are enough of a guide, alongside sacred knowledge (often embodied in customary law) and core international law on individual and collective rights (that is, legal safeguards in their original state; not watered down for the sake of commerce). Our fundamental human responsibility is to cherish and defend life for the sake of children, *all children*, meaning:

- *Air*: can they breathe air free of industrial contaminants?
- *Water*: can they access and drink water free of industrial pollution?
- *Soil*: can they access and consume wholefoods free of industrial chemicals and corporate engineering?
- *Sun*: can we adults reverse the climate change caused by industry and, thus, by our own consumer habits?

All of these core life elements are now extremely out of balance due to industrial economics, including ongoing colonialism. If our corporate/consumer world continues to hurtle on unchecked, life as we know it is in peril. Those of us living the consumer lifestyle must register this. We cannot delay making profound personal and societal changes to bring integrity to our relationships – within ourselves and with fellow humanity.[24]

BOX 9.7 | **Climate change: Odd bedfellow of 'eco' tourism**

Cheesemans' Ecology Safaris long ago issued 'A plea for the perpetuation of biodiversity and a planet inhabitable to all.' Their 1992 brochure warned that we are responsible for global warming. Unfortunately, few appeals of this type make the link between climate change and clients' air travel or land transport. One traveller reports: 'On my last safari, my wife and I drove 1300 miles [2090km] in a sturdy Land Cruiser, accompanied only by a guide' (Davis, 1999, p18). Thanks to such long-haul tourism, Mount Kilimanjaro, a safari favourite, is now 'stripped of its snowcap for the first time in 11,000 years' (Lovell, 2005).

Early warning systems

According to Indigenous Peoples, we are at a turning point in human relations with the sacred, including our relationships with each other and the natural realm. Decisions made by this generation of leaders will vibrate around the world as never before in history, through economic globalization. We are already witnessing this. Scientists have been unable to coherently explain the increased destruction by wind, drought, fire, floods and earthquakes. These are no longer natural occurrences, but abnormal events triggered by new scales of reckless consumption (including the current oil spree) and our crazy self-absorption.

Some Indigenous Peoples looking on bluntly say that their cultures are our early-warning system. Sacred knowledge passed down over millennia addresses life systems, including human behaviour. Continent to continent, the common principle of ancestral title is that rights must flow from responsibility. Some clans are named after animals as a remembrance of this connection. The frog clan, for instance, is reminded that the Earth sustains all frog relations: from four-legged, winged ones and water creatures to human (Lewis, 2001).

In consumer society, we look at rights and responsibilities differently. Industrial science talks in terms of 'indicator species' as if we humans are not one. Disappearing frogs, butterflies and coral reefs are recognized as indicators of biodiversity loss, instead of our own lifestyle choices. Societally, there is little emphasis on lifestyle other than to upgrade it. We have a narrow range of behaviour modification when something in life systems goes awry. In the midst of current climate change and cancer outbreaks, there are no sanctions against using household petrochemicals. Instead, we are told (by corporate media) to buy cars, trust in the usual consumer products and book a holiday to get our 'perspective' back. Buy now, *pay later*.

Globalization has shielded most of us in the corporate/consumer world from truth and consequences. When Indigenous Peoples are exploited or exterminated in the name of 'progress', the grim evidence is hidden away. But today this wall of invisibility is tumbling down, thanks to truths gradually reaching us via determined messengers. The UN has been forced to acknowledge Indigenous Peoples' critical role in maintaining biodiversity. And Indigenous leaders who manage to reach the UN stage are frank about what is endangering life systems. Information is available to us in the alternative media, if we have the courage to look.

When we abuse Indigenous Peoples for the sake of economics, we also abuse the four sacred life elements, discussed above. Indigenous Peoples, their cultures and their ancestral lands are indivisible. A blow to any one of them is a blow to them all. It is a severe blow to life systems as well. Every decision by us to shrug off rightful commerce, rooted in responsibility, accumulates into a heavy toll. The only counterbalance today is Indigenous Peoples, who remain the guardians of their life-sustaining ancestral lands. At this very moment, they are summoning us to listen.

A precautionary approach

Our corporate governments are belligerent in their pursuit of 'economic globalization'. Through UNESCO they started the Universal Ethics Project in 1997. However, Francesco Frangialli, secretary-general of the World Tourism Organization (WTO-OMT), still has the nerve to promote tourism as a 'smokeless industry' (Frangialli, 2002). And the World Heritage Committee (WHC) calls its new expert group on climate change 'early action' (ENS, 2005).

In 2005 the WHC left melting Mount Everest off the *List of World Heritage in Danger*. With this decision the alleged 'precautionary approach' of the CBD sank to yet another low. Presumably, bad publicity would put too much pressure on our precious Northern economy. Especially bad news the size of Everest: our beloved symbol in the North of conquered, tamed nature and of rescued 'poor' people (now supposedly happy porters).

Our tendency today is to lean on certification schemes in order to ease our ethics homework. If we understood the origins of certification, it would not so readily soothe our conscience. Certification and other awards are chiefly about moving product. Most companies find certification beneficial when it helps them to carve out a value-added niche or to outfox lobby groups. As a result, many known 'offenders' benefit from certification. Certification schemes get tainted by association, particularly as accreditation becomes more top down.

Following the beleaguered UN International Year of Ecotourism (IYE) in 2002, and the UN's adoption of weak guidelines on tourism and biodiversity under the CBD in 2004, major international institutions are exploring tourism certification with sudden cause. Lead organizations include the WTO-OMT, UNEP and TIES, joined by the Rainforest Alliance (US). As before the IYE, it is unlikely that the proponents of industrial 'eco' tourism, – or any well-funded intermediary organizations, – will ask the tough questions regarding sustainability. UN agencies are propagating 'a single common approach' (see www.tourism.unctad.org).

Available precedents show the limitations of voluntary certification. In the forest sector, some smaller companies are engaging Forest Stewardship Council (FSC) accredited certifiers;[25] but the major licensees lean towards looser standards under bodies such as the International Organization for Standardization (ISO) (FERN, 2001). In the organic farming sector, 'certification now services big business better than [dedicated producers] and consumers' (Chop, 2003, p19). There is nothing to suggest that tourism certification will go a better course.

Many NGOs are dedicated to undoing the damage of industry-biased certification. Organizations such as the Working Group on Tourism and Development (AKTE) in Switzerland) and Tourism Concern (UK) are advocating fair trade tourism. ITRI in the US, meanwhile, is promoting Indigenous-led certification. But Anita Pleumarom (2003) of the Tourism Investigation and Monitoring Team (TIM Team) in Thailand has challenged these NGO colleagues, saying: 'I have [not] seen any clear proposals on how fair trade initiatives could make corporations involved in the tourism sector liable for unfair, predatory and unlawful practices.' It is *our own travel lust* that shelters and keeps the most problematic of corporate infrastructure.

In industrial tourism, there is essentially no 'fair trade' because the industry cross-cuts various global economies, world regions and colonial legal regimes. Scrupulous companies cannot stop others from riding their shirttail and penetrating vulnerable areas or Indigenous territories declared 'no go'. Airlines will not shut down to avert climate change or to assist Indigenous Peoples whose territories are now sinking below sea level (see Gygax and Auran-Clapot, 2003). Few tourists will shed our consumer lifestyle or the conventional corporate investments that enable travel. So, how can we codify abuse? Why would we legitimize an abusive, life-destructive web of commerce?

> Fair trade does not begin to address such fundamental questions. Even at its most inclusive, most transparent, and most capacity-expanding, it merely improves indigenous peoples' access to an imposed economic system that cannot accomodate fundamentally different ideas about ownership, community, or social relations (Lutz, 2005, p5).

Fair trade theories have limited applicability to tourism. The tenets of fair trade were developed to apply to trade in products, not peoples or cultures. Safeguarding the latter is a far more encompassing question than nifty, single-issue agreements. It hinges upon Indigenous Peoples' self-determination in a holistic sense. Today, many Indigenous leaders are finding that this requires a multi-tiered strategy, combining legal, political, negotiations, direct action and spiritual components. Indigenous Peoples must engage the corporate/consumer world on multiple, interlinked fronts. NGOs and industry bodies such as the WTO-OMT TIES are hardly the ones to guide this process.

BOX 9.8   Sustainable tourism: Current industry standards

In contemplating what constitutes sustainable tourism:
    ... it is important to bear in mind that:
    1   Indigenous Peoples' territories are the target of the vast majority of ecotourism.
    2   Indigenous cultures themselves have been increasingly commercialized by third parties as such niche markets are developed.
    3   Indigenous Peoples often are the service backbone of the industry, though usually on paternalistic and/or exploitative terms which contravene international treaties for Indigenous and human rights.
These are the current industry standards (Johnston, 2000, p173).

Usually, there is no 'better' or 'best' when it comes to certification because third-party exercises in certification are market-based, and infringe upon ancestral title and rights. Safeguards exist when Indigenous Peoples can exercise their ancestral title, in its full scope and meaning through mandated leadership (see Chapters 2 and 3). Consent is then granted or denied through proper cultural channels involving the Elders. Decisions are made at a territorial level on the basis of sacred knowledge – after comprehensive review of tourism impacts upon Indigenous Peoples, humanity and life systems globally.

Beliefs and interpretation

Understanding the sacred

Although time is short for us to avert wide-scale industrial suicide, we are a very long way from any breakthroughs in communication on sustainable use.

When Indigenous Peoples say that the land or a certain area is sacred, the majority of us living the consumer way read this as political posturing. The assumption is that Indigenous Peoples just want a slice of the economic pie. Most individuals supporting economic growth and globalization believe that the pie is irresistibly appetizing. We see neither our own paternalism, nor the real nutritional value of the pie. Who and what does it feed? Children's author Madeleine L'Engle gives us a glimpse in the story *A Wrinkle in Time* (L'Engle, 1973).

Indigenous Peoples viewed as holding out on industry proposals are generally considered backward or prey to poor advice from environmentalists. They are often seen as having a victim complex and, thus, as needing to score a point. Sometimes companies openly liken them to a demanding child. In business circles, this racism manifests as scorn for Indigenous Peoples' governance ability and business aptitude. Overtures like consultation smack of such thinking; most aim to give just enough lip service to 'reconciliation' in order to crack stubborn communities.

Indigenous Peoples have reiterated that the sacred is not negotiable. Where resistance to industry transgressions is possible, whole families, communities and tribes have united to safeguard ancestral lands for future generations. There is no 10 per cent tithe as in European traditions; rather, everything is given to uphold life covenants. Among many Indigenous Peoples it is said that the constitution is written in the land.

Today, Indigenous Peoples are speaking about sovereignty not just to world governments, but also to global industries. Many Indigenous leaders are outspoken about corporate imperialism and the perils it poses, especially now that economic globalization so flagrantly crosses sacred life thresholds. Some see the day fast approaching when Earth systems and life cycles as we know them will shut down, reminding us of the Creator's sovereignty and teaching all humanity a harsh lesson on ownership and sustainable use.[26]

Sacred versus sustainable

Among Indigenous Peoples the words 'sacred' and 'sustainable' are fundamentally one. 'Sacred' refers to the belief that this physical world comes from the Creator, with its own immutable laws of connection and balance. It means that we cannot presume to own, buy, sell or remake any part of Creation.

Whereas sustainability is an inter-generational concept among the world's Indigenous Peoples, it remains self-focused in global consumer society. The world economy is driven by the ideology of 'resources'. Anything viewed as a resource (whether 'natural' resource or human 'capital') is considered there for the taking.[27] This has led to the infamous *terra nullius* doctrine of 'developing' Indigenous customary lands as if they were free to claim. Worldwide, those with business drive are still speeding to the corporate registry.

The businessman expecting a lifespan of 80 years wants to make his 'mark' in time to enjoy the fruits of his labour. On this life path there is both a heavy ecological toll and staggering impacts on fellow humanity.[28] Upon death, an estate of perceived belongings is left to offspring or relatives; however, what is bequeathed in posterity is a swathe of industrial impacts. Even so, we continue to pride ourselves as being 'industrious'.

Indigenous leaders know the business-oriented language of sustainability used in national politics and governments' foreign affairs. They will use the word 'sustainable' as a tool for cross-cultural communication. Still, their effort to translate sacred knowledge for dialogues on sustainability is a tedious task. In government talk shops, the mental gymnastics are endless – by design, the province of lawyers and number crunchers.

Between world governments diplomacy is more about image than substance. Politicians are conditioned to read between the lines and play policy off policy. This institutional culture gets projected onto Indigenous leaders addressing nation states on the topic of sustainability. Government delegations keep waiting for Indigenous Peoples to show their supposed true colours and 'get on with business'. Behind every Indigenous face they see a lurking consumer. They assume that Indigenous Peoples are adequately assimilated to want the dream blitzed at them through development propaganda and mass media.

Indigenous Peoples who have freed themselves from colonial thinking are very clear about their sense of what and who they are dealing with under the industry guise of 'eco' tourism. *All industries*, including the conservation industry (whether dealing with cultural or natural 'heritage'), share the same basic formula for business. Behind the marketing jingles of creations like ecotourism, most business interests subscribe to standard notions of profit and profit-making. We are nowhere near a shift in attitude.

BOX 9.9 | **Hopi discipline**

WARNING WARNING
    NO OUTSIDE WHITE VISITORS
    ALLOWED BECAUSE OF YOUR
    FAILURE TO OBEY THE LAWS
    OF OUR TRIBE AS WELL AS THE
    LAWS OF YOUR OWN.
Sign outside the Hopi village of Oraibi, Arizona, US, 1979)

Sacred jobs

The ecotourism industry is in denial of its impacts on cultural and biological diversity. The grim feedback from Indigenous Peoples is not registering on corporate radar screens as a serious issue. Why?

Today, jobs are treated as sacred. In consumer society, the workplace has become our universal sacred site. Jobs provide the currency to hold status and to belong. They bind consumers and corporations in a pact for social survival. This union blurs all common sense about sustainable relationships. Governments profiting off the confusion cannot be relied upon to restore any balance or order.

On today's job sites, the hunter goes forth, forgetting that when the 'Web of Life' is stretched too far strands will break. The hunter has given away what it means to be a hunter. He no longer prepares his own hunt in a sacred manner. Things that used to be watched – such as the season and availability – now matter little except in the context of share prices, dividends, bank interest rates or salary. Discretion is handed over to world corporations under the umbrella of impact assessment.

Companies are now entrusted with the proverbial hunt. Their focus is on shareholder return, not healthy co-existence. In the tourism industry, this translates into exponential forecasts for growth. Sustainability is measured by the volume of visitors and their per capita spending; if these economic quotas fall short, industry will not entertain other pillars of sustainability – for example, ecological, social, cultural or timeless ethical considerations. In times of both abundance and scarcity, the corporate hunter is single-minded about profit.

International talks on biodiversity conservation have not changed accepted sustainability equations. Traditional knowledge is imbedded in the CBD as a formality. Nevertheless, business interests have clung to the crumbling world (that is, corporate) 'order'. Now, they are surrounded by instability: political, ecological, psychological and spiritual. Under siege, the in preoccupation with economic growth is increasing. In corporate/consumer society, money means decision-making power – until Earth and life thresholds snap.

The chaos will continue to build until we each realize that it is time to discipline our own selves. Who are *we*? We are the global consumer class. We keep filling our shopping basket with industry 'goods'. *We are the least discerning, most dependent and confused persons in history.* We tread on sacred lands with dim memory of the life they support. We clamber across sacred sites as if they have lost their original relevance.

Conclusion

Today we are told there is a growing world economy. There is no shortage of affluent philosophers praising free market 'advances'; for instance, plantation crops and patented prescription drugs. But we need to ask who reaps these privatized benefits (that is, profits), at whose exploitation and to whose ultimate demise.

Sustainability can be thought of as a sacred blanket. If different threads of planning and management are brought together as a sustainability strategy, the blanket can have impressive texture for a while. But true texture and hold come from the core relationships that bind the blanket. Outcomes depend on whether these relationships are superficial or meaningful, and if those involved are conniving or caring.

Industry standards must address what it means to hurt and to heal. Our globalized economy generates intense pain for the majority of the world's people, particularly Indigenous Peoples. The consumerism feeding it stems from a more insidious form of pain: our spiritual disconnection. Professionalism marked by personal detachment and corporate culture is no way to mend such rifts. We need to waken our common humanity, not sanitize it.

Bureaucratic and institutionalized thinking on sustainability needs to end. As professionals, business owners, workers and tourists, we have not begun to assess our blind spots. It is time to observe what we do and why. It is one thing to undertake impressive sounding studies, programmes or 'eco' trips; it is quite another to divest ourselves of lurking prejudices and to seek understanding before making choices that affect others' lives more than our own.

The issues of sustainability run much deeper than our intellect. For a meaningful debate on sustainable tourism– or sustainability in *any industry* – we must be willing to get dirty, be wrong and stay real. What we discover about ourselves in this process may shock us. Outside our chronic consumerism there is a whole orbit of interdependence that we have yet to explore. If we can get past our sense of personal entitlement, this world would be a place of true abundance.

Beyond consumer milestones like holidays, there is another life vista. Spiritually, each of us is so much more than a consumer. Consumerism is a racially loaded corporate agenda, weak on coexistence and other expressions of cultural diversity. When we choose healthy interdependence outside it (for example, in our own community, family and/or garden), both our world and the world at large become a gentler, truly richer place.

It is incumbent on us all to open up to understanding. This is a narrow road. In order to travel it, we must abstain from 'consumer' holidays and search out opportunities for *real connection* and purpose. This is a very personal journey, but the crux of sustainability. Will your life contribute to the oppression of peoples and the endangerment of life systems, or be an instrument to uplift humanity?

Recommended reading

- Bakan, J. (2004) *The Corporation: The Pathological Pursuit of Profit and Power*, Free Press (also see film by same name: www.thecorporation.com)
- Berman, M. (1988) *The Reenchantment of the World*, Bantam Books, New York
- Dalai Lama, His Holiness (1999) *Ethics for the New Millennium*, Riverhead Books, New York
- *The Ecologist* journal, www.theecologist.org
- Environment News Service, daily electronic bulletins, www.ENS-NEWS.COM
- *Worldwatch* journal, Worldwatch Institute, www.worldwatch.org
- WWF-International (World Wide Fund for Nature International) (2004) *Living Planet Report 2004*, www.panda.org/livingplanet

Figure 9.1 **Sustainability checklist: Tourism and biodiversity conservation in Indigenous territories**

INDIGENOUS TITLE & RIGHTS
Consistent with international law on the rights of peoples

DISCIPLINED APPROACH
Subservient to life systems not corporate baselines

PRECAUTIONARY PRINCIPLE
Relationships based on mutual respect and understanding

SUSTAINABLE USE
Guided by sacred knowledge and Elders protocol

Figure 9.2 **Alarm bells for culture loss: What community feelings say about tourism**

Before assuming that tourism is 'good for the people' find out if local communities voice frustration, and pay attention to any words that might indicate 'business as usual', for example:

- Consulted, compensated, tokenized
- Deceived, misled, misinformed
- Bullied, intimidated, threatened
- Relocated, reserved, institutionalized
- Exploited, indentured, abused
- Marginalized, repressed, oppressed
- Labelled, degraded, humiliated
- Assimilated, exhibited, sexualized
- Discounted, belittled, stereotyped

Figure 9.3 **Questions to ask: Discerning the truth about 'eco' tourism**

'Yes' Indicates higher likelihood of sustainable tourism
'No' Indicates a red flag

World Policy Bodies
- Is there a non-partisan track record of correcting known 'development' abuses?
- Is the policy process itself sustainable, ie rights compliant?
- Do existing, interim and/or new policies align with Indigenous Peoples' rights?
- Are institution staff sensitized to rights-related issues and their link to sustainability?
- Is there an effective grievance mechanism for Indigenous Peoples within the policy process?

Industry and Companies
- Does comprehensive community planning precede tourism marketing?
- Are the Indigenous People(s) assured free and prior informed consent over all marketing?
- Are the core criteria and indicators for sustainability defined by the Indigenous People(s)?
- Do provisions for monitoring and evaluation have the guidance and blessing of Elders?
- Do staff receive ongoing cross-cultural training directly from the affected Indigenous People(s)?

Destination Country
- Is the state responsive to Indigenous grievances about international process? Eg UN, OAS, WTO, IUCN
- Has it made a sincere and sustained effort towards the decolonization of Indigenous Peoples?
- Does it engage in meaningful talks with Indigenous leadership toward interim measures to protect rights?
- Does it respect and effectively protect Indigenous Peoples living in voluntary isolation?
- Do national 'best practices' uphold Indigenous Peoples' rights?

Development Agencies
- Do the Indigenous People(s) themselves freely ask for third party presence and/or assistance?
- Do third parties heed cultural protocols and customary law?
- Do they remove themselves if requested by the Indigenous People(s)?
- Is there a strategic plan, jointly developed at the community level, to help frame cross-cultural dialogues?
- Do internal codes of conduct prohibit paternalism and back room decision making?

Tourists
- Do the tourists identify with Indigenous Peoples at eye level?
- Do they know the history of genocide linked to feeling 'better than' Indigenous Peoples?
- Are they aware that Indigenous Peoples have sophisticated knowledge systems, including prophecies?
- Can they think beyond the economic exchange of tourism, to see the relationship in all its dimensions?
- Is there any debriefing for the tourists together with the Indigenous Peoples, post trip?

Figure 9.4 **How to evaluate local tourism benefits:**
Indicators for sustainable 'eco' tourism in Indigenous territories

SAMPLE PROCESS
    1 *Standard* – established according to sacred knowledge of life systems
    2 *Goal* – defined through a legitimate community planning process
    3 *Indicators* – developed to be relevant to Elders and other customary authorities
    4 *Methods* – decided on the basis of cultural protocol

STANDARD: Self determination with respect to tourism
Goal: Ability to undertake collective decision-making as a People, including the right to say 'no'
Indicators:
- Industry compliance with international law concerning Indigenous Peoples' rights
- Maintenance of traditional resource rights, as a family, community and People
- Compatibility of company activities with customary law and cultural protocol
- Prevalence of outside 'experts' and interests in tourism planning and management

Methods:
- Assess terms of reference for dialogue, funding, consultants and pilot projects
- Compare theoretical protection for rights (eg legislation) versus actual situation (eg policy or practice)
- Audit changes in management structures over time
- Monitor the quality of legal agreements and voluntary gestures by industry

STANDARD: Integrity in the local tourism economy
Goal: New relationships based on mutual respect and understanding
Indicators:
- Uninterrupted access and use for Indigenous Peoples within own ancestral territory
- Adequate resources (eg food) for communal purposes, e.g. Elders, feasts, trade
- Generous return on tangible and intangible services, including the guardianship of biodiversity
- Not reliant on 'court action' or other campaigns to defend rights

Methods:
- Perform 'full cost' accounting of all tourism activities
- Assess level of direct funding available to Indigenous Peoples for governance, business and innovation
- Map changes in property rights distribution over time, and types of transfer or allocation made
- Monitor false and racist accusations such as 'poaching' or 'squatting'

STANDARD: Equitable diversification of local economy and livelihoods
Goal: Healthy interdependence
Indicators:
- Quality of protocol agreements
- Degree of respect for permitting capacity of Indigenous governance bodies
- Level of community-controlled investment
- Types of market targeted and ability to prevent unwanted market shifts

Methods:
- Develop indicators for economic development based on customary knowledge of sustainable use
- Monitor the fulfilment of commitments made in protocol agreements
- Compare funds distributed to communal royalties, corporate profits, 3rd party service contracts and taxation
- Track % of profits accruing to conservation versus business, who controls this budget and for what

Figure 9.5 **Rights and responsibilities**

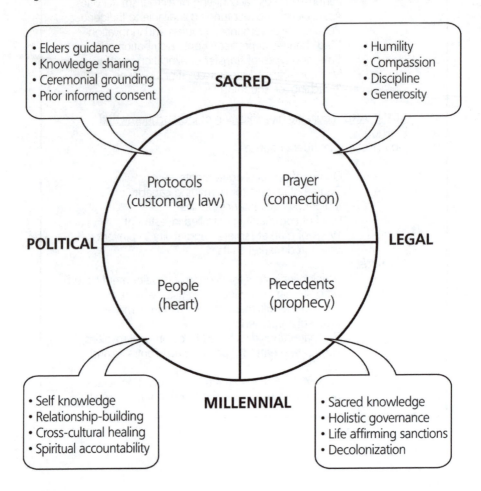

Figure 9.6 **Porter at Panama City Airport, Panama: Summing up the colonial reality of tourism**

Chapter 10

United Nations

**I venture to suggest to you that we have now reached almost the
end of our resources in speech-making, and it is not enough
that our ears be feasted ... but it is necessary that our
hearts have got to be touched.**

(Mahatma Ghandi, quoted in Fischer, 1950, p134)

The Hopi prophecy delivered to the United Nations (UN), and received by
the Hopi themselves millennia ago, describes two paths in life: one spiritual
and one materialistic. It speaks about knowledge and about individual choices.
The Hopi have shared it with the world believing that we are at a critical juncture. Four times they approached the United Nations General Assembly, to
warn that the '*Bahanna*' ('white') way of materialism will lead to chaos and our
own self-destruction (Mails, 1997, p175). Their overtures were rejected until
December 1992 when the UN conceded to host the *Cry of The Earth* gathering in New York (see Wittenberg Center, 1993).[1] By then optics on Indigenous
'issues' had changed; at the Rio Earth Summit, traditional knowledge had
become political currency.

   The Hopi are not the only Indigenous People to warn of the testing
times and possible danger soon to come if we do not salvage our spiritual
selves. In 1990, the Kogi of Colombia issued a documentary film through
BBC to 'give us a final warning' (Ereira, 2001, p35). This film was conceived
by the *Mamos*, the Kogi spiritual authorities, out of profound sadness and concern for humanity's present course. 'We are the Elder Brothers, with knowledge of all things, material and spiritual. We know what you have done. You
have sold the clouds. Open your eyes' (Ereira, 2001, p35). Like the Hopi, the
Kogi speak of our widespread annihilation – a purification of the Earth – if
we continue to flout sacred law.

Charting our humanity

Developments at the UN attest to this historical crossroad. Several negotiations are under way on environmental standards, addressing dilemmas identified in the 1987 *Brundtland Report* on sustainable development (WCED, 1987). While many initiatives for so-called 'sustainability' appear productive, few align with sacred life principles. The commanding framework is money (that is, economic growth). Indigenous prophecies warn that this economic orienteering will fail. We all live in the same precious Earth envelope; it now is coming apart at the seams due to our habitual – sometimes frantic – consumerism.

One sign of this malaise is the form of follow-up taken by the UN with Indigenous Peoples. During 1993, the UN Year of the World's Indigenous People motivated new partnerships. The theme of partnership carried forward through the UN Decade of Indigenous People, 1995–2004. Traditional knowledge became a feature of the *UN Convention on Biological Diversity* (CBD) and subsequently a focal point for agency programming. This has created a perception of even-handedness, if not of favour, towards Indigenous Peoples. At the World Ecotourism Summit (WES) in 2002, Klaus Toepfer, head of the United Nations Environment Programme (UNEP), very sincerely reported:

> There is a concentration already within the UN on Indigenous knowledge. This is a huge step forward and a signal to the global community to be aware of this. Certainly, with regard to Indigenous Peoples, I believe we are on a very, very good track. I really believe Indigenous Peoples' issues are high on the agenda now (Toepfer, 2002).

Nonetheless, the UN vision for dialogue on 'sustainable development' is not what it seems. There is a commercial substrate to *all* consultations with Indigenous Peoples.

The UN now has a labyrinth of programming on Indigenous 'issues'. Although Indigenous Peoples can finally address world governments on the UN stage, there is no seat there for them. At Cry of the Earth in 1993, Manuel Hoyungowa, grandson of earlier Hopi messenger Manuel Hoyungowa, made it clear that Indigenous Peoples were still not welcome at the UN (Hoyungowa, 1993). Today, as when the Hopi started knocking at the door of the UN in 1949, the same situation exists (see Boxes 10.1 and 10.2). In 2002, the United Nations Permanent Forum on Indigenous Issues (UNPF) commenced.[2] But throughout the UN system there is a distinct policy of subjugating Indigenous Peoples. Being high on the agenda is not synonymous with a role in shaping it.

The UN remains impenetrable for Indigenous leadership and Elders wishing to establish a proper governance relationship. The house of nations does not recognize Indigenous nations. Nor does it understand them. It is a system where sovereignty is secular (as opposed to spiritual) and private property law is supreme. In this environment, mutual regard often falters. Exchanges are guarded, alliances are tactical and stature is relative. Such scuffling defies the circle of life. It leaves no prospect of even basic dialogue on sustainable use, let alone sacred knowledge, with Indigenous Peoples.

We are told by Indigenous Peoples such as the Hopi and Kogi to reconnect as one family or lose all. If we continue to snub or tokenize Indigenous leaders on the critical governance questions of our time (air, water, soil and sun), there will be chaos. Indigenous Peoples hold the balance to industrial thinking and to our consumer appetite.[3] The UN needs to heed this. It must drop the patronizing, watered-down consultations on 'Indigenous knowledge' and start *real* dialogue on healing the relationships that endanger life. Final warnings are a blood red flag.

Checking our pulse

To understand where the UN is going in this particular chapter of history, we must look at the global tourism industry. It is no coincidence that tourism is high on the UN agenda today. Ecotourism is a last bastion, a means of completing what colonialism started. It provides a way to commercialize not just remaining 'biodiversity', but also the so-called 'intangible' heritage of Indigenous Peoples: culture itself.

According to industry, 'sustainable' tourism will shower blessings on far-flung communities, now typecast as the rural 'poor'. Our consumer monoculture will be their salvation. In practice, however, most Indigenous Peoples experience industrial ecotourism as a potent form of culture loss. In spite of this, the UN made tourism a darling sector through its International Year of Ecotourism (IYE) in 2002. Tourism entered the CBD dialogue as a form of 'sustainable use'.

The IYE announcement prompted an international outcry from grassroots groups. Most notable was the Third World Network's (TWN) campaign to scrap the IYE (TWN et al, 2002). In Asia, Indigenous Peoples gained access to the regional WES preparatory meeting, but only after non-governmental organizations (NGOs) rattled the organizers, saying: 'it really is inexcusable that the WTO-OMT [World Tourism Organization] … refuses to adhere to democratic principles and defies all efforts to remove the serious conflict of interests that has evolved around the IYE' (TWN et al, 2001). Indigenous participants then issued their own statement: 'we traveled from far away places to talk with you, only to find out that conclusions ready to be imposed on us have already been ironed out even before we arrived to this conference' (Chiang Mai, 2002). Identical concerns were voiced by the few Indigenous delegates who made it to the WES. Fiji elevated the issues, declaring its opposition to the imbalanced *Quebec Declaration* of UNEP and the WTO-OMT (see www.world-tourism.org/sustainable/IYE/quebec/anglais/declaration.html).

Globally, there is a macabre underbelly to the ecotourism economy. In the *Oxford Dictionary* macabre means 'dance of death'. Government negotiations on trade, environment and human rights are fast becoming part of this dance. Decisions in forums such as the CBD, United Nations Commission on Sustainable Development (CSD) and the World Commission on Protected Areas (WCPA) suggest precautions, but have left a paper trail allowing for industry expansion. To world governments, 'sustainable' tourism is still synonymous with economic growth. So, whose common good are the UN and the World Conservation Union (IUCN) protecting?

Through 'eco' tourism, world economic powers are pushing their agenda of economic rationalization onto 'underdeveloped' regions. Countervailing measures to biodiversity 'conservation' adopted within the CBD process – and parallel bodies such as the World Trade Organization (WTO) and the World Intellectual Property Organization (WIPO) – virtually ensure industry 'success'. Indigenous Peoples are not recognized as *peoples* (that is, rights holders) in the legal and lawful sense of the term. Alhough biodiversity is supposedly a priority, countries find more profit in vice than virtue.

The veneer of promise in the ecotourism industry is wafer-thin after three decades of abuse. As 'development' agencies push tourism to ward off debtor insolvency in the South, and governments rev up to privatize so-called 'protected' areas, ecotourism is becoming more deceptive than ever. At the UN, recent policy marketing has turned tourism into a perverse celebration of cultural diversity and poverty elimination. We are led to believe that those industry giants pimping Indigenous cultures and lands (in other words, cultural and biological diversity) will protect them (Pleumarom, 2003).

When sacred knowledge, sacred sites and sacred ceremonies can be appropriated for sale as 'eco-tours' or other incarnations of 'heritage' tourism, then we are close to liquidating the very life balance that sustains us. This is well under way, so we are indeed close. It leads to a form of insolvency that markets cannot ride, science cannot fix and we can barely fathom. Artists have written and sung about this to wake up the consumer masses.[4] Even Aesop's fable of the two frogs talks about our self(ish) destruction. But we still, for the most part, choose complicity through silence.

BOX 10.1	**UN Convention on Biological Diversity (CBD) lacks Indigenous Peoples' representation**

We must respectfully notify the CBD Secretariat that, to date, there is no mechanism for true Indigenous Peoples' participation in the *UN Convention on Biological Diversity*. The vast majority of Indigenous Peoples have absolutely *no knowledge* of the convention or how it affects their collective rights as Peoples under international law. This is an extremely serious situation because governments are now nearly ten years into negotiations. Therefore, we must deliver the message today that the pretending must stop... It is completely false for the Secretariat, or governments signing onto the convention, to suggest that Indigenous Peoples of the world have access to this process. *It also is inappropriate and unrealistic for the Secretariat or governments to expect the International Indigenous Forum on Biodiversity to speak on behalf of all Indigenous Peoples.* This consultation system creates an image of consensus-building, which is not supported by fact. Most Indigenous Peoples' leadership and their Elders remain *absolutely unaware* of your inter-government process on biodiversity.

(Tribal Chief Mike Leach, St'at'imc Chiefs Council; Leach, 2002)

UN Convention on Biological Diversity

Policy development on tourism

In 1997, the subject of tourism and biodiversity entered the UN consciousness. A handful of delegates began to collect around UN cafeteria tables, dreaming up pathways for the international dialogue on sustainable tourism. Usually, the circle included an NGO or two with an inside track on available funding. It was clear from the guardedness of these conversations that tourism and biodiversity would soon be a big business. Wish lists submitted to funders included workshops and more workshops, supported by 'best practice' studies. Many of the ideas circulated held promise of Indigenous Peoples' direct involvement. It all sounded legitimate and groundbreaking enough, but fell short on basic principles. Those Indigenous Peoples whose cultures and lands are mass-marketed through ecotourism were nowhere to be seen.

In 2002 the IYE arrived and there was still no meaningful voice for affected Indigenous Peoples in the UN debate on sustainable tourism. When tourism entered the 1998 round of UN negotiations on biodiversity, little effort was made to communicate implications to Indigenous Peoples (Johnston,

1999).[5] 'Expert' meetings on tourism got under way, with limited Indigenous participation. The CBD Secretariat understood that Indigenous Peoples should be involved, but seemed to underestimate the price of letting the process 'fall into place'. This left Germany, the main funder, to piece together the dialogue. It invited faces who had become familiar in the course of UN sessions or through its own development assistance projects. Only a few parties to the CBD took this tourism initiative seriously; but there were enough players to loosely call it a process.

Today, the international dialogue on tourism and biodiversity continues to operate largely by default. It cannot claim to have visibility among affected Indigenous Peoples worldwide. Nor can it profess to involve an adequate cross-section of 'experts' on sustainable tourism. The meetings have, without exception, been last minute affairs, even to those on the UN rumour circuit.[6] Attendance seems to have consisted primarily of whoever is readily available, few of whom are conversant with the CBD or Indigenous Peoples' vital role in biodiversity conservation.[7] Tourism NGOs, shut out of the CBD process on tourism until March 2000, have tried to play catch-up.[8] Even under old paradigms of participation, it would be hard to say that this process is 'as good as it gets'.

On the ground in communities targeted for so-called 'sustainable' tourism, the CBD is obscure. At the 2000 International NGOs' Workshop on Tourism and Biological Diversity in Berlin, one participant asked: 'Does the CBD liberate us or constrict us?' This is a complex question requiring detailed knowledge of UN processes. The complexity alone makes the process a liability. It is not just a matter of reading and understanding the CBD text, but of sitting inside the political debates on implementation, now occurring between governments. Governments themselves are utilizing the CBD for cross purposes. It is not uncommon for some governments to discretely flip flop their negotiating positions several times within a week, or between different UN affiliated bodies, to further their broader foreign policy objectives (see Box 10.5). The goal is *maximum* commercial access to Indigenous ancestral territories.

Indigenous Peoples wanting to understand whether the CBD affords any real protection would need to know the nature of such UN debates, which governments have the most to gain from manipulating the process, and how controversial issues like 'traditional knowledge' are packaged for negotiation. Only after full immersion in this hothouse can Indigenous leaders discern if the CBD belongs in their toolbox for protecting rights. Often, what newcomers find is that the CBD is mercurial. In some cases, it creates useful lobbying leverage, but in others it poses a hazard. The rights of Indigenous Peoples are far from secure, or even supported, under the CBD.

> **BOX 10.2**
>
> **International Indigenous Forum on Biodiversity (IIFB): Protecting or negotiating away sacred lands and sacred knowledge?**
>
> The traditional authorities of most of our peoples maintain the fundamental principles of our laws... However, throughout the CBD process I have seen – with real concern – that the Indigenous representatives meeting in the Indigenous Forum seem to deviate very easily from our principles, getting closer and closer to what seems like a dangerous process of accommodating what is imposed by the laws of trade and privatization of life... I want to be very emphatic in saying that we, the representatives of Indigenous Peoples ... have an enormous responsibility to defend the rights of *all* Indigenous Peoples in the world, including those of the thousands of peoples whose own wise men and women, drawing on their own laws, are saying that they want to live as Indigenous Peoples and that there is no place in their world for privatizing or doing business with life, with our mother Earth, or with our knowledge.
>
> The Fifth Indigenous Forum presented a document [to the UN] on Article 8(j) and related provisions... This document ... [did not] take into account all the positions discussed ... so therefore it cannot be considered a consensus proposal ... and prepares the way to mortally harming the future of Indigenous Peoples throughout the world.
>
> (Lorenzo Muelas Hurtado, Guambiano people, Movement of Indigenous Authorities of Colombia; Hurtado, 2000)

UN Guidelines on biodiversity and tourism

At the 2004 Seventh Conference of the Parties (COP7) in Malaysia, signatories to the CBD adopted global guidelines on tourism and biodiversity. The process to develop these guidelines began amicably in 1998 with a German government proposal,[9] but became saddled with controversy once Germany's strategy seemed to change in 2000 to 'success at any cost'.[10] At this point, discussions became needlessly polarized. Irregularities of process forced observer NGOs to fundamentally challenge the course of talks, exposing how a potentially good process turned bad.

From the beginning, the main concern among most tourism NGOs was that any process for global guidelines should respect the rights of Indigenous Peoples. Germany's proposal advocated that the guidelines should be undertaken in partnership with industry, with 'adequate attention' directed to Indigenous interests (not *rights*). At the CBD Ministerial Roundtable on

Tourism in 1998, countries pledged to 'take into consideration' and 'deal with' Indigenous and local communities. However, the references to Indigenous Peoples were patronizing. Governments were cautioned about the danger of letting participation 'fall unreasonably short of the ideal' (Johnston, 1998a).

To understand where the process lost integrity, we must fast forward to 2001. During that year the CBD Secretariat hosted the 'experts' Workshop on Biological Diversity and Tourism in Santo Domingo to begin finalizing international guidelines. Like previous meetings on the topic, this one was funded largely by Germany.[11] Although the emphasis was on vulnerable ecosystems, there was no acknowledgment that Indigenous territories are vulnerable *because of* industrial 'eco' tourism. Nothing in the meeting set up reflected the damage by so called 'eco' or 'sustainable' tourism to Indigenous Peoples, their cultures or ancestral lands[12] (and, thus to life systems on Earth). A few NGOs were invited, some of them Indigenous organizations. However, Indigenous Peoples' mandated leaders are only now beginning to find out about this process and the guidelines, after the fact.

In Santo Domingo, a vocal contingent of NGOs spoke in support of Indigenous rights.[13] This was an uncomfortable task, given that the proper role for NGOs on these matters is to support direct submissions of Indigenous leadership. By this stage, however, the optics on Indigenous participation in guidelines development had become utterly misleading. The CBD process on tourism was being carried by 'champions' who seemed increasingly dismissive of any mention of Indigenous rights. This made it important for witness NGOs to break the silence. Although the CBD Secretariat buoyed the meeting with balanced chairing, attitudes on the floor showed where the process was at. Some delegates were openly hostile towards the notion of cultural sustainability and towards CBD provisions for 'traditional' knowledge'.[14]

The Santo Domingo meeting could have launched a rich cross-cultural dialogue on sustainable tourism. Instead, it split on issues of Indigenous

---

BOX 10.3   *Akwe:kon Guidelines*: **Micro-managing the sacred**

The celebrated *UN Convention on Biological Diversity* (CBD) guidelines on impact assessment for sacred sites and Indigenous territories, called the *Akwe:kon Guidelines* (2004),[16] are part of grand political theatre. They were forged in a profane institutional setting without respect for cultural protocols. Actual custodians of well-known sacred sites, and of connected teachings, were never present in the guidelines process. Thus, 'negotiations' proceeded without appropriate consent and involvement of authorities and spiritual Elders, who understand and safeguard sacred knowledge. How obvious must our folly be before we wake up?

rights. While the resulting guidelines seem technically competent, they are highly damaging to Indigenous self-determination and, thus, to cultural diversity. Such an outcome was flagged heading into the process.[15] What no one foresaw was the extent to which the 'Guidelines Team' would push a process that was so visibly flawed.[17]

Surviving the 'Indigenous' guidelines

The real bane of the CBD process on biodiversity and tourism was a short-cut taken by the CBD Secretariat. On 18 April 2001, the German NGO Ecological Tourism in Europe (ETE) revealed to colleagues that a parallel set of UN guidelines had been drawn up specific to Indigenous Peoples' territories. ETE reported that these 'Indigenous' guidelines were superb. In actual fact, they are a travesty of Indigenous rights. There was no process at all with Indigenous Peoples to develop them. The content opens the way for rights infringement on multiple levels.

The *UN Draft Guidelines for the Conduct of Tourism in Territories Traditionally Occupied or Used by Indigenous and Local Communities* (known in UN lingo as UNEP/CBD/WS-Tourism/2) became a nightmare for the CBD Secretariat. The document was initially in the participants' package for the UN Workshop on Biodiversity and Tourism in Santo Domingo. However, when a group of NGOs expressed concern about the origin of these guidelines, the secretariat withdrew them. Factual information on their authorship was withheld. The secretariat gave three differing answers when pressed for information; it was not until the third and final day of the Santo Domingo meeting that it admitted they were a product of the secretariat itself.[18]

This document became known among concerned tourism NGOs as the 'mystery guidelines', and since Santo Domingo there has been an utter hush about them within the UN. When the CBD Secretariat attended the IFB preparatory meeting for the next Working Group on Article 8(j) (concerning 'traditional knowledge'), it was asked by the International Support Centre for Sustainable Tourism (ISCST) to address the guidelines for the benefit of those present, and to provide a copy to all Indigenous delegates. The secretariat ducked this question and spoke instead about the showcased umbrella guidelines on tourism of biodiversity. No copies of the document in question were circulated and none has yet to be released by the secretariat across Indigenous Peoples' communication channels.[19] All that lingers are questions about the document and its authorship.[20]

The CBD Secretariat should have been frank about its mistake. It is supposed to be an impartial facilitator of the CBD proceedings. While it is evident to all that the UN has inherent limitations, creating guidelines in the shadows specifically for Indigenous territories is a disturbing precedent. This incident is a wake-up call to the UN. If it wishes to function as a gathering place for honest dialogue on rights and responsibilities (including sustainability), its conduct must be without prejudice. Otherwise, the UN might as well declare itself a world trade agency.

Lessons lost and learned

Did the main CBD arena learn any lessons from the fiasco over the nicknamed 'mystery guidelines'? No. Proper Indigenous Peoples' involvement in developing the UN's umbrella on biodiversity and tourism was not sought, even though Indigenous cultures and territories are the main attraction globally for the 'eco' tourism industry. Instead, the presence and participation of NGOs in Santo Domingo, some Indigenous, was construed as acceptance of the guidelines' content – *without these terms of participation being communicated.*

None of the coordinating agencies or their consultants, with the exception of UNEP later on, took an interest in improving the process. Rather than look at ways to strengthen talks, the 'Guidelines Team' seemed to bank on appearances. ETE was retained to help shepherd the guidelines further along, creating an impression of NGO-consensus to support them.

In September 2001, ETE called a meeting of NGOs in New Delhi, partnering with the local NGO Equations for credibility. This was an important step in stage-managing the growing controversies. By this time, both the *UN Guidelines on Tourism and Biodiversity* and the IYE were on quicksand in the eyes of most NGOs involved as observers. Equations had hoped to open a space for effectively airing grassroots concerns. Afterward, however, Equations joined other NGOs in raising the concern that ETE and UNEP had misrepresented the event as being pro-guidelines and part of the IYE. UNEP was chastised for this 'ethically questionable method' of promoting so-called ecotourism (Third World Network et al, 2002).

The next phase of marketing the guidelines cut to the chase and dealt with the necessary political correctness around Indigenous Peoples. At the eighth Subsidiary Body on Scientific, Technical and Technological Advice (SBSTTA) to the CBD in 2003, an individual *said to* represent the Kuna of Panama was brought on stage by the Guidelines Team to make the final sales pitch – as if endorsement from world Indigenous Peoples existed. When government 'experts' accepted the guidelines moments later, the team hugged and whooped as if the process was something to be proud of.

In reality, there were embarrassing moments for the CBD Secretariat leading up to this initial government acceptance of the guidelines in March 2003. NGOs had submitted a number of statements exposing the collapse of good faith with respect to Indigenous Peoples (ISCST et al, 2001). These were brushed off, but nonetheless viewed as a threat to the process; fury and indignation were expressed from the very top down. How dare anyone say that the emperor is without clothes?

When UNEP hosted an event on tourism during the eighth SBSTTA in 2003, it was told by the CBD Secretariat, Germany and ETE (all invited speakers) that NGO involvement offering a dissenting opinion would be unacceptable and cause for their withdrawal. At this moment, the process became openly undemocratic. UNEP was pressured to stifle debate and it very apologetically asked for ISCST to step down as a speaker, though the organization had been cordially invited by UNEP and already was listed on the event poster.

The irony was that, by then, NGOs voicing concern about the CBD process on tourism saw no value in being redundant. ISCST was already was working with NGO partners internationally to support Indigenous leadership in creating an alternate route to safeguard Indigenous Peoples' rights. Thus, after discussion with home leadership within the St'at'imc nation,[21] the ISCST withdrew from the UNEP speaker's list in order to help redirect relationship-building. The St'at'imc Chiefs laughed in good humour, saying: 'Welcome to the club. Now you are being treated like an Indian.'

BOX 10.4 **World Commission on Protected Areas (WCPA) Tourism Task Force: Called to task**

During the World Parks Congress (WPC) in 2003, Indigenous leaders requested proper protocol from the WCPA Tourism Task Force and met with its chairs to explain why (see Gavidi et al, 2003)). Afterwards, a WCPA representative wrote privately to one Chief – slandering other involved Chiefs, planting rumours and saying that some Chiefs had been manipulated. She called the Chiefs' statement a private 'ambush' and downgraded the concerns about Indigenous *rights* to 'semantics'. This kind of institutional response utterly dismisses the gravity of issues pertaining to life on Earth, which are raised by Indigenous Peoples. When it happens at the executive level, we should fundamentally question the governance and decision making systems we have in place.

The hot potato of Indigenous rights

NGOs made a final appeal to salvage the CBD process on tourism in 2004 during COP7 in Kuala Lumpur. Their appeal backed the CBD Indigenous Caucus, which, following the guidance from Chiefs at the 2003 World Parks Congress (WPC) (see Gavidi et al, 2003), had requested that adoption of the tourism guidelines be deferred to COP8 in 2006. Deferral would have ensured that the guidelines address *cultural* sustainability, giving them legitimacy.

By this time, UNEP had stepped in to correct the irregularities of process, supporting the International Indigenous Leadership Gathering on Sustainable Tourism to be hosted by the St'at'imc People in Canada during

2005.[22] Klaus Toepfer stated: 'UNEP is aware of the need to build the capacity of Indigenous Peoples to fully participate in decisions regarding the development of tourism on their land' (Toepfer, 2003). This meeting, organized according to cultural protocols, would be the first opportunity for Indigenous leaders worldwide to evaluate the serious issues raised by the IYE and CBD tourism talks. The St'at'imc had called together affected Indigenous Peoples to deliberate how to guide the international community on bringing a conscience to the tourism industry. This endeavour was endorsed at its inception by the government of Fiji, the Great Council of Chiefs in Fiji, and Maasai Chiefs in Kenya and Tanzania, among many others.

In Kuala Lumpur, 'civil society' merely requested that world governments welcome the guidance of Indigenous leaders in 2005 before adopting the guidelines. Nonetheless, NGOs found their statement in support of Indigenous Peoples blocked (Johnston, 2004b and c) until steps were taken to save face for the process. Statement signatories such as TWN, the Tourism Investigation and Monitoring Team (TIM Team) and the Ecumenical Coalition on Tourism stood ready for a press conference if procedural amends were not immediately made by the UN. Yet, the fuss was never over NGOs getting heard; it was about creating a proper, lawful and welcoming space for Indigenous Peoples' leadership to be able to table concrete recommendations.

How deep did the institutional resistance go? On the surface, it appeared that the CBD Secretariat needed to shore up this particular process on tourism. However, the real conflict was over policy and procedures for Indigenous Peoples' involvement, which could spill across the whole UN. The Indigenous Leadership Gathering (eventually rescheduled for 19–25 March 2006), open to properly *mandated* Indigenous leaders, offered the very kind of Indigenous Peoples' representation that the UN has tried to avoid. It provided for real *Peoples'* representation, which has been systematically undermined in both the CBD Indigenous Caucus (the International Indigenous Forum on Biodiversity, or the IIFB) and other government-funded Indigenous 'expert' bodies within the UN and its affiliates (see Boxes 10.1 and 10.2).

For the UN, optics on its handling of Indigenous 'issues' remain a touchy, unresolved matter with high financial stakes for world governments and global corporations. The tourism industry has looked to the UN for user-friendly rules of access to biodiversity rich areas. It now has them, thanks to a clever closing act at COP7 orchestrated by the German Ministry of Environment.

'Indigenous' figureheads figured out

The CBD process on tourism shows what happens when policy development becomes more about products than principles. By 2004, Germany's role as champion of the UN process on tourism appeared driven by budget and a need for project deliverables. While the German Bundestag supports Indigenous Peoples' ancestral title and rights (German Bundestag, 2001), its Environment Ministry proceeded in the opposite direction, ignoring all warnings from NGOs abroad that the draft CBD tourism guidelines would *endanger* Indigenous Peoples. At COP7 in Kuala Lumpur, the German Environment Ministry and its colleagues pointedly skipped the IIFB's insightful workshop on tourism.

As mentioned earlier, Germany had arranged for a seeming representative of the Kuna (Panama) to praise the draft CBD tourism guidelines at the eighth SBSTTA in 2003,[23] giving the impression of Indigenous Peoples' support. The speaker characterized the draft CBD tourism guidelines as a valuable 'stakeholder' tool and 'a tremendous opportunity to utilize the *rapid growth* of tourism as the vehicle for sowing conservation, sustainable use and equity throughout the world [emphasis added]' (Muller, 2003, p8). These remarks came within a UN technical body which few Indigenous delegates are sponsored to attend. However, bystanders familiar with international law on Indigenous rights suspected immediately that this statement may not have been approved by the Kuna General Congress. It was entirely out of character with Indigenous Peoples' own submissions to the UN.

When COP7 opened in 2004, the Kuna were again held up by Germany as evidence of world Indigenous Peoples' supposed support for (and knowledge of) the draft CBD tourism guidelines. The German Environment Ministry distributed hundreds of copies of an impressive looking 'implementation' case study concerning the Kuna territory, known as Kuna Yala. This case study was produced expressly for COP7 to promote the UN's formal adoption of the guidelines. It was created with the heavy involvement of the same NGO delegate alleged to represent the Kuna. This individual had shown up at the meeting of tourism NGOs in Berlin just before COP5 in 2000, representing Conservation International (CI) and *opposing* measures of protection for Indigenous Peoples. At the WES in 2002, he had handed out business cards as a Canada-based tour guide, announcing that he was on the expert/advisory group formed to draft the CBD guidelines. Over time, some NGOs began to wonder if the Kuna knew much about these UN shenanigans.

Although the German case study admits that *moni* (the Kuna's borrowed word for money) has undermined Kuna culture, it also notes without much concern that Panama spent US$10 million on tourism marketing in 2002, in the hope of attracting more than 1 million tourists (Muller et al, 2003, pp28–29). Furthermore, Kuna Yala arrivals were expected to surge since 90 per cent of Panama's inventoried coastal attractions lie there (Muller et al, 2003, p30). Where is the *sustainability* in this, particularly cultural sustainability? It is mentioned briefly that the Kuna felt the UN guidelines 'don't recognize [Indigenous Peoples'] autonomy in resource control'. Nonetheless, the guidelines are summed up as 'an excellent coordinating framework' (Muller et al, 2003, p51) – but for whom?

From the perspective of Indigenous Peoples' rights, this German case study is disappointing. The process behind it is a particular concern. Independent follow-up indicates that the Kuna General Congress had no idea that participating in this study would mean being used for marketing UN guidelines on tourism that are potentially *harmful* to Indigenous Peoples. A senior Kuna technical worker says:

> This individual has no mandate at all to speak on behalf of or in association with the Kuna... He has taken advantage of the Kuna name to present several initiatives [not of the Kuna] ... by assuming representation of Kuna NGOs that appear weak. The rapport with our traditional authorities is not good.

The implications of participating in the German study were apparently not understood by the Kuna General Congress (that is, the Kuna Chiefs). This means that free and prior informed consent (PIC) was lacking.

BOX 10.5   Foreign policy manoeuvres

Governments with a high financial stake in how Indigenous rights are handled by the United Nations (UN) are strong on diplomacy, but blunt in their economic objectives. Within *UN Convention on Biological Diversity* (CBD) negotiations, there is often simultaneous policy-making and policy breaking, especially by Canada. At the fourth Subsidiary Body on Scientific, Technical and Technological Advice (SBSTTA) in 1999, Canada advocated that the cultural and spiritual impacts of tourism should be included in the assessment and monitoring of tourism (working group 2), then sabotaged this by opposing the principle of prior informed consent (*off record* in the government contact group), which is vital to Indigenous self-determination. Canada routinely plays both sides of the fence with respect to Indigenous Peoples, depending upon how much mileage is achievable in public relations (international image) versus domestic problem- solving (the Indigenous land 'question').

Prior informed consent defeated

The *UN Guidelines on Tourism and Biodiversity* were never intended to assure PIC by Indigenous Peoples. They are a conventional consultation tool, bringing the usual risk of extinguishing Indigenous rights (see Chapter 8). Several NGOs at the workshop in Santo Domingo reminded bureaucrats that Indigenous PIC must be a core principle. After the controversies there, the CBD Secretariat issued a fancy brochure for COP6 (The Hague) stating that Indigenous Peoples 'must be … approached for prior informed consent' (CBD Secretariat and UNEP, 2002, p9). However, on the day of adoption in 2004, Canada predictably requested that PIC be removed from the guidelines, saying: 'Prior informed consent is a sensitive issue for our country… There is a lack of logic in seeking the prior informed consent of people you are trying to notify' (that is, subjugate).[24] Brazil backed this request, having earmarked US$200 million for a promotional campaign called Pro-EcoTour in 1999. This cemented the *UN Guidelines on Tourism and Biodiversity* as an instrument for industry access to Indigenous territories.

The CBD Secretariat, in defence of the guidelines process, stated in Kuala Lumpur that it had conducted electronic consultations over two years and received comments from the CBD Indigenous Caucus (IIFB). It emphasized that some signatories to the controversial NGOs' statement there had been funded to attend the Santo Domingo workshop. None of this signals any real regard for Indigenous Peoples of the world. Why?

- The Santo Domingo workshop was announced just eight weeks ahead of time. The UN did not notify or invite affected Indigenous Peoples such as the customary authorities at Uluru, Machu Picchu, Chiang Mai or Hawai'i. Indigenous Peoples in global 'eco' tourism belts and at 'World Heritage' destinations, whose cultures and ancestral territories are vulnerable to tourism, were never included.
- The United Nations Development Programme (UNDP) reported in 1998 that in developing countries only 0.05 per cent of people have access to the internet (Carter, 1999). Among Southern Indigenous Peoples, this figure is substantially lower due to geographic, financial and language barriers; in the economic North, where most Indigenous Peoples live in developing world conditions, access rates are not significantly higher.
- Indigenous Peoples' and NGO representatives whose travel expenses are covered for UN meetings should not be under obligation to endorse the government programmes or initiatives under discussion. This would mean the loss of democracy and freedom of speech. No one should have to relinquish their own conscience, or forsake those they represent or support, in order to accept funding for participation.
- The IIFB is not representative of Indigenous Peoples of the world. There are no nomination criteria; participants are essentially self-nominated, though funding agencies also influence its make-up. As such, many members partake without any

real mandate or connection to cultural protocol official. This is known to many working on 'Indigenous issues' at the UN, including colonial governments such as Canada and Australia. Nevertheless, the CBD Secretariat made the IIFB an official advisory body, as if Indigenous Peoples' represention and government due diligence have been satisfactory (see Chapter 8).

- The IIFB produced consensus statements at COP7, consistent with the statement made by mandated Chiefs and other recognized Indigenous leaders during the WPC in 2003 (Gavidi et al, 2003), which attest to the UN's poor process on tourism. While the CBD process on tourism started in 1997, it was not until COP7 in 2004 that the IIFB had any capacity to conduct its own workshop on tourism.[25] The tourism guidelines were by then already wrapped up.

Given that the 'biodiversity' and 'sustainability' issues before us today are not just life-altering but *life-threatening*, we surely can do better:

> For decades, governments have tried to divide Indigenous Peoples or dilute their commentary by funding people who can speak but will not speak too much. On the biodiversity front, this has happened; now, Indigenous Peoples are starting to find out not only that something called the CBD exists, but that some government-funded 'indigenous representatives' have by their sheer presence endorsed a process that undermines traditional resource rights. The question being asked is: who do they represent and how were they appointed? Within Indigenous nations, there are long-standing cultural protocols for selecting and developing leadership (Johnston, 2000).

Nevertheless, asking for better is apparently too much. At the WES in 2002 the World Tourism Organization (WTO-OMT) scolded NGOs, saying: 'You have a bad attitude.'[26] The institutional outlook improved briefly following the WPC in 2003, when Achim Steiner, director general of the IUCN, acknowledged: 'An event without some heat and controversy is an event without relevance − without soul' (Steiner, 2003). But by COP7, the controversy on tourism deemed healthy by Steiner was again suppressed (Johnston, 2004b and c). Who gave the UN licence to baulk at upholding Indigenous rights? Since when was life not worth defending?

> **BOX 10.6** | **United Nations Draft Declaration on the Rights of Indigenous People: An expensive show**
>
> To develop a declaration that will have no real impact in law is to give false hope and expectations to Peoples whose lives are full of false hopes and broken promises. We do not want empty promises. We require real and tangible action from the United Nations for our survival as First Nations Peoples.
>
> (Michael Anderson, chairman of the Gumilaroi Nation, Australia, and convenor of the Sovereign Union of Aboriginal Peoples; Anderson, 1999, p9)

Reviving core principles

A process so lost in principle cannot be a beacon for balanced relationships. At some point such a process falls on its own inconsistencies amid all the cover-ups.

Unfortunately, such blunders of process are not isolated incidents inside the UN. The WTO-OMT is still coasting on its 1999 *Global Code of Ethics for Tourism*, said to cover all facets of sustainability including cultural protection (see Chapter 3). Its claims sound rather appalling once we hear how the process evolved and see the 'conflicting and contradictory nature of the text':[27]

> [The code] was initially drafted by entities known to safeguard the interests of the industry... [The WTO-OMT has] tried to project that [it] is a comprehensive document capable of addressing the complex web of tourism issues ... they refuse to see any whiff of tensions or contradictions within the code that could come in the way of its easy acceptance and implementation... [However,] The code is callously insensitive to the enormous problems created as a result of the incorporation of local communities into the market economy (Sreekumar and Gayathri, 2004, pp67–71).

When the WTO-OMT convened the first meeting of its Committee on Sustainable Development of Tourism in Thailand in 2004, there was a conspicuous absence of Indigenous Peoples; yet its study on sustainable tourism indicators specifically addresses 'traditional communities' as a type of *destination* (Manning, 2004). These indiscretions echo those made under the CBD. It is another worrisome performance, given the acute financial interest of corporations in 'biodiversity'.

It is time for the UN to operationalize core principles of the 1997 *Berlin Declaration on Sustainable Tourism*, which was signed by UNEP, the CBD

Secretariat, the Global Environment Facility (GEF), the IUCN plus various countries. Point 16 asserts that 'tourism should be restricted and, where necessary, prevented in ecologically and culturally sensitive areas'. This statement puts a spotlight on the need to define what is culturally sustainable. It provides a clear protocol for industry practice in and around Indigenous Peoples' ancestral territories, especially vis-à-vis sacred knowledge. In doing so, it strips away the entitlement of 'experts'.

While Germany maintains that the *UN Guidelines on Tourism and Biodiversity* reflect all previous codes of conduct, including the *Berlin Declaration*, this simply is not true. The survey of instruments prepared by ETE as background to the guidelines does not refer to any Indigenous Peoples' statements central to discussions of sustainable use, only a select few NGO proclamations (Meyer and Garbe, 2001).[28] Cultural sustainability was the notorious moot in Santo Domingo. *Within the CBD guidelines on tourism there are no meaningful measures to protect cultural sustainability (that is, ancestral title)*, although some NGO meeting participants urged this as the baseline.

There is no way to achieve cultural sustainability in Indigenous territories (the biodiversity 'rich' areas globally), except through mandated Indigenous leaders, their Elders, spiritial guardians and other customary authorities. This is a learning curve that the UN, world governments and their own 'experts' have yet to embrace. After being warned by Indigenous Peoples of the costs of selling all, world 'leaders' proffered negotiations on 'traditional knowledge' (that is, sanitized sacred knowledge) via the CBD. Article 8(j) and related provisions of the CBD do address 'Indigenous knowledge and innovation systems'. This seems an elaborate concession but is a ruse for extinguishing ancestral title.

As the UN parades its Indigenous 'success stories' we need to be mindful of what it stands for. While one arm of the UN vows to safeguard the intrinsic beauty and building blocks of life, another teases them apart. This is the way that the UN habitually operates. It gives lip service to sacred knowledge but is content to let industry and corporate science race to the outer limits, selling seabed methane and biotechnology as answers to our time. In 2001, UNEP admitted that it could not provide an update on its own menu of tourism programmes, let alone those known to be under consideration by the United Nations Commission on Human Rights (UNCHR).

In such times of darkness one penetrating ray of light shows the true layout of society. Last decade this ray of light shone not once but twice. The Hopi and Kogi messages were both direct admonishments, sent to the corporate world and those of us living the consumer way. Today, neither the Hopi nor the Kogi sit inside CBD talks. What does this tell us? Just how long will we pretend to be sincere, knowledgeable and caring?

Time for an overhaul

Peeking into the UN

Currently, two major systems of law exist in the realm of industry. There is the law of nation states, which drives the world economy using linear concepts of ownership and accountability. There is also customary law as practised by Indigenous Peoples, which generally embraces the world community from a perspective of interdependence and *mutual* sustainability. Most 'eco' tourism satisfies only the first set of laws. When does something legal become unlawful?

The CBD process on tourism has stumbled along – producing agendas, timelines and outputs before effective terms of reference for Indigenous Peoples' participation exist. Respected NGO advocates such as Nina Rao (Equations, India), Anita Pleumarom (Tourism Investigation and Monitoring Team, or TIM Team, Thailand) Deborah McLaren (Indigenous Tourism Rights International, or ITRI, US) and Tan Chi Kiong of the Ecumenical Coalition on Tourism (ECOT), Hong Kong) have worked overtime to issue a message of concern. But the institutional machinery of the UN threw up protective barricades, as if no lessons remain about structuring a participatory debate. Ron Mader, moderator of internet forums on tourism, has observed: 'In many cases, to discuss [certain issues] at all means being blacklisted' (Mader, 2002). The UN decided to promote tourism through the IYE, and most on the revenue chain have applauded.

Regarding the CBD framework and process at large, there are a few points to ponder:

- *The CBD is pro-industry, not pro-biodiversity.* There is a recurrence within the CBD, and other policy fora of this nature, of supposed 'experts' steering a pro-industry process and agenda, which Indigenous Peoples are expected to embrace.
- *The CBD has no real ecosystem approach.* Indigenous Peoples and Indigenous communities most immediately impacted by biodiversity-intensive industries (for example, ecotourism and the pharmaceuticals industry) have no knowledge of the process or its implications, let alone how to influence the process or protect against it.
- *Article 8(j) and related provisions give false comfort.* There still is no system to alert Indigenous Peoples as to what is being negotiated, how they can monitor or contribute to the debate, and who is accountable for facilitating their involvement.

- *The CBD does not protect Indigenous rights.* Outputs look consistent with the spirit, principle and letter of applicable international law but are phrased to avoid the core commitments of international law.

While world governments negotiate commercial access to culture, sacred sites and Indigenous territories at the UN, most Indigenous Peoples lack the basic information and resources necessary to demand due process. Concerns submitted in the interim by the small contingent of Indigenous 'representatives' are linguistically massaged by lawyers until their life force is suppressed. It is like a moulting process. The discourse looks intact because of the usage of words like 'traditional knowledge'; but all that is left is a hollow casing.

BOX 10.7   Cultural diversity or genocide?

Should we welcome the UN's new *Universal Declaration on Cultural Diversity*? During 2004, the United Nations Educational, Scientific and Cultural Organization (UNESCO) organized a dialogue on cultural diversity and tourism, addressing spirituality. But next door in the United Nations Commission on Human Rights (UNCHR) it is reported that 'isolated native communities are facing "true cultural genocide"' (Cevallos, 2003). Meanwhile, Belgium has 'blamed North America for the world's worst ever genocide over its killing of [15 million] Indigenous Peoples', indicating that 'the extermination continues today' (Logan, 2004). Several Indigenous Peoples such as the San in Botswana and the Maya in Guatemala now have genocide cases ready for international courts. Nevertheless, the UN still pushes the *same* industrial 'development' model that is responsible for the genocide. What the UN claims to protect via the *UN Convention on Biological Diversity* (CBD) it is actually destroying.

Prying off our blinkers

The economic mandate of the UN, and the pressure to meet corporate timelines for UN business, have made us captive globally to an industry system. We are all, to some degree, inoculated against knowing – if we participate in and benefit from the corporate/consumer economy. We have no idea of just how misinformed we are. The term 'biodiversity' suggests much less of a life crisis than what industry has unleashed around us.

UN deliberations on 'biodiversity' and related trade topics are held in scattered places without full transcripts. Canada and Australia – with the backing of New Zealand, the US and the UK – are using this process to lead the way to the global extinguishment of Indigenous Peoples' rights, the cornerstone of so-called 'biodiversity conservation'. In remote corners of the UN labyrinth, they have orchestrated an assault on Indigenous Peoples' ancestral lands, with dire implications for life systems on Earth. There are few observers present who know the technicalities or diplomatic language of this rights infringement, who are able to bear witness.

As colonial nation states, the UN itself and their respective business partners moan about Indigenous Peoples being unrealistic, they are nevertheless forced by international conventions to feign respect. Indigenous Peoples are now icons for fair play across the UN, the IUCN and the WTO (via WIPO). It is an interesting, albeit horrific, game to watch. Countries like Brazil 'have led the way to create legal treaties to protect human rights defenders, and yet these same principles are not enforced in their own countries' (AI, 2003). Amid this, CI praises Brazil for supposedly taking the global lead in the national promotion of 'eco' tourism (Hillel, 1999).

Amnesty International (AI) has 'called on governments to take immediate and concrete actions to turn their rhetoric on multiculturalism and indigenous rights into reality', reminding governments 'of the commitments they made at the World Conference Against Racism ... which set specific goals for actions on Indigenous Peoples' rights' (Cultural Survival, 2002). In spite of this the government antics continue. In 2002, ITRI organized the regional conference on Indigenous Peoples and Sustainable Tourism in Mexico; all through the preparations it felt strung along by UNEP, which in the end never supported the event but, regardless, cast it as part of the IYE. When UNEP finally agreed to fund the 2006 International Indigenous Leadership Gathering on Sustainable Tourism, it allotted just US$10,000 – hardly equivalent to its big IYE splash benefiting industry.

There are steep barriers to Indigenous Peoples taking their stories, shared plight and sacred life message to the international arena. Likewise, there is unacceptable pressure on them to meet the corporate calendar. How can Indigenous leaders comment upon commercial negotiations at the UN or elsewhere that intimately concern their Peoples, if the process is foreign and enabling funds are scarce? Usually, this is out of reach. Among those who do attend, some are 'so wary that they [argue] for not supporting the negotiation process at all' (GRAIN, 2004, p25).

This inhospitable institutional environment compels many groups to try to fill the gap, often in the clutches of the UN. ITRI had to resort to using its pre-drafted *Oaxaca Statement* at the WES in 2002, despite grassroots dissatisfaction over how it was formulated – or it would miss the 'consultation' window. The IIFB never got on its feet in the CBD process on tourism until COP7 in 2004, just when the talks were winding down. In many cases it might be best to abstain in order to avoid perpetuating the UN treadmill. However, in the back eddies of UN's highly corporate proceedings it can seem crazy not to undertake some form of damage control. Some Indigenous leaders watching the makeshift 'representation' are worried by the whole affair. 'The Earth is our mother and for that reason we cannot even think of exploiting or negotiating with her' (Hurtado, 2000, p2).

It is time to take the mystique out of UN processes supporting economic globalization and thoughtless industrialization. Decisions that unhinge life systems are being handled far too loosely by the UN. From now on, we need court reporter transcripts of all 'diplomatic' transactions on the UN floor – particularly those by colonial governments and their cohorts, whoever they may be. *The Cry of the Earth* has been issued (see www.wittenbergcenter.org) and we do not have time to rely upon witnesses to report and corroborate the trade-offs or deals. Nor should we have to ferret out the truths of UN business.

BOX 10.8   The United Nations: House of cards

The United Nations (UN) is like a casino. It is a corporate house, funded by governments and sustained by economic growth. As such, the house always wins. Indigenous Peoples will make inroads in some rounds, securing what seem like successes – such as the new United Nations Permanent Forum on Indigenous Issues (UNPF). But what the UN seemingly awards to Indigenous Peoples is taken away by its other hand. This begs our scrutiny. Can we really gamble with *life systems*? For how long will we give corporations the upper hand?

Prospects for a shift

In UN forums, Indigenous Peoples have observed mounting apprehension among world governments towards their submissions – particularly on ancestral title, which entails customary law for sustainability. World governments know that Indigenous rights and international environmental standards are routinely overridden. They want to look forward to profit, not become mired in present or past issues like liability and compensation. Thus, as the CBD process on tourism progressed, it became evident that many feared the outcomes of Indigenous Peoples' analysis. There was a level of protectionism which had no rational explanation other than the corporate bottom line.

Policy is a non-Indigenous phenomenon that lacks both the long time horizon and solemnity of ancestral title. In protected areas, our sanctuary mentality and poor track record show just how porous policy is. One way for us to understand these contradictions and shortcomings, and why they grow to such proportions, is to reflect on our own make-up. We are said to have both right- and left-brain lobes, each assigned a different purpose. If we function from only one, we will be imbalanced. The same applies to policy-makers.

In government forums policy flows from left brain thinking. Yet, inside ourselves we are provided all that we need to get centred. Nothing is missing in our sacred make-up. We tend to forget this, giving in to the 'ready made' trappings of consumer society and dropping our own filters. This can include disowning our 'soft' side – the part of us associated with intuition and instinct – especially on the job. Instead of filtering decisions through all layers of our consciousness, we become lazy and default to more superficial reflection.

Today, the UN balance sheet on 'biodiversity' is utterly jumbled. It has taken something which embodies *life*, renamed it and tried to squeeze out profit. We now have subsidized biodiversity losses for years longer than any good business manager would run a deficit. Regardless, the UN continues as a house of mirrors. In 2002, UNEP head Klaus Toepfer said that 'the "wealth"' of animal and plant life nurtured by Indigenous Peoples for generations, for ages' amounts to a 'treasure trove of … industrial products for the 21st century' (UNEP, 2002). On this corporate course there is no requital.

Our dilemma is not about whether to retrofit the UN. We would need the right material for that daunting a task. If the UN comprised *peoples*, not corporations or industry proxies, we could make headway. But this is not the case. So we must begin with our own innate humanity. If we realign our own life then it is possible to create balanced alternatives outside ourselves. After all, our right lobe (that is, our 'connected' intuitive self) is all about being creative.

This somewhat paraphrases the shift that many Indigenous Peoples now say is possible. Mayan cosmology and prophecy explains it in great detail. So do the Native American medicine wheel and many other teachings of sacred knowledge. But we seldom stop to listen, or change channels from left to right. So it remains to be determined if we will opt to know these brothers and sisters on the 'Tree of Life', or continue to block them or lock them away for what they reflect back to us.

Today, under government regimes, the reminders to reconnect spiritually are being threatened. In the US, the National Park Service listed a ceremonial sweat lodge as a 'demonstration structure' (Tippetts, 2001). In Australia, the Aboriginal Tent Embassy was evicted again in 2003, the keepers of its sacred fire called squatters (Fickling, 2003). That same year the office of *Oxlajuj Ajpop* (Conference of Ministers of Mayan Spirituality) in Guatemala was ransacked and six Mayan spiritual leaders were murdered.

These various incidents could be seen as random. However, they are escalating as global industries become impatient to access the lands of Indigenous Peoples. So long as they keep repeating, the CBD and other UN tools for heritage 'conservation' are without footing. Countries cannot claim to protect biodiversity while seeking to intimidate or exterminate its custodians.

> **BOX 10.9** **Sacred not for sale**
>
> Whenever human beings act with bad intentions, sooner or later they will have to drink their own poison. Because no one can cut a tree without killing the leaves, and in the web of life, no one can throw rocks without disturbing the peace and the balance of the water. This is why ... when our sacred sites are invaded by the smell of white men, the end will be near, not only for the U'wa, but also for the *riowa* [whites]. (Letter from the U'wa, Colombia, to the world, 2000)

Thus far, we have been slow to absorb the issues. During 1978, Wiradjuri leader Kevin Gilbert was awarded the National Book Council Award in Australia. In 2002, the Aymara activist Oscar Olivera of Bolivia was awarded the Goldman Prize for South America. But there are daily accounts of persecution of Indigenous Peoples worldwide. Elder Irene Billy of the Secwepemc in Canada has been jailed for her role in the Skwelkwek'welt Protection Centre, guarding her people's ancestral lands from tourism. In Chile, a group of Mapuche were convicted of 'terrorism' in 2004, also for resisting the appropriation and commercialization of their lands.

In corporate/consumer society, the ethic too often is: 'What's mine is mine, and what's yours is mine too.' But we all have it in us to passionately and compassionately defend the sacred. Some of us just turn away.

Conclusion

We have been told by the Hopi that: 'We are at a most critical time in human history. It is a crossroads at which the outcome of our actions will decide the fate of life on Earth' (Hoyungowa, 1993). Arvol Lookinghorse, 19th-Generation Keeper of the Sacred white Buffalo Calf Pipe, carried a kindred message to the UN on behalf of the Lakota:

> Now, we are in a critical stage of our spiritual and moral and technological development as nations. All life is precariously balanced. We must remember that all things on Mother Earth have spirit and are intricately connected.

A decade later, the World Bank issued a treatise on biodiversity called *Faith in Conservation* (see Palmer and Finlay, 2003); but its policies are unchanged.

Inside the UN and other reaches of the corporate world, there is resistance and impatience towards hearing out Indigenous Peoples. Some feel that

Indigenous Peoples are catered to in biodiversity talks. Some feel the emphasis on 'Indigenous knowledge systems' is overblown and unwarranted. And others simply want to set aside the niceties and get on with business. Very few of us grasp that life systems are dangling by a thread or remember inside ourselves what sacred knowledge is.

In 2001, the World Heritage Committee decided to keep its club closed to Indigenous Peoples.[29] This slight to sacred knowledge, although calculated, is merely symptomatic of economic globalization. What is more remarkable is our own disinterest in knowing what goes on for the sake of global trade (in other words, for our consumer whims). We like what industrial governments feeds us. We gobble up industry's cockeyed explanations and excuses. A genuine life crisis is here and we don't get it.

Currently, within the UN, rules for apportioning Indigenous territories and cultural 'assets' (so-called biodiversity) are being negotiated. Many government delegates believe that these talks are taking the 'high road', and they are right. In the Hopi teachings, the high road is the road of materialism. Thus, what we have is a civilized process for a tremendous lack of civility.

The Hopi and Kogi Elders have appealed to us to recall our sacred contracts and to rekindle sacred relationships – inside our own self, between races and with the land. They call on each of us to examine our own heart and to look into the heart of world 'leaders'. We need to look at the reflection of our consumer society in the gasping Earth, and in the situation of exploited peoples, to understand not just what is amiss but *why*.

Through our investments, lifestyles and attitudes we are lost in self-reverence. We live for economics, while there are sacred laws which no fortune can bend. When we flirt with ecological thresholds there comes a point where human ingenuity fails to cover up. When we systematically oppress others, it ultimately harms one and all. But we can choose regeneration by healing our spiritual confusion and its divisions such as race, class and gender discrimination.

Between Indigenous prophecy, and our own discomfort at contemplating 'new' ways of thinking and relating, there lies important ground to cover. This is the ground of values and attitudes. It may suit our comfort zones to confine policy talks to impersonal and scientific language. However, sacred knowledge provides for restoring balance on *all levels*, not just in the physical (that is, 'environmental') realm.

As a society are due for a complete psychological and spiritual shift. It is now inescapable and will come by force (some say cataclysm) if we do not approach it with grace. If we let our sacred core atrophy, it does not augur well for either Creation as we have known it, or for the present generations of children.

We are living in a time of critical choice. Can we remember how to pray in our own way (to feel gratitude, thanks and humility), live simply and share? Can we celebrate life rather than acquisitions? In this decade we will either lock into chaos or cultivate mutual respect, empathy and understanding. It is up to us to enliven and sanctify our humanity. How this chapter ends is our decision. The sacred lies in our own free will – the daily choices we each make.

Recommended reading

- Alfred, G. T. and Corntassel, J. (2004) 'A decade of rhetoric for Indigenous Peoples', *Indigenous News Digest*, no 822, item 4, 20 January
- Ayres, E. (2004) 'The hidden shame of the global industrial economy', *World Watch*, vol 17, no 1, January/February, pp20–29
- BBC (British Broadcasting Corporation) (1990) *From the Heart of the World: The Elder Brother's Warning*, Documentary produced for BBC by Alan Ereira of Sunstone Films
- Hurtado, L. M. (2000) *The International Indigenous Forum on Biodiversity: Negotiating Away the Resources and Traditional Knowledge of Indigenous Peoples?* Statement by Movimiento Autoridades Indígenas de Colombia. Fifth Conference of the Parties to the UN Convention on Biological Diversity, Nairobi, Kenya, 19 May, available at www.biodiv.org
- Leach, M., Tribal Chief (2002) *Participation of Indigenous Peoples in the CBD Process*, Statement by the St'at'imc Chiefs Council to Working Group II, Participatory Mechanisms for Indigenous Peoples and Local Communities, Ad Hoc Open-ended Intersessional Working Group on Article 8(j) United Nations Convention on Biological Diversity, Montreal, Canada, 5 February, available at www.biodiv.org
- Pleumarom, A. (2003) ' Our World is not for Sale! The Disturbing Implications of Privatization in the Tourism Trade', Paper presented at the International Seminar on Tourism: Unfair Practices – Equitable Options, hosted by DANTE, Network for Sustainable Tourism Development, December, Hannover, Germany, available from the Tourism Investigation and Monitoring (TIM) Team, Thailand, www.twnside.org.sg/tour.htm
- UNGA (United Nations General Assembly) (1993) *'Cry of the Earth': The Legacy of First Nations* – The Prophecies of Turtle Island, UNGA, New York, 22 November

Appendices

Appendix 1
Tourism Among Indigenous Peoples: Identifying What is Culturally Sustainable

Vulnerability	Sustainability
Expert driven	Elders guided
Corporate science	Ancestral title and rights
Industrial economics	Livelihoods upholding cultural diversity
Corporate profit formulas	Relationships honouring our interdependence
Quantitative measures of 'success'	Cultural indicators of living in balance
Compliance with national ecotourism plans, emphasizing economic interests	Compliance with customary law and international law on Indigenous Peoples' full body of rights
Third-party certification	Protocol agreements made in good faith, vouched for by the People
Political promises – for example, poverty relief	Spiritual contracts – for example, empathy and compassion
Material goals pursued	Sacred life relationships sustained
Policy – based on short-term thinking	Ceremony – transmitting millennial knowledge
Biodiversity managed	Creation understood

Appendix 2
Indicators of Unsustainable Tourism: What to Avoid

- Policy-making is market driven and serves conventional tourism.
- Tourists bank and invest in economic sectors responsible for the oppression of peoples and/or loss of biodiversity.
- Travel logistics require air transport or other heavy reliance upon life-choking carbon fuels.
- Ancestral title and rights of Indigenous Peoples are ignored, downplayed or otherwise violated.
- Racism permeates the business interactions at any level of the tourism economy.
- National tourism receipts sustain a colonial system or pay off debts to neo-colonial countries.
- Industry success is measured in terms of economic growth, not healthy and humane interdependence.
- 'Best practices' are sales-oriented instead of fostering long-term ethical relationship-building.
- Consultations, negotiations and partnerships continue to take an exploitative course.
- High level of concern expressed by Indigenous leadership and/ or observer non-governmental organizations (NGOs) regarding government policy and/or management.
- Elders and other customary knowledge-keepers remain peripheral to decisions and problem-solving.

Always ask Indigenous Peoples for their direct guidance – and their specific requests – concerning travel to their ancestral territory, in advance of making any travel or tourism plans.

Appendix 3
Indicators of Sustainable Tourism: What to Applaud

- Government abandons its predatory role, in favour of guardianship for future generations.
- Terms of reference for decision-making adhere to international law on the individual and collective rights of Indigenous Peoples.
- Protocol agreements for dialogue and business are negotiated with appropriate customary authorities.
- Love, compassion and respect govern the planning and problem-solving.
- Policy is grounded in a profound cross-cultural understanding of sustainability.
- Management is neither appropriated by, nor handed over to, 'experts'.
- The ethics of free and prior informed consent (PIC) and 'do no harm' are consistently applied.
- Community readiness is genuine and is based on comprehensive, current and relevant information.
- Tourism exchanges foster mutual regard, empathy and fellowship not dependency or inequity.
- Ecological impacts are evaluated on the basis of life systems, not illusory snapshots of single ecosystems.
- Conflict resolution mechanisms are compatible with sacred knowledge and customary law.

Always ask Indigenous Peoples for their direct guidance – and their specific requests – concerning travel to their ancestral territory, in advance of making any travel or tourism plans.

Appendix 4
The Four Pillars of Sustainable Tourism: Bridging Corporate Science and Indigenous Peoples' Knowledge

There are four major issues requiring our attention if negative 'eco' tourism trends that seriously impact Indigenous Peoples and global life systems are to be reversed, allowing for sustainable tourism:

1   *International law*: in international law, Indigenous Peoples have two tiers of rights. There are collective rights as peoples, called Indigenous rights, which are derived from the historical occupancy and use of ancestral lands. There are also individual rights known as human rights. Both categories of rights are inalienable. It is therefore incorrect to categorize Indigenous Peoples' submissions on tourism development as interests or demands. Self-determination and prior informed consent (PIC) are recognized rights, not political statements or a negotiating position. Sustainable tourism will respect and support the full body of international law concerning Indigenous Peoples.

2   *Ancestral title*: ancestral title is the core of Indigenous rights. Considerable misinformation exists concerning Indigenous title to ancestral lands. Within Indigenous cultures the land is understood as a trust from the Creator. There is a sacred duty to protect the land for future generations. The United Nations (UN) has recognized Indigenous Peoples' distinct relationship with the land as central to cultural survival. Yet, a number of government initiatives are under way which compromise this relationship, including 'protected' areas. Sustainable tourism will reinforce ancestral title, while accommodating co-existing title between Indigenous Peoples and colonial nation states.

3   *Customary laws*: customary laws are an expression of Indigenous title to ancestral lands. These laws create a balance with the land, with one another as human beings and with all aspects of Creation. Today, this system for governance is often referred to as 'traditional knowledge' (or sacred knowledge, because it concerns sacred life relationships). It involves personal accountability on all levels, including spiritual. Sustainable tourism will comply with applicable customary laws.

4   *Protocol*: cultural protocol underlies the implementation of customary laws. It is governed by the Elders, who received this knowledge from their ancestors, and provides a clear framework for decision-making, now and into the future. Sustainable tourism will strengthen rather than undermine Indigenous cultural protocol.

Appendix 4 (continued)

When these points are addressed with sincerity it is possible to build a foundation of mutual respect and understanding, which extends to the economic realm. The first step towards such a shift in relationships is to be open to the meaning and significance of these points, and to realize the sacred principle of connection. With humility, reverence and listening to one another balance can be restored.

Source: adapted from a submission to the World Ecotourism Summit, Quebec City, May 2002, by Alison Johnston on behalf of the International Support Centre for Sustainable Tourism (ISCST)

Appendix 5
Cross-Cultural Protocol for Tourists: Sample

- Find out the real cost of your trip and who bears it, starting with climate change.
- Rethink whether you need to travel to regain your centre and feel alive.
- If you decide to holiday, know what your travel supports politically and navigate with conscience.
- Learn the real history of your destination, through the Indigenous Peoples' own history of colonization.
- Enquire with Indigenous organizations regarding regional issues of concern to Indigenous Peoples.
- Request permission to visit Indigenous territories directly from the concerned Indigenous People(s).
- Confirm before purchasing a tour whether the business is truly owned and operated by the Indigenous People(s), or if they are used as a front.
- If travelling with an intermediary, request confirmation that it has followed proper cultural protocol to obtain permits for entry and for all activities.
- Verify the conduct of businesses and non-governmental organizations (NGOs) offering 'eco' tourism, with groups such as Indigenous Tourism Rights International (ITRI) (see www.tourismrights.org), before buying any third-party services or products.
- Avoid travel companies that give a false image of their relationship with Indigenous Peoples.
- Seek clarification and guidance from Indigenous People(s) locally regarding appropriate protocols for visit.
- Determine from the Indigenous People(s) if access to advertised sacred sites and ceremonies is welcome and, if so, what customary laws need to be observed (for example, gender rules).
- Decline to participate in any activity that you would consider intrusive if roles were reversed.
- Purchase nothing of suspicious origins; search out community made items from the artisans themselves, from a community-cooperative or from a legitimate cultural centre.
- Report unethical and exploitative commercial offerings to organizations like Cultural Survival (see www.cs.org) and Survival International (see www.survival-international.org).
- Move beyond a time-bound sense of exchange, and ask the Indigenous Peoples' leadership about other ways to leave a positive impact locally.

Appendix 5 (continued)

- Contribute financially to the Indigenous Peoples' struggle for fundamental rights; do this in a form useful to the people, respecting their right to self-determination.
- Support the operational budget of the host Indigenous Peoples' office.
- Enquire if they would like a donation made to any other Indigenous Peoples' organization(s) internationally.
- Refrain from other exchanges (for example, gift giving) unless the Elders identify a specific communal contribution benefiting all.
- Contribute the equivalent of your travel budget to the Indigenous Peoples' own travel fund, to facilitate their access to the United Nations (UN) and other international avenues for protecting rights.
- Shift your donations for conservation from 'environment' groups to the Indigenous Peoples whose ancestral lands are concerned.
- Donate your air miles for Indigenous leaders and Elders to undertake travels, as needed, for further protection of their people's rights.
- Change your consumer habits and lifestyle, reflecting upon racism and poverty as well as Earth thresholds.
- Commit to your own joyful spiritual practice and lead a disciplined spiritual life.

Appendix 6
Cross-Cultural Protocol for Consultants and Other 'Professionals': Sample

- Learn about the processes of colonization and how they continue today.
- Ask yourself how you contribute to colonization, in its various manifestations worldwide.
- Search your heart to know what is moving you to work on 'conservation' or 'development' issues.
- Know your own preconceptions, prejudices or formative past experiences concerning Indigenous Peoples.
- Inventory your personal qualities that you feel would help or hinder working with Indigenous Peoples.
- Reflect upon your willingness to enter new ground professionally, into areas bound more by heart than head.
- Decide if you are comfortable participating in cross-cultural family, community and ceremonial events.
- Be honest about your ability to respect and participate in spiritual tradition(s) other than your own.
- Reject contracts that could undermine or compromise Indigenous Peoples' rights.
- Respect cultural protocols, even if your peers do not.
- Offer a community rate to make yourself available directly to Indigenous Peoples, if your skills fit.
- Provide pro bono assistance to Indigenous Peoples, when called upon to be of service.
- Sit down with the Elders, and other customary authorities, and listen.
- Be aware that when you go home, locals still experience ongoing racism, discrimination and colonial poverty.
- Remember that the sacred life connections and honour the trust put in you as a 'consultant'.
- Be yourself, not the 'Earth suit' or credentials that you wear.
- Bring all of you to your vocation, embracing the spiritual significance of your work.
- Challenge modes of business that endanger today's children and global life systems.
- Strive to be open and compassionate, not better or right.
- Ask the hard questions and avoid easy answers, at the risk of unsettling those around you.
- Speak the deepest truth at all times, about what you know and don't know.
- Ground yourself spiritually to avoid losing courage amid controversy.

Appendix 7
Cross-Cultural Protocol for Non-Governmental Organizations (NGOs): Sample

- Deliver training on Indigenous rights throughout your organization, under appropriate guidance.
- Work in Indigenous territories on an invitation basis only; verify free and prior informed consent (PIC) for any projects or programmes impacting Indigenous Peoples globally.
- Develop your programmes together with affected Indigenous Peoples.
- Confirm that you are working with representative Indigenous leadership.
- Practise respect and humility in order to establish a climate of mutual learning.
- Disclose your personal stake in a project before proposing or proposing or discussing any collaboration.
- Provide background on your partners and funding agencies, and all applicable agreements.
- Be transparent about your related budgets, management fees and salaries.
- Reveal other desired benefits – for example, the ability to develop 'best practices' or publish papers.
- Give a list of your past associations with Indigenous Peoples to enable independent character checks on your work.
- Prepare a memorandum of understanding and other cross-cultural protocol agreements at the outset.
- Stick to agreed roles and responsibilities, avoiding any politics or work tangents that may affect Indigenous Peoples' rights.
- Play a technical support role, with a view to becoming obsolete.
- Honour confidentiality requests, erring on the side of caution.
- Address double standards, especially any perks, privileges or benefits within the 'development' hierarchy.
- Determine mutually agreed mechanisms for grievances, conflict resolution and healing.
- Suspend a project when requested by Indigenous People(s); replace any workers with non-respectful attitudes.
- Identify remedial training necessary for your staff and volunteers, together with appropriate Indigenous leaders.
- Confirm the strengths and weaknesses of your projects with all involved and affected Indigenous People(s).

Appendix 7 (continued)

- Refer all reports naming Indigenous People(s) to them for their courtesy review and advance approval or rejection.
- Share with your peers what you learn about cross-cultural work, after first clearing it with concerned Indigenous People(s).
- Give all contact details for your funders, enabling affected Indigenous Peoples to report to them independently.

Appendix 8
Cross-Cultural Protocol for Industry and Corporations: Sample

- Know the endangered health of the Earth, via Indigenous Peoples' sacred knowledge and other alarm bells such as the *Living Planet Report* (WWF-International, 2004) and the *Millennium Report* (MEAB, 2005).
- Look at the counter-arguments to economic growth and globalization spilling from the grassroots.
- Reflect upon industry's role in advancing the instability of life systems on Earth.
- Digest the implications for your leadership in industry, as the oil era hurtles forward and impacts accumulate.
- Brave a glimpse of who suffers globally in this economy and why.
- See the boomerang effect now underway as climate change, industrial toxins and denial close in on us all.
- Re-evaluate your position on the economics of exploitation, with children in mind.
- Screen your own business proposals for hints of 'business as usual'.
- Proceed with a new understanding of profit, consumerism and sustainable life relationships.
- Enquire with Indigenous People(s) about proper cultural protocol for initiating dialogue with respect to their ancestral lands.
- Understand their economic goals, principles for trade and applicable customary law on sustainable use.
- Submit a formal invitation stating the proposed business relationship, including your relevant past experience and references; use a format meaningful to the people and their communities.
- Ask if and how the company can support a community-level assessment of the proposal.
- Enter into a protocol agreement if there is mutual interest in exploring a possible business relationship.
- Commence a joint process to brainstorm and evaluate the prospects for collaboration.
- Disclose your full operational considerations – for example, market share, competition profit margins and limitations (past and future).
- Discuss any controversial issues in order to reach a shared understanding of best practices.
- Ensure readiness to negotiate among the people and/or communities as a whole via their mandated leaders and oppropriate customary authorities.

Appendix 8 (continued)

- Enter into a memorandum of understanding on climate goals for the negotiations, addressing necessary cross-cultural training.
- Provide the means for Indigenous leaders to get any eventual agreement vetted by other Indigenous Peoples experienced with your industry, and with industry at large before final deals are made.
- Undertake responsible marketing – no early birds or unwelcome terms of visitation.
- Respect cultural protocol, customary laws and international law on the rights of Indigenous Peoples.

Appendix 9
Cross-Cultural Protocol for World Governments: Sample

- Uphold the spirit and letter of international law on Indigenous Peoples' rights.
- Use the United Nations (UN) process with integrity.
- Practice diplomacy as if your children were the most vulnerable.
- Respect sustainability as a matter of life and living.
- Heed the symbiosis between Indigenous Peoples and 'biodiversity'.
- Connect the concept of cultural diversity to Indigenous Peoples' land rights.
- Understand that 'traditional knowledge' flows from an indivisible heritage, to which ancestral title to the land is core.
- Guarantee that negotiations and decision-making on trade, environment and heritage are without prejudice to Indigenous Peoples' rights.
- Identify legislation, policy and practices that contravene international law on Indigenous Peoples' rights.
- Implement interim measures to safeguard life systems, while correcting standards and dialogues that affect Indigenous Peoples.
- Engage in dialogue first with those Indigenous leaders who hold the harshest mirror up to the UN, the World Trade Organization (WTO) and affiliates.
- Establish a strategic review of the existing process for dialogue, on a consensus basis with these Indigenous leaders.
- Tackle the question of what makes the dialogue process itself sustainable, especially vis-à-vis cultural sustainability.
- Circle back to the principle of a 'precautionary approach' in the dialogue process itself.
- Confirm that participating Indigenous leaders are representative, via procedures determined by Indigenous Peoples.
- Ensure that the chair is neutral and jointly selected with Indigenous Peoples in all talks affecting their ancestral title and rights.
- Determine respective capacity-building needs that must be addressed for cross-cultural understanding.
- Decide together how these barriers to dialogue will be eased, and how conflict will be resolved, prior to talks commencing.
- Acknowledge that capacity funding for Indigenous Peoples must be self-directed and that recipients are not beholden in any way to the dialogue process.

Appendix 9 (continued)

- Agree to shared roles and responsibilities for keeping respect and empathy in the dialogue process.
- Disclose full details on any consultants and staff hired to handle issues affecting Indigenous Peoples.
- Set emergency reporting procedures on all developments and dialogues that may impact Indigenous Peoples and/or their ancestral territory.

Appendix 10
Biodiversity Loss: Our Cycle of Grief and Healing

What losses would we grieve upon realizing the severity of biodiversity loss? How would we heal the chaos and dysfunction? Below are four levels of loss for us to contemplate:

1   Losses in economic terms – challenging us in the mental realm
     Grief over our loss of lifestyle
     - Indicator: collapse of economic sectors due to abuse of Earth systems;
     - Impacts: loss of perceived self, loss of assumed autonomy, loss of professed innocence;
     - Our potential reaction: Clinging to the mantra of biodiversity economics;
     - Danger: protectionism;
     Healing: the principle of generosity

2   Losses in ecological terms – challenging us in the physical realm
     Grief over our loss of comforts
     - Indicator: failure of Industrial Revolution science to restore disrupted Earth cycles;
     - Impacts: loss of options, loss of illusion of control, loss of ability to posture;
     - Our potential reaction: denial of the seriousness of this crisis;
     - Danger: hoarding;
     Healing: the principle of humility

3   Losses in social terms – challenging us in the emotional realm
     Grief over our loss of consumerism
     - Indicator: breakdown of social structures marketed to the world as 'progress';
     - Impacts: loss of tolerance, loss of empathy, loss of our humanity;
     - Our potential reaction: regrouping at any cost;
     - Danger: increased human rights violations;
     Healing: the principle of love

4   Losses in cultural terms – challenging us in the spiritual realm
     Grief over our loss of individualism
     - Indicator: desire for knowledge (for example, real life meaning, purpose and wisdom);

Appendix 10 (continued)

- Impacts: loss of ego, loss of attitude, loss of arrogance;
- Our potential reaction: returning to familiar external things (for example, consumerism);
- Danger: fundamentalism.

Healing: the principle of connection

Appendix 11
Principles for Relationship-Building: Moving Towards Sacred Contracts

I enter into this agreement with my heart open to the Creator, bound by my own gratitude for Life and for the Creation that surrounds me.

I know your People to be my sisters and brothers, whom I will care for like my own.

I feel my personal connection to the lands that surround and nurture me, and I will nurture them.

I recognize my capacity to err in judgement, especially when my mind and heart are disconnected. I will make personal amends – opening myself to guidance and instruction when this happens.

I acknowledge the limitations of my own knowledge, and will seek and surrender to the wisdom of the Creator.

I respect the beauty of our diversity as Peoples, including our distinct traditions and languages that carry all we presently know and understand.

I will endeavour to listen to, learn from and respect my neighbours' way of expression.

I understand my journey and duty in life to be more than what is sometimes visible to me. I will find the courage to follow the signs put before me so that

I can fulfil my birth covenant with the Creator.

Source: adapted from a presentation to the United Nations Commission on Human Rights (UNCHR), Geneva, July 1999, by Alison Johnston on behalf of the International Support Centre for Sustainable Tourism (ISCST)

Notes

Chapter 1

1   See Association for the Study of Peak Oil and Gas (www.peakoil.net), the
Post Carbon Institute (www.postcarbon.org) and Worldwatch Institute Energy
Library (www.worldwatch.org/topics/energy/energy).

2   The Xhosa (South Africa) earn two and a half times the average local wage by
directly hosting tourists (Foroohar, 2002). Some Maasai communities (Kenya),
hosting cultural exchanges on their own terms, have had similar success (www.
wildland.com).

3   Donor countries are pushing trade liberalization through the *General Agreement
on Tariffs and Trade* (GATT). They have negotiated instruments such as the
UN Convention on Biological Diversity (CBD) to assist. This same corporate
regime is now being applied directly to 'conservation' utilizing so-called 'eco'
tourism. The United Nations Environment Programme (UNEP) describes this
diplomatically, saying: 'As development and conservation aid to developing
countries becomes increasingly restricted, ecotourism becomes an important
tool for alleviating poverty and sustaining protected areas' (Hillel, 2002).
However, the bottom line is that donor countries want privatization to maximize
revenue growth.

4   Bringing 'sustainability' to the practice of 'eco' tourism has been a
monumentally slow process. Over a decade ago, Special Expeditions (US)
discussed the ongoing ambiguity in its newsletter (O'Brien, 1994).

5   The Nature Conservancy is a sprawling NGO with an annual budget of
US$731 miilion. It is in the industry of ecotourism, with ecotourism projects in
15 countries (www.nature.org/conservationjourneys). Other mega-conservation
groups, such as the Sierra Club and the World Wide Fund for Nature (WWF-
International), also offer trips to help publicize their respective cause(s). See
www.sierraclub.org/outings and www.worldwildlife.org/expeditions/or www.
worldwildlife.org/travel. While these groups' conservation objectives differ from
Indigenous peoples' own priorities for ancestral lands, they often steer touristic
local activities due to their size, public reputation and government contacts.

6   Tourism Concern of England raised the prospect of the UN International Year

of Ecotourism (IYE), encouraging 'yet more development in fragile areas of the world, without addressing the problems that already exist' (Davies, 2002, p16). This same concern had been submitted by NGOs to the UN in 1998 when the process on tourism and biodiversity first began (ISCST et al, 1998).

7   'The World Tourism Organization estimates that international tourism will continue to grow by an average of 4.1 per cent per year up to 2020.' This increase would mean 'more than 1 billion people on the move by the year 2010 and 1.56 billion in 2020' (The Nature Conservancy, 2003, p3). In air travel alone, this amounts to a destructive economy of scale.

8   'According to the World Tourism Organization, more than 30 per cent of all international tourists nowadays travel to developing countries' (Netherlands Committee for IUCN, 2003). 'Tourism is the main source of foreign currency for 38 per cent of countries' (CI, 2003, pv).

9   Industrialized peoples dominate the global consumer class. This '20 per cent of the world's people ... consumes 70 to 80 per cent of the world's resources' (Prugh and Assadourian, 2003, p17).

10 According to Foroohar (2002), 'Travelocity and Expedia are now among the ten largest US distributors of travel products.' The Expedia website is owned by Microsoft Corporation.

11 All but Conservation International (CI) reached consensus on this point. A few NGOs, such as the organizer Ecological Tourism in Europe (ETE), had a weak understanding of issues of concern to Indigenous Peoples, but seemed to find mileage in the concept.

12 Lists of 'top' ecotourism destinations are regularly published. Though they mainly feature Indigenous territories, there may be scant mention of Indigenous Peoples. *Lufthansa Magazine*, for instance, compiled a wildlife-only trip list called 'The Seven Wonders of the Animal World' (Miersch, 1998, p18). *Adventure* magazine selected 25 'classic trips' (Benning, 2003), naming only the Arawete and neighbouring tribes (Brazil) and the Tsaaten people (Mongolia), although most trips identified occur within Indigenous territories.

Nonetheless, some popular travel magazines are highlighting destinations specifically because of cultural intrigue. *Outside* magazine has issued a compilation of 'Coolest Trips' and 'Top Ten Trends', which includes industry trips among the Embera (Panama), Nung (Vietnam) Garifuna (Honduras) and several other Indigenous Peoples (Blakesley, 2003). This kind of editorial coverage by high-circulation magazines forewarns of heavy impacts.

Although ecotourism literature is replete with unauthorized industry products featuring Indigenous territories and Indigenous cultures, some reporters after the IYE are keenly aware (namely, all the campaigns that it sparked *against* ecotourism) of the dangers of mismanaged 'eco' tourism. Singer (2003) indicates several Indigenous-owned and controlled operations in her synopsis of the world's best eco-lodges.

13 Ironically, these pinnacles are often linked to awareness of their own mortality – for example, turning 40, empty-nesting or retiring.

14 Often, what looks like industry withdrawal is just a strategic shift to another site. In Peru, industry activities along the Inca Trail long brought as many as 900 hikers per day (Lisagor, 2003, p92) – approximately 66,000 annually (Benning, 2003). Since 2003 there has been a limit of 450 hikers daily. Following this cap on tourist permits for trekking to Machu Picchu, many ecotourism companies attempted to replace this itinerary. Some companies have turned to alternative 'Inca Trails', leading to Machu Picchu (Benning, 2003). Others are replicating

'Inca Trail' treks along another mountain corridor in the Cordillera Vilcabamba (Blakesley et al, 2003, p60). This has troubling implications for new trekking routes. Tourist traffic along the Inca Trail has been so destructive that Kurt Kutay, owner of the widely respected company Wildland Adventures, says: 'If you're looking for a wilderness experience, go somewhere else' (Lisagor, 2003, p92).

15   Excellent information is now available on promoting fair working conditions for porters. Porters Progress in Nepal is a porter-run and administrated organization, with videos available (www.portersprogress.org). Their work inspired Porteadores Inka Ñan (known as the Inka Porter Project) in Peru, whose programming is also driven by the porters themselves (www.peruweb. org/porters). Valuable support organizations include Tourism Concern (www. tourismconcern.org.uk), known for its porters campaign, and the International Porter Protection Group (www.ippg.net).

16   The website of Papua New Guinea, for example, highlights the country's cultural diversity and provides extensive background on its many Indigenous Peoples. See www.pngtourism.org.pg.

17   According to the United Nations Educational, Scientific and Cultural Organization (UNESCO), 'Ecotourism is part of the sustainable development paradigm' (Bridgewater, 2003). What this means is that it serves economic growth.

18   It is misleading to define affluence on income grounds alone. Factors such as leisure time, access to consumer credit and future income-earning potential all play into net affluence. From a global perspective, anyone who can afford to travel is affluent.

19   'According to a calculation model (developed by the University of Liege), one person flying [from Western Europe] to Thailand uses 680kg of fuel' (Netherlands Committee for IUCN, 2003).

20   Ethics Professor Arthur Schaefer of the University of Manitoba notes: 'We need to realize that when we go to these places, we're spreading the virus of western capitalism, values and lifestyle' (Canadian Press, 2004).

21   Any arrival of 'eco-' tourists involves an injection of consumerism. Many travellers who are comparatively low on money (for example, university students or other 'backpackers') are rich in time and flexibility, and choose to linger in a community. Through gestures and body language, they often convey the same social attitudes as their wealthier counterparts. In practice, both groups pose similar cross-cultural challenges for Indigenous Peoples.

22   Eco-tours often enter the holiday mix as so-called 'trips of a lifetime'. Many describe this as a shift from 'tourist' to 'traveller', reflecting 'the accumulated wisdom of a lifetime spent circling the globe' (*Condé Nast Traveler*, 1999, p106). This highlights the fact that specialty travel decisions typically are made by frequent fliers. Their purchase of an 'eco' tourism holiday often has little to do with ecological principles.

23   *Travel & Leisure* magazine reports that 'eco-tours have established themselves as a classic element of the modern itinerary' (Theroux, 2001, p62).

24   Some of the best commentary on travel motives comes from travellers' own testimonies. Many writers have written about their lifestyle angst, mentioning travel. In an editorial for *Utne* magazine (January–February, 2004) American journalist Jay Walljasper wrote: 'I began travelling overseas in search of examples of positive social change.' Canadian author Will Ferguson told *House & Home* magazine (November, 2003) that he 'sees [travel] as a form of therapy

and feels most travellers are either "trying to find something or lose something"'. A common thread in such testimonies is the healing power of travel in times of personal turmoil.

25   See Chapter 4 for a discussion on 'The Transformative Power of Travel'.

26   In many countries where ecotourism growth is strong, domestic tourism is equal to, or even greater than, international arrivals (Christ et al, 2003). In countries such as Mexico, South Africa and Thailand where class and race relations can be tense, and class attitudes are readily expressed by some travellers, there is high demand for an experience 'bubble'. Patronage of Indigenous-owned and managed tourism enterprises is not likely to be significant among this segment of the travel market.

27   The Cofán have lost their tourism income due to the US-backed conflict in Colombia, which is connected to oil exploration. Many Cofán families are earning less than US$50 per year now. See www.cofan.org.

28   Refer to papers authored by Kurt Kutay (Kutay, 1989, 1991) of Wildland Adventures; Ray Ashton (Ashton, 1992) of Ashton Biodiversity Research Preservation Institute, Inc; and Malcolm and Linda Lillywhite (Lillywhite and Lillywhite, 1992) of Domestic Technologies International, Inc.

Chapter 2

1   Two venues commonly accessed by Indigenous Peoples are the Working Group on Indigenous Populations of the United Nations Sub-commission on the Promotion and Protection of Human Rights (Geneva, Switzerland) and the UN Permanent Forum on Indigenous Issues (New York City, US). The Sub-commission now has a formal Working Group on Transnational Corporations.

2   Some Indigenous Peoples have staged demonstrations outside major stock exchanges or gained entrance to company annual meetings. Others have conducted or joined consumer campaigns against individual corporations, utilizing documentary films and other visual tools. One famous example is the successful campaign against giant retailer Home Depot by the Carrier Sekani (Hamilton, 2003; Hoekstra, 2003), stopping sales of old-growth wood. A similar boycott was launched against Delta Hotels by the Secwepemc (see www.secwepemc.org) in protest of the company's investment at Sun Peaks ski resort on Secwepemc ancestral lands (TINN, 2003).

3   Today, governments and industry turn to multinational law firms such as Webber Wentzel Bowens (WWB) for help in settling this 'fray' (see www.wwb.co.za). WWB describes itself as 'ideally placed to provide a wide range of advice on all issues related to tourism development' (WWB, 2003, p2). This firm marketed its services at the 2003 World Parks Congress, advertising its ability to deal with land rights issues. In 2002, it acted for parties to a new 'eco' lodge development at the Madikwe Game Reserve, including the local communities. 'Interesting provisions specific to this agreement included making allowances for possible land claims that could be made on the reserve, and creating an effective mechanism to protect the parties involved should this happen' (WWB, 2003, p5). Is this kind of precedent useful? It can be if other Indigenous Peoples can access the precedent agreement(s) and make contact with the involved communities for direct commentary. However, most legal proceedings are protected by client privilege, and many have built-in mechanisms gagging disclosure or communications. Although WWB and similar firms may have

a 'pro bono unit' to earn the trust of communities, this can serve more as an ingenious way of attracting new business (for example, 'stakeholder' groups) than to benefit Indigenous Peoples at large.

4   During 2003, Conservation International (CI) mentioned the principle of prior informed consent in its report on *Tourism and Biodiversity*, but only in relation to capacity-building (Christ et al, 2003, p36). Its report was prescriptive rather than reflective of inherent local rights or cultural protocol. Recommendations revolved around a classic stakeholder approach.

5   Many Indigenous Peoples refer to bilateral talks as a government-to-government process. It brings together the respective leadership (that is, formally recognized leaders) in a mutually respectful process with clear ground rules. The principle applies equally to corporate situations, bringing the CEO and/or equivalent stature executive(s) into dialogue with customary authorities, such as the Chief(s), Matriarch(s) and/or Elders.

6   The UN study on treaties (Martinez, 1999, p46) states clearly that the burden of proof regarding Indigenous Peoples' collective rights lies with world governments (in other words, colonial nation states) and not with colonial Indigenous Peoples.

7   These racist attitudes are a carry-over of the notorious *Papal Bulls*, issued by the Vatican in 1452 and 1493, which viewed Indigenous Peoples as heathens – to be subdued by 'perpetual slavery'. On the 500th anniversary of Columbus' arrival in the Americas, Indigenous Peoples renewed pressure on the Vatican to repudiate this doctrine (American Indian Institute, 1992). However, it remains on the books and in full force and effect today.

8   See press release by Tourism Concern (2005) detailing 'slavery' conditions for ecotourism porters worldwide.

9   The 'saviour' complex of the ecotourism industry can touch even the best of partnerships. In Peru, Rainforest Expeditions says that the joint venture *Posada Amazonas* eco-lodge 'has prompted the Ese'ejas to undertake their own conservation efforts' (Singer, 2003, p86). Although this kind of comment conveys sincere enthusiasm, it also belittles customary governance systems. There is often little reflection on why customary practices are abandoned, or how tourism now contributes to colonial dispossession.

10   See Environment News Service at www.ens-news.com.

11   According to the Pentagon (US Department of Defense) report on climate change, made public in February 2004, abrupt climate change poses more of threat to world security than 'terrorists' (see Schwartz and Randall, 2003).

12   Article 8(j) of the *UN Convention on Biological Diversity* obliges contracting parties to 'respect, preserve and maintain' traditional knowledge systems and encourage equitable sharing of benefits arising from any application (CBD, 1992, p9). The caveat is that all provisions are subject to national legislation. This reflects the overriding premise of the CBD: that states have sovereign rights over their own biological resources (CBD, 1992, p2). It is an economic baseline, violating both the principle and practice of ancestral title (that is, true sustainable use – linking rights, *responsibilities* and generations).

13   Air New Zealand uses the slogan 'The World's Warmest Welcome'. It has run print advertisements conjuring a friendly image of the Maori saying: 'When we touch noses, or *hongi*, we're sharing the breath of life. With gentle presses we offer peace, friendship and hospitality. It's a traditional welcome that is 100 per cent New Zealand.' See the April 2000 issue of *Travel & Leisure* (p93).

Chapter 3

1   One of the identified problems in the tourism sector is the benefits to foreigners
        (McNeely, 1999). There are grave inequities between those of us who can
        afford to travel and Indigenous Peoples locked into mass tourism by systemic
        discrimination. These stem from long-standing colonial attitudes about place
        and role in society. In the business world, Indigenous Peoples are generally
        welcome as labourers but not as peers. Such racism has yet to be meaningfully
        recognized as a factor in sustainability.

2   'Manifest destiny' was the political phrase used during the 1840s to promote
        the continental expansion of the US. This policy, together with England's
        extinguishment agenda in Canada, resulted in what Belgium calls 'the world's
        worst ever genocide' (Logan, 2004). The American Indian Genocide Museum is
        now under way in Houston, Texas.

3   Not long ago it was contentious and divisive to say that Indigenous Peoples
        seldom benefit from ecotourism. Today, prominent industry spokespersons are
        admitting that promises of community participation and benefit-sharing have
        been shallow, especially towards Indigenous Peoples. Martha Honey, executive
        director of The International Ecotourism Society (TIES), states: 'Under the
        rubric of ecotourism, far too many indigenous communities have continued to
        lose their land, found jobs to be often menial and training minimal, and seen
        far too much "leakage" of tourism dollars' (Honey, 2004). Hitesh Mehta, a US-
        based consultant and board member of TIES, concurs: 'The local people are
        seldom included in the initial planning or in the assessment of [an eco-lodge's]
        impacts. Yet, they are the ones who know the resources and whose culture needs
        to be respected' (Singer, 2003, p90).

4   Due to the positive association now between tourism and biodiversity among
        world governments, development assistance policies increasingly favour tourism.
        Little of the available funding, however, directly reaches Indigenous Peoples.
        Most goes to consultants overseeing 'best practice' studies and pilot projects,
        or is channelled through NGOs for case studies. Indigenous Peoples have little
        means to challenge these funding decisions, even in the midst of widespread
        opportunism by third parties.

        Parallel to this, there is a dearth of private-sector funding for Indigenous
        Peoples wishing to establish their own tourism enterprise. Under colonial
        policies, the unlawful displacement, resettlement and disenfranchisement of
        Indigenous Peoples from ancestral lands has created domestic legal blocks to
        Indigenous entrepreneurship. Indigenous Peoples are considered 'landless' and
        without collateral. All the while, corporations derive profits from their ancestral
        lands, free of royalty obligations.

5   Industry is constantly scanning the globe for 'exotic' product offerings. Products
        featuring Indigenous people(s) who are recently contacted or on the brink of
        extinction are worth more in market terms. This puts isolated communities at
        risk of curiosity seekers and industry speculation.

6   The theme of the 1998 World Congress on Adventure Travel and Ecotourism
        was 'Adventure Travel is for Everyone'. This slogan assumes that everyone has
        the basic choice of whether to partake in tourism. However, few Indigenous
        Peoples in popular travel destinations have this freedom of choice. Most
        tour companies offering adventure and nature activities traverse Indigenous
        territories without consideration for consent or cultural protocol.

7   In most countries, the revenue objectives of government, termed 'financial sustainability', take precedence over other facets of so-called 'sustainable' development. Governments want to maximize industry growth rates, tax revenues and economic spin off. The ecotourism industry's success in this regard has earned it amnesty from regulation of environment or social justice standards in most world jurisdictions. There is *de facto* acceptance of industry profiteering.

8   The *Bangkok Post* (2003) reports that 'New tourism-related security initiatives are mushrooming, such as iJET Travel Risk Management', which provides 'travel intelligence' and 'crisis management services'. These services enhance profit by protecting consumer confidence in the travel industry. However, their reliance on intelligence specialists could quickly veer in another direction if government or industry discomfort with Indigenous Peoples' land rights increases. Already, many countries such as the 'brother nations' of Canada, Australia and the US have police surveillance units dedicated to watching Indigenous 'radicals' and 'extremists'. Since 2000, concerns over civil liberties have been expressed by a number of parties worried about looming 'Big Brother' scenarios.

9   Few seemingly 'enlightened' efforts to link Indigenous Peoples with the ecotourism industry result in new relationships. Many individuals believing they support Indigenous self-determination are, in fact, reinforcing industry trends. For example, some argue that 'A vibrant and successful Indigenous ecotourism sector will greatly strengthen ecotourism as a global industry' (Mader, 2002, p12). Such arguments sound valid, but position culture as product for the purpose of economic growth. Despite these concerns, The Nature Conservancy (TNC, 2003) and other conservation NGOs promoting ecotourism still speak of 'cultural resources'.

10   Some Indigenous Peoples are accused of 'poaching' threatened species. In conservation circles, there is little awareness of colonial policy and its implications. Even though Indigenous Peoples are belittled into situations of poverty, 'their' poverty (not *our* consumption) is blamed for environmental degradation. We extol 'traditional knowledge' while viewing Indigenous Peoples (not ourselves) as poachers.

11   In Venezuela, for example, Indigenous Peoples say that government development policy is responsible for not just culture loss but also ethnic cleansing: 'The government calls this development. We call it extermination' (Survival, 2001).

12   Both Australia and New Zealand have been reprimanded at the UN under the International Convention on the Elimination of All Forms of Racial Discrimination. In Canada, the federal government is closely monitored by Amnesty International on subjects ranging from policing brutality to the treatment of Aboriginal women.

13   The *General Agreement on Trade in Services* (GATS) is administered under the WTO. At the 2004 World Social Forum in Mumbai, India, international tourism NGOs disseminated a brochure warning that 'The unquestioning acceptance by tourism policy-makers of [this] package ... prescribed by international institutions such as the World Bank, the International Monetary Fund and the World Trade Organization as the "mantra" for development of the Global South is alarming' (Equations et al, 2004). For Indigenous Peoples, GATS compounds other threats in the globalized trade regime, such as the agenda of the World Intellectual Property Organization (WIPO).

14   Culture loss is most precipitous for Indigenous Peoples living some distance from the consumer economy, whose lands and/or cultures are suddenly targeted

for tourism. This has not stopped ecotourism companies from hunting out such new turf. Travel magazines routinely feature trips promising the opportunity to 'meet isolated tribes in Amazonia' (Benning, 2003, p49). World Expeditions offers a trip off the back roads of Papua New Guinea, where 'villagers rarely, if ever, see outsiders' (Blakesley et al, 2003, p46). Some conservation NGOs may be treading on equally risky ground. The Nature Conservancy (TNC, 2003) describes its Lashihai-Wenhai ecotourism project in China as having 'isolated and fascinating communities'.

15   Indigenous Peoples' organizations, such as the Indigenous Network on Economics Trade and Indigenous Environment Network, have been particularly vocal against the privatization of water. The struggle for access to water in Cochabamba, Bolivia, is profiled in the film entitled *The Corporation*.

16   A myriad of small travel companies targeting Indigenous ancestral lands, cultures and ceremonies advertise primarily over the internet, out of sight of most Indigenous Peoples. Many of these companies run small print advertisements in specialty magazines like *Shaman's Drum*, directing consumers to their website. There have been numerous reports of charlatanism in connection with such advertising.

17   Institutions such as the United Nations Development Programme (UNDP) have supported various countries' efforts (for example, Panama) to identify 'heritage routes' for national tourism promotion. Often these routes take on an ethnic theme without actually benefiting the Indigenous Peoples or Indigenous communities in question.

18   Some institutions, such as The Nature Conservancy (TNC, 2003) and Conservation International (CI, 2003), insist that ecotourism can educate about the value of cultural diversity. However, many such groups enter relationships with Indigenous Peoples on terms that are seen to undermine culture (see Chapter 7).

19   One ecotourism trip over the Larapinta Trail in Australia is described in terms of 'sacred Aboriginal sites' (Benning, 2003, p59). To counter such anonymity, the Anangu of nearby Uluru, Australia, have specifically instructed visitors via their website to address them by their proper name (see www.deh.gov.au/parks/uluru).

20   After the Kogi delivered their message to the world via a BBC documentary in 1990 (discussed in Chapter 10), they shut the gates to their ancestral territory in order to protect the ceremonies necessary for world balance (Ereira, 2001). This closure was enacted via a formal declaration barring outside visitation. It is a precautionary step based on customary law, facilitated by their high mountain territory.

Given this clear act of self-determination, one of the greatest misdeeds of the ecotourism industry today is that the Kogi remain on its destination horizon. *Outside* magazine laments the travel safety advisories on Colombia, saying that travellers are missing 'Encounters with the pre-Columbian Kogi people' (Blakesley, 2003, p49). This kind of editorial puts the Kogi squarely on the world ecotourism map, vulnerable to future industry harassment and disturbance by independent travellers.

The same issue of *Outside* notes that politically unstable Venezuela is 'equipped for an 'eco[travel]-renaissance'' (Lisagor, 2003, p93). This is mentioned with reference to a trip among the Pemón, accessing their sacred sites. Typically, industry treads into these areas without first understanding cultural protocols or the global balance at stake.

21 Thomas E. Mails has noted that 'Some researchers ... take particular delight in revealing that this is the way it "really" was' (Mails, 1997, p240).

22 In some situations, tourism 'creates empathy and we become defenders of the rights of people in remote places' (Canadian Press, 2004). Groups like the Ethical Traveler alliance (see www.ethicaltraveler.com) show the possibility for healthy connection between Indigenous Peoples and tourists. This group is 'a global community of tourists dedicated to putting its economic power and ethical clout to work' (Schumaier, 2003, p42). It is volunteer staffed and has a membership of approximately 1000 individuals from 15 countries. Campaigns have included boycott threats and other pressure tactics.

23 These sacred contracts are personalized within the family and community. They carry an obligation to look after future generations. This is fulfilled by exercising ancestral title. Governments, however, are threatened by such self-determination. Ironically, Indigenous self-determination means caring and sharing as opposed to being self-focused like consumer society (see Chapter 2).

Chapter 4

1 Corporations are using cultural images to advertise products without the remotest link to culture. In 2002, Sony issued a magazine add showing Maori-looking 'savages' to sell its Pentium computer software. In 2004, Hyundai dressed female models in skimpy 'buckskin' clothes and feather headdresses to sell its Tucson sport utility vehicle.

2 Most studies of ecotourism grossly underestimate the impacts of industry on Indigenous Peoples. There is a perception that tourist arrivals are comparatively low and benign because the 'natural spaces' seem wide open and verdant. However, impacts depend upon precisely where the tourists insert themselves vis-à-vis communities and their disposition towards local customary law.

3 The Four Seasons resort in Scottsdale, Arizona, US, features Native American heated stone massage as a 'signature' treatment; the Four Seasons hotel in Sydney, Australia, offers *kodo* massage incorporating Aboriginal techniques; and the Four Seasons spa in Punta Mita, Mexico, uses the agave extract and sage oil because of their known 'curative powers' (Ebbutt, 2003).

4 Aveda works with the Yawanawa in Brazil and others to source botanical ingredients for its spa products on mutually beneficial terms (www.aveda.com). This is an interesting brand strategy, given that Aveda was acquired by cosmetics giant Estée Lauder in 1997.

5 This statement was made at the UN by the US delegate in the government contact group on biodiversity and tourism during the Subsidiary Body on Scientific, Technical and Technological Advice (SBSTTA) of the *UN Convention on Biological Diversity* (CBD) in June 1999. None of the other participating governments countered this submission. The consensus stuck, even though attending Indigenous representatives had stated undisputable facts to the contrary.

6 See the UK's *Country Living* (2003) November, pp10–11.

7 See *Condé Nast Traveler* (1999) July, p25.

8 One common sight is the tourist rush to air-conditioned stores or the central tourist market to stock up on gifts before the flight home. In regions with high cultural diversity, these outlets usually have a cross section of Indigenous 'crafts' sold at a high mark-up. In Panama City, the Hilton gift shop sells Kuna *molas* (beautiful appliqué textiles) for US$50, the tourist market prices them at

US$25 and the Kuna women's co-operative asks US$10–$12 for comparable samples. The Kuala Lumpur central market has extravagantly higher mark-ups on Indigenous handicrafts; many items are priced at well over ten times the community price.

9   See website of the European Network for Indigenous Australian Rights: www. eniar.org. Reports of IPRs abuse have not substantially decreased, although Australian court decisions and copyright laws promise improvement.

10   In 1998, Lea & Perrins Worcestershire Sauce circulated a magazine advertisement showing a tribal portrait with the caption: 'You'll Be Shocked To Find Out What a Borneo Tribal Chief Put Lea & Perrins On'. Such advertisements may be seen to depict Indigenous Peoples in compromised ways, debasing Indigenous cultures.

11   Virtual tours are a nascent industry. Companies crafting them 'still have few to no competitors' (Wilson, 2004). As such, the market is poised for a surge in business, especially vis-à-vis ecotourism, which represents a niche within this niche. This creates market incentives for unscrupulous photography within Indigenous territories.

12   The River League travel company, for example, arranges for clients in Brazil to 'join members of the Arawete, Asurini, and Xipaya tribes to fish for piranha, track jaguars and learn rainforest lore' (Benning, 2003, p53). Jaguar tracking, though currently a dormant issue in terms of controversy, will likely become a focal point of future discussions on cultural sustainability. The jaguar is a sacred animal to many tribes in the Amazon Basin.

13   The book *Amazon: From the Floodplains to the Clouds* (Webb, 1997) shows a photograph of New York businessmen from the international real estate firm Julien J. Studley Inc. in the midst of an 'Indigenous' initiation ceremony in Manaus, Brazil, for 'Best New Salesman of the Year'. The executives completing the ritual were the company's 50 most productive salespeople. The trip was their reward for high performance.

14   The so-called 'corporate shaman' has its roots in retreat centres that sprang up, melding spirituality and business. Takoja Retreats of New Mexico, for example, advertised get-aways during the early 1990s for small corporations; its programmes blended Taoist and Native American spirituality.

15   The August 2002 issue of *National Geographic Adventure* features an article on Real de Catorce, Mexico, where the Huichol are famed for their ceremonial use of peyote (Salak, 2002). The author herself observes that outsiders' forays into Huichol territory are unwelcome. Yet this article, placed in a prominent travel magazine, will increase visitation. See Furst and Schaefer (1996) for a discussion of implications.

16   The magazine *Shaman's Drum* carries such advertisements, with the frequent warning 'Buyers Beware' due to the number of fake so-called Indigenous products.

17   The procession includes German tourists who annually 'participate in an Arapaho-style sun dance the Crows hold, which involves fasting and dancing but not the chest and back piercing common in the Lakota ceremony'. Two Bulls (2003) notes that 'This year, the tourists got more than they bargained for. This year, they went home scarred for life.' The hosts' decision to honour their Lakota ancestry crossed the visitors' comfort zone.

18   In one staged vision quest of Japanese tourists visiting Colorado in 1989, participants were provided elaborate meals and had posh tents and vehicles for

daily refuge (Giago, 2003). This disregarded *han-ble-c'i-ya* protocol, which is to be alone with the Creator and give up food and water for four complete days. It also was insensitive to the realities of life on colonial reserves, where severe post-colonial poverty is everywhere.

19   In North America and Europe, the men's movement has embraced both drumming and the *inipi* (sweat lodge) ceremony. Some members laughingly swap stories of their experience, like irreverently rigging the sacred *inipi* with car exhaust pipes. It is this kind of attitude that has led to the closure of *inipi* and other Lakota sacred rites to outsiders.

20   See the *Lakota Oyate Declaration of War Against Exploiters of Lakota Spirituality* at www.lakotaoyate.com.

21   According to government, 'The medicinal plant trade is the single largest cause of forest degradation in South Africa' (Davies, 2003). It is known that commercial gatherers are the problem, not local *inyangas* (herbalists) and *sangomas* (diviners).

22   Pharmaceuticals screening for new medications cost in the range of Cdn$500 million (Greenwald, 1998). Starting from scratch, companies would recuperate their costs for research and development on only three out of ten medicines.

23   Yuppies is the term used to describe the young urban professionals' demographic, which now overlaps in spending style with empty-nesting baby boomers. The paradox is that these affluent groups, consuming pirated medicines and herbal remedies, tend to fit the 'eco' tourist profile.

24   Similar practices exist industry to industry. For example, European film-makers casually entering an Indigenous community in Ecuador in 1999 attempted to give a short-wave radio worth just a few hundred dollars as a final exchange for filming privileges.

25   In 1999, an inappropriate overture was made by a senior Canadian government researcher (holding a PhD) to the Haisla people, in conjunction with the Kitlope watershed, a jointly managed protected area established between the Haisla and provincial/federal authorities.

26   One case involved a well-known Harvard-educated ethno-botanist who had worked for the World Wide Fund for Nature (WWF-International), the Smithsonian Institution and Conservation International (CI) – interestingly, all organizations fingered by Indigenous Peoples as bio-plunderers. Plotkin (1993) describes his experience taking *epena* snuff under the guidance of a shaman in a Yanomamo village in Venezuela. His detailed account was widely circulated in the book *Tales of a Shaman Apprentice* (Plotkin, 1994).

27   There is an active link between archaeology and ecotourism. The 'discovery' of Machu Picchu in 1911 led to mass commercialization of this sacred site by the tourism industry. Now the same tourism phenomenon threatens to engulf the 'lost city' of Victoria in Peru, allegedly discovered in 1999 (Blakesley, 2003, p60).

28   Earthwatch issued a 'Call for Proposals in Indigenous Knowledge' in 2003. According to this dispatch, its past-funded projects 'chronicle the use and knowledge of medicinal plants in Argentina, Brazil, Kenya and India'.

29   Greenforce, dedicated to 'wildlife conservation expeditions', provides research teams to support government projects in the South. Work has included both inventorying flora and assessing the economic viability of ecotourism. Its community interaction in places like Sabah in Malaysia and Bahuaja Research Station in Peru consists primarily of teaching English. This kind of liaison may encourage economic integration, bringing culture loss.

30   The Smithsonian Institution has been blasted by Indigenous Peoples'
organizations for many repatriation-related issues, most recently its
International Cooperative Biodiversity Groups Program (ICBG) in Panama.
ICBG is a bio-prospecting operation openly pursuing drug discovery in concert
with research into socio-cultural anthropology. For public relations, ICBG
funnels some proceeds to needy NGOs and communities through the Nature
Foundation. See www.stri.org.

31   The Ese'eja operate *Posada Amazonas* on a 60:40 basis with Rainforest
Expeditions. Under this type of contractual arrangement, the Ese'eja have
full control over disclosures about medicinal plants. However, such a formally
structured agreement is rare between Indigenous Peoples and the tourism
industry. Normally, communities are 'chatted up' by industry and consent to
ethno-botanical activities without understanding the full ramifications.

32   The Omaere Garden in Ecuador, the first ethno-botanical reserve in Latin
America, was created in 1993 and is managed by Indigenous Peoples of the
Pastaza region. The Terra Nova Medicinal Plant Reserve in Belize is operated
by the Belize Association of Traditional Healers. An African counterpart is the
Ikukhanya Kwelange Village in South Africa. Tourists visiting these areas can
go on guided tours with local knowledge keepers.

33   While this volume was being written, a book and film entitled *The Corporation*
were issued, making the parallel argument that corporations fit the profile of
a psychopath. Readers should refer to Balkan (2004) and Achbar (2005) for an
excellent discussion of global corporate standards.

34   In 2003, WIPO announced that it would fast track a framework for the
'protection' of TK and TCEs, including policy objectives and principles. This
was contradicted by WIPO (2004), saying that the IGC's mandate 'doesn't
provide for any specific result'. The IGC's mandate is to promote an aggressive
regime of IPRs. A 'lack of clear rules protecting TK creates risks for companies,
which prefer closing deals under well established, reliable and enforceable rules'
(WIPO, 2003, p4).

35   'The overall conclusion is that the IPRs system is the problem – and that it is
dangerous and wrong to dress the *problem* as the solution. If WIPO wants to do
something useful, it should concentrate on preventing the IPRs system from
trampling on Indigenous Peoples' rights in the first place' (GRAIN, 2004, p16).

36   A number of resource organizations such as the Meridien Institute are
recommended as impartial facilitators when conflict flares. Other institutions
like the World Conservation Union (IUCN) market their services as peace
brokers. While such services can be invaluable to settling regular environmental
disputes, they do not have a place in dialogues where Indigenous rights are
central. There is a poor cross-cultural fit and often conflict of interest too. Better
results are achieved when facilitators are nominated by Indigenous Peoples
themselves and then chosen through consensus with other involved parties.

37   This definition of 'transfigure' comes from *The Pocket Oxford Dictionary*, first
published by Oxford University Press in 1969 (Fowler, 1977).

Chapter 5

1   See Johnson (2004) for an insightful discussion on this movement to beautify
urban landscapes.

2   If urbanity was defined by behavioural traits – such as identifying with the
consumer lifestyle or being preoccupied with consumer wants – this figure
would be substantially higher. Television is wired into far-flung places. Where

television cannot reach, 'eco' tourists now carry the consumer message.

3   Where tourists go, consumer infrastructure soon follows. In Bodh Gaya, India, 'Not only are the teachings attracting more and more people … but also more flashy, so-called luxury hotels. Ironically, Gautama Buddha gave up a life of princely opulence to live as a simple ascetic' (Kanetsuka, 2002, p38).

4   See New Mexico 'Land of Enchantment' advertising campaign in *Organic Style* (2003) March/April, p51.

5   The Sanctuary on Camelback Mountain in Paradise Valley, Arizona, US, featured as a spiritual retreat in *Yoga* magazine, is described as sitting next to an ancient rock outcropping in an area 'once considered sacred to the indigenous people of the land' (Weintraub, 2004, p40). There are many such cases where the current ceremonial significance of a sacred site is not acknowledged. In Mexico, companies such as Sheraton Hotels and Resorts and Club Med have located near pyramids, characterized by industry as 'ruins'.

6   Anthropologist Martin Gray, in his book *Places of Peace and Power*, noted: 'Moses experienced divine revelation on Mount Sinai, Mohammed upon Mount Hara, Christ in a cave at Quarantana and Buddha beneath the Bodhi Tree' (cited in Scheer, 2001, p3).

7   In a most unusual outcome, the Canadian government purchased the 'private' land for return to proper cultural care. This coincided with heated forestry disputes in the territory of the Okanagan, which for economic reasons the federal and provincial authorities were eager to diffuse.

8   Autochthonous means 'sprung from the land'. This reflects the understanding that if the land is abused, it will be mirrored in the people because all is connected.

9   See CI's brochure entitled *Sacred Land: Refuge for Nature* (CI, 2003). CI points out that mass tourism is destabilizing 'Tibetan sacred land protection' systems, yet promotes protected areas funded by donor-led ecotourism.

10   The 2001 *In the Light of Reverence* project was created by the Earth Island Institute. During August 2001, it aired on cable television to 3 million viewers. In 2003, it was screened at the World Parks Congress in Durban, South Africa (see www.sacredland.org).

11   The US federal Bureau of Indian Affairs has conducted community classes on 'Archaeological Law Enforcement'. But how often do we see the US government subjected to criminal or civil penalties for its ongoing approval of sacred sites destruction?

12   Decision-making falls to the World Heritage Committee, comprised of 21 countries each serving a six-year term. Three advisory bodies guide the committee:

        1   World Conservation Union (IUCN);
        2   International Council on Monuments and Sites (ICOMOS); and
        3   International Centre for the Study of the Preservation and Restoration of Cultural Property (ICCROM).

Each submits recommendations via the coordinating World Heritage Centre (WHC), established in 1992.

13   Article 4(1) states that the rights of Indigenous Peoples should be respected. Article 4(2) elaborates, saying : 'the needs and wishes of some communities or indigenous peoples to restrict or manage physical, spiritual or intellectual access to certain cultural practices, knowledge, beliefs, activities, artefacts or sites should be respected'.

14   The manual contains some light discussion of Indigenous Peoples. For example,

it acknowledges that 'while site staff may legitimately regard certain valleys, rock formations or archaeological sites as natural or anthropological resources, such sites may be sacred to the host communities (Pedersen, 2002, p38). These references, however, are couched in policies and procedures that deny Indigenous Peoples any role in decision-making.

15   During recent decades, a number of Christian missions have been criticized for subverting Indigenous cultures. Many prominent evangelical groups equate Indigenous cultures with the devil. Their targets range from the Maya in Guatemala to the Akha in Thailand. Often, evangelism dovetails with government policy of assimilating Indigenous Peoples.

16   Sacred sites appropriation is a form of genocide used to re-colonize, integrate and assimilate Indigenous Peoples. 'If these sacred places are destroyed, those who base their beliefs on them will cease to exist as a people and a culture' (Seventh Generation Fund, 2001).

17   Peru's National Institute of Culture approved filming at Machu Picchu by beer company Cervesur, a subsidiary of Peruvian beer giant Backus and Johnston. The American publicity firm J. Walter Thompson shot the commercial. The latter's negligent use of a crane led to a large chip in the *Inti Watana*. This sundial, called the 'hitching post for the sun', is central to Inka sacred calendars and their oral history on sustainable use.

18   Unlike many Indigenous Peoples, the Pemón have secured jobs as guides to their own sacred sites at various waterfalls. Angel-Eco Tours, for example, offers trips where clients live 'in camp' with the Pemón while exploring the rainforest (Lisagor, 2003). In such cases, conclusions on local tourism benefits should not be drawn hastily. The Pemón's acceptance of certain tourism jobs by no means signals a healthy relationship with the national ecotourism industry. The Pemón and neighbouring tribes say there is no prior informed consent (PIC) for government development plans; they equate government policy with genocide (Survival, 2001).

19   '*Apus* is the Quechua word for "Spirits" not "Gods". The sun, the mountains, the wind are the spirits of the Earth emanating from the Creator' (Yachay Washi, 2001, p4).

20   'A pilgrimage is an outer journey to an inner experience. It is an itinerary designed with the hope of finding or enhancing one's spiritual bearings' (Scheer, 2001, p3).

21   There have been a number of public commentaries on how racism affects group behaviour and public policy. In the Hollywood movie *The English Patient*, it is suggested that nuclear bombs would never have hit Hiroshima if the people were white. Similarly, mass relocation of 12,000 Navajo and Hopi from the sacred Black Mesa area in the US 'would never have arisen ... if the people involved had been Anglo-Americans' (Scudder, 1998).

22   In 1996 The National Geographic Society hosted the month-long exhibition *Peru's Ice Maiden Unveiled* at its Washington, DC, headquarters. The Indigenous NGO Yachay Wasi challenged: 'Will American scientists and their American non-profit sponsors respect Indigenous Peoples' spiritual heritage in foreign countries?' (Samuel, 2002).

23   During 2002, Peruvian archaeologists unearthed a full Inka burial site at Machu Picchu, the first such 'bonanza' in a nearly a century. They announced that 'the burial find [would] be put on display where it was found to encourage tourism' (Vargas, 2002). The following year, Peru requested Yale University to return

similar 'cultural assets', but tacitly supported a roving exhibition of the burial remains during 2003–2005 (Associated Press, 2003).

24   This advertisement was featured prominently in international airports and in-flight magazines for consecutive years during the late 1990s. It inadvertently promotes two myths. The first myth is that sacred sites such as Machu Picchu are a remnant of *extinct* Indigenous Peoples. The second myth is that such sites remain largely 'untouched' by tourism. Many companies using this type of imagery and vocabulary have absorbed and perpetuated it unknowingly. Immersion in a colonial paradigm imparts a sense of entitlement, whether we are a company or consumer.

25   Machu Picchu is now open to locals free of charge on Sundays. This does not facilitate customary access, nor does it enable private ceremonial use. It simply expects local Indigenous Peoples to conform to the Christian calendar and feel comfortable amid weekend crowds.

26   North American and European companies long benefited from these obscene labour practices on the Inca Trail. Industry abuse led to a porter strike in 2001, which achieved a minimum wage of US$8 per day and maximum weight limit of 20kg (Lisagor, 2003).

27   Some tour operators previously featuring Machu Picchu have branched out to the 'ruins' at the 'lost city' of Victoria in the Cordillera Vilcabamba. Wilderness Travel takes clients for a 64km trek to Victoria over 'ancient Incan walkways'. For now, 'you'll have the excavated homes and ceremonial sites all to yourself' (Blakesley et al, 2003, p60). But the shift signifies a repeating pattern of industry appropriation of Indigenous Peoples' cultural sites.

28   See brochure entitled *Environment Protection and Biodiversity Conservation Act: Australia's Environment Law,* issued by the Department of the Environment and Heritage. This was one of Australia's featured handouts at the 2004 *UN Convention on Biological Diversity* (CBD) 6th Conference of the Parties in Kuala Lumpur, Malaysia.

29   See *Travel & Leisure* (2001) September, p113.

30   See *Condé Nast Traveler* (1999) July, p57.

Chapter 6

1   Indigenous Peoples must sometimes work with professionals of this commercial worldview, if outside technical services are necessary to help protect and exercise ancestral title. Lawyers, for example, are commonly required. In the legal domain, there are huge variances between colonial law and customary law. Most lawyers working on so-called 'land claims' view land as real estate. Such was the case in South Africa, when a law firm assisting with restitution of lands inside Kruger Park called the land in question a 'piece of real estate' and 'prize track' (WWB, 2003, p5). Viewing land through this lens is a far cry from understanding the land as sacred.

In government dialogues on biodiversity, the same commercial language is used. Often, it comes from the mouths of champions for 'conservation'. At the 2003 World Parks Congress, Queen Noor of Jordon referred to the Earth as 'our largest piece of real estate'. Many such individuals are too buffered from the full chain of impacts of industrial development to realize the danger of their remarks. They sincerely believe in a private-sector solution, seeing biodiversity loss as a management issue rather than a social ailment.

2   Wal-Mart is the largest multinational corporation in the world and is considered
       a model for economic globalization. It has also been granted the dubious
       honour of being named worst corporate human rights offender globally by
       The Ecologist magazine. Given this discrepancy, it is interesting that Wal-Mart
       is singled out in a positive light to encourage corporations to appoint a 'chief
       spiritual officer' (Religion News Service, 2004).

3   For details and a good discussion of implications, refer to news postings by
       Oilwatch of Ecuador; see www.oilwatch.org.ec.

4   In 2003, police in India killed 15 to 20 Adivasis for occupying their ancestral
       forest lands, annexed as the Wayanad Wildlife Sanctuary, and declaring them
       a self-governing area. India had agreed in 2001 to address their supposed
       'landlessness'. Authorities now claim to 'have cleared a wildlife sanctuary which
       was illegally occupied' (WRM, 2003).

5   Poverty has become the main excuse for promoting tourism in protected areas.
       'In the South, tourism is often the overriding justification for governments to
       support the creation of new protected areas' (Christ et al, 2003, p4). However,
       in practice, poverty alleviation is a gross domestic product (GDP) goal, not a
       community concept. To facilitate industrialization and national debt repayment,
       Indigenous peoples are removed from their ancestral lands. This facilitates so-
       called 'development', while throwing Indigenous Peoples into poverty. In the
       end, industry is said to fix what industry creates.

6   At the World Ecotourism Summit (WES) in 2002, the head of Parks Canada
       stated: 'This generation is the *last* to be able to create protected areas because
       the land available is a finite resource.'

7   There is an international cover-up of Canada and Australia's ongoing violations
       of Indigenous rights. In 2004, Canadian Louise Arbour was appointed as
       United Nations High Commissioner on Human Rights, and Australian Mike
       Smith was appointed chairman of the United Nations Commission on Human
       Rights. Yet, Canada, like Australia, has been grilled by the United Nation's
       Committee on the Elimination of Racial Discrimination. During 2002 and
       2003, Amnesty International told the UN that Canada is not adequately
       addressing the rights of Indigenous Peoples.

8   TILCEPA is a joint working group of the World Commission on Protected
       Areas (WCPA) and the Commission on Environmental, Economic and Social
       Policy (CEESP) of the World Conservation Union (IUCN), defined in full as the
       Theme on Indigenous and Local Communities, Equity and Protected Areas. It
       was established in 2000, and grew out of the Task Force on Local Communities
       and Protected Areas, launched in 1999. TILCEPA's mandate is to seek 'the full
       and effective recognition of the rights and responsibilities of local communities
       in the development and implementation of [relevant] conservation policies and
       strategies'. This mandate flows from past IUCN resolutions and statements.
              This initiative initially drew together a diverse group of professionals;
       following the World Parks Congress in 2003, its Indigenous membership grew.
       However, TILCEPA is not an Indigenous Peoples' initiative, nor are there
       protocols in place governing its interactions with Indigenous Peoples. The group
       still operates largely on its own discretion and initiative, without a transparent
       or adequately representative process with Indigenous Peoples. Its programming,
       therefore, has received mixed reviews and is still lacking any harmonization
       between 'expertise' and 'sacred knowledge'. See www.tilcepa.org.

9 TILCEPA's work resulted in the Fifth World Parks Congress (WPC) Recommendation 5.26, calling for recognition and support of community conservation areas (CCAs). During 2004, the *UN Convention on Biological Diversity* (CBD) Work Programme on protected areas recognized CCAs. TILCEPA followed up with a resolution to the IUCN World Conservation Congress, urging the IUCN to provide leadership on the matter, and requesting the WCPA to incorporate CCAs within its work programme.

10 Indigenous delegates' closing statement at the Fifth World Park Congress in Durban, South Africa, in 2003 stated:

> The declaration of protected areas on Indigenous territories without our consent and engagement has resulted in our dispossession and resettlement, the violation of our rights, the displacement of our peoples, the loss of our sacred sites and the slow but continuous loss of our cultures, as well as impoverishment. It is thus difficult to talk about benefits for Indigenous Peoples when protected areas are being declared on our territories unilaterally. First, we were dispossessed in the name of kings and emperors, later in the name of state development and now in the name of conservation... To overcome this history of dispossession and exclusion and violence against Indigenous Peoples in protected areas, Indigenous Peoples here at the WPC propose the establishment of a high-level, independent Truth and Reconciliation Commission on Indigenous peoples and Protected Areas.'

11 The initial privatization push came from the World Bank through its funding for national protected areas systems – explicitly linking parks and ecotourism. Conservation groups such as Conservation International (CI), the World Wide Fund for Nature (WWF-International) and The Nature Conservancy (TNC) jumped aboard, capitalizing on prescribed structural adjustments by brokering 'debt for nature' swaps. The *Brundtland Report* (WCED, 1987) gave moral authority to their early work. Today, the likes of Nelson Mandela have been recruited to help the cause along (TIM Team, 2003). However, the goal has always been a conventional conservation economy, with an emphasis on economics not 'conservation'.

12 The cost of Clayoquot's hallmark 'scientific' panel was absorbed primarily to protect the provincial forest economy from boycotts. Internationally, such conservation measures are most prevalent in flashpoint areas of conflict, where community advocacy campaigns or civil disobedience threaten the economic agenda of government.

13 Weekly household purchases and activities by the average consumer support both sweatshops and child labour, as well as mass pollution, pesticides and genetic modification. Our groceries, clothing and transport rank among the most serious human rights issues. This is the reality we need to contend with, inside ourselves.

14 Precedents in the tourism sector indicate a trend of endangerment. Popular tourism sites like Stonehenge in England, Lascaux Cave in France and the Great Barrier Reef in Australia have been rapidly degraded by tourism and subject to strict tourism limitations (Foroohar, 2002). Other sites such as Machu Picchu in Peru and Masai Mara in Kenya are in jeopardy and crying out for interventions. These destinations all need protection from tourism. Yet, they all

remain on the so-called 'eco' tourism radar screen. What does this foreshadow for protected areas?

15   The 1997 *Delgamuukw* decision of the Supreme Court of Canada, recognizing the existence of Aboriginal title, is still not implemented. Nor are other seminal court rulings following the *Delgamuukw* precedent.

16   Shareholders of the Olympic Bid Corporation include the Canadian federal government, British Columbia, Vancouver and Whistler.

17   Neither the Aboriginal Participation Work Group nor the Aboriginal Secretariat, established in 2001 to facilitate the Olympic bid, is properly representative. Both involve just Lil'wat, instead of the St'at'imc Nation. Under international law, a community cannot hold or protect Aboriginal title and rights; it is the *people* or Indigenous nation as a whole who have this legal status. Canada is well aware of these intricacies, but cultivated division nonetheless.

18   When the province issued a cutting permit to Ainsworth Lumber in 1999, and company foresters presented the St'at'imc with simulations of visual impacts geared to tourists, the St'at'imc told them: 'Not only will we see the impact but we will *feel* it' (John, 2003). St'at'imc women ordered the erection of a protection camp beside the logging equipment, humorously named The Delgamuukw Inn. All 11 St'at'imc communities supported the camp. It echoed the *Stagyn* fight; there were more death threats and a Chief was thrown into the ditch by loggers.

19   The 2001 letter from the German Bundestag to Canada stated:

> We understand that the Supreme Court of Canada recognizes those collective and inherent land rights of indigenous peoples as Aboriginal title in the 1997 Delgamuukw decision and request that your government negotiate with First Nations over the consequences of the now recognized co-existence of Aboriginal and Crown titles over all the traditional territories of nations that have not signed treaties. Nevertheless, it appears that your Minister for Indian Affairs continues to negotiate under the 1986 *Comprehensive Claims Policy* according to which Indigenous Peoples have to cede, release and surrender their title to their traditional territories and are granted parts back in return. Such a policy does not fully accommodate Aboriginal title, nor does it lead to the full participation of Indigenous Peoples in planning processes… We would therefore be very grateful if you could inform us of your opinion on this highly sensitive issue and hope that some of our suggestions can be taken up in further negotiations in your country.

20   *Gold Rush Days* is not a culturally or historically sensitive promotion. An equivalent would be a community festival called Slavery Days in the American south or Massacre Days in Australia.

21   Indigenous Peoples such as the Awá of Brazil have been killed by loggers, miners or 'hit men' for safeguarding ancestral lands. The Amazon Alliance calls this an act of genocide. See www.survival-international.org, www.cs.org and www.amazonalliance.org for ongoing cases.

22   Similar tactics are employed with Indigenous Peoples worldwide. One observer familiar with the situation of the Cofán in Ecuador notes: 'Around their territory, communities, with all other economic activities shattered, are unusually receptive to oil pay-offs to operate on their lands.'

23   The 2010 winter Olympic Games are expected to stimulate Cdn$10.7 billion

in new business for the provincial economy in British Columbia (*Western Native News*, 2004). Cultural tourism, entwined with 'eco' tourism, is a central pillar of provincial plans for related economic growth. In June 2003, just prior to the IOC's award of the 2010 Olympics, the governments of Canada and British Columbia announced Cdn$7.7 million of funding for the St'at'imc community of Lil'wat and its Halkomelem counterpart to build a cultural centre in the Whistler ski resort, a growing hub for the global ecotourism industry. (This funding was increased by an additional Cdn$3 million in September 2005, under the province's latest 'New Relationship' scheme.) The centre will showcase 'Aboriginal cultures from British Columbia, Canada and other parts of the world' (INAC, 2003). Its design includes dedicated eco-tour buildings.

24   TILCEPA was split over whether to support this statement which arose from its panel on communities and tourism organized by TILCEPA. When the involved Chiefs and Elder Ruby Dunstan gave an advance reading of the statement to TILCEPA, prior to its release, the session chair wanted to scrap the statement. Other TILCEPA members on the floor realized its value to Indigenous self-determination and argued passionately to support it. While TILCEPA is supposedly a support group to Indigenous Peoples, it is actually an arm of the IUCN, an inter-governmental body. Such organizations can play into colonial hands if their protocol with Indigenous Peoples is not set straight. Under no circumstances should their membership take it upon themselves to censor Indigenous Peoples.

Chapter 7

1   It is important to monitor the seeming breakthroughs in order to see how consistent efforts are. Conservation International (CI), an organization that has received substantial criticism from numerous Indigenous Peoples and NGOs over its promotion of ecotourism, has recently made efforts to support community-owned, operated and managed enterprises among Indigenous Peoples. For example, it is working with the Bukakhwe San Bushmen in Botswana on the Gudigwa Camp project and with the Kayapo in Brazil to secure the border of the Área Indígena Kayapo. When such organizations dabble in initiatives like this, are 'new' principles (for example, self-determination) applied programme-wide or only to some showcased projects? Normally there is weak follow-through due to competing agendas.

2   Geoffrey Wall points out the tendency 'for agencies to use the term "joint management" in the context of lesser arrangements where Aboriginal people have little power in decision-making' (Wall, 1999, p9; see also Chapter 6).

3   In the 'Community tourism' web discussion hosted by www.planeta.com in 2002, Balám stated: 'The less useful training we see is related to "guide training", where we see many projects lacking of social consensus and not related to a communal objective. Most of these training programmes are promoted by conservation NGOs.'

4   This 'playing the field' is most visible in the mining sector, where Indigenous Peoples and NGOs have confronted companies such as Alcan Aluminium, Barrack Gold and De Beers Diamonds for human rights abuses and other rights infringements. It is just as prevalent in tourism, but is better masked. One interesting development in 2004 was De Beers's sponsorship of the Canadian National Exhibition Pow Wow; this sponsorship announcement came shortly after *The Ecologist* cover screamed 'Dying for De Beers', protesting genocide

against the Bushmen (Botswana). See the September 2003 issue of *The Ecologist*, then read www.indianmarketing.com/cne.

5   In corporate culture, great use is made of psychological profiling. Tools such as Meyers Briggs or True Colours typecasting are regularly used to match personnel to projects or to promote team building. While such tools are valuable instruments for improving communication, it is difficult to prevent their unethical use.

6   See *Dumbing Us Down: The Hidden Curriculum of Compulsory Schooling* by John Taylor Gatto (2002).

7   In April 2004, The International Ecotourism Society (TIES) (US) co-hosted The Travellers' Philanthropy Conference, together with the Center on Ecotourism and Sustainable Development (US) and Conservation International (CI) (TIES, 2004). Philanthropy has long been a built-in feature of the ecotourism concept. Its impact upon Indigenous Peoples depends upon whether 'charitable' contributions support self-determination, or simply lubricate the way for industrialization. 'Conservation' and 'development' – which donors like to fund – are both colonial concepts. Thus, donations may mask the fact that communities cast as 'hosts' are actually 'targets', caught in industry's cross hairs.

8   Private collections of wealthy 'industrialists' are often put on public display or housed for 'scholars' through private institutions such as the Amerind Foundation (see www.amerind.org). These collections remain a thorny issue as Indigenous Peoples worldwide fight for repatriation of their cultural and, inherently, spiritual heritage.

9   For law firms, landing an industry client or facilitating a 'multi-stakeholder' tourism deal can be lucrative, either in project fees or visibility on the world stage. In South Africa, the Makuleke Communal Property Association of Kruger Park relied upon their *pro bono* legal team to '[manage] the call for proposals, the bidding process, the choice of preferred bidder' then '[lead] the negotiations, along with the drafting of various concession agreements' (WWB, 2003, p3). This created the foundation for four new luxury safari lodges on a profit-sharing basis. Although the law firm in question volunteered its time, it now has a reputation within the tourism industry for securing this type of deal, as well as exposure as a success story to the lodges' wealthy industry-connected clientele.

10   US President George W. Bush categorized NGOs as an enemy in his first televised speech following the tragic events of 11 September 2001 (which brought down the World Trade Center in New York). His naming of NGOs at this time must be viewed in the broader picture. Bush had just returned from the UN negotiations on climate change, where NGOs blasted his administration for withholding support for the *Kyoto Protocol*.

11   At the World Ecotourism Summit (WES) in 2002, the World Tourism Organization (WTO-OMT) was aware that most Indigenous delegates attending the summit had a limited background in UN dialogues on tourism; instead of ensuring an atmosphere of openness, it tried to create a wedge between these individuals and vocal NGOs, who were demanding a better process for Indigenous Peoples. The Indigenous delegates had a ten-minute audience with the WTO-OMT, while NGOs received a separate hearing of almost an hour. To many, it seemed that these two separate tracks of dialogue were intended to prevent 'contamination'.

    By 2004, attempts to cultivate differences were much more blatant.

During the *UN Convention on Biological Diversity* (CBD) proceedings in Kuala Lumpur, where the controversial CBD draft guidelines on tourism took centre stage, overt 'divide and conquer' tactics were used. After the Indigenous Caucus delivered a statement to world governments, which reflected the very same concerns raised by NGOs, certain members of the Caucus were approached 'off the record' by emissaries of the CBD Secretariat. In this closed discussion of political trade-offs, it was suggested that the Indigenous Caucus statement on tourism lacked foundation and consensus. In fact, the Indigenous Caucus statement had undergone three days of discussion and review inside the Caucus. It also reflected directions from Chiefs which had been submitted to the 2003 World Parks Congress in South Africa (see Gavidi et al, 2003).

12   NGOs capture the bulk of funding available to assist Indigenous Peoples. Many overseeing tourism 'development' deliver community training, shaped by either their own goals or by funder terms of reference. Frequently, the most basic and urgent training needs are ignored; the training focus is business-oriented rather than rights-oriented. The Nature Conservancy (TNC, 2003), for example, offers community training as guides and tour operators. In such scenarios, it is rare to see a *prerequisite* phase of training on rights. Indigenous Peoples approached by NGOs seldom know their rights or tourism-specific rights issues. This means that most NGOs are commencing training programmes without first ensuring prior informed consent (PIC). To correct this, the involved Indigenous people(s) must have capacity to organize a preliminary round of training for themselves on rights, featuring guest Indigenous leaders or Indigenous rights-support organizations as necessary. Otherwise, NGO trainers step in with training programmes beset with conflict of interest.

13   At the United Nations Commission on Sustainable Development (CSD) in April 1999, TIES participated as a member of the NGOs' caucus.

14   In the tourism sector, hotels and other establishments serving a wealthy international clientele (the global consumer class) often pay domestic staff with servant wages. They also may bar 'undesirables' (for example, local vendors) from tourist zones in order to guard exclusivity and create a privileged atmosphere. This type of practice continues to be the industry standard despite the glaring overtones of human rights abuse. It is often just as prevalent in 'locally' owned establishments as those owned by multinational companies or expatriates, due to class, race and gender discrimination.

15   The feature article on *La Ruta Maya* in *National Geographic* (Garrett, 1989) made no reference to regional human rights problems (Lack, 1990), 'reinforcing the notion that tourism is not only benign, but that it is a positive force for the preservation of the Maya, both ancient and contemporary, and that much the same holds true for ... nature and biosphere reserves' (Daltabuit and Pi-Sunyer, 1990, p12).

16   Stated goals included development of marginalized regions and communities; poverty alleviation for local Maya communities; and community participation in decision-making and implementation (SECTUR, 1990, 1991, 1992; Toriello, 1992).

17   By 1991, several mainstream travel companies in Europe and North America advertised tours to Mundo Maya. In 1992, there were *Mundo Maya* brochures ready in five languages for the annual International Tourism Bourse Trade Fair in Berlin, courtesy of the European Economic Community (EEC). Tourists

began to arrive before even a management apparatus was in place.

18   Companies such as Club Med and Camino Real helped to launch *Mundo Maya*. Mexico's privately funded mega-projects programme (*Travel Weekly*, 1991) included the *Villas Archaeologicas* at Palenque (Gaines, 1990).

19   In 1991, for example, CI negotiated a US$4 million deal with Mexico to expand the El Triunfo Biosphere Reserve. See Choudry (2003) in *Seedling* and Weinberg (2003) in *Native Americas*.

20   Projects such as *Mayarema* (Gardner, 1991), *Centro Maya* (Damsker et al, 1992) and a similar 'eco-development' initiative at Dzilam Reserve (Moreno, 1991) all integrated ecotourism.

21   When the MacArthur Foundation sponsored a conference in 1992 to discuss the formation of a 'conservation cooperation zone' in the Petén (Scott, 1992), it was conservationists, scientists and academic groups active in 'eco' tourism who attended.

22   In this second phase of *Mundo Maya*, the tourism ministers of member countries have formed the Mundo Maya Alliance, together with CI (US), Counterpart International (US) and The National Geographic Society (US). This signals even greater leverage by corporate-style NGOs in *Mundo Maya* programming. Previously, the *Organización Mundo Maya* (OMM) had engaged NGOs second hand through the national ecotourism councils.

Chapter 8

1   See Abocar (2004) and Calamai (2004) regarding the situation of the Inuit in the Arctic regions of Canada, Russia, Greenland and the US.

2   During the 1990s the World Trade Organization (WTO), the Global Environment Fund (GEF) and the International Monetary Fund (IMF) all opened discussion forums with Indigenous Peoples. 'These are landmark meetings because they never could have taken place a decade earlier' (World Bank, 1999). Government negotiations had been sealed to Indigenous Peoples until the pivotal Earth Summit in Rio de Janeiro in 1992. Today, the political climate has changed to such an extent that the World Bank's Operations Evaluations Department solicits feedback from Indigenous Peoples on its policies, programmes and projects. The Inter-American Development Bank (IADB), meanwhile, has compiled a Database on Indigenous Legislation in the Americas. To this day, however, all of these major financial institutions have a well documented track record of violating Indigenous rights.

3   It is no coincidence that the *General Agreement on Trade in Services* (GATS) and the *UN Convention on Biological Diversity* (CBD) are being advanced simultaneously. These two agreements contravene one another: the former ensuring individual rights (corporate-style trade), while the latter supposedly protects collective rights (including biodiversity). However, industry trade objectives are expedited by CBD posturing on 'traditional' knowledge and sustainable use. See analysis by the Gaia Foundation and Genetic Resources Action International (1998).

4   During 2000, the World Wide Fund for Nature (WWF-International) teamed up with the respected NGO Terralingua to issue the *Map of Indigenous and Traditional Peoples in Ecoregions*. In this report, WWF-International provides some insightful commentary on consultation *faux pas* (WWF-International, 2000, p56). However, it is a tricky read since WWF-International sees no intrinsic problem with NGOs (all stakeholders) directing consultations in the territories

of Indigenous Peoples (that is, rights holders). WWF-International's position – although it gives limited, strategic support to Indigenous Peoples' right to self-determination (WWF-International, 2000, p27) – is that Indigenous Peoples are mere stakeholders in conservation.

5   According to Conservation International (CI): 'Most tourism development is driven by the private sector', followed by multilateral and bilateral development agencies. 'Other stakeholders also have important roles; but their actual contribution depends on their ability to influence the central players' (Christ et al, 2003, pvii). This analysis of 'key players' tacitly admits the struggle of Indigenous Peoples in stakeholder talks, where Indigenous rights are overshadowed by commercial interests.

6   Lorenzo Muelas Hurtado (Movimiento Autoridades Indígenas, Colombia), Michael Anderson (Gumilaroi Nation, Australia) and Tribal Chief Mike Leach (St'at'imc Nation, Canada) are among countless Indigenous leaders who are outspoken on false consultation. Many say that false Indigenous 'representatives' put on display by colonial governments are just as damaging as the stakeholder process in which they participate (see Chapter 10).

7   At the Fifth Conference of the Parties (COP5) in Nairobi, there were, on average, 15 Indigenous delegates on hand to monitor the late night CBD Article 8(j) proceedings on traditional knowledge. This weak 'representation' enables governments to deliver compromised consultation products, such as the CBD draft guidelines on tourism, geared to industry interests.

8   One notable case of this took place within the Global Biodiversity Forum discussion on tourism, linked to the CBD. An Indigenous delegate instructed his colleague not to raise the right to self-determination within forum dialogues because it is 'too political'. This incident illustrated how some regularly funded individuals choose their platforms carefully so as not to jeopardize their funding or position as a sought-after 'representative' or 'expert'. Realistically, the term 'biodiversity' is far from apolitical. Many see the CBD and its provisions for traditional knowledge as an astute political move in favour of globalized trade.

9   The Maasai, Maori and countless other Indigenous Peoples have seen national governments buy off apparent 'leaders' using financial incentives. See Braddock (2004) and Olol-Dapash (1999, 2001).

10   There have been cases where the Indigenous Caucus at CBD meetings and related policy forums is chaired or co-chaired by such an individual. While certain country delegations and allied institutions usually know the situation, fellow Indigenous representatives who are present often have no means of verifying claims made by Indigenous 'representatives' from other continents. Year after year, the travesty continues because most governments in the know are more concerned about creating an impression of consultation than delivering a sound mechanism for dialogue. This can discredit the entire process in the eyes of mandated Indigenous leadership who later receive news of the proceedings.

11   At meetings of the World Trade Organization (WTO), social justice keeps re-emerging as a cross-cutting theme. Regardless of what industrial interests maintain, there is the irrepressible protest voice of civil society groups. The wellspring of commentary from these lobby groups indicates that the industrial way and economic growth come at an incomprehensible cost (such as climate change, child labour, systemic poverty, loss of genetic diversity and endangered food security).

12   Many eco-lodges boasting community involvement are structured as 'build, operate, transfer (BOT) agreements, whereby once the concession periods have expired, the community will become the owners of the fixed assets and improvements, and will have acquired the skills necessary to manage the business themselves' (WWB, 2003, p3). Kapawi in Ecuador and Posada Amazonas in Peru, which both provide for community transfer after 20 years, are often referenced as the industry standard. However, in South Africa, the deal structured between Wilderness Safaris and the Makuleke Communal Property Association by the law firm Webber Wentzel Bowens (WWB) 'is structured to last for 45 years' (WWB, 2003, p3). Few Indigenous Peoples or Indigenous communities entering into such agreements know pertinent industry statistics prior to signing agreements.

13   Within the public and private sectors, 'negotiations resourcing' is readily available to access resources, as part of project financing. This 'investment' is written of as a business cost to be offset by future profits. Indigenous Peoples, on the other hand, have no comparable financial ability to negotiate or monitor third-party proceedings of concern to them. They have no recognized assets to borrow against and cannot count on future royalties as collateral, due to government disregard for ancestral title and land rights.

14   Frequently, industry interests maintain discreet control under the guise of 'partnership'. In Colombia, projects of The Nature Conservancy (TNC) and the World Bank in the territory of the Kogi People are administered by a local NGO, the Fondación Pro-Sierra Nevada de Santa Marta. The Kogi experience is that 'what is given with one hand, Younger Brother takes away with another' (Ereira, 2001, p37).

Chapter 9

1   See the US Pentagon report on global climate change publicized in February 2004 (Schwartz and Randall, 2003) and the Arctic Council report on climate change released in November 2004 (Arctic Council, 2004, www.arctic-council. org). Also refer to September 2004 issue of *National Geographic* (National Geographic Society, 2004).

2   'On a global scale, biodiversity is being lost at a rate many times higher than natural extinction' (Christ et al, 2003, pvi).

3   Many resort establishments anchoring regional 'eco' tourism continue to release chemicals such as bleach, chemical fertilizers and herbicides into the ecosystem. They also affect other 'supplier' ecosystems; for example, it is said that 1.25 pounds of agricultural chemicals is used to produce a single set of conventional queen-sized bed sheets. If we multiply this by the number of beds in a typical resort, and the frequency of linen replacement, we get a broader picture of how chemical-intensive most tourist accommodation is.

4   Most government, industry and institutional bodies working on sustainable tourism adhere to the premise of economic growth. Most have resisted feedback indicating that growth models are problematic. Sustainable tourism, according to the United Nations Environment Programme (UNEP) and Conservation International (CI), 'draws on the principles of ecotourism' (Christ et al, 2003, p6). However, the global ecotourism industry has already discredited industry application of these principles. Sector to sector in the global economy, the industrial model functions on the *same* business logic.

5   According to UNEP, we already know that global warming threatens tourism in coastal and mountain areas, that loss of biological diversity will affect nature-based tourism, and that local water and air pollution is beginning to limit tourism in some areas (Aloisi de Larderel, 1999). UNEP views fresh corporate leadership as a solution. Nonetheless, there is resounding unity in the industrial world for economic growth – that is, more of the same.

6   Space tourism is nascent, taking dialogue on 'sustainable use' to another pitch. Two businessmen, one American and one South African, became the world's first space tourists (MacGregor, 2002). Today, an American company operating in Tonga is marketing week-long rocket trips into space as a form of elite travel (*The Globe and Mail*, 2002). On 21 June 2004, the first privately funded rocket was successfully launched, making such trips imminent. Whereas initial product offerings were 'high end', between US$2 million to US$20 million apiece, space travel is already being packaged for volume sales – for example, US$100,000 per ticket for as little as 15 minutes in orbit (Muir, 2004). Why is this troubling? Before exercising restraint and earning credibility in our immediate biosphere, we have expanded into new horizons.

7   During 2002, a peak year of terrorism fears, global tourism actually hit a record. 'For the first time, the number of international arrivals broke the 700 million mark, reaching nearly 715 million … a 3.1 per cent rise from 2001' (News Services, 2003). By April 2004, international air travel had returned to 'pre-terrorism' levels; the International Air Transport Association (IATA) forecasted a 'modest profit of US$3.2 billion' by the world's major airlines on international routes (Canadian Press, 2004). Now, slashed fares mean that even more people are travelling. At current rates, air travel contributes approximately 5 per cent of global carbon emissions (Christ et al, 2003, p32). Although warnings on global warming were issued to the aviation industry by 'expert' bodies such as the UK's Royal Commission on Environmental Pollution (Clover, 2002), the European Union (EU) has opted for an 'open skies' policy (Jones, 2003).

8   In the tourism sector: 'We are speaking of costs and benefits in a primarily financial language' (Vellas, 2002) – without much social or cross-cultural dimension, much less a spiritual context.

9   Current studies on ecotourism impacts, amassed over 20-plus years, recount a library of industry problems. However, since these studies were completed, the composite of the ecotourism industry has changed. A number of companies now remark upon the 'softening' of ecotourism. Second-generation eco-tourists are described as more demanding in terms of 'creature comforts' and less interested in nature interpretation (Theroux, 2001, p66). This means that current studies are outdated and should not be used for industry projections. Industry impacts (costs) will be much greater than existing data suggests.

10   Standards for impact assessment are a major concern of most NGOs advocating for sustainable tourism. Several respected NGOs have observed that: 'The industry is more interested in undertaking benefit analysis than any real cost/benefit analysis' (Pleumarom, 1999). This observation is based on a series of developments. In deliberations on tourism and biodiversity under the Fourth Subsidiary Body on Scientific, Technical and Technological Advice (SBSTTA) of the *UN Convention on Biological Diversity* (CBD) in June 1999, the focus in the government Contact Group was the positive impacts of tourism. Brochures for the International Year of Ecotourism (IYE) in 2004 emphasized the promotion

of tourism (WTO-OMT and UNEP, 2002), as did deliberations on tourism at the second Earth Summit in Johannesburg in 2002 (WSSD, 2002, paragraph 42). There is wide divergence between most NGO conceptualizations of sustainable tourism and government or institutional definitions.

11   In the same edition of ECOCLUB the editor, Antonis Petropoulis, unwittingly printed evidence to the contrary: 'In Laos it's all changing very quickly. Ten years ago you could see the Akha in their traditional costumes everywhere. Now, it's almost all gone except deep inside the countryside … it's an art to have tourists going into a village again and again and not have them leave a negative impact' (Gray et al, 2004). The ECOCLUB website, found at www.ecoclub. com, is recognized in Europe as the 'Best Responsible Tourism Site' via the Travel and Tourism Web Awards but is steeped in an industry perspective.

12   Article 8(j) and related provisions of the CBD are primarily motivated by trade imperatives. Most governments who have signed the CBD also signed the *General Agreement on Tariffs and Trade* (GATT) under the World Trade Organization. For the latter to proceed smoothly, there must be an appearance of environmental and social responsibility. Governments banked on 'traditional' knowledge to help put this batch of negotiations beyond reproach. To date, this has proved a worthwhile gamble. Most Indigenous Peoples worldwide remain unaware of the CBD and its worth as a tool, either for or against their collective rights (Leach, 2002).

13   Provisions for 'traditional' knowledge in Article 8(j) of the CBD are subject to national legislation. This caveat makes Indigenous Peoples subordinate to colonial law, undercutting their status as 'peoples' with distinct rights in international law. So, while collective rights are alluded to in the CBD, they are, in fact, rendered invalid and useless by its wording.

14   NGOs such as Equations in India, the Ecumenical Coalition on Tourism (ECOT) in Hong Kong, Indigenous Tourism Rights International (ITRI) in the US and the International Support Centre for Sustainable Tourism (ISCST) in Canada expressed concern to the UN about the promotional bias of the institutional programme of work on 'sustainable' tourism. They warned that proposed case studies would be meaningless without capacity provisions for affected Indigenous Peoples.

15   This government consensus was communicated in the Contact Group on tourism at the Fourth Subsidiary Body on Scientific, Technical and Technological Advice (SBSTTA 4) in 1999.

16   The Theme on Indigenous and Local Communities, Equity and Protected Areas (TILCEPA) of the World Conservation Union (IUCN) sponsored the Fifth World Parks Congress (WPC) session on tourism and communities and requested the the International Support Centre for Sustainable Tourism (ISCST) to organize and convene the event. Indigenous Peoples from Fiji, Kenya, Ecuador and Canada were represented. All had 9 to 12 months' notice of their funded participation and were able to prepare accordingly. See Chapter 10 for other steps taken directly under the CBD for Indigenous Peoples' input to the dialogue on sustainable tourism during 1999–2004.

17   Indigenous Peoples were not invited to the UN's first coordinated meeting on sustainable tourism at WTO-OMT headquarters in November 2004, nor could they easily access UNEP Governing Council discussions on tourism in February 2006.

18   This submission was made in Working Group 2 at the Fourth Subsidiary Body on Scientific, Technical and Technological Advice (SBSTTA 4) in 1999 in Montreal, Canada.

19   Haida Environmental, for instance, is a private consulting firm established for environmental impact assessments utilizing 'traditional knowledge'.

20   In 1999, the United Nations Commission on Sustainable Development (CSD) conducted a special session on 'sustainable' tourism, with emphasis on consumer behaviour. Ironically, this dialogue on sustainability occurred in Manhattan, New York, the world navel according to consumption-obsessed *Vogue* magazine and *Architectural Digest*.

21   Helen and Scott Nearing's books *The Good Life* (Nearing and Nearing, 1990) and *Loving and Leaving the Good Life* (Nearing and Nearing, 1992) provide one of the counter-examples, illustrating a couple's effort to forge their vocation and lifestyle outside the confines of consumerism.

22   This precept of medicine identified the human body as sacred, while other expressions of sacredness were being disavowed. Now, even this principle of the industrial era has been transgressed; today, genetic engineering tinkers with life building blocks and life systems at utterly unknown risk (Traavik, 2002). This is the final blow of corporate science. Pesticides, hormones and other dangerous food additives are the diet of children in consumer society.

23   Indigenous Peoples targeted to 'host' groups of tourists typically do not travel. Most are shut out of this economic bracket by systemic discrimination. In rare cases, loopholes to colonialism are found enabling some economic footing; but those whose relationship with the land remains strong tend to live a disciplined life and stay put.

24   Jane Goodall, in her book *Reason for Hope: A Spiritual Journey*, sums it up well: 'We do not, I think, have much time. And these changes must be made by us, you and me. If we go on leaving it to others, shipwreck is inevitable' (Goodall, 1999, p232).

25   Forest Stewardship Council (FSC) accreditation is based on ten principles, principle 3 being Indigenous Peoples' rights (FERN, 2001, p56).

26   Concerns expressed by Indigenous Peoples are shared by many others monitoring the 'sustainability' of the global economy. Since the 1970s, a number of non-Indigenous scholars and activists have commented at length upon the ultimately cataclysmic costs of industrial-style economics. The most poignantly named study is David W. Ehrenfeld's (1978) *The Arrogance of Humanism*. The discourse has also crossed into religious debate. In 1999, the Dalai Lama published a seminal work called *Ethics for the New Millennium*.

27   The book *Ishmael* by Daniel Quinn (1992) explains the notion of 'takers' and 'leavers'. It is a modern-day fable about 'biodiversity' and our consumer society's incessant taking.

28   The serious impacts of economic globalization on politically marginalized peoples and the 'environment' are well documented worldwide, for those who care to look. These include rampant violations of human rights, as well as the continued dispossession of Indigenous Peoples' ancestral lands through government and industry collusion. Respected journals such as *The Ecologist* (UK), *Resurgence* (Malaysia) and *Cultural Survival Quarterly* (US) are a good place to start reading.

Chapter 10

1   This *Cry of the Earth* spiritual gathering should not be confused with the subsequent *Call of the Earth*, an Indigenous 'experts' initiative launched in December 2002 (see www.earthcall.org).

2   See Alfred and Corntassel (2004) for a synopsis of advances made by Indigenous Peoples at the UN during 1995–2004.

3   Many would like to refute this on lack of evidence; however, recent mapping of remaining biodiversity worldwide attests to the customary governance of Indigenous Peoples:

> There is no doubt that Indigenous Peoples are causing environmental harm in some cases, and that this comes from a breakdown of traditional institutions, or the operation of traditional institutions at new scales that are not sustainable. All too true … but they are the terminal expression, not the root cause' (Hardison, 2004).

4   Artists such as Tracy Chapman (for example, 'Material World'), Bruce Cockburn ('If a Tree Falls') and Simon and Garfunkel ('Sound of Silence') have sent a clear message to the consumer world. Our problem is that we wait for someone with a PhD to verify things, then debate 'expert' opinions in endless scepticism. Where is our common sense?

5   Tourism, though not specified as a sector in the *UN Convention on Biological Diversity* (CBD), was the subject of a ministerial roundtable at the Fourth Conference of the Parties (COP4) in Bratislava in May 1998. The roundtable addressed Germany's proposal to launch a process for global tourism guidelines under the CBD. While governments were alerted to this proposal, equal diligence was not given to notifying affected Indigenous Peoples. Few Indigenous delegates expected to be in Bratislava had advance knowledge; consequently, they could prepare neither community-level interventions nor a coordinated response. Indigenous leadership outside the CBD (the world majority of Indigenous Peoples) was altogether bypassed. This oversight was serious, given that sustainable tourism is said to rest upon the participation of local communities.

6   Deliberations on tourism under the CBD proceeded at a careless pace, ignoring the precautionary principle of the convention. The 2000 International NGOs' Workshop on Tourism and Biological Diversity in Berlin happened just two months before COP5 in Nairobi. This time crunch made it difficult for many participating NGOs to take the CBD process seriously. Community-based NGOs could not undertake suitable outreach. As such, the workshop served more to create a speaking platform for the host NGO, Ecological Tourism in Europe (ETE), than to launch a principled process among NGOs. Likewise, the 2001 CBD Santo Domingo Workshop on Tourism and Biodiversity, an 'experts' event, was officially announced little over six weeks ahead. On that timeline, invited NGOs could only attempt to mitigate the impacts of a rushed process. Those linked to real community constituencies focused on requesting compliance with international law, especially concerning Indigenous Peoples. This type of advocacy should not be necessary within a UN process. Nevertheless, the scenario would play out again at the 2001 follow-up NGOs meeting in New Delhi. The event was organized by the same NGO, ETE, to help market the draft CBD guidelines. Its hasty organization troubled many NGOs, and shut out any possibility of legitimate Indigenous Peoples' involvement. There was no time to refer the invitation to mandated Indigenous

leadership or to undertake appropriate consultation with Elders. Among NGOs, abiding by the UN calendar continues as a barrier to dialogue; it breeds competitiveness and may reward misconduct.

7   At both the Vilm worskshop in November 1999 and the Santo Domingo workshop in June 2001, the group composition was poorly suited to the task. Few of the invited 'experts' had seen background materials on the CBD dialogue on tourism, such as previous analysis and recommendations. Many, including in some instances facilitators, were not familiar with even the language of the CBD. In Vilm, this resulted in scattered dialogue. In Santo Domingo, the result was open intolerance among some delegates towards Article 8(j). Criteria for 'expert' selection did not become any more transparent in follow-up work on the CBD tourism guidelines, leading up to COP7 in Malaysia during 2004. The process for guidelines development suffered from an increasingly narrow and Northern base of 'expertise' – reflecting less and less any sincere concern for the rights of Indigenous Peoples.

8   Even though the CBD dialogue on tourism began in 1997, with the *Berlin Declaration on Sustainable Tourism* and a side event at the inter-sessional meeting on Article 8(j) in Madrid, provisions for suitable NGO involvement were nil until March 2000. ISCST was the only tourism NGO present at CBD proceedings on tourism from 1997 onward. Observer NGOs such as the International Support Centre for Sustainable Tourism (ISCST), Third World Network (TWN) and, later on, the Rethinking Tourism Project (now Indigenous Tourism Rights International) did their best on limited budgets or volunteer capacity to communicate implications of the CBD process on tourism to a grassroots audience. However, workshops hosted by Germany in Heidelberg during 1998 and in Vilm during 1999 to support its proposal for global guidelines under the CBD had limited NGO participation. It was the 2000 International NGOs' Workshop on Tourism and Biological Diversity in Berlin that gave most NGOs their first glimpse of CBD proceedings. At this event, ISCST was asked by the host Ecological Tourism in Europe (ETE), to provide a formal briefing to participating NGOs, and to facilitate the drafting of an NGO statement for COP5 in Nairobi. Following this Berlin event, ETE was retained by Germany to continue in a coordinating role, undertaking consultancies to support the draft CBD tourism guidelines. By this time there had been a turnover in assigned staff and consultants in the German government. Scoring a home run for the CBD guidelines became more important to Germany than ensuring a grounded process for their development. Whereas initial disregard for NGOs had largely been an oversight, there now seemed to be a new pattern of deliberate exclusion. ETE was funded by Germany to carry the CBD guidelines forward, creating an impression within the CBD negotiations of NGO endorsement. During this period, ETE did not disclose the extent of this role to fellow NGOs. What developed was a conflict of interest on the part of ETE that several international NGOs were aware of. However, most other NGOs had no enabling funds to plug into the CBD process, and therefore either unplugged entirely or relied upon joint intervention statements to communicate their disappointment with the process. Those seen as supportive of Indigenous Peoples, or asking for a transparent and inclusive process, were ostracized and labelled. An important lesson for NGOs from this experience is the need for internal healing and relationship-building among them before jumping into reactive mode with respect to policy development.

9   At COP4 in Bratislava in 1998, Germany tabled a proposal that global tourism

guidelines be formulated under the CBD. This initial proposal was debated at the Ministerial Roundtable on Tourism, but was rejected as redundant. The tourism debate then transferred to the United Nations Commission on Sustainable Development (CSD) in 1999, where it was decided that the CBD Secretariat should undertake a process to develop guidelines. Who was involved in the drafting, as advisers, always remained very shadowy. Midway, many observer NGOs felt that the Secretariat had more invested in acceptance and adoption of the guidelines than their effective ground implementation. However, the guidelines may become a basis nationally for legislation (de Comarmond, 2002). Indigenous Peoples will have to contend with the guidelines for considerable time, unless countervailing measures are taken to protect Indigenous rights (ISCST, Rethinking Tourism Project et al, 2001).

10   During 2000, the German Ministry of Environment assumed responsibility from the development ministry Gesellschaft für Technische Zusammenarbeit (GTZ), for promoting the CBD dialogue on tourism. With this handover, dialogue became much less transparent and cooperative. Suddenly, German bureaucrats were taking positions on tourism within the CBD process that contradicted the German Bundestag's support to Indigenous Peoples concerning ancestral title and rights (German Bundestag, 2001).

11   While tourism was now a formal work programme under the CBD, the guidelines process remained a signature initiative of Germany. This raises the question of how far the German travel industry nudged its government to take a frontline role in advancing new 'sustainable' tourism markets. Touristic Union International (TUI), a prominent German tour wholesaler, was present alongside the German government to launch its global guidelines proposal at COP4 in Bratislava during 1998. Yet, it was not until the Eighth Subsidiary Body on Scientific, Technical and Technological Advice (SBSTTA) in 2003, when debate on the guidelines was closing, that Germany tried to create the impression of a common front with Indigenous Peoples. So, whose interests is Germany serving with respect to Indigenous territories? Behind its appearance of supporting Indigenous Peoples within the CBD, there has been a flagrant lack of courtesy and due diligence with respect to Indigenous rights.

12   During the Ministerial Roundtable on Tourism at COP4 in Bratislava during 1998, the Austrian minister said with refreshing frankness that 'sustainable tourism offers new market opportunities'. This reality has been hushed ever since in all CBD proceedings on tourism. As stated in Bratislava (Johnston, 1998a): 'The temptation exists for these opportunities to be further capitalized upon to the detriment of biodiversity and local land and resource rights. The tourism industry's propensity toward unrestricted growth and its commoditization of Indigenous cultures must be recognized as clearly unsustainable.'

13   This NGO contingent consisted of Alison Johnston from Canada for the International Support Centre for Sustainable Tourism (ISCST), Deborah McLaren from the USA for the Rethinking Tourism Project (now Indigenous Tourism Rights International, ITRA) and Nina Rao from India for Equations, who is Southern Co-chair of the Caucus of NGOs at the United Nations Commission on Sustainable Development (CSD). After discussions among international tourism NGOs in Berlin during 2000, their respective offices had attempted to share the early workload of supporting the self-determination of Indigenous Peoples. Tan Chi Kiong from Hong Kong of the Ecumenical Coalition on Tourism (ECOT) and his colleagues, unable to attend the UN

workshop in Santo Domingo, also worked tirelessly to raise awareness and capacity with respect to Indigenous rights. These groups would all take their message concerning rights-related issues to the World Ecotourism Summit (WES) during 2002 in Quebec City.

14   Many delegates in Santo Domingo were unfamiliar with the content and course of CBD negotiations on Article 8(j) and related provisions for 'traditional' knowledge. There was an aggressive reaction by some to any mention of cultural sustainability. It was perceived as a pet issue rather than a rights issue or technical question. Those expressing outrage had to be informed that the concept of cultural diversity is central to the CBD.

15   At COP4 in Bratislava, *Eco*, the NGOs' paper distributed to world governments, warned that 'There is a danger that any mechanism designated by the Conference of the Parties (COP) to draft guidelines will flounder in clichés and thereby facilitate continued self-regulation by the industry' (Johnston, 1998a). This message was reiterated at the United Nations Commission on Human Rights (UNCHR):

> It is imperative that Indigenous Peoples monitor tourism discussions within the CBD, as the proposed guidelines initiative has high initial support from the tourism industry. This is a clear indication that any guidelines formulated would not challenge the status quo. Industry certification based on such a diluted outcome could give tourism monopolies a measure of protection against charges of misconduct (Johnston, 1998b).

16   The *Akwe:kon Guidelines* were commissioned by world governments under the CBD in May 2000. They were elaborated over the next four years in conjunction with the Working Group on Article 8(j), which addresses 'traditional' knowledge. The completed guidelines were issued by the CBD Secretariat in February 2004. Download the guidelines at www.biodiv.org.

17   The CBD process on tourism was weakened by minimal Indigenous Peoples' involvement. The United Nations Environment Programme (UNEP) (Higuero, 1999) had stipulated guiding principles, namely that the guidelines should be based on case studies; be user-friendly; undergo peer review at a global expert workshop; and undergo stakeholder review at a national level. However, the process did not pass this 'principles' test with respect to Indigenous Peoples. Even if Indigenous leadership worldwide had been alerted to the process, which they were not, the process itself was inaccessible. Drafts of the guidelines were funnelled through the Subsidiary Body on Scientific, Technical and Technological Advice (SBSTTA), which few Indigenous Peoples' representatives could afford to attend. Meanwhile, no funding was provided for Indigenous Peoples' case studies on tourism until 2003. Their delegated role is Article 8(j), which operates on a very constricted and colonial interpretation of 'traditional knowledge'. This combination of factors meant that the CBD process on tourism proceeded without representative commentary from Indigenous Peoples. The guidelines reflect government, 'expert' and consultant reports on sustainable use and are not at all 'user friendly' to communities. This process differed markedly from the World Parks Congress in 2003, where explicit provision and funding was made available for 'counterpoint' arguments from Indigenous leadership.

18   The three NGO representatives demanding information on the guidelines were the International Support Centre for Sustainable Tourism (ISCST), the Rethinking Tourism Project (now ITRI) and Nina Rao, Southern Co-chair of

the United Nations Commission on Sustainable Development (CSD) NGOs Caucus on Tourism. All three signed a statement to the seventh Subsidiary Body on Scientific, Technical and Technological Advice (SBSTTA) in November 2001, detailing the fiasco of the *UN Draft Guidelines for the Conduct of Tourism in Territories Traditionally Occupied or Used by Indigenous and Local Communities* and requesting due process (ISCST, Rethinking Tourism Project et al, 2001). ISCST presented a follow-up statement at the Working Group on Article 8(j) in February 2002, in relation to CBD participatory mechanisms. This statement reported as follows:

> In Santo Domingo, a second set of guidelines was briefly circulated... The [CBD] Secretariat said that the Working Group on Article 8(j) produced these guidelines, which are specific to Indigenous Peoples. Yet *no* Indigenous Peoples' leadership globally, let alone Indigenous Peoples' organizations working on tourism, knew of their development, or participated in their development. The Secretariat released it briefly, then backtracked upon being advised in Santo Domingo that it would hold no legitimacy for Indigenous Peoples (ISCST, 2002).

19   The CBD Secretariat responded to criticism of its process on biodiversity and tourism by issuing a promotional booklet called *Biological Diversity and Tourism: Development of Guidelines for Sustainable Tourism in Vulnerable Ecosystems* (CBD Secretariat and UNEP, 2002). This publication was released at COP6 in The Hague during 2002. While it stipulates Indigenous prior informed consent (PIC), this is inadequate to make up lost ground vis-à-vis Indigenous Peoples. Indeed, the booklet may prove highly counter-productive for the Secretariat. Its introduction makes inappropriate reference to Indigenous Peoples and the coveted commercial value of their ancestral lands as 'destinations':

> ... in order to reflect the true richness of local biological and natural resources, as perceived, described and interpreted by indigenous and local communities, the brochure is illustrated with images of biological diversity as portrayed in native art. We hope that, in this way, the reader will gain an image of tourist destinations and the value and beauty of their biological diversity that is different from that conventionally conveyed in tourism-related materials (Zedan, 2002).

20   Allegations have been made that the Canadian Justice Department was consulted in the preparation of the hotly disputed UN *Draft Guidelines for the Conduct of Tourism in Territories Traditionally Occupied or Used by Indigenous and Local Communities*. This has not been verified; but the guidelines text does reflect a fully domesticated (that is, colonial) approach and body of law on rights – consistent with Canada's policy of extinguishment.

21   The International Support Centre for Sustainable Tourism (ISCST) is located on reserve in the territory of the St'at'imc People in Canada. The day that the United Nations Environment Programme (UNEP) called ISCST to communicate its dilemma, there was a meeting of the Lillooet Tribal Council, enabling discussion by the Chiefs of the issues. The St'at'imc leadership was not surprised that ISCST had been uninvited from the UNEP workshop due to peer pressure, nor that an obscure Indigenous organization had seemingly been recruited to make the final sales pitch on the guidelines. These were all foibles that the leaders had seen before and fully expected to see again.

22   UNEP was informed of this meeting in October 2001 and confirmed support in
      May 2003.
          UNEP contributed 4 per cent of the overall budget in order to leverage
      funding from other sources.
23   The presentation had its desired effect. It was following this presentation on the
      draft CBD tourism guidelines that the Subsidiary Body on Scientific, Technical
      and Technological Advice (SBSTTA) recommended their adoption by world
      governments at COP7 in 2004.
24   In 1999, Canada wrote the initial dialogue paper on tourism for SBSTTA. One
      Indigenous delegate at the 2002 World Ecotourism Summit, who has worked
      with the Assembly of First Nations in Canada, stated that Canada was also
      central to writing the original draft of the CBD tourism guidelines. Canada
      then maintained a background role on tourism issues, surfacing at the crucial
      moment in 2004 to ensure that the principle of PIC was removed prior to UN
      adoption of the guidelines. This is the consistent policy of Canada. At the
      Fifth Conference of the Parties (COP5) during 2000 in Nairobi, Canada struck
      PIC from the deliberations on Article 8(j). Canada, despite its fiduciary duty
      to Indigenous Peoples, has effectively utilized the international arena to water
      down PIC to consultation in order to contain Indigenous Peoples' rights.
25   Previously, NGOs acting as a support to Indigenous Peoples had held workshops
      during CBD sessions in an attempt to raise awareness on tourism issues within
      the IIFB. This includes workshops convened by Cultural Survival Canada
      in 1997, by ITRI in 2000 and by ISCST in 2002 and 2003. However, these
      workshops were all 'external' events made possible by NGO capacity. None of
      them arose from the IIFB as a group, nor (more importantly) from proper, direct
      representation by affected Indigenous Peoples.
26   This comment was made by the WTO-OMT representative during the
      UNEP/WTO-OMT official meeting with NGOs. It was made in response to
      the NGOs' statement, which emphasized a precautionary approach on tourism,
      particularly proper protocol with Indigenous Peoples.
27   When the WTO-OMT became a UN agency in 2003, it was easy to see that
      government talks on 'sustainable' tourism would nosedive further. Multinational
      corporations rule the WTO-OMT Business Council. They also run the
      Environment Task Force of the International Air Transport Association
      (or IATA) and are heavyweight observers to the Committee on Aviation
      Environmental Protection of the International Civil Aviation Organization
      (ICAO). Global corporations have been allowed to clench the reins of policy
      development, putting us all at risk.
28   Ecological Tourism in Europe (ETE) referenced nine different documents
      arising from NGO initiatives on sustainable tourism. While the mentioned
      documents are all valuable, none would apply in Indigenous territories except,
      perhaps, as a formally invited annexe to customary law. Indigenous Peoples
      worldwide have encountered difficulties with NGOs taking charge on issues
      which, by protocol, should be addressed through appropriate channels by, or at
      least together with, mandated Indigenous leadership.
29   The World Heritage Centre (WHC) outright rejected the principle of
      establishing a World Heritage Indigenous Peoples Council of Experts
      (WHIPCOE) as a consultative body or reporting mechanism. Instead, it
      'encouraged professional research and exchange of views on the subject' (WHC,
      2001, p57). This decision, aside from being paternalistic, assumes that we have

References

Prologue

Miller, A. (2002) Quoted in Oprah Editorial, April, p42

Chapter 1

ABC Network (2002) 'Indigenous culture is Australia's greatest treasure: Ruddock', 7 April, www.abc.net.au

Aloisi de Larderel, J. (1999) Presentation on behalf of United Nations Environment Programme, Division of Technology, Industry & Economics. International Institute of Peace Through Tourism Conference. Glasgow, UK, October 1999

Ananthaswamy, A. (2004) 'Massive growth of ecotourism worries biologists', *New Scientist*, 4 March, www.newscientist.com

Andreef, M. (2002) 'Where to go for thrills – If money is no object', *The Vancouver Sun*, November 30, pE13

Ashley, C., Godwin, H. and Roe, D. (2001) *Pro-Poor Tourism Strategies: Expanding Opportunities for the Poor*, Pro-Poor Tourism Briefing No 1, Overseas Development Institute, Institute for Environment and Development and the Centre for Responsible Tourism, London, UK

Ashton, R. (1992) 'World trends in tourism and conservation (ecotourism)', *Proceedings of the 1992 World Congress on Adventure Travel and Ecotourism*, Adventure Travel Society, Englewood, London, UK

Ashton, R. (1999) 'Working for a Successful Ecotourism Story: The Case of Punta Sal National Park'. In Singh, T. V. & Singh, S. (eds) Tourism Development in Critical Environments, Cognizant Communications Corp., New York, pp89–101

ATTC (Aboriginal Tourism Team Canada) (2003) '$2.9 billion of economic activity for aboriginal tourism', Turtle Island Native Network, 25 April, www.turtleisland.org

References

Baker, M. (2004) 'Child-sex stalkers find an indulgent new frontier', *Sydney Morning Herald*, 12 June, www.smh.com.au/articles/2004/

Bellett, G. (2003) 'Airlines fight back to reclaim losses', *The Vancouver Sun*, Business Section, 6 May, pD5

Benning, J. (2003) 'Wild horizons', *Adventure*, February, pp49–63

Blakesley, M., Marr, A., McDowell, D. et al (2003) '*Outside* destinations special', *Outside*, March 2003, pp44–60

Bridgewater, P. (2003) Presentation on behalf of Man and Biosphere Programme of United Nations Educational, Scientific and Cultural Organization (UNESCO) at side event of government of Germany, Subsidiary Body on Scientific, Technical and Technological Advice (SBSTTA) to the Convention on Biological Diversity (CBD), 12 March

Canadian Press (2003) 'UN talks on Indigenous rights declaration deadlocked', *The Globe and Mail*, September, www.globeandmail.com

Canadian Press (2004) 'Eco-tourism harmful: Prof.', *The Province*, Travel Section, 30 March, pA32

Christ, C., Hillel, O., Matus, S. and Sweeting, J. (2003) *Tourism and Biodiversity: Mapping Tourism's Global Footprint*, UNEP and Conservation International

CI (Conservation International) (2002) *Ecotourism*, Brochure prepared for the World Parks Congress in Durban, South Africa, Washington, DC

Clover, C. (2002) 'British experts call for end to cheap flights', *The Vancouver Sun*, Travel Section, 30 November 30, pE3

Condé Nast Traveler (1999) 'Trips of a lifetime', *Condé Nast Traveler*, August, pp105–113

Davies, S. W. (2002) 'Ecotourism', *Holland Herald*, In-flight magazine of KLM Airlines, April, pp14–26

Davis, W. (1999) 'A tribute to those who conserve: Safaris are not only magical, they are useful', *High Life*, In-flight magazine of British Airways, October, p18

ETE (Ecological Tourism in Europe) *Compilation and Analysis of Existing International Documents Relating to Sustainable Tourism*, UNEP/CBD/WS-Tourism/INF/1, Prepared for the United Nations Workshop on Biological Diversity and Tourism, Santo Domingo, Bonn, April 2001

Equations (India), Ecumenical Coalition on Tourism (Hong Kong), Tourism Watch (Germany) and AKTE (Arbeitskreis Tourismus und Entwicklung, Switzerland) (2004) *Who Really Benefits from Tourism?* Statement of Concern of the Tourism Interventions Group at the Fourth World Social Forum in Mumbai, India

Foroohar, R. (2002) 'Getting off the beaten track', *Newsweek*, spring, 22 July

Gee, D. (2002) 'Final night in Africa', *The Province*, 10 January, pB4

George, J. (2004) 'Must tourists destroy the things they love?, *Nunatsiaq News*, 24 September, www.nunatsiaq.com/news/nunavut

Griffin, K. (2003) '"World's greatest traveller" keeps special spots secret', *The Vancouver Sun*, 29 November, ppI1, I4

Hillel, O. (2002) 'Ecotourism: A possible tool for sustainable development', *CBD News*, vol 2, no 1, January/July, p7

Hinch, T. (1999) Panelist Presentation. Conference of International Institute of Peace Through Tourism, Glasgow, UK, October

Hochman, D. (2001) 'Outback stabbing', *Entertainment Weekly: Forecast Double*, pp24–31

Honey, M. (2004) 'Letter from TIES executive director', *Eco Currents*, Newsletter of The International Ecotourism Society (TIES), first quarter, p2

ISCST (International Support Centre for Sustainable Tourism), Cultural Survival Canada, Environment Liaison Centre International, Forest Peoples' Programme et al (1998) *NGO Joint Statement On the Ministerial Proposal for Global Guidelines on Sustainable Tourism*, Fourth Conference of the Parties (COP4) to the Convention on Biological Diversity (CBD), Bratislava, Slovakia, 7 May

Jones, L. (2003) 'Air France – KLM deal seen as spur for more', Bloomberg News, reprinted in *The Vancouver Sun*, Business Section, 1 October, pD13

Kutay, K. (1989) 'The new ethic in adventure travel', *Buzzworm*, summer, pp31–36

Kutay, K. (1991) 'Ecotourism revisited', *Buzzworm*, March/April, p91

Lillywhite, M. and Lillywhite, L. (1992) *Low Impact Tourism: A Natural Resource Management and Economic Development Strategy for Indigenous Communities*, Report completed for the US Agency for International Development (USAID) by Domestic Technologies, Evergreen, Colorado

Lisagor, K. (2003) 'On the beaten track', *Outside*, March, pp92–93

Mader, R. (2002) *Sustainable Development of Ecotourism Conference: Final Report*, April, www.planeta.com/ecotravel/tour/2002ecotourismreport.html

Mejia, Y. (2002) Presentation from floor. World Ecotourism, May, Quebec City, Canada

Meyer, M. and Garbe, C. (2001) 'Compilation and analysis of existing international documents relating to sustainable tourism', prepared by Ecological Tourism for Europe for the Workshop on Biological Diversity and Tourism, Santo Domingo, 4–7 June (UNEP/CBD/WS-Tourism/INF/1)

Miersch, M. (1998) 'Brave the elements to produce breathtaking documentaries', *Lufthansa Magazine*, May, pp13–18

The Nation (2003) 'Kayan girls want to be more than just tourist attractions', 24 December, reprinted in *New Frontiers*, newsletter of Tourism Investigation and Monitoring Team (TIM Team) (Thailand), November/December, pp6–7

Netherlands Committee for the IUCN (World Conservation Union) (2003) *The Dutch, Nature and Tourism*, Interpretive Map, Amsterdam

Nierenberg, D. (2003) 'Populations of large ocean fish decimated', *World Watch*, vol 16, no 5, September/October, p9

O'Brien, T. (1994) 'Redefining ecotourism: A concept comes of age', *The Special Expeditions Traveler*, summer, p1

Ogilvie, C. (2003) 'Chiefs seek to "control" Canada's use of Natives in tourism', *The Province*, 3 December, pA12

Palomo, M. (1999) Presentation on behalf of the Philippine Rural Recontruction Movement 'Going Native' debate on Indigenous Peoples and Tourism, Hosted by the Netherlands Centre for Indigenous Peoples, Amsterdam, 9 December

Phillippines representative. (1999) Evening side event organized by The International Ecotourism Society, UN Commission on Sustainable Development, April, New York, US

Potts, R. (2003) 'The hidden valley', *Condé Nast Traveler*, January, pp115–125, 219–223

The Province (2001) 'Africa: A hot spot', 4 November, pC14

Prugh, T. and Assadourian, E. (2003) 'What is sustainability, anyway?' *World Watch*, vol 16, no 5, September/October, pp10–21

Rao, N. (2002) UNEP Side Meeting with Indigenous Peoples & Non-government Organizations. World Ecotourism Summit, May, Quebec City, Canada

Reguly, E. (2001) 'Airline chaos may devolve flying back to an elite activity', *The Globe and Mail*, Business Section, 13 November, pB17

Reichel-Dolmatoff, G. (1999) 'A view from the headwaters', *The Ecologist*, July, pp276–280

Séguin, R. (2003) 'Canada criticized for bid to amend rights deal', *The Globe and Mail*, 26 September, www.globeandmail.com

Shaw, J. (2003) 'Bioprospecting: Corporations profit from Indigenous genes', *In These Times*, vol 28, issue 2, 26 November, www.inthesetimes.com

Sides, H. (2003) 'Beast master', *Outside*, November, pp107–113

Singer, N. (2003) 'Resort to virtue: The world's ten best eco-lodges', *Outside*, March, pp83–91

Spears, T. (2002) 'Ruin yourself', *The Vancouver Sun*, 16 February, pG10

Strachan, A. (2001) 'Survival skills', *The Vancouver Sun*, 27 January, ppH6–7

Tan, C. K. (2003) 'Ecumenical Coalition on Tourism (ECOT) Concept Paper' for World Social Forum 2004, Hong Kong, October

Theroux, M. (2001) 'The ecotrip: It's not easy being green', *Travel and Leisure*, September, pp61–68

TNC (The Nature Conservancy) (2003) *Special Report: Ecotourism*, Brochure prepared for World Parks Congress in Durban, South Africa, TNC, Arlington, Virginia, US

Toepfer, K. (2002) UNEP Side Meeting with Indigenous Peoples and Non-Government Organizations, World Ecotourism Summit, May 2002, Quebec City, Canada

Tremblay, T (2001) Cited in 'Prof's university course explains what TV's *Survivor* is really all about', Canadian Press, *The Province*, 8 April, pA32

UN (United Nations) 'Indigenous lands severely damaged by development, mining, tourism, Permanent Forum told as debate begins on environment', Press Release HR/4664, Second Session of United Nations Permanent Forum (UNPF) on Indigenous Issues, New York, US

UNDP (United Nations Development Programme) (2003) 'Biodiversity vital for achieving Millennium Development Goals, London meeting concludes', 5 March, www.undp.org

The Vancouver Sun (2004) 'Natural resources top performers', Business Section, 12 March, pG4

Western Canada Wilderness Committee (1997) 'Ecotourism means more jobs than logging', *EcoForum*, Journal of the Environment Liaison Centre International, Nairobi, Kenya, vol 21, no 3, October, p14

Williams, P. and Dossa, K. B. (1996) *Ethnic Tourism: Native Interest Travel Markets for Canada*, Centre des Hautes Etudes Touristiques, France

WTO-OMT (1997) *Tourism 20/20 Vision: A New Forecast from the World Tourism Organization*, WTO-OMT, Madrid

WTO-OMT and UNEP (World Tourism Organization and United Nations Environment Programme) (2002) *International Year of Ecotourism: 2002*, Promotional brochure, WTO and UNEP, Madrid and Paris

WWB (Webber Wentzel Bowens) *WWB Brief*, Corporate newsletter published for clients and distributed at the 2003 World Parks Congress, no 14, September, pp1–6

Chapter 2

Agence France Press (2004) 'Tourism in PNG: Expect the unexpected', 15 August, www.channelnewsasia.com

AI (Amnesty International) (2003) 'Americas: Human rights defenders – persecution reaching emergency proportions', Press release, 10 November

American Indian Institute (ed) (1992) 'Discovery, heathens, slavery, religious freedoms', Communique no 15, formulated by the Traditional Circle of Indian Elders and Youth, Sapa Dawn Center, Welm, Washington, DC

Auran-Clapot, J. and Gygax, J. (2003) *The Grievances of Indigenous Peoples in South Africa and Namibia against Globalisation*, Report from the 2003 United Nations Working Group on Indigenous Populations, 21–25 July, www.ngocongo.org

Ayres, E. (2004) 'The hidden shame of the global industrial economy', *Worldwatch*, vol 17, no 1, pp20–29

BBC (British Broadcasting Corporation) (2004) 'Herbal remedies "threatens plants"', BBC News, London, UK, 8 January

Braddock, J. (2004) *New Zealand Labour Government Cuts Off Maori Claims to the Foreshore*, Distributed via the Protecting Knowledge List Server of the Union of British Columbia Indian Chiefs, British Columbia, Canada, 10 June

CBD (Convention on Biological Diversity) (1992) *Convention on Biological Diversity: Text and Annexes*, Secretariat of the CBD, Montreal, Canada

Christ, C., Hillel, O., Matus, S. and Sweeting, J. (2003) *Tourism and Biodiversity: Mapping Tourism's Global Footprint*, Conservation International, Washington, DC, US

Christian World Service (2004) 'Press Release: Christian World Service says listen to Maori on the foreshore and seabed', 10 May 10, www.scoop.co.nz

CI (Conservation International) (2003) *Ecotourism*, Brochure prepared for the World Parks Congress in Durban, South Africa, CI, Washington, DC, US

Cultural Survival (2002) 'Indigenous organizations request halt on highland development in Thailand', *Cultural Survival Weekly Indigenous News*, 25 October

Cultural Survival (2004a) 'Native Hawaiians to protest illegal occupation of Hawai'i', *Cultural Survival Weekly Indigenous News*, 14 January, www.cs.org

Cultural Survival (2004b) 'South Africa: Human Rights Commission to investigate alleged abuse of Khomani San', *Cultural Survival Weekly Indigenous News*, 1 September, www.cs.org

Daes, E.-I. (1997) *Indigenous Peoples and Their Relationship to Land*, UN Economic and Social Council, Commission on Human Rights, 20 June

Daily Express (2004) 'MP urges survey on idle Native land', Circulated by Canadian Indigenous Biodiversity Network, 17 August

Darai, S. (2004) 'Reclassification of Indigenous people in Nepal', *Cultural Survival Weekly Indigenous News*, 25 June, www.cs.org

Davies, S. W. (2002) 'Ecotourism', *Holland Herald*, In-flight magazine of KLM Airlines, April, pp14–26

DFID (UK Department for International Development) (1999) *Tourism and Poverty Elimination: Untapped Potential*, Brochure prepared for United Nations Commission on Sustainable Development (CSD), New York, US, April

Forest Trends (2003) *A New Agenda for Forest Conservation and Poverty Reduction: Making Markets Work for Low-Income Producers*, Forest Trends, Washington, DC, US, www.forest-trends.org

Gonzalez, G. (2005) '"War on terror" zeroes in on Indigenous Peoples', www.ipsnews.net, 6 June

Hamilton, G. (2003) 'First Nations call for boycott of lumber: Tribal council wants Home Depot not to buy from Canfor and others', *The Vancouver Sun*, 21 April

Heiltsuk Tribal Council (2001) 'Press release: Heiltsuk Win Koeye', 30 March, www.heiltsuk.com

Hoekstra, G. (2003) 'Carrier Sekani target Home Depot in forest policy fight', *Prince George Citizen*, 8 April

HRW (Human Rights Watch) (2004) 'Discrimination against Dalits in Nepal', press release on website www.hrw.org

Indigenous Peoples' Biodiversity Network (1996) Proceedings From the Indigenous Peoples' Workshop on Developing a Framework for the Protection of Knowledge & Practices of Indigenous Communities, 2–3 May, Ottawa, Canada

Iwand, W. M. (2003) 'Tourism: unfair practices – equitable options', Presentation on tourism industry and poverty alleviation, International preparatory seminar for 2004 World Social Forum, organized by DANTE tourism network, Hanover, Germany, 8 December

IWGIA (International Work Group for Indigenous Affairs) (2004) *The Indigenous World 2004*, Copenhagen, Denmark

Johnston, A. (2000) 'Indigenous peoples and ecotourism: Bringing Indigenous knowledge and rights into the sustainability equation', *Tourism Recreation Research*, vol 25, no 2, pp89–96

Kutay, K. (2003) 'Maasailand cultural Safari: Beyond the looking glass', *Wildland Adventures Wild News*, August

Lisagor, K. (2003) 'On the beaten track', *Outside*, March, pp92–93

McNeely, J. (1999) Presentation from floor on behalf of IUCN. Sectoral Discussion on Tourism. 14th Global Biodiversity Forum, Montreal, Canada, 18 June, 1999

Martinez, M. A. (1999) *Study on Treaties, Agreements and Other Constructive Arrangements between States and Indigenous Populations*, United Nations Economic and Social Council, Commission on Human Rights, 22 June

Mbaria, J. (2003) '"Respectful" tourists among the Maasai', *The East African*, 6 October, pA2

MERC (Maasai Environmental Resource Coalition) (2004) *The Killing Fields of Loliondo*, www.maasaierc.org 2004

Mumba, Justice Florence of Zambia (2004) International Judicial Colloquium, Suva, Fiji, 9 August

Mutu, M. (2003) 'Battle brews in New Zealand over Maori Rights', Interview by Gillian Bradford, 21 September, www.abc.net.au

NEFIN (Nepal Federation of Indigenous Nationalities) (2003) Resolution from Fifth National Congress of NEFIN, 23–25 August

New Zealand Herald (2004) 'Australia, Canada likely to lead way, not Fiji', 3 January, www.nzherald.co.nz

Norris, J. (2005) 'UN criticizes foreshore law', www.stuff.co.nz, 14 March

Ole Ndasko, N. (2003) Letter from Indigenous Rights for Survival International (Tanzania) to International Institute for Peace Through Tourism (Vermont), 30 November

References

Ole Tiampiati, M. (2004) 'Loita and Purko Maasai resist IUCN Plans for the Naimina Enkiyio', *Cultural Survival Weekly Indigenous News*, 25 June

Olol-Dapash, M. (1999) 'In the hands of government: The last Maasai journey', *Cultural Survival Quarterly*, vol 23, no 4, 31 December, www.culturalsurvival.org

Olol-Dapash, M. (2001) 'Maasai autonomy and sovereignty in Kenya and Tanzania', *Cultural Survival Quarterly*, vol 25, no 1, 30 April, www.culturalsurvival.org

Olol-Dapash, M. (2004) Personal communication, 22 June

Olol-Dapash, M. (2005) Quoted on website of the Ogiek People of East Africa, www.ogiek.org

Olol-Dapash, M. and Kutay, K. (2005) 'The Maasai People: Indigenous stewards living among parks, ranches and tourism', *Eco Currents*, pp3–6, www.ecotourism.org

Oman, K. (2004) 'Debate continues over articles in draft declaration', *Cultural Survival Weekly Indigenous News*, 24 September, www.cs.org

Rao, N. (2002) UNEP Side Meeting with Indigenous Peoples & Non-government Organizations. World Ecotourism Summit, May, Quebec City, Canada

Schulte-Tenckhoff, I. (1999) 'Lecture on the rights of Indigenous peoples: An International Perspective', Indigenous Governance Programme, University of Victoria, British Columbia, Canada, 18 March

Schwartz, P. and Randall, D. (2003) *An Abrupt Climate Change Scenario and Its Implications for United States National Security*, US Department of Defense, Washington, DC, US

Seattle Times (2003) 'Fiji tribes may regain beach control', Distributed via the Protecting Knowledge List Server of the Union of British Columbia Indian Chiefs, British Columbia, Canada, 21 November

Séguin, R. (2003) 'Canada criticized for bid to amend rights deal', *The Globe and Mail*, 26 September, www.globeandmail.com

Shaw, J. (2003) 'Bioprospecting: Corporations profit from Indigenous genes', *In These Times*, vol 28, issue 2, 26 November, www.inthesetimes.com

Simon, D. (2004) 'Australian human rights chair "a shame", says Aborigine', www.eniar.org, 7 January

Singer, N. (2003) 'Resort to virtue: The world's ten best eco-lodges', *Outside*, March, pp83–91

Smoke, M. (1999) Roundtable Discussion on Indigenous Peoples and Tourism, Conference of the International Institute for Peace through Tourism, Glasgow, UK, October

Stuff (2004) 'Government says Fiji foreshore law not a precedent for New Zealand', 3 January, www.stuff.co.nz

Survival International (2004) *Collective Rights: UK Government Rejects Collective Rights for Tribal Peoples*, Brochure, March, www.survival-international.org

Suzuki, D. (1997) *The Sacred Balance: Rediscovering Our Place in Nature*. Greystone Books, Vancouver, Canada

Tan, C. K. (2004) *Ecumenical Coalition on Tourism (ECOT) Concept Paper for World Social Forum 2004*, Issued at Activists Strategy Meeting on Tourism organized by ECOT, 22–23 January, Mumbai

TINN (Turtle Island Native Network) (2003) 'Support for sun peaks protests deals political blow', *TINN Discussion*, 31 January, www.turtleisland.org

TNC (The Nature Conservancy) (2003) *Special Report: Ecotourism*, Brochure prepared for World Parks Congress in Durban, South Africa, TNC, Arlington, Virginia, US

Tourism Concern (2005) 'Trekking wrongs: Porter's rights', press release, www.tourismconcern.org.uk

Valencia, F. (2005) Statement by the coordinator of human rights, Association of Indigenous Councils of Northern Cauca

The Vancouver Sun (2004) 'Natural resources top performers', Business Section, pG4, 12 March

UNDP (2003) 'Biodiversity vital for achieving Millennium Development Goals, London meeting concludes', 5 March, www.undp.org

Vellas, F. (2002) Report on Costs & Benefits of Ecotourism, World Ecotourism Summit, May, Quebec City, Canada

Willcocks, P. (2004) 'First Nations learn from enviro campaigns, target Olympics', various community papers, The Dogwood Initiative, Canada, 26 May

WRM (World Rainforest Movement) (2004) 'Kenya: The Maasai stand up to IUCN displacement attempts from their forest', *World Rainforest Movement Bulletin*, no 84, July

WWB (Webber Wentzel Bowens) *WWB Brief*, Corporate newsletter published for clients and distributed at the 2003 World Parks Congress, no 14, September, pp1–6

Zápara (Asociación de la Nacionalidad Zápara) (2000) 'Declaration of the Ancestral Territory of the Zápara', Puyo, Ecuador, December

Chapter 3

Abia Yala (1999) 'The virus of tourism', Special Issue on Tourism among Indigenous Peoples in the Americas, August, p1

Acosta, T. E. (2003) 'Mandate of the Indigenous peoples', Statement on behalf of TONATIERRA (www.tonatierra.org) and CONIC (Council of Indigenous Organizations and Nations of the Continent), Circulated by the Union of British Columbia Indian Chiefs, British Columbia, Canada, March

Associated Press (2002) 'Africa reclaims lost daughter', *The Vancouver Sun*, Travel Section, 4 May, pG2

References

The Bangkok Post (2003) 'Tourism "vulnerable"', Reprinted in *New Frontiers*, Newsletter of the Tourism Investigation and Monitoring Team, September–October

Barlett, D. L. and Steele, J. B. (2002) 'Dirty dealing: Indian casinos are making millions for their investors and providing little to the poor', *Time*, 8 December, www.time.com

Barton, A. J. (2003) 'Service travel: A Blackfeet experience', *Native Peoples*, vol 16, no 3, March/ April, p24

Benning, J. (2003) 'Wild horizons', *Adventure*, February, pp49–63

Berman, M. (1988) *The Reenchantment of the World*, Bantam Books, New York

Blakesley, M., Marr, A. et al (2003) '*Outside* destinations special', *Outside*, March, pp44–60

Blangy, S. (2005/2006) *Indigenous Destination Guidebook*, Indigène Editions, France, www.indigene-editions.fr

Canadian Press (2004) 'Eco-tourism harmful: Prof.', Travel Section, *The Province*, 30 March, pA32

Capra, F. (1988) *The Turning Point: Science, Society and the Rising Culture*, Bantam Books, New York, US

Centre for Tourism Research and Development and the Institute of Tourism and Hotel Management (2002) *The International Conference on Tourism Development, Community and Conservation: Shaping Eco-tourism for the Third Millennium*, Invitation package, 28 February–2 March, Bundelkhand University, Jhansi, India

Cernea, M. M. (1991) 'Knowledge from social science for development policies and projects,' in Cernea, M. M. (ed) *Putting People First: Sociological Variables in Rural Development*, Oxford University Press, Oxford, UK, pp1–41

Christ, C., Hillel, O., Matus, S. and Sweeting, J. (2003) *Tourism and Biodiversity: Mapping Tourism's Global Footprint*, Conservation International, Washington, DC, US

CI (Conservation International) *Ecotourism*, Brochure prepared for the World Parks Congress in Durban, South Africa, CI, Washington, DC, US

Daes, E. I. (1996) *Supplementary Report of the Special Rapporteur on the Protection of the Heritage of Indigenous Peoples*, United Nations Sub-commission on the Prevention of Discrimination and the Protection of Minorities, 48th session, Geneva, Switzerland

Daes, E. I. (1997) *Indigenous Peoples and Their Relationship to Land*, United Nations Economic and Social Council, Commission on Human Rights, Geneva, Switzerland, 20 June

Daley, J. (2003) 'On a mission from God', *Outside*, November, p36

Daly, H. E. and Cobb, J. B. (1989) *For the Common Good: Redirecting the Economy Towards Community, the Environment and a Sustainable Future*, Beacon Press, Boston, Mass, US

Davis, W. (2004) 'Keepers of the world', *The National Geographic*, October, pp50–69 de Kadt, E. (1979) 'Social planning for tourism in the developing countries', *Annals of Tourism Research*, January/March, pp36–48

Equations (2004) *Who Really Benefits from Tourism?* Ecumenical Coalition on Tourism and Tourism Watch, World Social Forum, Mumbai, India

Ereira, A. (2001) 'Back to the heart of lightness', *The Ecologist*, vol 31, no 6, July/August, pp34–38

Fitzhenry, E. (2002) 'The embodiment of Enkai: The Mau Forest and Maasai spirituality', *Cultural Survival Voices*, vol 1.3, 1 June

Flores, G. (2005) 'Honduras: Repression against Garífuna people', statement issued by OFRANEH (the Honduran Black Peoples' Fraternal Organization), La Ceiba, Honduras, 23 March

Gardner, A. (1997) 'Cultural tourism: A love–hate relationship', *Tok Blong Pasifik*, September/December, vol 51, no 3/4, pp14–15

George, J. (2004) 'Must tourists destroy the things they love?' *Nunatsiaq News*, 24 September, www.nunatsiaq.com/news/nunavut

Heaton, H. (2004) 'An ecotourism challenge: The South–North tourism route', *Cultural Survival Quarterly*, vol 28, no 2, 15 June, pp54–56

Honey, M. (2004) 'Letter from TIES executive director', *Eco Currents*, Newsletter of The International Ecotourism Society (TIES), first quarter, p2

IPSM (Indigenous Peoples Solidarity Movement) (2004) 'Solidarity picket for Secwepemc Aboriginal title and rights', Press release, March, www.skwelkwekelt.org

Isaacson, R. (2002) 'Dravidian dream: Travel Tamil Nadu', *Geographical*, November, pp101–104

IWGIA (International Work Group for Indigenous Affairs) (2004) *The Indigenous World 2004*, IWGIA, Copenhagen, Denmark

Johnston, A. (1998) *Report on the International Workshop on Indigenous Peoples and Development*, Ollantaytambo, Peru, 21–26 April 1997, completed in April 1998 on behalf of Cultural Survival Canada for submission to the Danish Ministry of Foreign Affairs, Copenhagen, Denmark

Jones, L. (2003) 'Air France – KLM deal seen as spur for more', Bloomberg News, reprinted in *The Vancouver Sun*, Business Section, 1 October 2003, pD13

Kaufman, S. (2004) 'Dispatches from a Macaw research trip', *Grist Magazine*, 4 March, www.gristmagazine.com

Leach M. (2002) Tribal Chief of T'it'qet, St'at'imc Nation, Canada. Interview. September

Lisagor, K. (2003) 'On the beaten track', *Outside*, March, pp92–93

Loeb, T. L. Jr. and Paredes, A. (1991) 'Modernization, tourism and change in a Mexican marketplace', *Tourism Recreation Research*, vol 16, no 2, pp31–43

Logan, M. (2004) 'Indigenous peoples day: Genocide it is', 9 August, www.ipsnews.net

References

Mackie, J. (2002) 'It began with a man who began backwards', *The Vancouver Sun*, 2 March, pA19

Mader, R. (2002) *Sustainable Development of Ecotourism Conference: Final Report*, April, www.planeta.com/ecotravel/tour/2002ecotourismreport.html

Mails, T. E. (1997) *The Hopi Survival Kit: The Prophecies, Instructions and Warnings Revealed by the Last Elders*, Penguin Books Ltd, London, UK

Malani, M. (2003) Presentation for Panel on Tourism and Communities, Fifth World Parks Congress, Durban, South Africa, September

Munsterhjelm, M. (2002) 'The First Nations of Taiwan', *Cultural Survival Quarterly*, summer, pp53–55

McNeely, J. (1999) Presentation from floor on behalf of IUCN to Opening Session of 14th Global Biodiversity Forum, Montreal, Canada, 18 June, 1999

Olol-Dapash, M. (2003) Presentation for Panel on Tourism and Communities, Fifth World Parks Congress, Durban, South Africa, September

Pambrun, J.-L. R. (1998) 'The Impact of the tourism industry on the Indigenous population of French Polynesia', *Indigenous Affairs*, vol 2, April/June, pp30–34

Pasimio, J. A. (2004) 'Ban Jalae Hilltribe Life and Culture Centre', *Chiang Mai News*, 4 October

Pleumarom, A. Tourism Investigation Monitoring Team presentation at evening side event during the UN Commission on Sustainable Development, April 1999, New York, US

Radhakrishnan, S. A. (2005) 'Eco-tourism centre to be set up in capital', distributed by Equations, 26 September, www.equitabletourism.org

Radhakrishnan, S. A. (2005) 'Eco-tourism centre to be set up in capital; distributed by Equations, 26 September, www.equitabletourism.org

Rana, D. S., Kainthola, S. and Naithani, P. S. (2003) 'The struggle for community-based conservation and equitable tourism in the Nanda Devi Biosphere Reserve in India', Paper presented at the Namche Conference, Nepal, 24–26 May

Rice, S. (2001) 'Best practices: Doing it the pueblo way', *National Geographic Traveler*, December, p30

Sahagun, L. (2003) 'Tribes buying back ancestral lands', *Los Angeles Times*, 20 October, www.latimes.com

Schulte-Tenckhoff, I. (1999) 'Lecture on the rights of Indigenous peoples: An international perspective', Indigenous Governance Programme, University of Victoria, British Columbia, Canada, 18 March

Schumaier, S. (2003) 'Fresh tracks: destinations', *Outside*, October, p42

Schurmann, H. (1981) 'The effect of international tourism on the regional development of third world countries', *Applied Geography and Development*, The Institute for Scientific Cooperation vol 18

Sherman, B. (2002) Presentation on behalf of Indian Country Tourism. World Ecotourism Summit, May, Quebec City, Canada

Sierra (2003) 'For the record', March/April, p13

Singer, N. (2003) 'Resort to virtue: The world's ten best eco-lodges', *Outside*, March, pp83–91

Smoke, M. (1999) Presentation on behalf of Indigenous Tourism International. Indigenous Tourism Workshop. Conference of International Institute of Peace Through Tourism, Glasgow, UK, October

Survival (2001) 'Death in the Lost World', Public service advertisement in *Shaman's Drum*, vol 59, p71

Tan, C. K. (2002) Statement on behalf of the Ecumenical Coalition on Third World Tourism. UNEP/WTO informal evening dialogue with NGOs. World Ecotourism Summit, May, Quebec City, Canada

Tebtebba Foundation (2003) *Indigenous Peoples and The World Summit on Sustainable Development*, The Philippines

Thoma, A. (2000) Presentation on floor. 1st International Meeting of Tourism NGOs on Biodiversity, in preparation for the Fifth Conference of the Parties to the UN Convention on Biological Diversity, Berlin, Germany, March

TNC (The Nature Conservancy) (2003) *Special Report: Ecotourism*, Brochure prepared for World Parks Congress in Durban, South Africa, TNC, Arlington, Virginia, US

Toepfer, K. (2002) UNEP Side Meeting with Indigenous Peoples and Non-Government Organizations, World Ecotourism Summit, May, Quebec City, Canada

Ward, D. (2002) 'Believe it! Pattison's billion-dollar baby', *The Vancouver Sun*, 2 March, pA1

WCED (World Commission on Environment and Development) (1987) *Our Common Future* (Brundtland Report), Oxford University Press, New York, US

WRM (World Rainforest Movement) (2003) 'India: Adivasis shot for claiming their ancestral homeland', *WRM Bulletin*, no 70, 21 May

Chapter 4

Achbar, M., Abbott, J. and Bakan, J. (2005) *The Corporation*, film by Big Picture Media Corporation, www.thecorporation.com

American Indian Movement (1984) 'Resolution made in the territory of the Sovereign Diné Nation, Window Rock, Arizona', 11 May, reprinted in *Cultural Survival Quarterly*, no 27(2), 15 June

Archer, F. (1999) Interview. Conducted during UN Commission on Human Rights, Working Group on Indigenous Populations, 17th Session, July

References

Bakan, J. (2004) *The Corporation: The Pathological Pursuit of Profit and Power*, Constable and Robinson Ltd, London, UK

BBC (British Broadcasting Corporation) (2004) 'Herbal remedies threaten plants', BBC News, www.news.bbc.co.uk, 8 January

Benning, J. (2003) 'Wild horizons', *Adventure*, February, pp49–63

Blakesley, M., Marr, A. et al (2003) '*Outside* destinations special', *Outside*, March, pp44–60

Bradley, D. (2001) 'Baskets past, present', The Press-Enterprise, July 2001. Obtained from Native News Listserver of the Union of BC Indian Chiefs, 15 July

Bruchac, J. (1993) 'Respecting the sacredness of sweatlodges', *Shaman's Drum*, no 32, summer, p2

Can West News Services (2003) 'Adventure spas for New Age travellers', *The Vancouver Sun*, Travel Section, 20 December, p18

CBC (Canadian Broadcasting Corporation) (2005) 'Playing Indian', CBC Radio One Ideas Program, 24 May, www.cbc.ca/ideas

Chlanda, E. (2000) 'Tourism Commission "ignores Aborigines"', *Alice Springs News*, 5 April, www.alicespringsnews.com.au

Christ, C., Hillel, O., Matus, S. and Sweeting, J. (2003) *Tourism and Biodiversity: Mapping Tourism's Global Footprint*, Conservation International, Washington, DC, US

Davies, R. (2003) 'Illegal gatherers threatening South African forests', Originally published on www.iol.co.za, 26 March, Re-circulated by the Indigenous Peoples' Secretariat (Canada) on the Convention on Biological Diversity

The Dominion Post (2003) 'Native species being plundered for medicines, scientist says', 22 February, republished on www.stuff.co.nz

Ebbutt, J. (2002–2003) 'A moment in time', *Four Seasons Spa: What's New and Noteworthy*, Brochure of Four Seasons Hotels and Resorts, Canada, pp8–14

Ellis, S. (2003) 'Editor's message', *Spa Enthusiast*, vol 2, no 1, spring, p2

Etienne, M. and Leacock, E. (1980) *Women and Colonization*, J. F. Bergin Publishers, Inc, New York, US

Fitness (2002) 'Fitness/beauty extra', Editorial on spa-style products, July, p64

Fowler, F. G. and Fowler, H. W. (1977) *The Pocket Oxford Dictionary of Current English*, Clarendon Press, Oxford, UK

Furst, P. T. and Schaefer, S. B. (1996) 'Peyote pilgrims and Don Juan seekers', in Furst, P. T. and Schaefer, S. B. (eds) *People of the Peyote: Huichol Indian History, Religion and Survival*, University of New Mexico Press, Albuquerque, US, pp503–521

Gaia Foundation and GRAIN (Genetic Resources Action International) (1998) 'Global trade and biodiversity in conflict', *Seedling*, no 1, April

Giago, T. (2003) 'Sacred ceremonies must be protected', Notes from Indian Country Weekly Column, *Lakota Journal*, 7 April, www.lakotajournal.com

Gilbert, E. (2003) *Broken Spears: A Maasai Journey*, Atlantic Monthly Press

GRAIN (Genetic Resources Action International) (2003) 'World patents for global domination?', *Seedling*, October, pp11–16

GRAIN (2004a) 'The great protection racket: Imposing IPRs on traditional knowledge', *Seedling*, January, pp13–17

GRAIN (2004b) 'Sharing a few crumbs with the San', *Seedling*, January, p9

Greenwald, J. (1998) 'Herbal healing', *Time*, Canadian edition, vol 152, no 21, 23 November, pp47–57

Hanstein, B. S. (2004) 'Aboriginal art – selling out Aboriginal culture: Yesterday and today?', Website of the European Network for Indigenous Australian Rights, www.eniar.org

Hardison, P. (2003) E-mail exchange on 'Traditional knowledge, science and the commons', Indigenous Knowledge List Server, University of Washington, US

Helliwell, T. (2003) 'Magical mystery tour of Kenya', *Issues Magazine*, August/September, p8

Henninger, M. (2002) 'Native care', *Condé Nast Traveler*, Word of Mouth editorial, October, p38

Janke, T. (2004) *Minding Culture: Case Studies on Intellectual Property and Traditional Knowledge*, World Intellectual Property Organization, Geneva, Switzerland

Linden, E. (2001) 'Can a spa trip change your life?', *Self*, April, p164

Macquarie University (2004) 'Indigenous knowledge and bioprospecting', International Conference, 21–24 April, Sydney, Australia

Malani, M. (2002) Presentation from floor on behalf of Government Fiji. World Ecotourism Summit, May, Quebec City, Canada

Malanowski, J. (2003) 'The future of travel', *Four Seasons, Four Decades*, Four Seasons Hotels and Resorts, Canada

Mead, A. T. P. (1995) 'Biodiversity, community integrity and the second colonialist wave', Abya Yala News, vol, 8, no 4, pp6–8

NTTC (Northern Territory Tourist Commission) (2005) Referenced on the website of Anangu Tours at Uluru, Australia, www.anangutours.com

O'Shane, T. (2003) Quoted in 'Get all bogus boomerangs off the market, says Aboriginal leader', press release by Arts Hubs Australia, 10 April, reprinted at www.eniar.org

Phillips, V. (2000) Presentation from floor on behalf of Washington State University. Protecting Knowledge: Traditional Resource Rights in the New Millennium. Conference hosted by the Union of BC Indian Chiefs, Vancouver, Canada, 23–26

Pleumarom, A. (1999) Tourism Investigation Monitoring Team presentation at evening side event during the UN Commission on Sustainable Development, April, New York, US

References

Plotkin, M. J. (1993) 'Blood of the moon, semen of the sun', *Shaman's Drum*, no 32, summer, pp32–41

Plotkin, M. J. (1994) *Tales of a Shaman Apprentice*, Penguin Books, New York, US

Posey, D. A. and Dutfield G. (1996) *Beyond Intellectual Property: Toward Traditional Resource Rights for Indigenous People & Local Communities*, International Development Research Centre, Canada

Red Cherries, B., Medicine man of the Cheyenne (2002) 'Submission to Cultural Heritage and Sacred Sites: World heritage from an Indigenous perspective', Side panel to the First' Session of the United Nations Permanent Forum (UNPF) on Indigenous Issues, organized by Yachay Wasi, New York, US, 15 May

Russell, A. M. (2004) 'Venture out: Canyon ranch health resort', Feature on No Snow Winter Retreats, *Shape*, January, pp32–34

Salak, K. (2002) 'Lost souls on the peyote trail', *National Geographic Adventure*, August, pp90–96, 106–108, 115

Schultes, B. (1999) Presentation on behalf of Indigenous Peoples Program of The Earth Council, at evening side event organized by The International Support Centre for Sustainable Tourism. UN Commission on Sustainable Development, April, New York, US

Schulz, A. (1999) Presentation on behalf of The Adventure Travel Society. Conference of International Institute of Peace Through Tourism, Glasgow, UK, October

Scripps, H. (2002) 'Shamans heal in the workplace', *The Province*, Business Section, 25 August, pC10

Sinclair, M. (1999) Presentation at workshop organized by The International Support Centre for Sustainable Tourism. UN Commission on Human Rights, Working Group on Indigenous Populations, 16th Session, July

Singer, N. (2003) 'Resort to virtue: The world's ten best eco-lodges', *Outside*, March, pp83–91

Toepfer, K. (2002) UNEP Side Meeting with Indigenous Peoples & Non-government Organizations. World Ecotourism Summit, May, Quebec City, Canada

Trask, H.-K. (1999) *From a Native Daughter: Colonialism and Sovereignty in Hawai'i*, University of Hawai'i Press, Honolulu

Two Bulls, M. (2003) 'Inside the sun dance', *Argus Leader*, 20 July, www.argusleader.com

Urbani, D. (2003) 'Native spirituality: Medicine cards can help to create a link with nature', www.desertnews.com, Reprinted by *Indigenous News* List Server, 6 January 2003

Velasco. J. (2002) Aymara of Peru. Report on UNEP/TIES Conference on Ecotourism in Lima. World Ecotourism Summit, May, Quebec City, Canada

Webb, A. (1997) *Amazon: From the Floodplains to the Clouds*, Monacelli Press, New York

Williams, P. and Dossa, K. B. (1996) *Ethnic Tourism: Native Interest Travel Markets for Canada*, Centre des Hautes Etudes Touristiques, France

Wilson, P. (2004) 'Virtual-tour websites put holidays on a hard drive', *The Vancouver Sun*, Business Section, 7 April, pD3

Wills, R. (2000) Presentation on Biopiracy. Protecting Knowledge Conference: Traditional Resource Rights in the New Millennium. Hosted by the Union of British Columbia Indian Chiefs. 23–26 February, Vancouver, Canada

WIPO (World Intellectual Property Organization) (2003a) 'Protection of traditional knowledge and genetic resources: A bottom up approach to development', *WIPO Magazine*, November/December

WIPO (2003b) 'Next steps for international protection of traditional knowledge in view', WIPO press release, Geneva, 21 July

WIPO (2004a) 'Learning the lessons of traditional knowledge: Broadening the base of intellectual property', *WIPO Magazine*, January/February

WIPO (2004b) 'Traditional knowledge: Policy and legal options', Intergovernmental Committee on Intellectual Property and Genetic Resources, Traditional Knowledge and Folklore, Sixth Session, Geneva, Switzerland, 15–19 March (WIPO/GRTKF/IC/6/4)

WIPO (2004c) 'WIPO director general welcomes growing recognition of Indigenous peoples' rights', Press release PR/2004/388, Geneva, Switzerland, 9 August

Wycoff, A. (2004) 'Venture out: Miraval life in balance resort and spa', Feature on No Snow Winter Retreats, *Shape*, January, p32

Chapter 5

ABC News (2003) 'Aborigines look to discourage Uluṟu climbers', 4 May, reprinted at www.eniar.org

AFP (Worldwide News Agency (2004) 'Dalai Lama helps sell India tourism', *The Province*, Travel Section, 21 March 21, p B8

Anthony, T. (2002) 'Chinese find Shangri-La and make plans to cash in', *The Vancouver Sun*, Front Section, 26 July, pA11

Associated Press (2000) 'Saving the sacred', 15 July, Redistributed via *Native News* internet service

Associated Press (2003) 'Peru wants Yale University to give back Machu Picchu relics', 6 March, Re-circulated via internet by Yachay Wasi

Blakesley, M., Marr, A. et al (2003) '*Outside* destinations special', *Outside*, March, pp44–60

Callan, K. (2002) 'Rock of ages: Aboriginals just want Uluṟu to rest in peace', *Outside Travel Guide*, p24

Cembalest, R. (2004) 'The high road in the Andes', *The New York Times*, 15 August, www.travel2.nytimes.com/2004/08/15

References

CI (Conservation International) (2003) *Ecotourism*, Brochure prepared for the World Parks Congress in Durban, South Africa, CI, Washington, DC, US

Condé Nast Traveler (1999) 'Y2K watch: It's good, it's bad, and it's coming at you', December, p86

DeTerville, A. (2002) Chair of International Alliance against Racism, Racial Discrimination, Xenophobia and Related Intolerance (IARR), 'Message to Indigenous peoples', Indigenous Sacred Sites Mailing List, 8 August

The Economist (2001) 'Tourism in Peru: Road to ruin', 21 July, p30

Edeli, D. and Hurwitz, Z. (2002) 'A tale of spiritual resistance: An anonymous narrative', *Cultural Survival Quarterly*, vol 26, no 4, www.cs.org

Ereira, A. (2001) 'Back to the heart of lightness', *The Ecologist*, vol 31, no 6, July/August, pp34–38

Genzlinger, N. (2001) 'If land is called sacred, bitter disputes can erupt', *The New York Times*, 14 August, Distributed via Union of British Columbia Indian Chiefs List Server, British Columbia, Canada

Gooch, B. (2001) 'Om-ward bound', *Travel and Leisure*, September, pp164–166

Henwood, M. (1999) Comment from floor, Conference on Aboriginal Tourism hosted by the Kwakiutl District Council, Alert Bay, Canada, January

Hinch, T. (1999) Panelist Presentation. Conference of International Institute of Peace Through Tourism, Glasgow, UK, October

Johnson, L. (2004) 'Guerilla gardening: Resistance is fertile', *Canadian Gardening*, April, pp114–118

Kadane, L. (2004) 'Gal-exclusive getaways attract exhausted career women', *The Vancouver Sun*, Travel Section, 3 July, pF7

Kanetsuka, K. (2002) 'Under the bodhi tree: Present-day Bodh Gaya attracts the holy and luxury hotels', *Shared Vision*, December, p38

Kluger, J. (2003) 'Spiritual retreat: Machu Picchu ... may have been nothing more than a royal vacation home', *Time*, 16 February, Re-circulated via internet by Yachay Wasi, www.yachaywasi. org

Koontz, K. (1998) 'Head trips', *Shape*, July, pp96–101, 150

KZN Wildlife (KwaZulu-Natal Wildlife) (2003) *San Rock Art of the Ukhahlamba*, Brochure on the Kamberg Rock Centre, South Africa

Laville, S. (2004) 'UNESCO sounds final warning for Inca city', *The Guardian*, 30 June 2004

Lisagor, K. (2003) 'On the beaten track', *Outside*, March, pp92–93

Los Angeles Times (2001) 'Machu Picchu attracts 2500 a day', Reprinted in *The Vancouver Sun*, Travel Section, 17 March, p15

Luxner, L. (2000) 'Machu Piccu gets a quick lift', *Americas*, vol 52, no 2, April, pp4–5

Mader, R. (2002) *Sustainable Development of Ecotourism Conference: Final Report*, April, www.planeta.com/ecotravel/tour/2002ecotourismreport.html

McCarthy, M. (2001) 'The inner journey spiritual travel', *Shared Vision*, May, pp24–28

McLeod, C. (2003) 'In the light of reverence: When every place is sacred', *The Sacred Land Reader*, www.sacredland.org/reader.html

Muqbil, I. (ed) (2004) 'The shape of brands to come', *Travel Impact Newswire*, vol 42, 29 June, pp1–6, www.travel-impact-newswire.com

Norrell, B. (2004) 'Petroglyphs among the most threatened sacred sites', *Indian Country Today*, 7 June, Recirculated on the *Indigenous News* electronic list server

Paekal, C. (2003) 'The coolest beast on Australia's rivers: Boatel', *The National Post*, 13 September, Travel Section, front page

Pedersen, A. (2002) *Managing Tourism at World Heritage Sites: A Practical Manual for World Heritage Site Managers*, UNESCO World Heritage Centre, Paris, France

The Province (2002) 'Remote kingdom wary of tourists', 8 November, pB10

RAIPON (Russian Association of Indigenous Peoples of the North) (2004) 'The conservation value of sacred sites of Indigenous peoples of the Arctic: A case study of northern Russia', Presentation at the Seventh Conference of the Parties (COP7) of the United Nations Convention on Biological Diversity (CBD), Kuala Lumpur, Malaysia, February

Regalado, A. (2005) 'Ukukus worry about glacier', *The Wall Street Journal*, 17 June, www.post-gazette.com

Salazar, C. (2000) 'Controversy on calamitous beer commercial shoot on Machu Picchu', Associated Press, 12 September, Circulated by the South and Meso American Indian Rights Center, US

Samuel, M.-D. (2002) 'Peru: Inka challenge', *Yachay Wasip 'Simin'*, vol 9, no 2, fall, p3

Scheer, R. (2001) 'Pilgrimage: A journey to self', *Common Ground*, February, p3

Scudder, T. (1998) 'Letter to Abdelfattah Amor, Special Rapporteur of the United Nations Commission on Human Rights', 30 January, Circulated by the Sovereign Dineh Nation

Seventh Generation Fund (2001) Background on Sacred Earth Conference, Disseminated by the Rethinking Tourism Project (US) on 11 March

Shown Harjo, S. (2002) *Report on Gathering to Protect Native Sacred Places: Consensus Position on Essential Elements of Public Policy to Protect Native Sacred Places*, Union of British Columbia Indian Chiefs List Server, British Columbia, Canada, 2 December

Sovereign Dineh Nation (1988) *Sovereign Dineh Nation Alert to Anthropologists*, Circulated by the South and Meso American Indian Rights Center, US, 19 October

Squires, N. (2005) 'Gas sniffing epidemic plagues Aborigines in shadow of Ayres Rock', *The Daily Telegraph*, 13 August

References

Survival (2001) 'Death in the lost world', Public service advertisement, *Shaman's Drum*, vol 59, p71

Taliman, V. (2002) 'Sacred landscapes', *Sierra*, Magazine of the Sierra Club, vol 87, no 6, November/December, pp36–43, 73

Taukane, E., President of the Federation of Indigenous Peoples of Mato Grosso (2002) Cited in 'Waura people fight for cavern in the Upper Xingu region', Reported by Amigos da Terra, 18 August, Circulated by the Amazon Alliance

TNC (The Nature Conservancy) (2003) *Special Report: Ecotourism*, Brochure prepared for World Parks Congress in Durban, South Africa, TNC, Arlington, Virginia, US

UNEP (United Nations Environment Programme) (2003) *Tourism Programme – Activities for 2003*, Division of Technology, Industry and Economics, Paris, France

UNESCO (United Nations Educational, Scientific and Cultural Organization) World Heritage Centre (2001) *Demonstration Project Linking Conservation and Tourism at Six World Heritage Sites*, UNESCO, Paris

UNESCO World Heritage Centre (2003) *The World Heritage Tourism Programme: Biodiversity Partnerships*, UNESCO, Paris

United Confederation of Taíno People and Ihuche Rareito Coalition (2002) Submission to the United Nations Permanent Forum (UNPF) on Indigenous Issues, New York, US, 15 May

United Nations Foundation (2004) 'Peru's Machu Picchu proposed for UNESCO endangered list', *UN Wire*, 30 June

The Vancouver Sun (2001) 'Vandalism: Official indifference destroying paintings', 28 July, pA16

Vargas, M. (2002) 'Peru finds Inca burial site at Machu Picchu', *Reuters*, 12 October

Weintraub, A. (2004) 'Spiritual retreats: Finding sanctuary', *Yoga*, January/February, p40

Wilson, D. (2000) 'Grandfather's story', *The Ecologist*, Issue on the Cosmic Covenant, vol 30, no 1, January/February, pp12–14

World Heritage Committee (2001) *Report on 25th Session*, Document WCH-01/CONF.208/24, Helsinki, Finland, 11–16 December

Yachay Wasi (2001) 'Declaration of Machu Picchu', *Yachay Wasip 'Simin'*, vol 8, no 2, summer/fall, p4

Yachay Wasi (2002) *Cultural Heritage and Sacred Sites: World Heritage from an Indigenous Perspective*, Report from Side Event to First United Nations Permanent Forum (UNPF) on Indigenous Issues, New York, US, 15 May

Chapter 6

Amazon Alliance for Indigenous and Traditional Peoples of the Amazon Basin (1999) Electronic list server communiqué, Washington, DC, US

Associated Press (2002) 'Californians fight over history', 22 July, Circulated by www.jsonline.com.

Bakan, J. (2004) *The Corporation: The Pathological Pursuit of Profit and Power*, Constable and Robinson Ltd, London, UK

Bettrán, J. (ed) *Indigenous and Traditional Peoples and Protected Areas: Principles, Guidelines and Case Studies*, The World Conservation Union, Gland, Switzerland

Berman, M. (1988) *The Reenchantment of the World*, Bantam Books, New York, US

Christ, C., Hillel, O., Matus, S. and Sweeting, J. (2003) *Tourism and Biodiversity: Mapping Tourism's Global Footprint*, Conservation International, Washington, DC, US

Colchester, M. (2003) *Salvaging Nature: Indigenous Peoples, Protected Areas and Biodiversity*, World Rainforest Movement (www.wrm.org.uy) and Forest Peoples Programme (www.forestpeoples. org)

Davies, S. W. (2002) 'Ecotourism', *Holland Herald*, In-flight magazine of KLM Airlines, April, pp14–26

Denbak, S. (2004) 'Presentation on regional tourism on behalf of Cadence Strategies Consulting Firm', Economic Development Conference, Lillooet, Canada, March

Dunstan, R. (2003a) Chief Emeritus and Chair of the Stein Valley Nlaka'pamux Heritage Park, Series of personal interviews, January–March

Dunstan, R. (2003b) 'Stein Valley Nlaka'pamux Heritage Park: A provincial park and living museum of cultural and natural history', Paper presented at 2003 World Parks Congress in Durban, South Africa

The Ecologist (2002) 'Dying for our oil', vol 31, no 10, December 2001/January 2002, p19

Epler Wood, M. (2002) Personal communication

Ereira, A. (2001) 'Back to the heart of lightness', *The Ecologist*, vol 31, no 6, July/August, pp34–38

Ferrari, M. F. and de Vera, D. (2003) *The Philippines: Indigenous Peoples' Rights Based Approach to Conservation*, Information bulletin of the Forest Peoples Programme, September, Moreton-in-Marsh, UK

Flores, G. (2002) Coordinator of OFRAEH (Honduran Black Peoples' Fraternal Organization), statement on behalf of the Garífunas of Honduras, 18 April

Forest Peoples Programme (1998) *Guyana Information Update*, 24 August, Circulated via the South and Meso American Indian Rights Center, Oakland, California, US

References

Foroohar, R. (2002) 'Getting off the beaten track', *Newsweek*, 22 July

Gavidi, O. Ratu, Malani, M. Ratu, Leach, M. Tribal Chief, Borman, R. Chief et al (2003) 'Tourism and communities: Can protected areas deliver benefits to local peoples?', Statement by Indigenous Leaders and support organizations to Fifth World Parks Congress, Durban, South Africa, available from sustour@axionet.com

Hebert, L. and Healey, S. (2003) *Coercive Conservation Practices in Sub-Saharan Africa*, International Human Rights Advocacy Centre, Denver, Col, US

Houlder, V. (2004) 'Forests thrive under control of Indigenous peoples', *The Financial Times*, 23 July, Reprinted in *Forest Conservation News Today*, www.forests.org

IADB (Inter-American Development Bank) 'Presentation to World Summit on Ecotourism', Quebec City, Canada, May

IFG (International Forum on Globalization) (2003) 'Map depicting the negative impacts of economic globalization on Indigenous peoples', www.ifg.org/programs/indig.htm

INAC (Indian and Northern Affairs Canada) (2003) 'Press release: Squamish and Lil'wat First Nations Cultural Centre', 22 June, Circulated via Turtle Island Native Network, www.turtleisland.org

John, G. (2003) Chief and Chairperson of St'at'imc Chiefs Council, personal interview

Johnston, A. (2001) 'Oh Canada, your home on Native land', *Native Americas*, vol 18, no 3/4, fall/winter, pp74–79

McNeely, J. (1999) Presentation from floor on behalf of IUCN. Sectoral Discussion on Tourism. 14th Global Biodiversity Forum, Montreal, Canada, 18 June

Nichiporuk, M. (2004) 'Presentation on Regional Tourism on behalf of Cariboo Chilcotin Coast Tourism Association', Economic Development Conference, Lillooet, Canada, March

The Province (2004) 'Oil demand expected to fall in 2005', Business Section, 14 July, pA30

Pynn, L. (2003) 'First Nations band members split over merits of hosting 2010 Olympics', *The Vancouver Sun*, 30 June, pA9

Ramsey, M. (2003) 'First Nations victory song provides Olympic send off', *The Vancouver Sun*, 30 June, Circulated by the Union of British Columbia Indian Chiefs, British Columbia, Canada

Rana, D. S. et al (2003) 'The struggle for community based conservation and equitable tourism in the Nanda Devi Biosphere Reserve in India', Paper presented at the Namche Conference: People, Parks and Mountain Ecotourism, Nepal 24–26 May

Religion News Service (2004) 'And here's ... the chief spiritual officer!', Issued by Religion News Service and reprinted in *Travel Impact Newswire*, 12 August

Sam, R. (2004) *Here is Our Story on Sutikalh*, available from the author by writing to sutikalh2003@telus.net

Staples, S. (2004) 'Scientists: our survival depends on "designer ecosystems"', *The Vancouver Sun*, 28 May, ppA1–A2

Stevenson, M. G. (2004) 'Decolonizing co-management in northern Canada', *Cultural Survival Quarterly*, vol 28, no 1, 15 March, www.culturalsurvival.org

Survival International (2002) *Parks and Peoples Report*, Survival International, London, www.survival-international.org

Tait, I. (2002) Presentation to the St'at'imc Nation on Canada's 2010 Winter Olympics bid, on behalf of Vancouver 2010 Bid Corporation, Lillooet, Canada

Telfer, D. (2003) 'Deep in the Malaysian jungle: Journey ... to meet the Orang Asli, the elusive "original people" of the rain forest', *The Gazette*, 15 February

TIM Team (Tourism Investigation and Monitoring Team) (2003) *Privatization of Africa's National Parks*, TIM-Team Clearing House, Thailand, 5 October

The U'wa (2003) 'Letter from the U'wa to the world', Reprinted in *Oilwatch Network Bulletin*, Resistance no 36, March

VPTE (Victoria Park Tent Embassy) (2000) *Media Release: Council Threatens Aboriginal Tent Embassy*, Issued 29 July via the Leftlink mailing list

WCED (World Commission on Environment and Development) (1987) *Our Common Future* (Brundtland Report), Oxford University Press, New York, US

Western Native News (2004) 'Tourism industry conference not to be missed', February, p3

WRM (World Rainforest Movement) (2003) 'India: Adivasis shot for claiming their ancestral homeland', *WRM Bulletin*, no 70, 21 May

WWB (Webber Wentzel Bowens) (2003) *WWB Brief*, Corporate newsletter published for clients and distributed at the 2003 World Parks Congress, no 14, September, pp1–6

Chapter 7

Anderson, M. (2000) 'Presentation at Traditional Resource Rights Conference', Gumilaroi Nation (Australia), Hosted by Union of British Columbia Indian Chiefs, Canada, January

Ashton, R. (1992a) Series of interviews during 1992 World Congress on Adventure Travel and Ecotourism, Whistler, British Columbia, Canada

Ashton, R. (1992b) 'World trends in tourism and conservation (ecotourism)', in *Proceedings of the 1992 World Congress on Adventure Travel and Ecotourism*, The Adventure Travel Society, Englewood, CO, US

Berman, J. (2003) 'Archaeologists recover Maya Attar from looters', www.voanews.com, 30 October

References

Bookbinder, M. P., Dinerstein, E., Rijal, A., Cauley, H. and Rajouria, A. (1998) 'Ecotourism's support for biodiversity conservation', *Conservation Biology*, vol 12, no 6, December, pp1399–1404

Brosnan, G. (2002) 'Central American Indians protest development plan', *Reuters*, 15 October

Buettner, D. (2003) 'Groundbreaker: A plan to save Guatemala's Mayan cities ... ', *Outside*, August, pp26–27

CCAD (Comisión Centroamericana de Ambiente y Desarollo) (2003) *Current Status of the Central American Protected Areas System*, prepared for First Mesoamerican Congress on Protected Areas, Managua, Nicaragua

Choudry, A. (2003) 'Privatizing nature, plundering biodiversity', *Seedling*, Journal of Genetic Resources Action International (GRAIN), Barcelona, October, pp17–21

Christ, C., Hillel, O., Matus, S. and Sweeting, J. (2003) *Tourism and Biodiversity: Mapping Tourism's Global Footprint*, Conservation International, Washington, DC, US

CI (Conservation International) (2003) *Ecotourism*, Brochure prepared for the World Parks Congress in Durban, South Africa, CI, Washington, DC, US

Counterpart International Inc (2004) Mundo Maya: Sustainable Tourism Project, press release, www.counterpart.org/news

Daltabuit, M. and Pi-Sunyer, O. (1990) 'Tourism development in Quintana Roo, Mexico', *Cultural Survival Quarterly*, vol 14, no 1, pp9–13

Damsker, M., Jesiolowski, J. and Quarles, W. (1992) 'Rainforesting by Rodale', *Organic Gardening*, vol 39, no 5, p19

Deen, T. (2003) 'Under fire, World Bank launches Indigenous peoples fund', Inter Press Service, 14 May, www.ips.com

The Ecologist (2003) 'Special report on the bushmen of the Kalahari', vol 33, pp27–43

Faust, B. (2003) Series of telephone interviews with Dr Betty Faust of the Anthropology Department of Oregon State University, Oregon, US, Spring.

Flores, G. (2005) 'Honduras: Repression against Garífuna people', statement issued by OFRANEH (the Honduran Black Peoples' Fraternal Organization), La Ceiba, Honduras, 23 March

Gaines, L. (1990) 'Mexico says "megaprojects" should lure arrivals and investors', *Travel Weekly*, vol 49, February, p11

Gardner, F. (1991) 'Who benefits from ecotourism?', *Earth Island Journal*, spring, p30

Garrett, B. (1989) 'La Ruta Maya', *National Geographic*, vol 176, no 4, pp424–479

Gatto, J. T. (2002) *Dumbing Us Down: The Hidden Curriculum of Compulsory Schooling*, New Society Publishers, Gabriola Island, Canada

Gavidi, O. Ratu, Malani, M. Ratu, Leach, M. Tribal Chief, Borman, R. Chief et al (2003) 'Tourism and communities: Can protected areas deliver benefits to local peoples?', Statement by Indigenous Leaders and support organizations to Fifth World Parks Congress, Durban, South Africa, available from sustour@axionet.com

Gibran, K. (1985) *The Prophet*, A.D. Donker (Pty) Limited, South Africa

Harrington, T. (1991) 'Tourism damages Amazon region', *The Christian Science Monitor*, August

INGUAT (Instituto Guatemalteco de Turismo) (1991) *Guatemala: Colourful and Friendly*, Brochure, Guatemala

Iyer, S. R. (2004) 'Global compact: Summit and counter-summit', *Third World Resurgence*, vol 167/168, July/August, pp9–13

Johnston, A. M. (1994) 'A critical review of alternative tourism: Full fare tourism? A case study of Mundo Maya', MA Thesis, University of British Columbia, Canada

Kinane, E. (2002) 'Plan Puebla Panama: Another scheme skewering Central America', 9 March, available from edkinane@a-znet.com

Kotzé, D. J. (1999) Presentation on behalf of South African Department of Environmental Affairs and Tourism, UN Commission on Sustainable Development, New York, US, April

Leibman, D. (1993) 'Guatemala: Tourism at the crossroads', *Friends of the Earth*, March 1993, p11

Lucas, K. (2001) 'Indigenous leaders lambast World Bank, IMF', Inter Press Service, 10 May, Distributed by Union of British Columbia Indian Chiefs, British Columbia, Canada, 6 July

McNeely, J. (1999) Presentation from floor on behalf of IUCN. Sectoral Discussion on Tourism. 14th Global Biodiversity Forum, Montreal, Canada, 18 June, 1999

Ole Sikar, T. (2002) Maasai of Tanzania. Report on UNEP/TIES Conference on Ecotourism Summit, May, Quebec City, Canada

OMM (Organización Mundo Maya) (1991) *Mundo Maya: Proyecto Regional*, OMM, Guatemala, May

OMM (1992a) *Executive Summary: Conceptual Framework and Objectives of the Mundo Maya Organization*, OMM, Guatemala

OMM (1992b) *Reformulación de Objectivos y Programas del Proyecto Mundo Maya*, OMM, Guatemala, 14 May

Oviedo, G. (1998) Informal commentary, United Nations Working Group on Indigenous Populations, Geneva, Switzerland

Rao, N. (2000) Submission from floor, International Meeting of Tourism NGOs, Convened by Ecological Tourism in Europe (ETE) as preparatory meeting for the Fifth Conference of the Parties (COP5) to the Convention on Biological Diversity (CBD), Berlin, Germany

Rivera, V. S. (2002) 'The Mesoamerican biological corridor and local participation', *Parks*, Journal of IUCN Protected Areas Programme, vol 12, no 2, pp42–54

Rome, A. (2003) 'An ecotourism exchange in the Amazon advances community-based ecotourism around the world', *The International Ecotourism Society Newsletter*, third quarter, p7

Scott, D. C. (1992) 'Saving the forest by changing attitudes', *The Christian Science Monitor*, 29 April, pp10–11

Seltzer, M. (2002) Presentation on behalf of Business for Sustainable Travel, World Ecotourism Summit, May, Quebec City, Canada

SECTUR (Secretária de Turismo de México) (1990) *Mundo Maya: Antecedentes y Perspectivas de un Circuito Turístico en el Sureste de México*, SECTUR, Mexico

SECTUR (1991) *México: El Mundo Maya*, Brochure, Mexico

SECTUR (1992) *Programa Mundo Maya*, SECTUR, Mexico

SECTUR (1993) *Avances del Programa Mundo Maya*, SECTUR, Mexico, December

SECTUR (2002) *Programa Mundo Maya*, SECTUR, Mexico, February

Shaman's Drum (2001) 'Campaign launched to stop mistreatment of Khwe Bushmen in Kalahari Game Reserve', Editorial, *Earth Circles*, no 59, pp14–15

Singer, N. (2003) 'Resort to virtue: The world's ten best eco-lodges', *Outside*, March, pp83–91

Stevenson, M. G. (2004) 'Decolonizing co-management in northern Canada', *Cultural Survival Quarterly*, vol 28

Survival International (2004) Bushmen Fundraising Appeal, London, UK, May

TIES (The International Ecotourism Society) (2004) 'Travelers' philanthropy conference: A big success', press release, 5 May, www.ecotourism.org

TNC (The Nature Conservancy) (2003) *Special Report: Ecotourism*, Brochure prepared for World Parks Congress in Durban, South Africa, TNC, Arlington, Virginia, US

Toepfer, K. (2002) UNEP Side Meeting with Indigenous Peoples and Non-Governmental Organizations, World Ecotourism Summit, May, Quebec City, Canada

Toriello, A. (1992) Series of interviews during 1992 World Congress on Adventure Travel and Ecotourism, Whistler, British Columbia, Canada

Trask, H. K. (2000) 'Tourism and the prostitution of Hawaiian culture', *Cultural Survival Quarterly*, Spring, pp21–22

Travel weekly (1991) 'Tourism minister plans strategy to hit 10 million visitor plateau', vol 50, 25 April, pM6

Wall, G. (1999) *Partnerships Involving Indigenous Peoples in the Management of Heritage Sites*, Department of Geography, University of Waterloo, Ontario, Canada

Weinberg, B. (1991) 'Guatemala: The hamburger connection to genocide?', in Weinberg, B. (ed) *War on the Land: Ecology and Politics in Central America*, Zed Books Ltd, New Jersey, US

Weinberg, B. (2003) 'The battle for Montes Azules: Conservation as counterinsurgency in the Chiapas rainforest', *Native Americas*, spring, pp40–53

Weiner, T. (2003) 'Mexican rebels confront tourism in Chiapas', *The New York Times*, 9 March, www.nytimes.com

WWB (Webber Wentzel Bowens) (2003) *WWB Brief*, Corporate newsletter published for clients and distributed at the 2003 World Parks Congress, no 14, September, pp1–6

Zinn, R. (2002) 'Plan Puebla Panama and the fight to preserve biodiversity and indigenous rights in Chiapas', 26 September, www.corpwatch.org

Chapter 8

ABC Network News (2002) 'Transcript: Traditional owners to manage more national parks', 21 November, www.abc.net.au

Abocar, A. (2004) 'Inuit "poisoned from afar" due to climate change', *Environmental News Network*, 13 May, www.enn.com

Alfred, T. (1999) *Peace, Power, Righteousness: An Indigenous Manifesto*, Oxford University Press, Canada

Anderson, M. (2000) Presentation on behalf of Gumilaroi Nation (Australia) at Traditional Resource Rights Conference, Hosted by Union of British Columbia Indian Chiefs, British Columbia, Canada, January

Ashton, R. E. (1999) 'Working for a successful ecotourism story: The case of Punta Sal National Park', in Singh, T. V. and Singh, S. (eds) *Tourism Development in Critical Environments*, Cognizant Communication Corp, New York, US, pp89–101

Barnett, A. (2004) 'Tribes attack UK over "destruction of homeland"', *The Observer*, 15 August, www.observer.guardian.co.uk

Braddock, J. (2004) 'New Zealand Labour government cuts off Maori claims to the foreshore', 10 June, Distributed via the Protecting Knowledge list server of the Union of British Columbia Indian Chiefs, British Columbia, Canada

Calamai, P. (2004) 'Inuit way of life in danger, report finds', *Toronto Star*, 21 August, www.thestart.com

Chandler, S. (2001) *Oral Report on Behalf of Quaker Committee on Aboriginal Affairs to St'at'imc Chiefs Council, spring 2003*, Canadian Department of Foreign Affairs and International Trade, Presentation to invited NGOs at consultation meeting in preparation for United Nations Commission on Human Rights (UNCHR) session on the *Draft Declaration on the Rights of Indigenous People*, Lillooet, Canada, November

Christ, C., Hillel, O., Matus, S. and Sweeting, J. (2003) *Tourism and Biodiversity: Mapping Tourism's Global Footprint*, Conservation International, Washington, DC, US

Ereira, A. (2001) 'Back to the heart of lightness', *The Ecologist*, vol 31, no 6, July/August, pp34–38

References

Fisher, R., Ury, W. and Patton, B. (1991) *Getting to Yes: Negotiating Agreement Without Giving In*, Penguin Books, New York, US

Fortier, F. (1998) WIPO Consultation with Indigenous Peoples, July, Geneva

Gaia Foundation and GRAIN (Genetic Resources Action International) (1998) 'Global trade and biodiversity in conflict', *Seedling*, April

Gavidi, O. Ratu, Malani, M. Ratu, Leach, M. Tribal Chief, Borman, R. Chief et al (2003) 'Tourism and communities: Can protected areas deliver benefits to local peoples?', Statement by Indigenous Leaders and support organizations to Fifth World Parks Congress, Durban, South Africa, available from sustour@axionet.com

Honey, M. (2004) 'Letter from TIES executive director', *Eco Currents*, Newsletter of The International Ecotourism Society (TIES), first quarter, p2

Iyer, S. R. (2004) 'Global compact: Summit and counter-summit', *Third World Resurgence*, vol 167/168, July/August, pp9–13

Johnston, A. (2000) 'Tourism and biocultural diversity: Designing policies, programs and activities consistent with Article 8(j) of the CBD', in Gündling. L., Korn, H. and Specht, R. (eds) *International Workshop: Case Studies on Sustainable Tourism and Biological Diversity*, German Federal Agency for Nature Conservation, Vilm, Germany

Laifungbam, R. (2003) *Committee on Indigenous Health: Briefing Reports to PFII 2003*, UN Permanent Forum on Indigenous Issues, New York, 13 June

Leach, M., Tribal Chief (2003) Interview, St'at'imc Nation, spring 2003

Malanes, M. (1999) 'Tourism killing world's Eighth Wonder', *Third World Resurgence*, no 103, March, pp17–19

MEAB (Millennium Ecosystem Assessment Board) (2005) 'Living beyond our means: Natural assets and human wellbeing', March, www.millenniumassessment.org

Ole Sakuda, N. (2004) Representative of Simba Maasai Outreach Organization, 'Biodiversity and Maasai sacred sites', Statement to United Nations Permanent Forum (UNPF) on Indigenous Issues, New York, US

Olol-Dapash, M. (1999) 'In the hands of the government: The last Maasai journey', *Cultural Survival Quarterly*, vol 23, no 4, 31 December, available at www.culturalsurvival.org/publications/csq

Olol-Dapash, M. (2001) 'Maasai autonomy and sovereignty in Kenya and Tanzania', *Cultural Survival Quarterly*, no 25, vol 1, 30 April, available at www.culturalsurvival.org/publications/csq

Posey, D. A. and Dutfield, G. (1996) *Beyond Intellectual Property: Toward Traditional Resource Rights for Indigenous Peoples and Local Communities*, International Development Research Centre, Ottawa, Canada

Price, T. (2002) 'Tuvalu: For a limited time only', *The Globe and Mail*, Travel Section, 7 December, pT3

Rizvi, H. (2003) '"Pay for destruction", Indigenous people tell corporations', Inter Press Service, 16 May, www.oneworld.net

Singer, N. (2003) 'Resort to virtue: The world's ten best eco-lodges', *Outside*, March, pp83–91

Smith, A. (1975) Submission to Union of British Columbia Indian Chiefs, British Columbia, Canada

Stein, S. (2003) 'The Alien Tort Claims Act in danger: Implications for global Indigenous rights', *Cultural Survival Weekly Indigenous News*, 27 June, www.culturalsurvival.org

Schulte-Tenckhoff, I. (1999) 'Lecture on the rights of Indigenous Peoples: An international perspective', Indigenous Governance Programme, University of Victoria, British Columbia, Canada, 18 March

Toohey, P. (2002) 'Loophole opens parks to land claims', *The Australian*, 26 October 26, Circulated by the Union of British Columbia Indian Chiefs, British Columbia, Canada

WCED (World Commission on Environment and Development) (1987) *Our Common Future* (Brundtland Report), Oxford University Press, New York, US

World Bank (1999) 'Opening presentation by World Bank staff', Workshop hosted by World Bank, United Nations Commission on Human Rights (UNCHR), Working Group on Indigenous Populations, 17th Session, July

WWB (Webber Wentzel Bowens) (2003) *WWB Brief*, Corporate newsletter published for clients and distributed at the 2003 World Parks Congress, no 14, September, pp1–6

WWF-International (World Wide Fund for Nature) (2000) *Map of Indigenous and Traditional Peoples in Ecoregions*, WWF, Gland, Switzerland, 23 November

Chapter 9

Aloisi de Larderel, J. (1999) Presentation on behalf of United Nations Environment Programme (UNEP), Division of Technology, Industry and Economics, International Institute of Peace through Tourism Conference, Glasgow, UK, October

Ananthaswamy, A. (2004) 'Massive growth of ecotourism worries biologists', *New Scientist*, 4 March, www.newscientist.com

Anderson, M. (1999) Statement for and on behalf of the Euahlayi Nyoongahburrah and the Sovereign Union (Australia), 'Globalisation and multinationals', WGIP, Geneva, Switzerland, July

The Arctic Council (2004) *Impacts of a Warming Climate: Arctic Climate Impact Assessment*, Cambridge University Press, Cambridge, UK

Ashton, R. E. (1999) 'Working for a successful ecotourism story: The case of Punta Sal National Park', in Singh, T. V. and Singh, S. (eds) *Tourism Development in Critical Environments*, Cognizant Communication Corp, New York, UK, pp89–101

Ashton, R. (2003) Planeta.com Electronic Forum on Tourism Certification, 22 October, www.planeta.com

References

Ayres, E. (2004) 'The hidden shame of the global industrial economy', *Worldwatch*, vol 17, no 1, pp20–29

Baer, L.-A. (1999) Presentation on behalf of Saami Council. Workshop on Tourism & Indigenous Peoples organized by the International Support Centre for Sustainable Tourism. UN Commission on Human Rights, Working Group on Indigenous Populations, 17th Session, July 28

Bellett, G. (2003) 'Airlines fight back to reclaim losses', *The Vancouver Sun*, Business Section, 6 May, pD5

Berman, M. (1988) *The Reenchantment of the World*, Bantam Books, New York, US

Bien, A. (2003) *A Simple User's Guide to Certification for Sustainable Tourism and Ecotourism*, The International Ecotourism Society (TIES), Released at the Fifth World Parks Congress, Durban, South Africa, September

Broswimmer, F. (2002) *Ecocide: A Short History of the Mass Extinction of Species*, Pluto Press, London, UK

Brown, N. (1999) Presentation on behalf of Friends of the United Nations. Conference of International Institute of Peace Through Tourism, Glasgow, UK, October

Bushell, R. (2000) 'Global issues for protected areas and nature-based tourism: Case studies of partnerships in Australia addressing some of these issues', in Gündling, L., Korn, H. and Specht, R. (eds) *International Workshop: Case Studies on Sustainable Tourism and Biological Diversity*, Federal Agency for Nature Conservation, Bonn, Germany, pp94–115

Canadian Press (2004) 'World air travel returns to levels before 2001 attacks', *The Vancouver Sun*, Travel Section, 1 April 1, pF8

Chop, H. (2003) 'Whose label? Organic certification now serves big business better than farmers and consumers', *Alternatives*, vol 29, no 4, fall, pp19–20

Christ, C., Hillel, O., Matus, S. and Sweeting, J. (2003) *Tourism and Biodiversity: Mapping Tourism's Global Footprint*, Conservation International, Washington, DC, US

Clover, C. (2002) 'British experts call for end to cheap flights', *The Vancouver Sun*, Travel Section, 30 November, pE3

CSD (United Nations Commission on Sustainable Development) (1999) *Draft Decision on Tourism and Sustainable Development*, Agenda Item 5, CSD, New York, US, 19–30 April

Davies, S. W. (2002) 'Ecotourism', *Holland Herald*, In-flight magazine of KLM Airlines, April, pp14–26

Davis, W. (1999) 'A tribute to those who conserve: Safaris are not only magical, they are useful', *High Life*, In-flight magazine of British Airways, October, p18

Eagles, P., McCool, S. F. and Haynes, C. D. (2002) *Sustainable Tourism in Protected Areas: Guidelines for Planning & Management*, World Conservation Union, Gland, Switzerland

Ehrenfeld, D. W. (1978) *The Arrogance of Humanism*, Oxford University Press, New York, US

ENS (Environment News Service) (2005) 'World Heritage Committee to decide global warming effects, Durban, South Africa', 18 July, www.ens-newswire.com

Epler Wood, M. (2003) 'Ethical marketing', *Epler Wood Report*, Epler Wood International Consulting Firm, Burlington, Vermont, May

FERN (Forests and the European Union Resource Network) (2001) *Behind the Logo: An Environmental and Social Assessment of Forest Certification Schemes*, FERN, www.fern.org, May

Gavidi, O. Ratu, Malani, M. Ratu, Leach, M. Tribal Chief, Borman, R. Chief et al (2003) 'Tourism and communities: Can protected areas deliver benefits to local peoples?', Statement by Indigenous Leaders and support organizations to Fifth World Parks Congress, Durban, South Africa, available from sustour@axionet.com

The Globe and Mail (2002) 'Tonga opens gateway to space tourism', Travel Section, 30 March, pT6

Goodall, J. with Berman, P. (1999) *Reason for Hope: A Spiritual Journey*, Warner Books, New York, US

Gray, D. D. and Tuffin, B. (2004) 'Ecotourism without tears', *Time Magazine*, Asia Edition, 16 February, available via Associated Press and quoted in *ECOCLUB*, no 58, March 2004, www.ecoclub.com

Gygax, J. and Auran-Clapot, J. (2003) 'Rising oceans: The life of Indigenous Peoples at stake', press release issued by CONGO (Conference of Non-governmental Organizations in Consultative Status with the United Nations) during Working Group on Indigenous Populations at UN Commission on Human Rights, Geneva, Switzerland, July, www.ngocongo.org/ngonew/indigenous49.htm

Higuero, I. (1999) Presentation on behalf of UNEP Biodiversity Unit, 14th Global Biodiversity Forum, Montreal, Canada, 19 June

Honey, M. (2004) 'Letter from TIES executive director', *Eco Currents*, Newsletter of The International Ecotourism Society (TIES), first quarter, p2

IUCN (World Conservation Union) (2003) *Protected Areas in 2003: Scenarios for an Uncertain Future*, Gland, Switzerland

IUCN (World Conservation Union), Earthwatch Institute and WBCSD (World Business Council for Sustainable Development) (2002) *Business and Biodiversity: The Handbook for Corporate Action*, available from the WBCSD at www.wbcsd.ch

Johnston, A. (2000) 'Tourism and biocultural diversity: Designing policies, programs and activities consistent with Article 8(j) of the CBD', in Gündling, L., Korn, H. and Specht, R. (eds) *International Workshop: Case Studies on Sustainable Tourism and Biological Diversity*, Federal Agency for Nature Conservation, Bonn, Germany

Jones, L. (2003) 'Air France – KLM deal seen as spur for more', *Bloomberg News*, Reprinted in *The Vancouver Sun*, Business Section, 1 October, pD13

Kirby, A. (2003) 'Rich "must pay to save nature"', BBC News Online, 21 May, www.news.bbc.co.uk

Laird, S. (1999) *Equitable Biodiversity Research Relationships in Practice: Written Agreements between Communities and Researchers*, Prepared for WWF-International (9Z0698/01), Gland, Switzerland, January

Lash, G. (1999) 'Submission on behalf of The International Ecotourism Society (TIES)', Dialogue Segment on Tourism – Promoting Broad-based Sustainable Development through Tourism while Safeguarding the Integrity of Local Cultures and Protecting the Environment, United Nations Commission on Sustainable Development (CSD), April, New York, US

Leach, M., Tribal Chief (1999) Interview, Lillooet, Canada, October

L'Engle, M. (1973) *A Wrinkle in Time*, Bantam Doubleday Dell, New York, US

Lewis, P. O. (2001) *Frog Girl*, Whitecap Books, Vancouver, Canada

Lovell, J. (2005) 'Photos show climate change as ministers meet in UK', Reuters, 14 March

Lutz, E. L. (2005) 'Is fair trade fair? *Cultural Survival Quarterly*, vol 29, no3

Lutg, E. L. (2005) 'Is Fair trade fair?' *Cultural Surival Quarterly*, Vol 29, No 3

MacGregor, K. (2002) 'First paying "Afronaut" blasts off', *The Globe and Mail*, 26 April, p1

MacKinnon, K. (1999) Presentation on behalf of the World Bank to Sectoral Discussion on Tourism, 14th Global Biodiversity Forum, Montreal, Canada, 18 June

Mader, R. (2002) *Sustainable Development of Ecotourism Conference: Final Report*, April, www.planeta.com/ecotravel/tour/2002ecotourismreport.html

Malanowski, J. (2003) 'The future of travel', *Four Seasons, Four Decades*, Four Seasons Hotels and Resorts Magazine Commemorative Issue

McIntosh, L. (2004) Personal communication

McNeely, J. (1999) Presentation on behalf of IUCN, Sectoral Discussion on Tourism, 14th Global Biodiversity Forum, Montreal, Canada, 18 June

MEAB (Millennium Ecosystem Assessment Board) (2005) 'Living beyond our means: Natural assets and human wellbeing', March, www.millennium assessment.org,

Muir, S. (ed) (2004) 'Bring your *Lonely Planet*', *The Vancouver Sun*, Business Section, 30 January, pG1

National Geographic Society (2004) Issue titled 'Global warning: Bulletins from a warmer world', *National Geographic*, vol 206, no 3

Nearing, H. and Nearing, S. (1990) *The Good Life*, Shocken Books, New York, US

Nearing, H. and Nearing, S. (1992) *Loving and Leaving the Good Life*, Chelsea Green Publishing, White River Publishing, Vermont, US

News Services (2003) 'Tourism record', *The Province*, Travel Section, 4 February, pB4

Nierenberg, D. (2003) 'Populations of large ocean fish decimated', *World Watch*, vol 16, no 5, September/October, p9

Ole Sikar, T., Maasai of Tanzania (2002) *Report on UNEP/TIES Conference on Ecotourism in East Africa*, World Ecotourism Summit, Quebec City, Canada, May

Pleumarom, A. (1999) Tourism Investigation Monitoring Team presentation at evening side event during the United Nations Commission on Sustainable Development (CSD), New York, US, April

Pleumarom, A. (2003) 'Our world is not for sale! The disturbing implications of privatization in the tourism trade', Paper presented at the International Seminar on Tourism: Unfair Practices – Equitable Options, Hosted by DANTE, Network for Sustainable Tourism Development, December, Hanover, Germany

Pleumarom, A. (2004) 'Ecotourism on nose-diving course', Third World Network Briefing Paper for the Seventh Conference of the Parties (COP7) to the Convention on Biological Diversity (CBD), Kuala Lumpur, Malaysia, February

Quinn, D. (1992) *Ishmael: An Adventure of the Mind and Spirit*, Bantam Books, New York, US

Ray, P. H. and Anderson, S. R. (2000) *The Cultural Creatives: How 50 Million People Are Changing the World*, Harmony Books, New York, US

Reguly, E. (2001) 'Airline chaos may devolve flying back to an elite activity', *The Globe and Mail*, Business Section, 13 November, pB17

Rifkin, I. (2003) *Spiritual Perspectives on Globalization: Making Sense of Economic and Cultural Upheaval*, Skylight Paths Publishing, Woodstock, Vermont, US

Schwartz, P. and Randall, D. (2003) *An Abrupt Climate Change Scenario and Its Implications for United States National Security*, US Department of Defense, Washington, DC, US

Suzuki, D. (2003) 'Leading the way to the sacred balance', *Health'N Vitality*, September, pp10–13

Suzuki, D. (2004) Keynote Presentation to World Governments, Opening Plenary, Seventh Conference of the Parties (COP7) to the Convention on Biological Diversity (CBD), Kuala Lumpur, Malaysia, February

Theroux, M. (2001) 'The ecotrip: It's not easy being green', *Travel and Leisure*, September, pp61–68

TNC (The Nature Conservancy) (2003) *Special Report: Ecotourism*, Brochure prepared for World Parks Congress in Durban, South Africa, TNC, Arlington, Virginia, US

Toepfer, K. (2002) UNEP Side Meeting with Indigenous Peoples and Non-Governmental Organizations, World Ecotourism Summit, May, Quebec City, Canada

Traavik, T. (2002) Scientific Director, Norwegian Institute of Gene Ecology, Presentation on Genetic Engineering and Biosafety, Third World Network Seminar: Biodiversity in Crisis, The Hague, The Netherlands, 14 April, Held in conjunction with Sixth Conference of the Parties (COP6) to the Convention on Biological Diversity (CBD)

UNEP (United Nations Environment Programme), Standard and Poor and SustainAbility (2004) UNEP press release, 'UN survey finds most companies not reporting on social, environmental risks', 1 November, available at www.un.org/news

Union of Concerned Scientists (1992) 'World scientists' warning to humanity', 18 November, Cambridge, Mass, www.worldtrans.org/whole/warning.html

The Vancouver Sun (2004) 'Shove over, Bub', Arts and Life Section, 6 November, pF5

Vellas, F. (2002) *Report on Costs and Benefits of Ecotourism*, World Ecotourism Summit, May, Quebec City, Canada

WBCSD (World Business Council for Sustainable Development) (2004) Press release, 'The business case for biodiversity', 2 November, Geneva, Switzerland

Williams, P. (1991) 'Ecotourism management challenges', *Fifth Annual Travel Review Conference Proceedings*, Travel and Tourism Research Association, (www.ttra.com), pp83–87

WRI (World Resources Institute) (2004) *State of the World Report 2004: Richer, Fatter and Not Much Happier*, WRI, Washington, DC, US

WSSD (World Summit on Sustainable Development) (2002) WSSD Final Report, 'Plan of implementation', paragraph 43, Johannesburg, see www.world-tourism.org/sustainable/wssd/implementation.htm

WTO-OMT and UNEP (2002) *International Year of Ecotourism: 2002*, promotional brochure prepared leading up to the World Ecotourism Summit in Quebec City, Canada

WWF-International (World Wide Fund for Nature International) (2004a) Press release, 'WWF update on alarming state of the world', 21 October, Gland, Switzerland

WWF-International (2004b) *World Wide Fund for Nature's (WWF's) Living Planet Report 2004*, WWF, Gland, Switzerland

Chapter 10

Alfred, G. T. and Corntassel, J. (2004) 'A decade of rhetoric for Indigenous peoples', *Indigenous News Digest No 822*, Item 4, 20 January

AI (Amnesty International) (2003) 'Americas – human rights defenders: Persecution reaching emergency proportions', Press release, 10 November

Anderson, M. (1999) Statement on sovereignty, Gumilaroi Nation (Australia), Working Group of the Commission on Human Rights to Elaborate a *Draft Declaration on the Rights of Indigenous Peoples*, Geneva, Switzerland, 26–30 July

Carter, I. (1999) E-mail contribution to discussion on indigenous knowledge facilitated by the World Bank, 18 March

CBD Secretariat and UNEP (2002) *Biological Diversity and Tourism: Development of Guidelines for Sustainable Tourism in Vulnerable Ecosystems*, Montreal, Canada, www.biodiv.org

Cevallos, D. (2003) 'Isolated Indigenous groups face extinction', Inter Press Service, 1 July, Distributed by the Amazon Alliance, www.OneWorld.net

Chiang Mai Group (2002) Statement on the Process of the Regional Meeting on Community Based Ecotourism in South East Asia, Chiang Mai, Thailand, 3–7 March

Cultural Survival (2002) 'Amnesty report marks Columbus day with call for greater recognition of Indigenous rights', *Cultural Survival Weekly Indigenous News*, 17 October

De Chavez, R. (1999) 'Globalization and tourism: Deadly mix for Indigenous peoples', *Tebtebba*, The Philippines, January/March

de Comarmond, S. (2002) Minister for Tourism and Transport, The Seychelles, Presentation to World Ecotourism Summit, Quebec City, Canada

Ereira, A. (2001) 'Back to the heart of lightness', *The Ecologist*, vol 31, no 6, July/August, pp34–38

Fickling, D. (2003) 'Days are numbered for Aboriginal "tent embassy"', *The Observer*, 10 August

Fischer, L. (1950) *The Life of Mahatma Gandhi*, Harper and Row Publishers, New York, US

Gavidi, O. Ratu, Malani, M. Ratu, Leach, M. Tribal Chief, Borman, R. Chief et al (2003) 'Tourism and communities: Can protected areas deliver benefits to local peoples?', Statement by Indigenous Leaders and support organizations to Fifth World Parks Congress, Durban, South Africa, available from sustour@axionet.com

German Bundestag (2001) Letter to Canadian Prime Minister John Chretien

GRAIN (Genetic Resources Action International) (2004) 'Biodiversity convention to develop "regime on benefit sharing"', *Seedling*, April, p25

Hardison, P. (2004) 'Coercive conservation versus none', Posting on the University of Georgia EANTH list server, 16 November

Hillel, O. (1999) Presentation on behalf of Conservation International (CI), Evening side event organized by The International Ecotourism Society (TIES), United Nations Commission on Sustainable Development (CSD), April, New York, US

Hoyungowa, M. (1993) 'Cry of the Earth', Prophecy message and statement delivered and submitted to the United Nations General Assembly (UNGA), 23 November, New York, US

Hurtado, L. M. (2000) *The International Indigenous Forum on Biodiversity: Negotiating Away the Resources and Traditional Knowledge of Indigenous Peoples?* Statement by Movimiento Autoridades Indígenas de Colombia. Fifth Conference of the Parties to the UN Convention on Biological Diversity, Nairobi, Kenya, 19 May 19, available at www.biodiv.org or sustour@axionet.com

IIFB (International Indigenous Forum on Biodiversity) (2004a) 'Tourism: our voices are not yet heard', *Indigenous Voices*, Daily bulletin of the IIFB during the Seventh Conference of the Parties (COP7) to the Convention on Biological Diversity (CBD), 16 February

IIFB (2004b) 'SOS. CBD tourism guidelines put Indigenous cultures at risk', *Indigenous Voices*, Daily bulletin of the IIFB during the Seventh Conference of the Parties (COP7) to the Convention on Biological Diversity (CBD), 18 February

ISCST (International Support Centre for Sustainable Tourism), Rethinking Tourism Project et al (2001) Joint NGO Statement to the Seventh Subsidiary Body on Scientific, Technical and Technological Advice (SBSTTA) to the Convention on Biological Diversity (CBD), Montreal, Canada, www.tourismrights.org

ISCST (2002) Statement on participatory mechanisms for Indigenous Peoples and local communities. Submitted to the Ad Hoc Open Ended Intersessional Working Group on Article 8(j), February, Montreal, Canada

Johnston, A. (1998a) 'Suitable parameters for the process to establish global tourism guidelines under the CBD', *Eco*, NGO journal produced during the Fourth Conference of the Parties (COP4) to the Convention on Biological Diversity (CBD), May

Johnston, A. (1998b) 'Policy and community-level issues concerning Indigenous peoples, tourism and biodiversity', Paper prepared for Workshop on Tourism and Indigenous Peoples, Co-hosted by International Support Centre for Sustainable Tourism and Indigenous Peoples Development Network, Working Group on Indigenous Populations, United Nations Commission on Human Rights (UNCHR), Geneva, Switzerland

Johnston, A. (1999) 'Threats and opportunities presented by international policy debates on tourism', *Cultural Survival Quarterly*, Special Issue on Protecting Indigenous Culture and Land through Ecotourism, summer, pp57–59

Johnston, A, (2000) 'Tourism and biodiversity conservation: Possibilities for partnership', *Contours*, Journal of the Ecumenical Coalition on Tourism, March

Johnston, A. (2004a) 'Tourism: No holiday from accountability', Information paper issued by IUCN, CEESP, TILCEPA, the St'at'imc Chiefs Council and ISCST, Seventh Conference of the Parties (COP7) to the Convention on Biological Diversity (CBD), Kuala Lumpur, Malaysia, 9–20 February

Johnston, A. (2004b) 'Throwing caution to the wind: The fiasco of the CBD tourism guidelines', *Eco*, Newsletter of the international NGO coalition issued by the Environment Liaison Centre International, vol 10, no 8, 18 February

Johnston, A. (2004c) 'Wake up call: The CBD guidelines on tourism', *Eco*, Newsletter of the international NGO coalition issued by the Environment Liaison Centre International, June

Leach, M., Tribal Chief (2002) *Participation of Indigenous Peoples in the CBD Process*, Statement by the St'at'imc Chiefs Council to Working Group II, Participatory Mechanisms for Indigenous Peoples and Local Communities, Ad Hoc Open-ended Inter-sessional Working Group on Article 8(j) United Nations Convention on Biological Diversity, Montreal, Canada, 5 February, available at www.biodiv.org or sustour@axionet.com

Logan, M. (2004) 'Genocide it is', Inter Press Service News Agency, 9 August

Mader, R. (2002) 'Response and more questions,' concerning the Reviewing Ecotourism Campaign, Asia, United Nations International Year of Ecotourism (IYE) list server, 11 January

Mails, T. E. (1997) *The Hopi Survival Kit: The Prophecies, Instructions and Warnings Revealed by the Last Elders*, Penguin Books Ltd, London, UK

Manning, E. W. (ed) (2004) *Indicators of Sustainable Development for Tourist Destinations: A Guidebook*, World Tourism Organization, Madrid, Spain

Meyer, M. and Garbe, C. (2001) *Compilation and Analysis of Existing International Documents Relating to Sustainable Tourism*, Prepared by Ecological Tourism in Europe (ETE) for the Convention on Biological Diversity (CBD) Workshop on Biological Diversity and Tourism, Santo Domingo, 4–7 June, UNEP/CBD/WS-Tourism/INF/1

Muller, S. (2003) Presentation on behalf of PEMASKY (Kuna NGO) to the to the Eighth Subsidiary Body on Scientific, Technical and Technological Advice (SBSTTA) to the Convention on Biological Diversity (CBD), Montreal, Canada, 13 March

Muller, S., Castillo, G. et al (2003) *Biodiversity and Tourism: The Case for Sustainable Use of the Marine Resources of Kuna Yala, Panama*, German Federal Agency for the Environment, Nature Protection and Nuclear Safety, Bonn, Germany

Palmer, M. and Finlay, V. (2003) *Faith in Conservation: New Approaches to Religions and the Environment*, World Bank, Washington, DC, US

Pleumarom, A. (2003) 'Our world is not for sale! The disturbing implications of privatization in the tourism trade', Paper presented at the International Seminar on Tourism: Unfair Practices – Equitable Options, Hosted by DANTE, Network for Sustainable Tourism Development, December, Hanover, Germany

Sreekumar, T. T. and Gayathri, V. (2004) 'Rights versus obligations: Civil society responses to child labour and child abuse in the service industries', Paper prepared for Activists Strategy Meeting on Tourism organized by ECOT, Mumbai, India, 22–23 January

Steiner, A. (2003) Letter to Tribal Chief Mike Leach, Follow-up to Fifth IUCN World Parks Congress, World Conservation Union (IUCN), Gland, Switzerland, 23 October

Tippetts, S. (2001) 'Park Service might tear down Piscataway Sweatlodge', Message circulated via internet, Disseminated by the Protecting Knowledge List Server of the Union of British Columbia Indian Chiefs, British Columbia, Canada, 9 February

Toepfer, K. (2002) UNEP Side Meeting with Indigenous Peoples and Non-Governmental Organizations, World Ecotourism Summit, May, Quebec City, Canada

Toepfer, K. (2003) Letter from United Nations Environment Programme (UNEP) to St'at'imc Chiefs Council, c/o International Support Centre for Sustainable Tourism, 9 May

TWN (Third World Network) et al (2001) 'Statement: Preparations for World Ecotourism Summit in Quebec and other IYE events', Participants of the TWN Seminar on Biodiversity and Intellectual Property Rights, Kuala Lumpur, 4 February

References

Third World Network, TIM Team, Sahabat Alam Malaysia and Consumers Association of Penang (2002) 'UN International Year of Ecotourism 2002: In a deep muddle – Scrap it!', *TIM Team Clearing House for Reviewing Ecotourism*, no 19

UNEP (United Nations Environment Programme) (2002) 'Big development projects need cultural impact assessments', Press release, 19 November

The U'wa (2003) 'Letter from the U'wa to the world', (2000), Reprinted in *Oilwatch Network Bulletin*, Resistance no 36, March

WCED (World Commission on Environment and Development) (1987) *Our Common Future* (Brundtland Report), Oxford University Press, New York, US

The Wittenberg Center for Alternative Resources (ed) (1993) 'Cry of the Earth: The legacy of first nations – The prophecies of Turtle Island', series of videotapes documenting the conference proceedings, available via www.wittenbergcenter.org

WHC (World Heritage Committee) (2001) Report of WHC meeting in Helsinki, Finland, 11–16 December, document WHC-01/CONF.208/24

Zedan, H. (2002) 'Foreword', *Biological Diversity and Tourism: Development of Guidelines for Sustainable Tourism in Vulnerable Ecosystems*, CBD and UNEP, available from CBD Secretariat, Montreal, Canada, www.biodiv.org

Index